Other books by Martha Brill Olcott

The Kazakhs

Central Asia's New States

*Getting It Wrong: Regional Cooperation
and the Commonwealth of Independent States*
(with Anders Åslund and Sherman Garnett)

Russia After Communism
(edited with Anders Åslund)

KAZAKHSTAN
Unfulfilled Promise

Martha Brill Olcott

CARNEGIE ENDOWMENT FOR INTERNATIONAL PEACE
Washington, D.C.

Carnegie Endowment for International Peace
1779 Massachusetts Avenue, N.W., Washington, D.C. 20036
202-483-7600   www.ceip.org

The Carnegie Endowment normally does not take institutional positions on public policy issues; the views and recommendations presented in this publication do not necessarily represent the views of the Carnegie Endowment, its officers, staff, or trustees.

To order, contact Carnegie's distributor:
The Brookings Institution Press
Department 029, Washington, D.C. 20042-0029, USA
1-800-275-1447 or 1-202-797-6258

Printed in the United States of America.
Composition by Oakland Street Publishing. Text set in ITC Berkeley.
Printed by Automated Graphic Systems, Inc.

Library of Congress Cataloging-in-Publication Data

Olcott, Martha Brill, 1949-
  Kazakhstan : unfulfilled promise / Martha Brill Olcott.
    p. cm.
Includes bibliographical references and index.
  ISBN 0-87003-189-9 (cloth : alk. paper) — ISBN 0-87003-188-0 (pbk. : alk. paper)
  1. Kazakhstan--Politics and government—1991- 2. Kazakhstan—Economic conditions—1991- 3. Kazakhstan--Ethnic relations. I. Title.
  DK908.8675 .O43 2002
  958.45'086—dc21
                                                          2001008724

9 8 7 6 5 4 3 2

Contents

Foreword

A decade ago few Westerners had heard of Kazakhstan, the second largest of the Soviet republics and a source of vast undeveloped oil, gas, and other mineral reserves. After independence in 1991, Kazakhstan started to appear in the Western news—first when the United States helped the Kazakhs dismantle their nuclear weapons, and later when Chevron and Exxon/Mobil signed agreements to develop major Kazakh onshore and offshore oil reserves. Now the country's vast size, its oil and gas, and its pivotal location make it of strategic importance to the United States, our Western allies, and Kazakhstan's two powerful neighbors: China and Russia.

The most multi-ethnic of all the states carved out of the Soviet Union, Kazakhstan has been led through its independence and up to the present day by Nursultan Nazarbayev, a president determined to make his country into a bridge between Europe and Asia. Kazakhstan though suffers many of the problems faced by Russia, with whom it shares a three-thousand-mile border to the north; it too has spent the last decade working to establish the structures and mechanisms that make civil society, markets, and government work. The extent to which Kazakhstan has succeeded in these endeavors and the degree to which it has veered toward the perils of corruption, authoritarianism, and the suppression of civil society are the subject of this book.

Martha Brill Olcott, a senior associate at the Carnegie Endowment and an internationally respected expert on Central Asia, looks at the first decade of Kazakhstan's existence in the context of its political and historical legacy, its geography, and its economic and social development. While the strategic prize of Caspian oil and gas reserves remains an important factor driving U.S. and other Western interests, Olcott shows that far more is at stake for both the people of the region and U.S. interests than the successful building of transit routes linking Kazakhstan's natural resources to the outside world.

The consolidation of political and economic power among a privileged elite and an increasing intolerance of political dissent became the distinguishing characteristics of Kazakhstan's state-building strategy in the late 1990s. Olcott argues that the United States and the international community must not disregard these developments. The spread of radical Islam and the rise of ethnic tensions have already posed serious problems for many of the states that emerged out of the Soviet collapse. Kazakhstan inhabits a complex part of the world in which its success or failure as a state will have wider implications for its neighbors.

As the world's attention focuses increasingly on Central and South Asia in the aftermath of the September 11, 2001, terrorist attacks, Olcott's trenchant analysis should be of particular interest to scholars and policy makers alike. We have seen that a failed state anywhere, but particularly in this part of the world, can have far-reaching consequences. This book could not be appearing at a more appropriate time.

Kazkhstan: Unfulfilled Promise will make an important contribution to understanding the pitfalls of state building and the dangers these pose for regional and global security. Perhaps nowhere was the granting of independence more bittersweet and the challenges of sustaining it more complex than in the case of Kazakhstan.

Jessica T. Mathews
President
Carnegie Endowment for International Peace

Acknowledgments

This volume has been nearly a decade in the making and would never have been possible without the financial support of a number of sources. The genesis of the project was a grant from the Smith Richardson Foundation, which provided support to the Foreign Policy Research Institute (in Philadelphia) for an early predecessor of this study in 1994. The Dean of Faculty's Office at Colgate University has also contributed to some of the research costs of the project. Mostly, though, this book is the result of the generous support of the Carnegie Endowment for International Peace and its Russian and Eurasian program. Some of my travel to Kazakhstan was provided by the Central Asian American Enterprise Fund, on whose board of directors I served from 1994 to 2000.

The opportunities that I had as a board member certainly contributed to a deepened understanding of how Kazakhstan's economy operates and first sensitized me to the many shades of gray that color its landscape. I also benefited from serving, albeit briefly and sporadically, as a consultant for several Western energy and gold-mining companies. This experience contributed to my understanding of the technical difficulties associated with developing Kazakhstan's resources as well as just how challenging it is to mount a world-class project in the Kazakh environment.

Kazakhstan is no longer a remote and forbidding place. Unlike in my earlier works, in this volume I am able to draw extensively on the written work of other Americans who have done fieldwork in Kazakhstan. There is a whole generation of young scholars who are making important contributions to the field; I have found the writings of Pauline Jones Luong (Yale University) and Bhavna Dave (University of London) particularly useful in this endeavor and have benefited from my conversations with them. At various stages of the project I have also benefited from consultations with William Fierman (Indiana University) and Gregory Gleason (University of New Mexico), and Sally Cummings, all of whom have spent long periods conducting research in Kazakhstan in recent years.

This volume could never have been produced without the advice and assistance of my colleagues and former colleagues at Carnegie, both in Washington and in Moscow, including Anders Åslund, Sherman Garnett, Alexei Malashenko, and Galina Vitkovskaya. I also would like to acknowledge research assistance by Judith Smelser and Maria Popova and the enormous energy put into this project by Erik Scott and Marat Umerov. All four have worked for me as junior fellows. I especially want to thank Natalia Udalova Zwart, who has helped with the project since the very beginning, and her successor at Carnegie, Marcus Fellman, who took over for Natalia in 2001.

As always I am particularly grateful for the support and intellectual guidance offered by my husband, Anthony Olcott, and for the forbearance of my three children, Hillary, Andrew, and Alison Olcott.

Acronyms

ADB	Asian Development Bank
AgipKCO	Agip Kazakhstan North Caspian Operating Company
AIPC	American International Petroleum Corporation
APFS	accumulative pension fund system
CENTRASBAT	Central Asian Peacekeeping Battalion
CIS	Commonwealth of Independent States
CNPC	China National Petroleum Corporation
CPC	Caspian Pipeline Consortium
CPSU	Communist Party of the Soviet Union
CSCE	Commission for Security and Cooperation in Europe
EAU	Euro-Asian Union
EBRD	European Bank for Reconstruction and Development
EFF	Extended Fund Facility
FDI	foreign direct investment
GDP	gross domestic product
GNP	gross national product
GUAM	Georgia, Ukraine, Azerbaijan, and Moldova
GUUAM	Georgia, Ukraine, Uzbekistan, Azerbaijan, and Moldova
ICA	Intergas Central Asia
IFES	International Foundation for Election Systems
IMF	International Monetary Fund
IPF	investment privatization funds
JV	joint ventures
KEGOC	Kazakhstan Electricity Grid Operating Company
KMRC	Kazakhstan Mineral Resources Corporation
KNB	National Security Committee
KTK	Commercial Television of Kazakhstan
NATO	North Atlantic Treaty Organization
NIS	newly independent states

NGO	nongovernmental organization
NMP	net material product
NKK	People's Congress of Kazakhstan
OKIOC	Offshore Kazakhstan International Operating Company, now known as AgipKCO
OPIC	Overseas Private Investment Corporation
ORT	Russian media/news organization
OSCE	Organization for Security and Cooperation in Europe
PNEK	People's Unity Party
PPF	private pension fund
PPP	purchasing power parity
PSA	production-sharing agreement
RAO–UES	Russia's Unified Energy Systems
RNPK	Republican People's Party of Kazakhstan
RSFSR	Russian Soviet Federative Socialist Republic
ShNOS	Shymkent Kumkolneftetorgsintez
SNEK	Union of the People's Unity, later renamed People's Unity Party
SPF	state pension fund
TDA	United States Trade and Development Agency
TNK	Tiumen Oil Company
UNDP	United Nations Development Program
USAID	United States Agency for International Development
USDA	United States Department of Agriculture
USIA	United States Information Agency
USSR	Union of Soviet Socialist Republics
VAT	value added tax
WTO	World Trade Organization

KAZAKHSTAN

1

Introducing Kazakhstan

The distinguished Nigerian novelist Chinua Achebe's observations about his own country can easily be applied to the current situation in Kazakhstan.

> The trouble with Nigeria is simply and squarely a failure of leadership. There is nothing basically wrong with the Nigerian character. There is nothing wrong with the Nigerian land or climate or water or air or anything else. The Nigerian problem is the unwillingness or inability of its leaders to rise to the responsibility, to the challenge of personal example, which are the hallmarks of true leadership.[1]

In some ways, Kazakhstan was never as fortunate as Nigeria because it is a landlocked state that began independence with a seriously damaged environment. The legacy of colonial rule in Kazakhstan is much more uneven than that in Nigeria; at least it seems that way to someone who is not a serious student of Africa and who seeks to compare the horrors of the Stalinist system with the insufficiencies of British rule. Yet Kazakhstan began its existence as an independent country with many advantages, both human and natural.

My purpose in writing this book is to provide a window into Kazakhstan by offering an explanation for how and why its first president, Nursultan Nazarbayev, established Kazakhstan's family-based system of rule, as well as the likely consequences of his actions. My goal is to show how the failure of leadership in Kazakhstan came about. By describing the political, economic, and social evolution of Kazakhstan during the first decade of independence and by providing a sense of how the country's population has viewed these developments, I show why the current system was not fore-ordained. This volume is for those interested both in Kazakhstan and in learning the details of its state-building efforts. It is also for readers who are concerned more generally with the process of transition from communism to independent statehood in the successor states of the Union of Soviet Socialist Republics (USSR).

Despite the absence of a strong democratic tradition in Kazakhstan, the country could have developed a pluralistic or quasi-pluralistic political system and a transparent market economy if its leaders had only shown the will to discipline themselves. In its first years, the country's ruling elite at least flirted with the idea of a transition to democracy and supported a thoroughgoing macroeconomic reform. But these promising beginnings were abandoned over time, and now the country shows every sign of developing into a family-run state. What is more, as in Nigeria, the United States and other Western powers are reluctant to press too hard for political and economic reforms for fear that their access to the country's valuable natural resources will be restricted. As I argue in this volume, however, the policy choices made in Kazakhstan over the past decade may destabilize local conditions and make long-term access to Kazakhstan's riches all the more difficult.

No single book can do justice to the complexities of state building in a country as large, as resource rich, and as ethnically diverse as Kazakhstan. In this volume I build on more than a quarter century's study of this former Soviet republic and its people. It is not my intention to reproduce or summarize my earlier writings on the history of Kazakhstan (*The Kazakhs*), or on the geopolitics of the area, which was the subject of *Central Asia's New States*.[2] Instead, I seek to bring to bear my more recent experiences in studying and traveling in the country and look in some depth at the past ten years of developments in Kazakhstan.

This book provides an introduction to the challenges that faced the leaders of Kazakhstan when the state gained independence a decade ago, why those leaders were reluctant to accept independence, how they tried to create a politically loyal population, what political institutions they used to do this, how they tried to manage the country's economic resources in the process, and what major social and political rifts developed over the past decade as a result of those policies. Finally, I look at what the next decade in Kazakhstan might look like, and specifically at what may happen when President Nazarbayev departs the political scene, as he must inevitably.

Why Kazakhstan Matters

The West has been drawn to the Caspian Sea with its billions of dollars of oil and gas reserves that seem all the more important in the aftermath of the September 11, 2001, attacks on the World Trade Center and Pentagon. The war on terrorism unleashed by these horrific events makes global dependence on Persian Gulf oil reserves seem more problematic, and the new resources in the Caspian region and in Russia even more attractive. Western businessmen and politicians had already been interested in the fate of Kazakhstan, Turkmenistan, and Azerbaijan, where the bulk of the Caspian reserves are found.

Of the three states, Kazakhstan's reserves are likely to prove to be the most significant, and while the country produces some eight hundred thousand barrels of oil daily, the country's leaders hold out hope that Kazakhstan will turn into another Saudi Arabia in the next two decades. The country has 70.52 trillion cubic feet of gas reserves and at least 16.4 billion barrels of oil reserves. The latter figure is likely to triple and could even increase sixfold if the most optimistic estimates of Kazakhstan's offshore reserves are fully proved.[3]

Kazakhstan has been of interest to U.S. policy makers since its independence because it was the only non-Slavic post-Soviet state to have inherited nuclear weapons. It was also the site of a projected multibillion-dollar American investment. Independence meant that Chevron's project to develop the vast Tengiz oil field in western Kazakhstan, the first such project of its kind, would require permission from government officials in Almaty instead of from Soviet officials in Moscow, with whom the venture had originally been negotiated.

The level of international interest in this vast nation, which is two-thirds the size of the continental United States, has steadily increased over time. While the claims that Central Asia will be a second Persian Gulf may turn out to be vast exaggerations, the Caspian basin reserves remain a potentially enormous windfall for Western energy companies and, with Russia, could serve as an important alternative to the Persian Gulf. Caspian oil has been exploited for nearly a century, but when the Soviet Union was intact,

Western experts had limited knowledge of just how vast those reserves were and little expectation of being able to play an active role in developing them.

Now, large Western oil companies believe it is critical to secure a part of the Caspian reserves, especially because the governments in Kazakhstan, Turkmenistan, and Azerbaijan seemed more interested in Western investment in their assets than did the government in Russia. This meant that the conventional wisdom in Western policy circles concerning these states quickly shifted 180 degrees, as Azerbaijan and the Central Asian states went from being inconvenient additions to the international scene to being potential strategic assets. In 1991 the possible collapse of the USSR was viewed as a threat to global security until just weeks before it happened, in part because of what were seen as the "unstable forces" that might be unleashed. The new states of Central Asia and the Caucasus lay on the edge of the "arc of crisis," a phrase frequently used in the late 1970s and 1980s to describe the area from the Indian subcontinent to the Horn of Africa.[4] This area, said to separate the stable Western world from a non-Western Muslim one, was precisely where Samuel Huntington later saw an impending "clash of civilizations."[5]

Instinctively, Western policy makers shied away from too direct an engagement in that part of the world, and so, initially, the international community was willing to grant Russia great latitude in the Soviet Union's former domains. The USSR was not simply a continuation of the Russian empire; it was also a postimperial multinational state. The international community had viewed Moscow's suppression of the empire's various nationalities to be part of the general denial of basic political freedoms to Soviet citizens and saw the democratization of the USSR as the remedy for it. There was fear that the breakup of the Soviet Union would set a dangerous precedent and create new risks that outweighed the injustices of perpetuating the Soviet system. Once the Soviet Union broke up, however, the international community did not support the idea that Russia should attempt to reconstitute it. In fact, to avoid the risks associated with this, many diplomats initially argued that Russia had legitimate geopolitical interests in the contiguous former colonies and could realize these if it would behave "responsibly."

Over time it became more difficult to interpret Russia's actions benignly. The 1994 invasion of Chechnya served as a bloody demonstration of what Russia was capable of, if provoked. Although not behaving nearly as ruthlessly beyond its borders as it did within its boundaries, Russia still used heavy-handed pressure to induce reluctant states to join the Commonwealth of Independent States (CIS).[6] While claiming neutrality, it unabashedly favored the Abkhaz secessionists over the Georgian government and helped the Armenians in their war against Azerbaijan. In this environment, Russia's attempts to dictate Kazakhstan's economic policy, especially in the oil and gas sectors, were seen by many in the West as overstepping the bounds of responsibility.

The Caspian region was described as vital to U.S. security. This stance was first made explicit by then U.S. Deputy Secretary of State Strobe Talbott in a July 1997 speech that he titled *A Farewell to Flashman*:

> The United States has a stake in their success. If reform in the nations of the Caucasus and Central Asia continues and ultimately succeeds, it will encourage similar progress in the other New Independent States of the former Soviet Union, including Russia and Ukraine. It will contribute to stability in a strategically vital region that borders China, Turkey, Iran, and Afghanistan, and that has growing economic and social ties with Pakistan and India. . . . It would matter profoundly to the United States if [internal and cross-border conflicts] were to happen in an area that sits on as much as two hundred billion barrels of oil. That is yet another reason why conflict resolution must be Job One for U.S. policy in the region: it is both the prerequisite for, and an accompaniment to, energy development.[7]

U.S. commitment to Kazakhstan and Central Asia has grown with time, and Strobe Talbott's words seem more prescient after the United States dispatched troops to Uzbekistan as part of a military operation in Afghanistan. Still, the challenges of state building in Kazakhstan have not been made simpler by the greater strategic importance of the region or by increased international interest in its oil wealth. In fact, I argue the opposite is true. As with leaders of so many other resource-rich states, demand for mineral reserves has placed extraordinary temptations before Kazakhstan's rulers, making Western arguments for good government that much harder to sell. As I discuss more fully in the concluding chapter, this creates a conundrum for U.S. policy makers. Caspian oil will be a strategic asset only if continued access to it can be ensured; with inland deposits, this requires that the host country as well as the transit states all be stable.

Thus, U.S. policy makers face the constant challenge of balancing long-term and short-term policy interests: the need to remain on good terms with the current rulers of oil-rich states, while trying to prevent them from destabilizing their own societies. For the Clinton administration, the former task was the more important, and short- and medium-term interests were dominant. The focus became "pipeline politics" (that is, the fight over the routes this oil would take to market). Securing the independence of the Caspian states was termed a priority, and President Bill Clinton cited the signing of a four-state pledge to create an East-West (Baku-Ceyhan) pipeline as one of the most significant foreign policy accomplishments of 1999.[8]

Clinton's message was quite different from that offered in late 1991 and 1992 when Secretary of State James Baker traveled the region trying to convince the Central Asian leaders to embrace the union of economic development and democratic principles. To make this point, when the USSR collapsed, the United States recognized the independence of all the successor states but authorized the immediate opening of only two embassies in the Central Asian region, in Kazakhstan and Kyrgyzstan. Certainly, the fact that Kazakhstan had nuclear weapons played no small part in U.S. decision making, but official U.S. statements emphasized that both Kazakhstan and Kyrgyzstan were being rewarded for their commitment to democratic and market reform.

Although embassies were later opened in all the newly independent states, the symbolism of the two-stage process by which the United States established full diplomatic relations was not lost on the leaders of the region. These actions implied certain preconditions for strong U.S. support. Independence had to be more than the mere transfer of power from Moscow to republic-level Communist Party officials, who by now had become national leaders. Power, and consequently a portion of the national wealth, had to be shared with the people.

This message, brought home in a range of ways during the first few years of independence, made all the region's leaders somewhat uncomfortable. The international assistance that the United States and other donor nations offered to these states targeted projects designed to promote structural economic reforms that create the legal environment necessary for the rule of law and the protection of private property. Kazakhstan and Kyrgyzstan received a disproportionate share of this aid because commitment to a radical restructuring of society remained greatest in those two countries. It was also assumed that Russia would serve as a model for the states of Central Asia because the Russians were seen as natural leaders in that part of the world and were assumed to be more deeply committed to the goals of economic and political reforms than were these new neighbors.

These early policies seriously underestimated the amount of social, political, and economic reconstruction that was necessary for any of the newly independent states to make the transition to sustainable statehood. It also underestimated the new states' suspicion of Russia, as well as Russia's lingering dreams of empire, or at least neo-imperial domination.

The subsequent change in U.S. and Western attitudes continues to affect the kinds of states that emerge in the region, and not necessarily for the better. In the short run it makes these states more likely to survive because Russia has effectively been warned not to become the neighborhood bully. Russia's potential influence in this region may always have been exaggerated. A U.S. military presence in Uzbekistan, however brief, seems certain to diminish any future military threats from Russia, although it may lead to a security void. In the long run the greatest sources of instability lie within the states themselves. Geopolitics alone does not dictate outcomes in the state-building process. If the income from the energy sector is not shared with the general population and if the region's leaders choose to use it primarily for their personal benefit, who will provide a buffer for them from their angry masses and from those neighbors who seek to be the patrons of disgruntled elements in the population? The George W. Bush administration may well find itself facing difficult choices in Kazakhstan and elsewhere in the Caspian region in the next few years.

There is much to the old adage that history would not keep repeating itself if we would only listen to it. It has taken the United States decades to recover from the damage done to relations with oil-producing states through its unsuccessful efforts to back those in power against the more radical forces that oppose them. The histories of both Iran and Iraq might have been much different had the U.S. foreign policies of the 1960s and 1970s been less focused on regime stability and more focused on the long-term political viability of these regimes. As we have seen in the Middle East, false steps with one state can have a serious impact on U.S. relations with an entire region and on the U.S. global strategy more generally.

The Cold War is at an end, and so too it seems is the post–Cold War. A new period of global vulnerability began the day terrorists brought down two of the world's tallest buildings by turning passenger jets into flying bombs. It is hard to imagine a more vivid example of the power of today's radical forces—or of the new financial interests ready to bankroll them. Today Afghanistan is the battlefield, and a long-smoldering conflict there will only increase the likelihood that the regimes in Central Asia will also become targets for radical Islamists seeking to oust secularists.

Corrupt regimes stimulate the development and popularity of radical forces, and as I make clear in this book, some of the early auguries are disturbing. Still headed by a Soviet-era figure, President Nursultan Nazarbayev, the Kazakhs have yet to cope with the inevitable challenge of transferring power to a new post-Soviet generation.[9] At the same time, the process of democratic institution building has all but halted in Kazakhstan after an initial phase in which Kazakh leaders had resigned themselves to taking such steps as the price of good relations with the West in general and the United States in particular. Over time the region's leaders have become more adept at rebuffing the implied conditionality of the early U.S. policy in the region, and U.S. pressure has also become less sustained, making these men less apologetic about their behavior. That the United States had to depend on the hospitality of Uzbekistan's strong-man President Islam Karimov to conduct a military foray into Afghanistan is likely to render democracy a harder sell to the region's leadership and to make the United States less vocal in its efforts to advance it.

All Central Asia's leaders, including President Nazarbayev, claim that the tradition and temperament of the Asian people make them little suited to democracy. This seems a gratuitous justification for consolidating power in the hands of the ruling elite. It is much more obviously the case that almost none of these men has any instinctive attraction to democracy; rather they seem to prefer replacing the grandiose public structures of the late Soviet era with new and more massive presidential palaces, mosques, and museums.

Independence has brought vast new temptations, and this is especially true in a resource-rich state like Kazakhstan. Kazakhstan's resources seem certain to be developed, but the conditions of corruption complicate the process. Promised tenders have often gone sour, and those who have seemingly won bids have sometimes been pushed into contractual default so that the Kazakh government can gain new concessions. Given the difficulties of shipping oil and gas from the region, the pace of development will be slower and more complicated than was initially predicted, leaving the United States continually to reevaluate its support for what could become an increasingly less attractive regime. The fighting in Afghanistan in the winter of 2001–2002 simply highlights the deteriorating security environment in the region more generally, which seems certain to provide Washington with a never-ending series of policy challenges.

That the United States chose to establish a military outpost in Uzbekistan in late 2001 need not be indicative of how U.S. policy makers would respond to a deteriorating political or economic situation in Kazakhstan. After all, the United States was not responding to an appeal by the Uzbeks to help preserve their domestic stability, but rather Uzbekistan became a strategic asset for the United States to achieve its overarching goals.

The challenge before these states remains one of enhancing their own viability. The second-term Clinton administration demonstrated a strong concern for the fate of Central Asia, and the Bush administration seems headed for even greater engagement, but neither independence nor U.S. policy has yet to contribute much to improve the lives of the Central Asians. The long-term security of these states requires that independence be something more than a transfer of power from Moscow to the new national capitals. It must also entail a meaningful transfer of rights and responsibilities to the population itself.

The Soviet Union fell apart largely because Moscow failed to meet both elite and mass expectations for promised economic and political reforms. The leaders of Kazakhstan have inherited these same challenges, along with a responsibility to manage billions of dollars in resources. Those dividing the spoils must also deal with a socially and politically traumatized population. True, the leaders of Kazakhstan and the other newly independent states may claim that they have not caused these traumas, but with income disparities growing and the disenfranchisement of the people increasing, Kazakhstan's leaders are quickly coming to the end of whatever grace period the granting of independence afforded them. The nation's Kazakhs still have great pride in their new national homeland, but most other nationalities living in the country have little sense of political empowerment. Although foreign investment is steadily increasing and the economy may have already passed its worst period, dreams of vast national wealth have yet to be realized. What lies ahead is far from clear, but as I make explicit here, during the first decade of statehood Kazakhstan's leaders squandered much of their opportunity to quickly right old Soviet wrongs.

Blessed with Resources but Cursed by Geography

With vast untapped fossil-fuel reserves, substantial gold deposits, and rich unmined veins of copper, chrome, and aluminum, Kazakhstan is a state of enormous potential natural wealth. In fact, a Soviet geologist once boasted that Kazakhstan was capable of exporting the entire periodic table of elements.[10] It also has enough developed farm and pastureland to meet the immediate needs of its population of nearly 15 million, of whom today slightly more than half are Kazakhs.[11] Given its natural resources, one would think that Kazakhstan's future is ensured, especially since it also has a diverse industrially based economy (largely in ferrous and nonferrous metallurgy), sufficient to insulate the country from the risks associated with resource-dependent development.

Despite all this, Kazakhstan began its existence as a fragile state and as a country of paradoxes, a state crippled by its history as well as by its geography. Both the Kazakhs and the Russians claim Kazakhstan as their homeland, and while the current legal system favors the claims of the former, a three-thousand-mile border with Russia creates a not-so-subtle reminder of the risks associated with these potentially conflicting claims.

Kazakhstan's economic potential is enormous because it combines natural and human resources. At the time of independence, Kazakhstan's economy and industrial plants were fully integrated with those of Russia. Not only did factories on both sides of the border supply one another, but the energy grids and supply lines also traditionally ran north-south rather than east-west. President Nazarbayev was well aware of the interdependency of Kazakhstan's economy with Russia's, and to a lesser extent with the economies of Kyrgyzstan and Uzbekistan. Given the limited exposure that he and his first group of advisers had to the conditions of a market economy, it was hard for him to imagine how foreign investment and international technical assistance could help break those ties.

As I detail in chapter 5, with time the Kazakh leader came to better understand the country's economic potential, spurred in large part by a level of international investor interest that far exceeded Nazarbayev's initial expectations. Kazakhstan has the highest per capita foreign investment in the CIS. According to the Kazakh government, the country has received some $13 billion in foreign direct investment (FDI) in its first decade of existence.[12] This figure is somewhat misleading because it reflects investment in planned projects as well as capital being directly injected into economic production. As of the end of 2000, half of these investments had gone into the oil and gas sector. The proportion of investment going into that sector is likely to increase as Kazakhstan's new oil fields move from an exploration to an exploitation phase.

I also discuss how, outside the oil and gas sector, foreign investment in Kazakhstan has been slower and more tentative than the government had hoped. Investment in the oil and gas sector itself is behind schedule, slowed in part because of the uncertainty of relations with Russia. Until the price of oil jumped unexpectedly, the oil and gas industries produced far more limited royalties and tax revenues, and still fewer jobs than were originally projected.

As I also detail in chapter 5, Kazakhstan has a difficult business climate that is keeping some potential investors away. The legal infrastructure governing foreign investment is far from complete. While the rights of foreign investors are now relatively well established compared to other states in the region, they have not yet been fully tested. The existing laws governing property change frequently, even if only subtly, putting most foreign investments at potential risk, and the profitability of most large projects requires the negotiation of legal exclusions and tax holidays. In the absence of an independent judiciary and commercial arbitration system, the concessions granted to investors cannot be guaranteed to survive the life of the projects. The allocation of contracts and resource development rights to foreigners has not always proceeded smoothly. Several big mineral resource extraction projects have been scandal-ridden after Western firms were pushed out of deals they thought were firm, or they were forced into expensive new negotiations. Stories of business people pulling out of smaller projects are also commonplace.

Similar problems have also crippled independent Kazakh entrepreneurs, erecting a formidable glass ceiling beyond which those lacking protection cannot venture. In some ways, and most troubling of all, the reach of the official family—including the president, his wife and her family, their daughters, and their sons-in-law—is increasing. Their holdings must now be reckoned with in most of the major sectors of the economy.

The consolidation of economic power in a few hands also threatens to disrupt the country's precarious ethnic balance. At independence Kazakhs accounted for only about 40 percent of the population of the country; about 37 percent of the population were ethnic Russians.

President Nazarbayev tried to turn the country's demography and geography into a national asset, after referring to his nation as a bridge between

Europe and Asia. Not only does the country straddle the two continents, but its history is rooted in the two civilizations and its population is nearly evenly divided between European and Asian peoples.[13]

Unfortunately, a skillful turn of phrase is not sufficient to create an international role for Kazakhstan. To date, as I explore at considerable length in chapter 3, this claim has proved to be little more than a public relations effort designed to make an asset of Kazakhstan's geographic and demographic positions and to raise the stature of the man who leads the nation. So, while Kazakhstan claims to be the most multinational of the Soviet successor states, with over a hundred nationalities represented in the republic, in reality the history of the past decade has been that of the political empowerment of one national group, the Kazakhs, at the expense of all others. Both Kazakh nationalists and the Kazakh population at large view independence as the restoration of Kazakh statehood.

The Kazakhs were a pastoral, nomadic people of Turko-Mongol stock who began to consolidate in the fifteenth century by organizing themselves into three groups, or *zhuzes*, commonly termed hordes. The Small Horde had its territory on what is now western Kazakhstan, the Middle Horde in north-central Kazakhstan, and the Great Horde in southern and southeastern Kazakhstan. Territorial domination was a relative concept for the Kazakhs, given the nature of the nomadic livestock breeding economy, although each Kazakh *aul* (the migratory unit) had fixed routes and pasturage during their annual migratory cycle. The three hordes were loosely unified from the first quarter of the sixteenth century to the last quarter of the seventeenth century. When Kalmyk Mongol tribesmen began moving west and started taking control of Kazakh pasturelands, the *khans* (chieftains) who ruled the Small and Middle Hordes sought protection from Russia's ruler, swearing allegiance to the Russian tsars in 1731 and 1740, respectively. The *khans,* however, did not anticipate that this allegiance would ultimately lead to the colonization of their lands and to a blurring of territorial boundaries between their people and the Russians. The Kazakhs understood it as an alliance of a weak ruler to a stronger one, but the Russians viewed it as the prelude to fuller control, which was exercised by the forcible conquest of the Kazakh lands in the late eighteenth and early nineteenth centuries.

Many Kazakhs maintain that from that time on their ancestors suffered at Russian hands, continuing up to the Alma Ata Uprising of 1986,[14] when Kazakh protesters were killed during demonstrations provoked by the replacement of longtime Kazakh party leader Dinmuhammad Kunayev by a Russian from outside the republic. In honor of this event, December 16 was chosen as Kazakhstan's independence day. Kazakh nationalists go so far as to accuse the Russians of making three separate attempts at genocide of the Kazakh people. The first was the famine of the 1890s, when after several harsh winters the Kazakhs were turned away from traditional pasturelands to make way for Russian settlers. The second began with the deportation of hundreds of thousands of Kazakhs in the aftermath of a failed anti-Russian uprising in 1916, which was then quickly followed by the famine and epidemics of the Civil War from 1918 to 1922. The worst Russian treatment of the Kazakhs resulted from the policies of collectivization in the 1930s, which left four to six million Kazakhs dead and irrevocably shattered their traditional pastoral livestock-based culture. The Kazakhs never fully recovered from this blow, because after World War II Soviet authorities once again drove Kazakhs from traditional lands in the northern part of the republic to make way for European settlers during the Virgin Lands drive of the 1950s. Even the name of the campaign was an irritant, for it implied, erroneously, that these steppe lands were vacant until Russian settlers were sent to farm them.

The Kazakh government has been working with Kazakh nationalists to think up ways to compensate the population for the injustices it and its ancestors suffered. As we see in chapter 6, the government has had a formal demography policy, including programs to resettle the Kazakh diaspora community and incentives for Kazakhs to have large families. These policies are designed to make the Kazakhs—currently constituting almost 54 percent of the population—the overwhelming majority population as quickly as possible and to secure ethnic Kazakh control of those parts of the country that were ethnic Russian enclaves. In the process Kazakhstan's government is not above gerrymandering electoral, and even territorial, districts to create Kazakh majorities wherever possible. Soviet administrative boundaries were designed to achieve one set of outcomes—effective management by Moscow—and the new Kazakh ones are designed to maximize control of the new national elite.

Most Kazakhs do not believe that the primary task of state building should be to redress the wrongs of history. They accept Kazakhstan as a multinational state and are generally willing to grant Russians the same rights as Kazakhs if those Russians are prepared to learn the history, language, and culture of the people for whom this new country is named.

The country's Russian population, however, is not willing to do this. More than a quarter of Kazakhstan's Russian population, upwards of two million since 1992, has left the country in little more than a decade rather than accept this change of status.[15] Ethnic Russians also feel aggrieved and are angry that the USSR simply disappeared, leaving them unaccountably transformed from a majority into a minority population.

Few of the country's ethnic Russians believe that the Kazakhs have any real claim to statehood, and most regard the Kazakhs as a late-emerging and incompletely developed people who would have had little or no sense of national identity had the Soviets not "given" them a homeland. Contemporary literature suggests that the prerevolutionary settlers saw themselves as frontiersmen, and at the time of independence only about half of Kazakhstan's Russian population had roots in the republic that went back more than fifty years. The majority of Russians were the descendants of Soviet-era settlers who either came or were sent to a remote part of their country. Most local Russians, however, have adopted the mind-set of the descendants of the early settlers who regard Kazakhstan as part of a Russian frontier region that had no precise boundary. For the Russians, the first postindependence constitution, adopted in January 1993, was a particular blow, referring as it did to Kazakhstan as being "the home of the Kazakh people."[16] Kazakhstan's Russian population had understood it to be the home of the Russian people as well. Those who lived in northern Kazakhstan believed that they had been living not just in the Soviet Union but on Russian soil since Kazakhstan had been a constituent part of the Russian Federation until 1936.

Such historical battles are of little interest to the remaining 20-odd percent of the population who are neither Kazakh nor Russian. They are more concerned with having the government maximize the discretionary rights of linguistic and cultural minorities. While many non-Kazakhs are most sympathetic to the Kazakhs' past maltreatment by the Russians, they see such grievances as being against governments that are now defunct, and so, they feel, these historical wrongs should not be righted at their personal expense.

In chapter 3, I explain how Kazakhstan's government has tried to respond to the challenge of the country's multi-ethnicity by designing a constitution that offers the representatives of all nationalities in Kazakhstan equal protection before the law. The country's leaders, however, are as much trapped by the vestiges of the Soviet understanding of nationality as are the country's citizens.

Nationality has a central place in Kazakhstan and naturally bestows on ethnic Kazakhs a position of relative privilege. One of the great ironies of the Soviet system was that although *nationalism* was always viewed as a major threat to the stability of the allegedly internationalist Soviet state, *nationality* was used as the primary sorting principle in Soviet society. Every young Soviet citizen acquired an internal passport at age sixteen, and from that point on his or her nationality was fixed for life. Generally, one took the nationality of one's father, although people of mixed parentage were sometimes able to choose. However, someone with two Ukrainian parents, for example, could not declare himself a Kazakh, even if he (and his parents and grandparents before him) had been born in Almaty.

Even in the Soviet period, a Ukrainian living in Kazakhstan would have felt some sense of living "abroad." Soviet publications written in Ukrainian might have been available at a cultural center but were not sold at newsstands, and of course local television and radio programs would have been only in the Russian or Kazakh languages. Travel to Ukraine was cheap but indirect, and telephone service was inexpensive but of poor quality. Children could be sent to Ukraine to study, increasing the likelihood of a job assignment in Ukraine upon graduation. Kazakhs and Russians were also free to go there, and many did. In fact, President Nazarbayev tried unsuccessfully to get his parents to allow him to go to the Kiev[17] Institute of Civilian Aviation in Ukraine.[18] His parents, though, pressed him to remain close to home, as was typical for a Kazakh child raised in a traditional rural setting.

The USSR was a place of paradoxes. The state set cultural and ideological homogenization as an explicit goal. At the same time, though, the state was organized into a federation with greatly enhanced rights for ethnic communities within the territories that bore their names. Thus, without intending to do so, the regime set up a system in which the boundaries between ethnic communities were made to appear immutable, and national communities saw the preservation of their cultural and linguistic differences as their primary goal. This system generally leveled the political salience of nationality for those peoples with historic legacies of nationhood and for those groups whose ethnic consciousness was redefined as a result of Stalin-era social engineering. Few Soviet peoples remained politically acquiescent during the late Gorbachev years, when the policies of *glasnost* and *perestroika* stimulated a heightened national consciousness and led to demands for political independence.[19]

This was not the case in Kazakhstan. As this book emphasizes, one of the main challenges to state building in Kazakhstan is that independence was not achieved as the culmination of a popular struggle. Independence was "awarded" at a gathering of Soviet republic leaders, from which Nazarbayev was absent.[20] For most people living in the Soviet Union, the collapse of the USSR exaggerated the importance of nationality over citizenship. It was rapid and unexpected and so demonstrated that citizenship is mutable. At the same time, ethnic identity, based on blood, seemed immutable and able to form a legitimate basis for political empowerment.

Given the potential volatility of Kazakhstan's demographic situation, initially Kazakhstan's rulers made some tentative efforts to model themselves after multi-ethnic states such as the United States, but they quickly tired of the effort, citing the inappropriateness of the comparison. I argue that this was a mistake. The myth of the United States as a "melting pot" has long been replaced by the recognition that some groups were forcibly incorporated, brought in as slaves, or had their homelands involuntarily annexed. There is also now the admission that not all groups have been equitably treated. Complete assimilation is no longer expected and has been replaced by a desire to balance political oneness with ethnic differentness. Reference to "we the people" of the United States no longer immediately evokes an image of a white Anglo-Saxon,[21] as citizenship is now expected to be ethnically blind, and groups appeal to U.S. authorities when they feel that the neutrality of the system is being violated.

In the post-Soviet world no one really expects the state to be neutral, but rather to favor those whose homeland the country "really" is. As I detail in chapters 2 and 3, this legacy of Soviet-era understandings of nationalism creates a real burden for Kazakhstan's leaders. State documents talk of the "Kazakhstani people," a reference to all the citizens of the state, but Kazakhstan's citizens do not think of themselves as one people.

Kazakhstan's constitution speaks of the equality of peoples regardless of nationality, a point that is repeatedly made by President Nazarbayev and other leading Kazakh figures. Yet few believe that these statements reflect the actual conditions in their country, and the appointment of an ethnic Kazakh to replace a non-Kazakh is almost always interpreted as an ethnic slight.

As I explain in chapter 6, life for local Russians contains daily small slights, which Kazakhs defend as simply natural parts of the state-building process. One of these was to switch the spelling of the country's official name from *Kazakhstan* to *Kazakstan* (in 1995), to better reflect Kazakh pronunciation (from *Kh* to *K* in the Cyrillic alphabet). Two years later the Kazakh government switched the spelling back to *Kazakhstan* in international usage but left the official spelling at home unchanged, a seemingly needless irritant. The Russian mass media retaliated by continuing to use the "Kh" throughout, claiming that the alternative was difficult to pronounce. Plans to switch written Kazakh from the Cyrillic alphabet to Latin script are exacerbating already sore feelings. But the biggest irritant, from the point of view of the Russians, is that they are being forced to learn and speak Kazakh, which the Kazakh constitution says must exist side-by-side with Russian and eventually come to dominate it.

Those who do not speak Kazakh are not appeased by formal declarations that preserve Russian as a language of "international communication."[22] In chapter 6, I also discuss the difficulties of making the Kazakh language and culture equal to Russian, to say nothing of replacing it, because at the time of independence almost no non-Kazakhs, and not even all ethnic Kazakhs, spoke Kazakh. Most Kazakhs, though, are sympathetic to the idea that the Kazakh language should have a place of privilege because Kazakhstan is the Kazakhs' home. More than any other kind of legislation, the new laws making Kazakh the official language of the state and mandating its use in a variety of public arenas clearly create a shift both in actual and perceived economic and political empowerment.

Gaining Confidence with Time

In this book I discuss how, with time, Kazakhstan's leaders have grown more confident in advancing the national cause of the Kazakh people and are doing so in a way that increasingly works to their own personal advantage. In chapter 2, I describe how Kazakhstan's leaders were convinced initially that their country's state-building strategy had to be driven by its location, requiring Kazakhstan to demonstrate continuing sensitivity to Russia's preferences for the kind of state their country should become.

At the time of independence Kazakhstan was more economically dependent upon Russia than was any other former Soviet republic. While Kazakhstan's dependence is being both reduced and redefined,[23] it will be far more difficult to circumvent the need to ship goods across Russia, heading both east and west. New or expanded transport links facilitate shipping across China to Asia, across the Caspian to Azerbaijan, and across Iran to

Europe, but the freight capacity of these routes will remain restricted well into the future. Using most of the new routes for shipping fossil fuel to markets is problematic, until at least 2005 or even later.

In chapter 5, I examine how, in the first years of independence, Kazakhstan's government had only partial control over the country's economic wealth. Chevron's development of the Tengiz oil field was delayed for several years until the major partners in the transaction gave Russia an economic interest in allowing the project to succeed. There was also the problem of the unresolved status of the Caspian Sea and Russia's earlier opposition to Kazakhstan's putting up for tender the development rights for these reserves. Leading Russian industrial interests also laid claim to equity shares in Kazakh projects in other sectors too, and as we see in chapter 5, they dominated ferrous metallurgy in Kazakhstan in the early years.

All this uncertainty initially made Western partners very cautious of investment in Kazakhstan, and although Kazakhstan is developing strong new economic strategic partnerships, Russia remains important because it is able to assert influence by leveraging the grievances of the local Russian community. Russia's leaders believe that they should enjoy postimperialist rights and privileges, including the ability to oversee the fate of their stranded co-nationals, and they were vocal about asserting this in the first years after the Soviet collapse. At that time, as I explain in chapter 5, Russia had only a minimal interest in repatriating Kazakhstan's Russians and was far more interested in pressing Kazakhstan's leaders to accept suitable terms for the citizenship of ethnic Russians in Kazakhstan.

The ethnic Russian population is Kazakhstan's Achilles' heel. Disrupting established trade patterns between Russian and Kazakh firms meant unemployment for ethnic Russians, who accounted for the majority of workers in Kazakhstan's factories and mines. The Kazakh government had no way to gauge the level of patience for decreasing standards of living of any part of the population. Improved economic relations with Russia served Kazakhstan's short-term interests but seemed likely to harm the long-term economic development of the country.

Kazakhstan's development strategy has been to try to balance the two options, seeking to promote Western investment and involvement while institutionalizing close economic ties with Russia. Although maximizing foreign investment requires implementing a free trade or at least a low-tariff regime, stabilizing economic relations with Russia may well entail accepting the economic interdependence of the two states and setting up preferential relations that foreign investors may find troubling. These two strategies are potentially at odds with each other, and Kazakhstan's economy is moving forward without fully addressing this basic contradiction.

Kazakhstan's foreign policy was also initially dominated by its desire not to antagonize Russia and a drive to integrate with it. The Kazakh government remained an advocate of a strong CIS long after most other leaders had grown disenchanted with it, and the Kazakhs also supported a variety of other plans that called for greater integration with Russia. Nonetheless the Kazakhs were regularly at odds with Russia's leadership because of Kazakh insistence that the proposed or existing CIS institutions be formed of equal partners.

In chapter 2, I also describe the tension that existed in the area of security relations. For the first years after independence the military forces of the two nations were closely intertwined, and it seemed clear that Russia's security needs would drive Kazakhstan's agenda. Kazakhstan's stance has become more independent in recent years. As the Nazarbayev government has striven to ingratiate itself with the United States and other Western nations, it has also begun to better understand the limitations of geography and so has been careful not to diminish its options vis-à-vis Moscow. Kazakhstan joined the Partnership for Peace, takes an active role in the North Atlantic Treaty Organization (NATO)–sponsored Central Asian Peacekeeping Battalion (CENTRASBAT), and has offered the United States access to its airspace and military facilities as Washington prepared for war in Afghanistan in 2001. At the same time the Nazarbayev government has negotiated a series of ever more inclusive agreements with Russia covering security as well as economic issues. Kazakhstan has also been an enthusiastic member of the new Shanghai Cooperation Organization.[24]

As I detail throughout the volume, in the course of the past decade, though, Kazakhstan's leadership has become less concerned with appeasing Russia and is no longer overly sensitive to the concerns of the ethnic Russians living in Kazakhstan. One important gesture in this regard was Nazarbayev's decision to move the capital of the nation from Almaty to Akmola (renamed Astana) on December 10, 1997. This action, which I describe at greater length in chapters 4 and 6, moves the nexus of power from the southeast corner to the north-central part of the country and thus much closer to Russia. It is no accident that Nazarbayev chose a visit by then Russian Prime Minister Viktor Chernomyrdin to declare the transfer of Kazakhstan's seat of power.[25]

Trapped between Western Pluralism and Asian Autocracy

With time Nazarbayev realized that Russia was growing weaker while Kazakhstan was growing stronger. These perceptions were reinforced by shifting international attitudes toward both Russia and Kazakhstan. The growing international interest in Kazakhstan has also had a real and negative impact on political institution building, which is my subject in chapter 4.

Outside powers have sent the Kazakhs conflicting signals over the past several years. On the one hand, the United States in particular and other Western powers somewhat more tentatively have pressed Kazakhstan to create a regime that upholds basic democratic traditions. These countries want Kazakhstan to employ practices such as the full enfranchisement of the population, equal civil rights for all ethnic groups, fair competition for political power between contending groups, and equality of economic and social opportunities across ethnic lines. At the same time, Western leaders are eager to ensure that their companies are well positioned to develop Kazakhstan's oil reserves. So, while they may be sympathetic to human rights and other political opposition groups that have seen their sphere of action sharply reduced in recent years, these same leaders are unlikely to do much more than invoke mild rebukes to the offending Kazakhs, and sometimes they are reluctant to do even that. Take for example the state visit of President Nazarbayev to the United Kingdom in November 2000, when he received the Order of St. Michael and St. George from Queen Elizabeth II, at the very time that Western newspapers were filled with articles of the theft of state assets by the Kazakh president and other family members.

The Kazakh leader, of course, has never admitted to any malfeasance. He claims that the Western press maliciously distorts the truth (see chapters 6 and 7) and tries to control his international image by keeping Western lawyers, lobbyists, and public relation firms on retainer. Publicly, the Kazakh leader explains that any shift in political emphasis that has occurred is necessary for the country to work out its national identity, and until that takes place, the country cannot withstand a succession crisis.

The truth is that Kazakhstan's leaders now feel that its valuable resources and the heightened Western interest in them give the Kazakhs the freedom to establish their primacy and to benefit personally from Kazakhstan's vast wealth. This has led the government to adopt a state-building strategy that emphasizes the need for political stability even at the expense of political participation. Over time, the Kazakh government has grown increasingly afraid of what popular empowerment can bring and has restricted the scope of electoral politics. It is my contention that no utility is derived from limiting political participation and that Kazakhstan's best state-building strategy would be to grant each of its ethnic groups equal access to the institutions of power in order to foster loyalty to the state. This does not mean that the government should not or does not want the population to be politically loyal. Its goal, though, is to insulate political outcomes from popular choice.

Even more important is that few of Kazakhstan's leaders truly believe that popular participation is necessary to legitimate the state. Most of them still believe as the old Soviets did, that popular will can be shaped through ideological indoctrination, and they simply underestimate the difficulty of the task (see chapter 3). The Soviet Union had a fully integrated ideological system, with media, education, and the arts all mobilized to serve the state's goals. As I show in subsequent chapters, the means currently at the disposal of the Kazakh elite are far more limited, restricted in part by its interest in developing a global reach for the economy.

Much of the elite consolidation of power has been justified as restoring Kazakh nationhood. Yet the nature of the unique historical role the Kazakhs intend to play is still unclear. The symbolic import of the government's message has been somewhat vaguely conveyed, the Kazakh government claiming that it seeks to combine European traditions with Asian ones.

The Kazakhs understand an Asian approach to be one that legitimates the policies of political crackdown when they serve the purpose of economic transformation. Once economic recovery is ensured, they promise that political democracy will be introduced. The evolution of South Korea, Taiwan, and Singapore is often cited as proof of the soundness of such a strategy, but as I argue, it is also not clear that the Kazakhs have the will for self-discipline that the "Asian tigers" have often demonstrated. Seeking to sacrifice due process in the name of economic necessity, Kazakh leaders also do not yet accept the need to be European, nor do they accept the contention that a civil society offers the legal infrastructure that is necessary for the protection of private property.

Ironically, the government's strong commitment to pursue macroeconomic change was initially used to justify a consolidation of power in the executive branch. President Nazarbayev argued that without such a consolidation, Kazakhstan would fail to develop the legal infrastructure necessary to secure private property and attract foreign investment. This was a point Nazarbayev hammered away at in the spring and summer of 1995 when he dissolved parliament and urged amending the constitution to make the parliament less fractious. Kazakhstan would be a strong presidential republic for a long time, he said in August 1995, because "we lack a parliamentary culture and traditions and a well-developed multiparty system."[26] Since his reelection as president in January 1999, there has been further talk of increasing the powers of the presidency, and even of making it hereditary, a decision that if taken will be done without an open popular debate.

Parliaments are by nature a brake on executive power, and what President Nazarbayev saw as a fractious parliament was one that others viewed as a legislature trying to learn how to do its job. The Kazakhstan parliament certainly held up government plans for privatization of the economy, but many parliamentarians blocked the government proposals not so much because they distrusted the institution of private property, but because they objected to the abuses of the allocation process.

As I demonstrate in chapter 4, there is no institution in Kazakhstan capable of providing legal protection or balancing the president's power. There is a story told that over drinks after a dinner in 1990, a Russian adviser, sent from Moscow to help with the problems of political institution building, chided Nazarbayev, saying that he seemed more of a benevolent dictator than a democrat. The Kazakh president is said to have responded that of all three words, the only one he understood was *dictator*.

Even if the tale is apocryphal, Nazarbayev seems to have tired of textbook-style democracy quickly once he learned how difficult it is to control. The Kazakh government maintains that the population has supported it in these efforts, often citing public opinion polls that show that people are more concerned with the maintenance of public order than with having a strong say in how their country is ruled. Nevertheless, President Nazarbayev has sought to maintain the fiction that Kazakhstan has a quasi-participatory model of rule. He has used public referendums to extend his term of office and constitutional reforms that substitute a weak bicameral legislature, elected by a complex and elaborate procedure, for a somewhat stronger unicameral one. He then ran for the presidency "on a competitive basis," having ensured that he faced no serious competition. Smarting from Western criticism, Nazarbayev promised to make the 1999 parliamentary elections more democratic, only to have those elections again fall short of international norms. Since then, he has taken steps to attempt a dynastic succession.

President Nazarbayev and his advisers have been trying to build the foundation for patriotism in Kazakhstan by guessing at what the population wants, rather than allowing the people to state their own desires. They justify this by arguing that popular rule might lead to the exacerbation of ethnic conflict. Although it is true that Kazakhstan is an ethnically divided society, the argument that ethnic differences would turn violent if the population were accorded greater rights of self-government is generally based on inappropriate analogies. Russians and Kazakhs have virtually always lived close to one another peacefully, and, with the exception of the 1916 uprising, ordinary Russians were never held responsible for the excesses of the previous state policy.[27]

Promoting political exclusion is always potentially dangerous since it requires a subject population that is either passive or loyal. Lacking that, the government must be confident that it has the capacity to make a sufficiently effective use of force to ensure the population's submission. It is far from clear whether any of these preconditions are in place in Kazakhstan. The many divisions that are beginning to typify Kazakhstan include: growing intra-ethnic splits within the Kazakh population that could compound interethnic ones, growing gaps between rich and poor, increasing regional differences, and the growing alienation of Islamic activists. While Kazakhstan has a growing and increasingly more visible security apparatus, the effectiveness of that apparatus is still untested, providing little evidence that it will be effective at anything more than suppressing isolated cases of dissent.

Western democratic theory is based on the premise that political participation makes people stakeholders and that this helps to create the sense of political community that forms the basis of political loyalty and patriotism. It may be convenient for Western leaders occasionally to ignore the ways that regimes try to insulate themselves from public pressure in oil- or other resource-rich states, but the affected populations need not indefinitely remain a submissive party to the indifference of their leaders and of other nations to their fates.

If people lack a sense of political community, they will feel no loyalty to the state in which they live, and public order will be ensured only as long as apathy prevails. Apathy, though, is a far less reliable political force than is patriotism. By promoting stability at the expense of participation, the Kazakh elite has effectively stunted the process of building a new Kazakh state and may eventually have to turn to the international community to become the guarantor of Kazakh independence.

2

Reluctantly Accepting Independence

Sensitive to the often unpleasant fates of small and ethnically divided states that border on more powerful ones, President Nazarbayev initially sought ways to trade sovereignty for Kazakh domination of a territorially integral Kazakhstan. Nazarbayev's goal was to level the playing field for Kazakhstan as much as possible so that his country would be no weaker than any of the other Soviet successor states. Nazarbayev feared that to press for a strong, Kazakh-dominated country was to risk antagonizing Russia and so to put the security of his newly independent country at risk. He did not want the ethnic Kazakhs to have less control of their country than did his former Soviet neighbors. Nazarbayev had the ambition to play the role of an international leader and wanted to ensure that Kazakhstan did not pass from the world's stage. In these early years, many, including the leaders of the newly independent nations themselves, saw independence as potentially illusory. Nazarbayev's solution was to influence his fellow presidents to develop a shared understanding of how to regulate relations with Russia to common advantage.

From the onset, Kazakhstan's leaders recognized that building a viable and stable independent state would require a great deal of diplomatic finesse since no one could easily protect this landlocked state from the effects of Russian displeasure. The juridical hurdle of statehood was crossed in late December 1991, when the international community recognized the republic of Kazakhstan. The psychological hurdle of statehood is decreasing with time but has not disappeared.

Most Russians see no natural dividing line between Kazakhstan and Russia, despite the fact that the Kazakhs believe there is. But with every passing year, even though they are still not fully delineated, the current borders take on more legitimacy. There remains, however, a lingering hope on the part of many Russians—and even some Kazakhs—that the two states and the two peoples will someday be formally reunited.

Russia's psychological barrier to accepting Kazakh statehood was a factor in interethnic relations in the republic even before independence, but it became much more salient once Kazakhstan's independence was proclaimed. Russia viewed the rising Kazakh ethnic sense of self-awareness and the ensuing distrust and frustration among the Russian population as a potentially explosive concoction, and one that Russia need not sit quietly by and tolerate.

The great military imbalance between Kazakhstan and Russia is an unequivocal warning that in the event of a conflict between Kazakhstan's two largest ethnic communities, Russia could easily partition Kazakhstan, taking the northern lands to which it claims historic rights. In the first years of independence it was not obvious how the international community would respond to such a usurpation of power, especially if Russia were to make skillful use of local Russians as surrogates and intervened for their protection. The Kazakh leadership was also acutely aware of its country's strong economic dependence on Russia, which was especially profound at the time of independence.

That President Nazarbayev was one of the most forceful advocates of the preservation of the USSR should be no surprise given Kazakhstan's vulnerable situation. After the demise of the USSR, no one worked harder than Nazarbayev to find a new formula for integrating the former Soviet republics into some form of effective multilateral organization, one in which each member state was effectively the equal of all others. Initially Nazarbayev believed that this was the best way to advance Kazakhstan's interests, but as he grew more confident of his own skills, as well as with Kazakhstan's inherent hold on statehood, the Kazakh leader became more interested in a junior partnership with Russia. Still, Nazarbayev's preoccupation with integration took precedence over the pursuit of economic development and political institution building.

Nazarbayev and Kazakhstan

It is difficult to separate the process of state building in Kazakhstan from the personality of its first and, as yet, only president. President Nazarbayev's advocacy of a policy of integration helped ensure its support by the population, even though such a strategy on the surface might have seemed antithetical to the interests of a newly independent state.

Nazarbayev's will has just about always been translated into state policy, initially because he was strongly supported by the population and later because he had created the institutions necessary to buffer him from popular criticism. Appointed Kazakhstan Communist Party first secretary in 1989, Nursultan Abishevich Nazarbayev assumed the title of president of his Soviet republic in March 1990, at the same time that most other republic first secretaries expanded the base of their authority. He ran unopposed in the popular election in December 1991 (his most likely competitor had failed to get the 100,000 petition signatures necessary for him to appear on the ballot) and received 98 percent of the vote, with more than 80 percent of eligible voters participating.[1] Next, he opted to avoid a more competitive election, scheduled for 1996, in favor of extending his term in office to December 2000 through a referendum held in April 1995. Then, in 1998 when President Nazarbayev became anxious about his popularity, he scheduled the presidential election to take place earlier, in January 1999. An antidemocratic election law passed to accommodate the timing change ensured that he would face only token opposition. It is hard to know whether the Kazakh president's fears were real or imaginary. Public opinion polls from late 1997 showed him as still having strong approval ratings.[2] At roughly the same time, though, only about a third of the population was reported to support his economic policies.[3] A year later, a petition circulated calling for his resignation, which received more than 20,000 signatures. The figure was an insignificant one in a country of nearly fifteen million, but the insult it conveyed was not.

Nevertheless, Nursultan Nazarbayev has always been by far Kazakhstan's most popular politician. In the first years of independence many saw Nazarbayev as embodying Kazakh statehood. Initially, conventional wisdom held that the country's stability was due in no small part to his tenure in office. Even many of Nazarbayev's most vocal critics would grant that, save for his presence in high office, Kazakhstan would likely have fallen victim to the same interethnic strife that occurred in so many other parts of the former Soviet Union.

Speculation on "what might have been" was quite natural in Kazakhstan, given that conditions there are not wholly dissimilar to those in other post-Soviet states that experienced interethnic disturbances. Comparisons are most frequently made with the situation in Moldova, and Nazarbayev always gets high marks when the relative passivity of Russian secessionists in northern Kazakhstan is compared with the early violence and lingering instability caused by Moldova's breakaway Transdniester Republic. The Russians of northern Kazakhstan are neither as well organized nor as defiant as those in the Transdniester region, and they have also received less support from the Russian political and military establishment.[4] Again, accurately or not, Nazarbayev's success at home and his prestige abroad are often cited as an explanation for why Kazakhstan avoided the civil strife experienced in Moldova in 1991–1992.

In fact, the years just before and after independence afforded Nazarbayev an opportunity to shine. Nazarbayev was probably the only Soviet party leader simultaneously to enjoy the strong support of his population, the respect of his fellow leaders, and the trust of Mikhail Gorbachev. Nazarbayev was reportedly being groomed for the post of either vice president or prime minister of the USSR at the time of the failed August 1991 coup. Nazarbayev was sensitive to the enormous change wrought by the August events and the potentially fatal weakening of the Gorbachev regime and the USSR itself.[5] Many fellow republic presidents turned to him in the coup's aftermath to try to broker a power-sharing agreement with the center. When that failed, he took up the initiative to redefine the CIS to include all the remaining Soviet republics and not simply Russia, Belarus, and Ukraine.[6]

A leader is fortunate when his personality and leadership traits are a particularly good fit for the nature of the society of which he has charge. Nazarbayev was certainly a man for his times in the last years of Soviet rule and the first years of independence. It is less apparent how well suited he is for handling the longer-term problems of Kazakhstan's transition to independence, which may help explain why Nazarbayev has backed away from an earlier commitment to introduce democratic or quasi-democratic institutions in Kazakhstan.

Nazarbayev's career experiences hold clues as to why he has backed away from his commitment to democracy and may also explain the roots of so many of his other policies in the first years of independence. Nazarbayev was a Soviet success story. A graduate of a Soviet technical junior college, his claim to "advanced" education is a correspondence degree from a regional higher party school.[7] Born in the village of Chemolgan in rural Alma Ata oblast in 1940,[8] the Kazakh president moved north for his first job, at the Karaganda Metallurgical Complex, where after ten years in a blast furnace production shop he switched to full-time Communist Party work. Nazarbayev was equally at ease in a Russian-dominated Communist Party milieu and the rural Kazakh community in which he was raised. He was able to develop the bureaucratic skills and the patronage necessary to rise to the top of Kazakhstan's party oligarchy in near record time. Nazarbayev was appointed prime minister of Kazakhstan at age forty-four.

Although a strong public proponent of Gorbachev's economic and political reform program, the young prime minister was passed over for appointment as republic first secretary in December 1986. This was presumably because of his earlier close association with Kazakh party leader and longtime Communist Party of the Soviet Union (CPSU) Politburo member Dinmuhammad Kunayev, who was one of the targets of the reformers' anticorruption campaign in the mid-1980s.[9] Despite Nazarbayev's often scathing criticism of his former mentor, Gorbachev decided to appoint Gennady Kolbin,[10] an ethnic Russian and oblast first secretary from central Russia to head Kazakhstan's Communist Party. Angry crowds gathered in downtown Alma Ata when word of Kolbin's appointment spread, and demonstrators clashed with hastily pulled together law enforcement forces, which consisted in part of local cadets.[11]

The events of those days must have been personally humiliating for Nazarbayev, who, in order to protect his own career chances, silently accepted Kolbin's appointment and made way for a CPSU central committee–appointed commission to investigate the disturbances. This committee eventually found that the instigators of the Alma Ata Uprising, as it came to be termed, were the children of the Kazakh elite, who were drunk and high on dope when they took to the streets to protest the curtailing of the Kunayev era that had so unfairly favored them. Nazarbayev, who finally succeeded Kolbin in June 1989, allowed this version to stand unchallenged until shortly before independence, which was declared on the fifth anniversary of the Alma Ata demonstrations.[12]

Nazarbayev's first goal in those years was to improve Gorbachev's opinion of him, and, especially after becoming first secretary, to strike a good deal for Kazakhstan as well. He succeeded quite well at both tasks. From the time of his appointment as Kazakhstan's first secretary to Gorbachev's final days in office, Nazarbayev was a useful ally to the former Soviet leader. Nazarbayev worked hard to carve out a reputation for himself in the years just after coming to power, by first closely studying the situation in Moscow and then carefully measuring his actions. The question of how economic authority should be divided between the center and the periphery was an issue of fiery debate when Nazarbayev was promoted to first secretary in June 1989. Anxious that Kazakhstan should gain at least a share of its vast mineral wealth, which was then exclusively under Moscow's control, the Kazakh leader became a forceful advocate of a middle position, calling for "a strong center and strong republics."[13] Effectively this meant that part of the hard currency revenues from the sale of Kazakhstan's resources would be credited directly to the republic's benefit, although the decisions affecting the development of these resources would still rest almost exclusively with Moscow. Part of this revenue, in turn, could be used for the development of a more diversified industrial economy within Kazakhstan, and the rest could be used simply to improve the local standard of living.

Moscow was only one focus of the Kazakh party leader's attention. No less important to Nazarbayev was strengthening his position within Kazakhstan and rewarding an elite who would serve him loyally. When Nazarbayev took control of Kazakhstan's Communist Party there were still many who viewed him as a brash and ruthless upstart, someone willing to forget old obligations if it helped advance his own career. By the time of his 1989 promotion, bloody demonstrations in Kazakhstan and elsewhere had sensitized the Gorbachev leadership to the need for Communist Party leaders at the republic level to enjoy local support if they were to be effective supervisors of the economic and political reform process.

The need to gain popular approval has been a challenge ever since, and one that Nazarbayev has never fully surmounted, largely because he has set enjoying the perquisites of power as a priority. There have been enormous changes in the structure of government in Kazakhstan over the past decade, and President Nazarbayev has changed his personal advisers several times in an effort to make Kazakhstan's government a professional one. The patterns of patronage that developed in his first years in office, though, continue to impede the implementation of economic and political reforms in the country. Charges of favoritism and corruption increasingly dog the presidency and the presidential entourage. Critics have alleged that the country is developing a tribal or clan system or one based on a family dynasty, while Nazarbayev's defenders counter that they are substituting a more "Kazakh" system in place of the Soviet one that preceded it. Both groups see the problem of patronage as a feature of transition, but as Nazarbayev's critics argue, corruption is now so deeply rooted that the turn to autocracy may prove irreversible.

Over time President Nazarbayev has grown more sophisticated as a political leader as well as seemingly more corrupt. When he took over as the head of Kazakhstan, public opinion already mattered. This lesson was driven home by the December 1986 Alma Ata riots and even more so by the great symbolic role that unrest quickly assumed in Kazakh political life.

Nazarbayev believes that public opinion can and must be managed, but he has been bedeviled by the question of just how much and when to heed the public. Still, he understood from the outset that to be a popular leader he would have to enjoy the strong support of Kazakhs, regardless of their political persuasion, and to be supported or at least tolerated by the country's non-Kazakh population as well. Nazarbayev's nationalism was initially the most temperate of any of the post-Soviet leaders, as he sought to define Kazakh nationalism in a way that was explicitly tolerant of the contributions of non-Kazakhs, and this in turn provided increased support for his policies of preserving strong ties among the post-Soviet states.

How sincere a Kazakh nationalist Nazarbayev was in these early years is hard to say. Even today, he sees the Soviet legacy as complex, although he is a far more vocal critic of the system that raised him than he was in the first years of independence. People change over time, and anyone with the amount of ambition that Nazarbayev had even during the Soviet period does well not to engage in too much psychological self-examination. Perhaps Nazarbayev always had a strong and suppressed sense of national identity, or maybe he simply found it convenient to nurture this identity in the past decade.

Creating a Place for the Kazakhs in Kazakhstan

His hunger for personal recognition as a great and strong president has also made Nazarbayev more of a Kazakh nationalist. The pursuit of integration seemed to make this more feasible as a strategy, for if Russia were placated on critical economic and security issues, then the Kazakh leader expected to have the flexibility necessary to pursue a domestic agenda more to his liking. Sensitive to prevailing ethnonational trends, Nazarbayev seems to have decided that it would somehow be easier to make Kazakhstan a strong Kazakh state rather than a strong multinational one.

While Nazarbayev's understanding of how to use the structure of the Kazakh state to his own advantage evolved steadily, the preeminent role of the Kazakhs in this state was never to be questioned. President Nazarbayev has made continual reference to his pride in being a Kazakh, his desire to honor his ancestors, and the need for those who live in the republic to respect the traditional Kazakh culture. Although he has often identified these values as a source of interethnic tolerance, his intent was to emphasize the special relation of Kazakhs to Kazakhstan. In a speech given in 1994, Nazarbayev stated:

> A nation cannot exist without a state, it vanishes. It is not our people's fault, but its trouble that it has become a minority in the land of its ancestors. It is quite appropriate if in some cases the interests of the indigenous nation, the Kazakhs, are given special emphasis in this state.[14]

Despite such statements, Nazarbayev tried, particularly at the outset, to promote the Kazakh people's special relation to their nation in a way that would not antagonize local Russians. In the Soviet era it was somewhat easier to argue this position since Russians could be urged to learn about and respect the Kazakhs' culture in the context of friendship among peoples.[15] The mention of special rights for the Kazakhs, however, has always been highly contentious for the local Russians, even in 1989 when the existence of the USSR offered Kazakhstan's Russian population the prospect of intervention by Moscow and the legal protection of Soviet legislation against encroachment on their linguistic and cultural rights.

Yet Nazarbayev understood that a failure to offer the promise of preferential treatment to his republic's titular nationality would risk enraging the republic's Kazakhs, who were still smarting over the various indignities that they had suffered throughout Soviet rule. Although before independence the Kazakhs were a minority in the republic that bore their name, the only such community in the former Soviet Union, they wanted to be granted the same cultural rights that the other principal Soviet nationalities were receiving. As was true elsewhere in the USSR, informal political groups with nationalist political agendas organized in Kazakhstan to press for legislation that would make Kazakh the official language of the republic.[16] In August 1989 their wish came true when a bill was passed that mandated a phased program for increasing Kazakh language instruction in republic schools while gradually shifting the conduct of local and republic government business into Kazakh. Regions that were more than 70 percent Kazakh were to shift immediately to doing business in Kazakh, and all the rest would have up to fifteen years to complete the transition. Russian groups, especially those in northern Kazakhstan, objected to the latter provision and to the requirement for proficiency in Kazakh for high school graduation beginning in 1992.

The language law that Kazakhstan adopted was far less comprehensive than the legislation passed in many other republics. Its aim was simply to create a public role for Kazakh that would somewhat reduce, but definitely not eliminate, the role of Russian. Unlike virtually everywhere else in the USSR, the two languages were given near parity in Kazakhstan. Elsewhere in Central Asia, only the Kyrgyz afforded Russian a nearly analogous position. In reality, before Kazakhstan's independence, the enhanced role for Kazakh was more than cancelled by Russian's continuing role as the official language of the USSR. After all, it was not as though the use of Russian were fated to die out in Kazakhstan, although this might have been the impression conveyed to the uninitiated by Russian nationalist objections.[17] Local Russian groups claimed that their objections stemmed from a desire to have their own cultural renaissance. In reality, however, they were campaigning against providing any role for the Kazakh language in Kazakhstan; they were against the very idea that Russians should have to learn Kazakh.

The fierceness of the battles over Kazakhstan's language law left Nazarbayev and those close to him with little doubt that even serious talk of independence could destabilize the situation in the republic. While censorship was eased during those years, opposition political groupings were able to register in the republic only if they formally disavowed the goal of independence for Kazakhstan.[18] To talk of independence was akin to treason.

Given the enormous undeveloped natural resources of the republic, Nazarbayev and the Kazakh Communist Party elite felt that even a piece of the pie would have been a good deal for Kazakhstan. Most other republics and autonomous regions had far less to gain from the power- and profit-sharing arrangements proposed by Moscow, and by mid-1990 it was already apparent that this formulation was no longer sufficient to meet the growing hunger for autonomy that was gripping those living in the USSR's regions.[19]

By that time the Baltic republics had reclaimed their independence, there was mounting public support for independence in Ukraine and Georgia, and calls for republic sovereignty were commonplace throughout most of the country.

By contrast, in Kazakhstan there were only vague mutterings about independence, and the small nationalist groups, Azat and Alash, focused on the need for greater cultural and religious autonomy, respectively.[20] In part, the generally cautious Kazakhs had been made more timorous by the savagery with which Gennady Kolbin had cracked down on anything that could have been even remotely construed as nationalist protest. Some even went so far as to refer to 1987–1988 (the Kolbin period) as a "mini 1938," thus comparing Kolbin's policies to those of Stalin during the great purge.[21] The appointment of Nursultan Nazarbayev was thus met with great relief in Kazakhstan, especially by ethnic Kazakh leaders. Sensitive to the precarious demographic balance in the republic, even many nationalist Kazakh intellectuals did not want to risk tarnishing Nazarbayev's reputation for fear that someone far less sympathetic to the Kazakh cause might be appointed by Moscow to replace him.

They also understood that Nazarbayev was succeeding in ingratiating himself with Gorbachev. Peace in the republic allowed Kazakhstan's leader to play an increasingly important role in USSR politics. Few in Kazakhstan yet believed that their republic could become an independent country, and certainly not one with anything resembling its Soviet republic boundaries. Every ethnic group wanted to preserve its ancestral lands, and for the nomadic Kazakhs the fact that few of them still live on their traditional northern pasturelands has been a long-standing grievance. To risk the complete loss of this territory, which at least still bore their name and the possibility of future resettlement, was to be avoided at almost any cost. Separatist talk was becoming common among the Russian population of northern Kazakhstan, and the new city governments elected in the northern cities in late 1989 included considerable separatist factions. Kazakhs feared the politicization of the local Russian population. Watching the nightly news, they were constantly reminded of how secessionist movements had already led to prolonged armed conflicts between the Azerbaijanis and Armenians as well as between the Georgians and the Abkhaz.[22] It did not take much imagination to envision the ever more nationalistic Russian population of northern Kazakhstan taking up arms at a time when Moldova's Russian population (living in the Transdniester region) was threatening armed secession. If the union did not survive, Kazakhs had good reason to fear that the territorial integrity of their republic could be threatened as well.

This helps to explain why Nursultan Nazarbayev, who had assumed the title of president of Kazakhstan in March 1990, became a stalwart supporter of rewriting the Treaty of Union, which had bound the Soviet republics together since 1922. Nazarbayev did not play a key role at the April 1991 Novo-Ogarevo meeting of republic leaders, which arrived at a new power-sharing formula that gave more power to the country's constituent units. His hard work in lobbying for the treaty, though, was a critical factor in mustering support for the agreement in a number of wavering republics.[23]

The acrimony of trying to get a declaration of sovereignty passed by the republic legislature in the fall of 1990 had to have spurred Nazarbayev in his efforts. The legislators who debated the bill had been elected in March 1990 in the first semicompetitive elections held for the republic parliament. The new parliamentary deputies were almost all people who were on the party *nomenklatura* lists,[24] but they proved far more fractious than had their predecessors. The new legislators were beginning to act like parliamentarians, as though the partially democratic electoral procedure that had brought them to office gave them a popular mandate.

A declaration of sovereignty was passed in October 1990 after a bitter debate that reflected the prevailing divisions in the republic.[25] While the document unequivocally asserted Kazakhstan's right to control its own resources and manage its political affairs, it tried to skirt the question of whether Kazakhstan was the homeland of the Kazakhs or whether it belonged equally to all the republic's various peoples. If it was the land of the Kazakhs, which the declaration of sovereignty weakly endorsed, then the Kazakh language and culture deserved a special place in the republic.

Although throughout 1990 it was simply unthinkable to Nazarbayev that his republic could become independent, by mid-1991 many previously unthinkable things were already occurring in the Soviet Union. Mikhail Gorbachev was beginning to act like a spent political force. One sign of this was his refusal to turn the presidency of the USSR into a popularly elected office, when Boris Yeltsin was willing to participate in a contested race for the presidency of Russia. The center of power was shifting from Moscow to the republics, but Gorbachev seemed unable to work out a compromise position that would leave economic reformers and advocates of republic power satisfied. In response to this, the Kazakh leader began to distance himself somewhat from Gorbachev and to court Russia's new president, Boris Yeltsin.

Nazarbayev became preoccupied with the search for a formula to keep the union together, which became even more important to him than defending Kazakhstan's interests against Moscow. Because of these efforts, Nazarbayev's prestige in general increased, not just in Kazakhstan but in the entire USSR. He became even more visible after the abortive Communist Party coup of August 1991 led to the scuttling of the new Treaty of Union on the very eve of its signing. Nazarbayev took the lead in calling for saving the country when Gorbachev convened USSR legislators in a special session held just after he was released from house arrest.[26]

Gorbachev lacked the legitimacy to rule successfully, while Nazarbayev's position within Kazakhstan in particular had been strengthened by the banning of the Communist Party in the aftermath of the failed coup. This act led to the transfer of millions of dollars of property from the Communist Party to Kazakhstan government coffers, including centrally located office buildings, institutes, hotels, and apartment buildings. The banning of the party also shifted new responsibilities to the government, giving the Kazakh president vast sources of patronage for filling the positions he created in the new government.

By late 1991 a form of secessionist fever had spread from the outlying republics to Russia. Once reformist and pro-market forces allied with Yeltsin, there was nothing to hold the old elite coalitions of the center together, and their dissolution led to that of the USSR itself. Nazarbayev spent much of the first two weeks of December trying to help Gorbachev broker a loose confederative structure to replace that of the USSR, but there simply were few takers left among the senior republic leaders. Although President Nazarbayev may have preferred that Kazakhstan remain within a redefined union, the events of the last half of 1991 had left him in a highly advantageous position to become the effective leader of an independent Kazakhstan.

Whatever ambivalent personal feelings the presidents of the various Soviet republics might have had about the divorce from Moscow, by December 1991 political expediency dictated that they each embrace independence with enthusiasm. Left with little choice, on December 16, 1991, Kazakhstan's leaders declared their country's independence. It was the final republic to do so, and Kazakhstan's parliament voted for independence eight days after Russia, Belarus, and Ukraine announced their withdrawal from the USSR.

In Search of a Winning Formula for Integration

There was a surreal air about the events of December 1991. The republics' juridical status had certainly changed, and all the newly independent states hurried to gain admission to the United Nations, as well as to nearly every other major international body that would have them. But many found it hard to believe that independence was real. The leaders of the newly independent states had long functioned in a political universe in which Moscow's will was law throughout the entire USSR, and its preferences were also generally viewed as diktat in a group of satellite states just beyond its borders. For the first months of independence many CIS leaders expected their states to become little more than clients of Russia, so they poised themselves to take rapid advantage of the new opportunities that they assumed would prove fleeting.

In large part because he recognized the elusiveness of this goal, Nazarbayev's first priority was to attain some form of reintegration of the former Soviet republics. This was not simply an exercise in nostalgia on Nazarbayev's part, but an effort to solve Kazakhstan's security dilemma. If Kazakhstan were still a part of a larger whole, then it would be less important to many of Kazakhstan's citizens just how the new state defined itself. Integration meant that those who were most disgruntled with Kazakhstan could still take comfort from their identification with the supranational entity that Nazarbayev hoped to form.

The urge to integrate was almost instinctive for Kazakhstan's leaders and citizens alike, regardless of their ethnic origin. There was little unanimity, though, on what price should be paid for this integration. Some in Kazakhstan would even have given up independence if a stable union with Russia would have resulted. In the early years of independence this was the position of Kazakhstan's most famous poet, Olzhas Suleimenov, who turned political activist in the late 1980s when he organized the vastly popular Nevada-Semipalatinsk antinuclear movement. Suleimenov, who went on to form his own political party, the People's Congress, advocated Kazakhstan's acceptance of a confederative status from Russia.[27]

Suleimenov enjoyed some support for this position, which would have traded juridical independence for rights of cultural, political, and economic autonomy over all Kazakhstan's current territory. President Nazarbayev and most members of Kazakhstan's ruling elite obviously did not view this as a fair trade. They believed that Kazakhstan should remain the equal of all the newly independent states, and they sought a solution in which Kazakhstan surrendered sovereignty on terms equal to those of other states.

In the first years of independence Nazarbayev thought that some surrender of sovereignty was inevitable, but he also felt that Russia's strategic advantage over Kazakhstan was maximized in bilateral arrangements. By contrast, he believed that multilateral settings afforded at least some chance for the newly independent states to parry Russia collectively to their mutual benefit.

Thus Nazarbayev dedicated himself to the task of finding a form of supranational successor to the Soviet Union that would be acceptable to his fellow CIS leaders. Although a strong advocate of Kazakhstan achieving the maximum profit from its economic resources, President Nazarbayev simultaneously tried to convince his fellow CIS leaders that reintegration was in everyone's best interest. He did this both within and outside the structure of the CIS. Nazarbayev was initially an advocate of a strong CIS, and he was less worried than were many other leaders that the development of multinational institutions within the framework of the CIS would be a formula for Russian domination. On the contrary, given the long border between the two, Kazakhstan's leaders believed that the lack of such structures would likely lead to greater Russian pressure on a bilateral basis.

President Nazarbayev was unsuccessful in getting his CIS colleagues to accept a strong multilateral organization, as were the Russians themselves. Initially Kazakhstan's and Russia's leaders shared an interest in preserving the territories of the former USSR as a geopolitical and economic space. Russia saw this as a means of remaining a great power, while Kazakhstan saw integration as the way to maximize its influence in the region and the world more generally.

To be sure, this showed a lack of imagination on Nazarbayev's part and a failure to appreciate the possibilities that existed for Kazakhstan as a sovereign state. He eventually moved away from the priority he placed on integration, a goal that was further handicapped by Russia's and Kazakhstan's contradictory understandings of how this should be advanced. Their differences in approach also caused President Nazarbayev to rethink the kind of integration that would be appropriate for Kazakhstan. It is highly unlikely that, even if Russia's and Kazakhstan's leaders had found a common position, they could have overcome the objections to a comprehensive and institution-based integration process that were and are still held by the leaders of most other post-Soviet successor states.

Nazarbayev found the process of trying to achieve integration with Russia frustrating. His argument was one of mutual advantage, which was largely undermined by Russia's access to and use of various security and economic pressure points in each of the post-Soviet successor states. Despite Russia's periodic use of these pressure points, Moscow never succeeded in getting the post-Soviet states to join in any sort of effective union, either in whole or in part. Russia's first effort, the September 1993 economic union of nine CIS states, led to the collapse of the ruble zone two months later. Three states (Azerbaijan, Georgia, and Ukraine) were unwilling to trade even limited economic autonomy for close economic and security relations with Russia. This rebuff, and the incompleteness of the union that resulted, made Russia demand virtually complete economic control over the states that remained within its direct economic orbit, those still inside the ruble zone. This was enough to drive all but war-torn Tajikistan out of it.

Russia's critics saw the CIS as a vehicle for ensuring Russian supremacy because Soviet successor states were not being asked to "contribute" their sovereignty on an equal basis. To remedy this, Nazarbayev suggested that the CIS be replaced by a new organization, a Euro-Asian Union (EAU), in which member states would adopt common policies at an intergovernmental parliamentary assembly and would share a common currency and common foreign economic policies. EAU decisions were to be based on a four-fifths majority, with each member state having an equal vote.[28] Nazarbayev wanted legislative ratification by the parliaments of member states for EAU agreements to have the force of law in order to preserve the juridical independence of each of the member states.

Such defenses of national sovereignty were not sufficient to mollify the Kazakh leader's fellow presidents. When Nazarbayev presented this idea at the CIS meeting of April 1994, it was met with little enthusiasm. This did not stop Nazarbayev from pushing forward with the idea, which he had formally introduced as a public document at the United Nations. CIS newspapers published some two hundred articles in support of the proposal, and the Kazakhs sponsored conferences in Russia and Almaty where it was debated. There was never, however, a groundswell of support. For a while the project enjoyed the endorsement of Kyrgyz leader Askar Akayev and Georgian President Eduard Shevarnadze, but both eventually backed away from it when Russia's leadership strongly disapproved.

Nazarbayev's proposals found only minimal support from the CIS's other presidents, who were less willing to trade sovereignty for security, or at least preferred to do so on the basis of comprehensive bilateral agreements. It must have been disturbing to the Kazakh leader to learn that he was so out of step with most of his CIS colleagues, who were willing to abandon Soviet-style solutions fully. The EAU was predicated on the need to preserve a single post-Soviet space, and this in itself was something that the presidents of many of the newly independent states found objectionable.

States such as Turkmenistan, Uzbekistan, and Moldova did not share land borders with Russia, and so their leaders felt far freer to imagine a post-Soviet future in which Russia played an ever-diminishing role. Azerbaijan had a similar vision, although it did have a small and potentially contentious border with Russia in Daghestan. The goal of these states was to make the post-Soviet world only one of the neighborhoods in which they lived and to develop ever-improving ties with a host of other neighboring states as well as their former Soviet "brothers." Each sought to do this in a slightly different way, but the leaders of these states believed that their flexibility in international affairs would be maximized if they based their relations with Russia on bilateral agreements. Probably the most painful defection from Kazakhstan's point of view was that of Ukraine. The Ukrainians had the Russians breathing down their necks every bit as much as the Kazakhs did. The prize for Ukraine, however, was membership in Europe, whereas Europe seemed far away from Kazakhstan, while China, a potentially far more menacing state, was just beyond its borders.

More damning, though, was Russian opposition to the plan. Kremlin leaders viewed Nazarbayev's suggestion as contrary to their own national interests. An EAU predicated on the idea of shared authority between sovereign states was in direct conflict with the Russian strategy of seeking multilateral frameworks that would institutionalize their own strategic and economic domination. Russia's formal response to Nazarbayev's plan came at the October 1994 CIS meeting, when its delegates tried to usurp and redefine his plan to make it supportive of strengthening the CIS rather than replacing it. At that time member states agreed to a six-point program that called for the closer integration of economic, political, and security relations within the CIS's own institutional arrangements. It provided no mechanisms for this to be achieved, however, and so they effectively made impossible the goals that they were formally supporting.

Since that time, there could be little doubt that Nazarbayev's proposals for the creation of an EAU were dead, although the Kazakh leader has continued to claim that such a union would be preferable to the CIS.[29] Partly,

Nazarbayev's timing had been unfortunate. The recent political rebirth of the Communist Party of Russia brought with it talk of the re-creation of a Soviet Union, which was extremely unsettling from the perspective of the leaders of the newly independent states. This tainted any talk of a new union, and there was no way that Nazarbayev wanted his union confused with a communist-inspired restoration of a Moscow-style diktat, in which any sovereignty that continued to exist would be purely symbolic.

The rise of the Communists also corresponded to a change in Russian government thinking about the policies that should be pursued toward the "near abroad," as the Soviet successor states were then collectively termed. In late 1994, the liberal-minded foreign minister, Andrei Kozyrev, pressed these states to define their strategic interests synonymously with those of Russia.[30] Throughout 1995 this trend in Russia's policies became ever more apparent, with Moscow claiming residual ownership rights in a number of key strategic resources, including energy. This affected all the Caspian Sea states, including Kazakhstan.

Kozyrev's policy became an increasingly dominant theme in bilateral relations between Russia and Kazakhstan, and in Russia's relations with other CIS states. By mid-1995 Russia was pushing hard for an expanded role within the CIS, and Russia's first choice was to use the CIS as an instrument for its coordination of the military and economic policies of the member states. Russia's security goals were now clear: international borders (those not with CIS states) were to be secured at least in part by Russian troops; conflicts within the CIS were to be negotiated by Russian-dominated multinational forces that were recognized (and if possible funded) by the United Nations; and Russian troops were to be based throughout the CIS. Russia, however, had real difficulty in achieving these objectives.

The Russian government continued to strive for a similar level of economic integration. To this end, it pushed for the establishment of the CIS's Interstate Economic Council (in 1994), which was supplanted in 1995 by the Customs Union. The special conditions on membership laid out by several states, particularly Ukraine, doomed this organization to little more than a paper existence from its very inception.

From this point, relations within the CIS developed in a two-tier system. When the economic union initiative faltered, the Russian government pushed for a four-nation deep integration treaty between Russia, Belarus, Kazakhstan, and Kyrgyzstan. Tajikistan later signed on as well. The treaty called for the development of a full economic union between those states, including the introduction of a single currency by the end of 1997, as well as the coordination of plans to develop natural resources and other critical sectors of the economy through the use of multinational corporations formed from union members wherever possible. The legal and educational establishments of member states were to strive toward full coordination as well, and the treaty mandated the development of an interstate legislative oversight council to supervise the entire process. The latter was established almost immediately, but it never succeeded in regularizing either trade relations or other economic policies.[31]

At the same time a group of states tried to back away from the CIS and formed a new multilateral organization, GUAM, to help them do so.[32] The leaders of Georgia, Ukraine, Azerbaijan, and Moldova began discussions on establishing a cooperative economic and security organization in late 1996 and formalized their plans at the October 1997 Organization for Security and Cooperation in Europe (OSCE) summit. Uzbekistan formally joined them in April 1999 during the NATO celebrations in Washington, and GUAM became GUUAM.[33] That organization began to recede in importance, however, after the election of Vladimir Voronin, a Russian communist, as the president of Moldova on April 4, 2001. Voronin's election coincided with Uzbekistan's reevaluation of its security needs and Tashkent's growing interest in improved bilateral relations with Russia. By this time, pressure on Kazakhstan to join GUUAM had almost fully abated.

Despite these developments, Russian leaders tried with some regularity to reinvigorate the CIS, although Boris Yeltsin's ill health did little to advance this cause. He insisted on presiding over the organization, even though his capacity for work was ever diminishing. A meeting of the heads of state, first scheduled for January 1998, was postponed several times before it was finally held on April 29 of that year in Moscow. In an effort to give greater credibility to the ailing Russian leader, it was agreed at that time that Yeltsin would remain chairman of the council until 2000.

The April 1998 summit appointed Russian businessman Boris Berezovsky as the executive secretary of the CIS. Believing that he possessed the charm and skills necessary to save the organization and make it more businesslike, Berezovsky launched an ambitious program of travel and consultation with CIS leaders, trying to find ways to better define and make mutually acceptable the CIS functions. For a while it looked as though the appointment of the energetic Berezovsky would serve to reenergize the flailing organization, at least as a forum in which the leaders of the post-Soviet states could meet and discuss common problems. Berezovsky's proposed changes, however, encountered broad resistance. In particular, the presidents of Turkmenistan and Uzbekistan opposed restructuring because they had no wish to strengthen the CIS administration. The CIS staff opposed the proposed personnel reductions and also objected to Berezovsky's market approach to economics. Others objected to Berezovsky's proposal that the representatives be seated hierarchically at summit meetings according to their country's contributions to the organization.[34]

After Vladimir Putin came to power in December 1999, yet another effort was made to reinvigorate the CIS. Nazarbayev worked with Putin to advance the case of integration, supporting the Russian president's efforts to launch the Euro-Asian Economic Community, a transformed and upgraded version of the Customs Union. The leaders of Belarus, Kazakhstan, Kyrgyzstan, Russia, and Tajikistan signed the documents endorsing this in Astana in October 2000. Putin actively sought closer ties with the former Soviet states of Central Asia, promoting military and technical cooperation under the auspices of the CIS Collective Security Treaty and the establishment of a regional antiterrorist center. By this time, though, Nazarbayev was much more confident about his ability to manage a bilateral relationship with Russia, although he nonetheless was quick to offer support for the new Russian president's efforts, noting that Kazakhstan pursued a policy of integration with all CIS countries and "especially with the Russian Federation."[35]

Seeking Accommodation with Russia

As already noted, initially Nazarbayev and Kazakhstan's senior leadership did not seem to be particularly troubled by Moscow's lingering control. Even a largely titular form of independence created enormous new opportunities for them. Nazarbayev, as well as others in positions of prominence, moved quickly to position trusted friends and family members in posts that managed the country's foreign economic relations so that state assets might become personal ones in case independence proved short-lived.[36] If independence was sustained, then Kazakhstan's wealth would come under the more permanent control of the local elite since they supervised the economic reform process that would transform state holdings into privately owned property.

Independence was also a great psychological victory for the republic's Kazakh population, which had long felt victimized by Russia's colonial policies and by Soviet nationality policy. Many of the Kazakhs' grievances were generations old, but the revelations that came out with *glasnost*, combined with the new political freedoms of *perestroika*, allowed these feelings of personal anger to begin to be expressed collectively. Although excited by its prospects, few of the Kazakhs had anticipated independence, and there was a general nervousness that the breakup of the USSR would somehow lead to disastrous consequences. In fact, an August 1992 survey supported by the U.S. Information Agency (USIA) found that 61 percent of the population of Kazakhstan believed that "it was a great misfortune that the Soviet Union no longer exists."[37]

Fate's victims for so much of their history, many Kazakhs were now terrified that independence would be their final undoing, that the new country's Russian population would try forcibly to split northern Kazakhstan from the rest of the country. The culture and tradition of the Kazakhs revolved around the control of their former grazing lands and the burial places of their forefathers. They recognized, as well, that many of Kazakhstan's Russians viewed the region in symbolic terms, seeing this to be Russia's frontier and their homeland, over which they were now losing control.

Involuntarily stripped of their Soviet citizenship, even local Russians with newer ties to the region viewed Kazakhstan's independence as an unpleasant surprise, but most were too stunned to know how to react. Their response was generally one of silent displeasure, especially because Russia's leaders were too preoccupied with their country's rebirth and newly changed status to offer much concrete defense of their "stranded co-nationals," other than to discourage them from attempting to move back to Russia proper.

Although President Nazarbayev understood that he had to maintain the support of the ethnic Kazakhs, he was also aware that Kazakhstan's security depended upon the continued quiescence of the country's large Russian population, as well as the more formal support of Kazakhstan's independence by Russia's leaders. The economy of northern Kazakhstan was fully interlinked with that of the neighboring Russian oblasts. Ending these links could mean economic hardships for the Russian-dominated parts of the republic and a worsening economic situation in the country more generally. This put Russia in an extremely advantageous position for extracting strategic and economic concessions from Kazakhstan. All Russia had to do was to issue veiled threats about what the improper treatment of Kazakhstan's Russian population might provoke, and the Kazakh leadership immediately became more malleable. This did not mean that Nazarbayev and his colleagues knuckled under to all Russia's demands, but the country's leadership was never allowed to escape its feeling of vulnerability.

The Kazakh president was quick to demonstrate that he was willing to "cut a good deal" with Russia and that Kazakhstan was content to remain within the protection of Russia's nuclear shield. He also rapidly reaffirmed that Kazakhstan had no interest in remaining a nuclear state and started to negotiate the dismantling of Kazakhstan's nuclear arsenal almost immediately after receiving independence. Certainly this won Kazakhstan many new friends in the West, especially in the United States, as the Americans were allowed to help Kazakhstan denuclearize.[38] The decision was also well received in Russia and in Kazakhstan. In addition to having more than thirteen hundred nuclear warheads on its soil, the former Soviet republic had been a major nuclear test site and was still reeling from *glasnost*-era revelations about the scale of the ecological damage done in the republic.

Over time, Kazakhstan's decision to give up its nuclear weapons provided a framework for the resolution of its security needs more generally. It brought the United States in early as an important foreign actor in the country, while Russia was generally able to count on Kazakhstan's friendship. Kazakhstan was a signatory to the CIS Collective Security Treaty in 1992 and renewed its membership in 1999, although by then Kazakhstan was participating actively in NATO-sponsored activities. Even more important though is the bilateral relationship with Russia. The foundation for Russian-Kazakhstan military cooperation is the 1992 treaty, On Friendship, Cooperation and Mutual Assistance, which provides the building blocks for close cooperation between the defense establishments of the two countries. Russia pledged to help the Kazakhs build their own military forces. In September 1994 Russia was granted the right to maintain military bases on Kazakhstan's soil and to move troops and military equipment across Kazakhstan's territory. In 1995 Russia was granted a role in the protection of Kazakhstan's border with China, which later reverted to exclusive Kazakh control.[39]

In the mid-1990s Kazakhstan began to distance itself somewhat from Russia, although in July 1998 the two countries signed a comprehensive security agreement, each agreeing to provide all necessary assistance, including military assistance, in the event of an attack on the other country, and in 2000 Kazakhstan once again agreed on close military cooperation with Russia.[40]

The Kazakhstan-Russian security relationship, however, has not been without problems. The most serious of the disagreements between the two countries was over the fate of Baikonur, the Soviet space center near the Kazakh city of Leninsk. In 1994, after two years of sometimes very acrimonious negotiations, the Kazakhs gave the Russians virtually complete jurisdictional rights to the city and space center for a mere $115 million a year, a sum that the Russians later applied against Kazakhstan's debts. Russia also retained the rights to the Balkhash missile attack early-warning center and the Sary Arka and Emba weapon test sites. The latter is slated to be under Russian control until 2005. Minimal numbers of Russian troops remain to staff Baikonur, Balkhash, the two weapon test sites, and the Russian border guard mission in Almaty.

The status of the Baikonur space center has regularly created difficulties in the Kazakh-Russian relationship, and the Russians have been loath to pay even the nominal rent that was eventually agreed upon, citing Kazakh's nonpayment of its interstate debt. Finally, in January 2000, a set of comprehensive agreements was reached between the new governments of Prime Minister Kasymzhomart Tokayev and the Russian acting president, Vladimir Putin, in which Russia transferred military aircraft and technology to the Kazakhs.[41] Almost simultaneously the Kazakhs turned over half ownership of the state electric company to the Russian United Electrical Systems to meet the state's debt to Russia. While negotiations seem to have favored Russia, with time the Kazakhs have grown somewhat more confident in the relationship. In October 1999 they even banned Russian launches from the space center for a four-month period after two explosions led to civilian casualties.

Kazakhstan's security relationship with Russia is further complicated by the former's active participation in the U.S.-sponsored NATO Partnership for Peace. Kazakhstan has allowed U.S. technical experts to play a leading role in the dismantling of its nuclear weapon systems and in the conversion of its defense establishment more generally. This has sometimes displeased Moscow, such as during an unscheduled 1994 U.S. airlift of weapon-grade uranium from Kazakhstan.[42] Kazakhstan was also a member of the NATO-sponsored CENTRASBAT,[43] which consisted of troops from Uzbekistan, Kazakhstan, and Kyrgyzstan that received training from U.S. military experts in the management of ethnic conflict. By the late 1990s U.S.-Kazakh bilateral relations, while having generally gone forth under the NATO umbrella, superseded CENTRASBAT in importance. These U.S. and other NATO efforts do not presuppose a Russian withdrawal from Kazakhstan, but they have led to U.S. troops engaging in exercises on Kazakhstan's soil.

Nevertheless, Russia remains Kazakhstan's dominant security partner. In March 2000 the Kazakh president signed an accord with Russia and Kyrgyzstan to organize a joint air defense system to advance the development of a joint air defense system for the CIS. As part of this agreement, Russia supplies Kazakhstan with fighter jets and missile defense systems, in addition to millions of dollars in arms that Russia exports to Kazakhstan yearly.[44] As Nazarbayev stated eight months later, "I never tire of repeating that Russia is Kazakhstan's closest ally, because this is the way the fate of our peoples has taken shape. This is the way geography and history ordered it."[45]

But relations between the two states are complicated, and economic relations are even more so than security ones. Russian officials have always felt that Moscow was entitled to residual rights in Kazakhstan, while the Kazakhs are more and more uncomfortable with granting the Russians special privileges. Initially the economies of Russia and Kazakhstan remained fully intertwined. As late as 1994, the first year for which such statistics were reported, 59.4 percent of Kazakhstan's exports went to Russia, and 46.7 percent of Kazakhstan's imports came from Russia.[46] The interdependence of the two economies was probably even greater in the preceding years. Russia was dependent upon Kazakhstan for raw materials—initially 100 percent of Kazakhstan's aluminum, iron ore, and chrome were sent to Russia—and Kazakhstan received just about all its industrial machinery and heavy equipment from Russia. In 1992 it was unthinkable to planners in both countries that one could make the transition to a market economy without accounting for the needs of the other. To do otherwise would be to risk disaster. Of course, it was always Kazakhstan's economy that was at the greater risk in the relationship since in its search for new and better partners it was still generally obliged to ship its goods across Russia.

Consequently, the Nazarbayev government decided that to ensure in particular the continued operation of its industries, Kazakhstan was prepared to absorb the shocks of Russian economic policy by remaining within the ruble zone. This marriage of economies of the two newly independent states was an unhappy one from the outset. Russia blamed part of its skyrocketing inflation on neighboring states that expected the delivery of rubles but that would not free prices at the same speed as Russia. For their part, Kazakh leaders complained of unfair trade policies that cut off deliveries to Kazakh enterprises as a punishment for the nonpayment of government debts that were still being negotiated by the two states. Kazakhstan eventually left the ruble zone in November 1993, when the price of membership became the transfer of the nation's gold reserves to Moscow. As I discuss in chapter 5, this decision led to a major reorientation of Kazakhstan's economic strategy.

Kazakhstan was particularly vulnerable in the energy sector, where Russia has most vigorously claimed equity rights because of prior Soviet investments. Kazakhstan's refineries were not linked by the USSR pipeline system to its principal deposits, nor did the refineries possess the technical capacity to process most of the country's oil. So, although an oil- and gas-rich state, Kazakhstan imported 28,299,700 tons of energy from the former Soviet Union in 1993, the majority of which came from Russia.[47]

In addition, Kazakhstan's hydroelectric plants serviced Russian industries to the north instead of Kazakh cities to the west or south. Western investment in the energy sector would ease this dependence, but plans for pipeline construction left Kazakhstan sandwiched between the Russian interest in profiting from fossil-fuel transit fees and U.S. desires to isolate Iran, the cheapest alternative route.

Meanwhile, the Kazakh leadership remained sensitive to the fact that demography had left the country with a potential time bomb. They feared that the large Russian population would well prove to have a shorter fuse than the Kazakh population, but no one wanted economic collapse to proceed to the point where the fuse of either group would be tested. Improved economic ties with Russia seemed the best way to ensure that this would not happen. Sovereignty might be compromised for stability, but Nazarbayev was unwilling to trade the territorial integrity of his country or accept vassal status with Russia as the price. He tried to shape economic and political reforms in ways that would make Kazakhstan the kind of state that would appeal to both Kazakhs and local Russians. To do this successfully required careful politicking at home and lobbying in Russia. With time, Nazarbayev's endorsements became little more than seemingly insignificant words.

Kazakh perceptions of dependency on Russia have been steadily changing since the mid-1990s. Once Nazarbayev understood that integration was not likely to be forthcoming and began to fear Russia less, he sought a more independent international stance for Kazakhstan and modified his country's policies to reflect a greater receptiveness to international advice. Kazakhstan's economic planners have taken close direction from World Bank and International Monetary Fund (IMF) consultants, but as they were reminded again after Russia's August 1998 financial crisis, for the next decade or two (at least), Kazakhstan's economic reform cannot occur along a wholly separate track from that of Russia's. How relations should be worked out between the two states has been the subject of continual negotiations, but virtually everyone involved in Kazakhstan's economy feels strongly that there cannot be permanent trade barriers between these two states.

The Kazakhs now believe, however, that they have to decide on the country's economic priorities without Russian guidance. It took time for Kazakhstan's economic reformers to understand that they could withstand Russia's economic blockades and shortages. Mass unemployment among Kazakhstan's Russian population also became a somewhat diminishing strategic risk, especially as large numbers of Russians, the majority from the industrial work force, began to leave the country. Most important, the Russians too began to cut themselves off from the Kazakhs. It became easier to defend the cause of macroeconomic reform despite its near-term hardships because Russia's three-thousand-mile border with Kazakhstan began to be delineated and secured by Russian troops.

By the late 1990s, Russia became firm in its resolve to establish a delineated border with Kazakhstan and to strengthen border controls, claiming the need to control the illegal passage of goods across its border caused by poor security. In time, the Kazakh elite came to appreciate that they had initially overestimated the nature of the threat that Russia posed to Kazakhstan's security and the extent to which Russia was prepared to risk its international position to prevail in the Kazakh republic. Even at its most acquiescent, the government of Kazakhstan did not roll over and play dead on command. Although the Kazakhs rarely just acceded to Russian demands, they have generally tried to make agreements that Russia found controversial quietly rather than bickering openly. This strategy has been characteristic of Kazakhstan's relations with large Western foreign investors as well.

Kazakh leaders have also begun to put more emphasis on cooperating with their Central Asian neighbors. Kazakhstan, Uzbekistan, and Kyrgyzstan agreed to make a Central Asian common economic space in January 1994. The Central Asian Economic Community did not include Russia but grew larger with the addition of Tajikistan in 1998. The Kazakh leaders would like to see this ineffectual union become stronger, and they believe that their country's interests would also be well served if the two other Caspian successor states, Azerbaijan and Turkmenistan, would join. This union was designed in part to counter Russia's influence, but it also exists to compensate for Russia's partial withdrawal. Russia has observer status in this organization.

Although cooperation within Central Asia is a necessary condition for regional stability, it cannot guarantee Kazakhstan's survival. This means that Kazakhstan will always have to have an eye on Russia's potential response. It is likely that Kazakhstan has declined to join GUUAM for this reason; GUUAM was explicitly designed to limit Russia's involvement in the strategic affairs of the member states. Nevertheless, Kazakhstan's understanding of its independence has changed dramatically in a few short years. Initially it did not believe that it had any rights as a state at all, but now it is pursuing an assertive state-building policy.

With time, Nazarbayev has come to understand Kazakhstan's potential as a country, although it is possible that he now overstates it. The Kazakh leader is said never to have traveled abroad before 1990. Given this, it is not hard to understand the hesitancy that he showed about Kazakhstan's "going it alone" as the USSR was collapsing. As he became more at ease with traveling the world, Nazarbayev's appraisal of his nation's potential role changed as well. In his mind at least, Kazakhstan is the jewel of the region, the wealthiest and most physically attractive of all the region's states.

Nazarbayev has never liked playing second fiddle to anyone and has bridled when unfavorable comparisons have been made between his state and any of its neighbors, or between the quality of his leadership and that of other post-Soviet leaders. He is confident that he can be a well-respected figure globally and believes himself more than the diplomatic equal of the inexperienced Vladimir Putin, an advantage he did not believe he enjoyed with Boris Yeltsin.

Nazarbayev is less enamored of trading sovereignty for security than he was a decade ago, but even now Kazakhstan's leader is willing to accept a greater trade-off of autonomy and security than are the leaders of most of the other newly independent states. While other states were content to let the CIS wither, Kazakhstan's policy makers had a very different understanding of the relation between economic and security needs. The Kazakh leaders believe that geography puts them at risk, and a strong Russian president could increase this sense of vulnerability. As long as Vladimir Putin continues to emphasize the need for Russia to assert its strategic interests in neighboring states,[48] President Nazarbayev will continue to emphasize the need for accommodation in his dealings with his northern neighbor. Still, accommodation is not synonymous with domination.

While publicly demanding an equal partnership with Russia, however, Kazakhstan's leader would be content with a well-structured relationship in which his country was Russia's junior partner. Kazakhstan has tried hard to nullify some of Russia's lopsided influence in the country, actively pursuing a highly diverse foreign policy strategy, which includes close ties with such disparate states as the United States and China. Nazarbayev seems well aware that such strategic partnerships exist at the behest of the stronger state rather than the weaker.

As the Kazakhs look less and less frequently to Russia, they are in fact becoming something of the junior partner that they want to be. Yet while publicly Kazakhstan's leaders often vigorously defend the right of Kazakhstan as a sovereign nation to define its own national interests, privately they admit that such calculations are generally made with an eye to Russia's likely response. What is most troublesome to the Kazakhs is not that they must occasionally cede to the Russian will, but that the Russians will almost never cede to Kazakh preferences.

3

The Challenge of Creating Kazakhstanis

Each of the Soviet successor states has struggled to define just who exactly are "the people," but in Kazakhstan such efforts were especially contentious. The country's leaders proudly boast that Kazakhstan is the most multinational of all the Soviet successor states, but few who live in the country seem proud of this ethnic diversity. Instead, it appears a source of stress for many. Outside observers sense that for Kazakhstan to survive and prosper, its population must develop a civic-based patriotism to a common homeland rather than an ethnic-based loyalty to the land of the Kazakhs (or, alternatively, of the Russians). This seems more difficult for the country's Kazakh-dominated leadership to understand than for its outsider advisers.

At the time of statehood, the country's two principal peoples, the Russians and the Kazakhs, each looked at the world in different ways, leaving the government with the challenge of bridging these differences. The government also sought to accommodate the worldviews of other ethnic minorities, so that all these diverse peoples would share common political goals. Kazakhstan's government has managed to keep the peace but has not given real meaning to the country's ethnic diversity. While claiming to speak for all, it has favored the interests of ethnic Kazakhs over the country's other ethnic communities. At the same time, as the country has become less democratic, President Nazarbayev and the ruling coterie have given everyone less voice in establishing the political norms and institutions that govern political life.

In a more democratic setting, feelings of personal political empowerment might have led to a diminished importance of ethnic differences, and so created more opportunities for ethnic accommodation. Even under such conditions, ethnicity would likely have continued to play an important role in influencing preferences for how the state should function. Yet Kazakhstan's rulers have tried to shape the nature of the Kazakh state with little popular involvement, preferring to imagine what it is that the people think and feel, rather than consult them.

Although the same elite has dominated the country for more than a decade, its understanding of how to balance the interests of Kazakhstan's two principal ethnic communities has changed. While continuing to embrace the rhetoric of ethnic tolerance that stresses the multinational nature of the state, the government now actively pursues policies that strengthen the Kazakhs' claim to cultural, political, and economic hegemony. These policies are geared to a future in which the Kazakhs will be a large enough majority to dominate the country.

President Nazarbayev and his close associates initially expected that the change in demographic balance would be gradual. The expectation was that the higher natural growth rate of the Kazakhs would be augmented by some in-migration of Kazakhs living elsewhere and an outmigration of those Russians who could not accommodate themselves to the changed political circumstances of the republic. Although the government sponsored the in-migration of Kazakhs, it also encouraged Russians to see a future for themselves in Kazakhstan and regularly reaffirmed this goal. One can only speculate on what factors motivated the Kazakh leadership, because few of these policies were well articulated. Certainly there was a fear that the Russians, living in ethnically consolidated enclaves, would opt for secession rather than outmigration. There was also a concern that Russia would not tolerate the outmigration of millions of Russians. In fact, when Russians initially began to leave the country, the Kazakh leadership went to great lengths to deny that they were leaving.

The demographic change has been a rapid one, caused largely by the departure of nearly one in four Russians. In addition, the population of Kazakhstan has been atypically mobile in the past decade, and the population makeup has been changing at the local and the national level. As local Russians started leaving Kazakhstan in increasing numbers, the Kazakh government began to rethink its strategy. Although Kazakhstan's government never targeted the Russians, most seem to have viewed their departure as a good thing, and slowly the policies of the government changed to make the most of their departure.

Over time Kazakhstan has become a more conspicuously Kazakh state, both in its composition and in its ideology. The Russian language remains in wide use, its legal status being only slowly eroded, more for practical reasons than for ideological ones. The state cannot afford to lose its educated and technologically skilled population, which still functions almost exclusively in Russian, regardless of ethnic origin. The Kazakhstan government's long-range plans call for English to become the international language of the next generation, and English language instruction was mandated for all schools by the end of 2000. But languages are not introduced by legislation as much as by large expenditures on education, which to date have by and large been lacking in Kazakhstan. Kazakh nationalists, however, are constantly pressuring the government to restrict the role that those not fluent in Kazakh can play in public life.

The weak showing of Kazakhstan's nationalist parties at the polls is not an accurate indicator of the public support of the nationalists' agenda.[1] It is more a product of the political system's favoritism toward progovernment parties and factions, and to some extent a measure of the popular distrust of the administrative capabilities of the Kazakh nationalist leaders. In fact, parts of the Kazakh nationalist agenda are viewed sympathetically by many Kazakhs, including those of the ruling elite, and most Kazakhs resist the idea that all ethnic communities have equal claims to political empowerment in multi-ethnic Kazakhstan. Kazakhstan is *their* homeland, even though there is considerable variation among the Kazakh population as to what this means precisely. The Kazakhs agree that they suffered at Russian hands for more than two centuries and that the reestablishment of the Kazakh state must compensate for that.

Given the deep-seated differences in political values between the country's two principal nationalities, it is a testament to the population's apathy that the country's social and political atmosphere has been so calm. The strategy that the government is pursuing remains potentially dangerous. By reducing the scope of individual political action and emphasizing the cultural and spiritual needs of the Kazakhs, the government is trying to prevent an economically and socially disaffected population from mobilizing across ethnic lines. It is also assuming that it can keep the population from mobilizing along ethnic ones. While the risk of ethnic discord seems in no way imminent, for all the talk of foreign threats, the greatest source of instability for Kazakhstan lies within the state itself.

Nationalism and Ethnic Identity in Kazakhstan

Ethnic differences that were latent in the Soviet era became suddenly apparent with the collapse of communist ideology. The Soviet system required that individuals preserve their *nationality*, the term used to denote ethnic identity, which was indicated on line five of the passport that each adult was obliged to carry and on most other official documents. Simultaneously, though, the totalitarian structure of the system demanded allegiance to the artificial sociopolitical construct of the Soviet Union rather than to an ethnic or territorial nation. Those for whom loyalty to the ethnonational community overshadowed their feelings for the Soviet fatherland risked repression by a state that searched determinedly for enemies.

The infrastructure of terror—the remains of the old Stalinist security system—decayed along with the ideology of communism, which allowed people more freedom to define their own loyalties. Many leaders felt that elevating national identity from an indicator of ethnicity to an ideological bond would facilitate the creation of new state allegiances. After all, nationalist aspirations for independence had played a critical role in undermining the stability of the economically and ideologically bankrupt USSR. Even in Kazakhstan, where until independence the ethnic Kazakhs were a minority, the ruling elite still viewed them as the only community inherently loyal and patriotic. Citizenship, however, was awarded to all permanent residents, creating two de facto classes of citizens from the outset.

Soviet political and economic practices left all the new states with sizable populations that were living outside what local politicians began to term peoples' *historic homelands*. Communist planners dispatched more people to some parts of the USSR than to others so that several of the new countries (Armenia, Uzbekistan, and Turkmenistan) were close enough to being mononational to make the emphasis on ethnic identity a potentially attractive foundation for national unity.

The emergence of nationalism as the basis of state ideology in most of the neighboring states intensified the problem of identity formation for Kazakhstan, whose boundaries are more than many others a product of administrative choices made during the Soviet period.[2] Kazakhstan was deliberately developed as a showcase of Soviet economic and social theories, and Kazakhstan's demographic situation was a product of those policies. Although Kazakh nationalists may be convinced that the metropolis's primary goal was to overwhelm them numerically, Moscow was motivated by more complex incentives, both economic and ideological. In fact, in various periods (especially in the 1920s and 1930s), the population sent to Kazakhstan was the object of punishment, as opposed to being a punishment for those among whom they were sent to live. It is fair to say, however, that the Russian and Soviet policy makers were not overly troubled by the dislocations suffered by the Kazakhs as a result of various resettlement policies.

In some other kind of state, a new form of civic pride or geographically based loyalty might have developed to unify all who lived in the Soviet republic of Kazakhstan. However, the omnipresent ideology of the Soviet Union rigidly fixed a person's ethnic identity while propagating and rewarding internationalism. As a result, people with strong ethnic loyalties from all the country's ethnic communities, including the Russians, always felt discriminated against during the Soviet era. Nationality was a given, but *nationalism,* believing that your ethnic community was somehow superior to all others, was a crime for which you could be jailed and, under Stalin, even executed. Such conditions served to leave people hypersensitized to the importance of advancing the cause of their ethnic communities, and this hypersensitivity has locked the people of Kazakhstan in a kind of political zero-sum game in which the advances of one ethnic group are understood as losses by the other.

Kazakhstan's leaders have been aware of their republic's riven nature since at least the mid-1970s and have made repeated efforts to elaborate policies and propaganda systems to incorporate the identities of both Russians and Kazakhs. Some progress was made during the Brezhnev era when longtime republic party boss, Dinmuhammad Kunayev, succeeded in creating a certain loyalty to the concept that one could be a *Kazakhstanets* ("Kazakhstaner"), or a person from Kazakhstan. This term had no ethnic connotation and was used to encourage pride in the republic as an important region of the Soviet Union, a distinctive and multi-ethnic part of the whole that was making vital contributions to the entirety of the USSR.

As the USSR weakened, however, and as the republic elites began to fight for greater control of the resources on their own territory, nationalism became a critical part of the vocabulary that justified this move toward sovereignty. Moscow, it was frequently charged, was preventing the local ethnic community from exercising its historic claim to a territory. For such a strategy to be successful, it had to be embraced by the head of a republic's Communist Party, and those who opted not to push for such a strategy risked ouster by an angry population.

This made the calculus of decision making difficult for Nursultan Nazarbayev. He was aware of the economic costs of continuing to cede the control of the wealth of his republic to Moscow, but he was equally conscious of the risks associated with advancing ethnonational claims to nationhood in Kazakhstan. As I have detailed, northern Kazakhstan in particular is a region with two antithetical histories: the Kazakhs believe that they were pushed from this land by advancing Russians, while the Russians consider it the edge of Russia's historical frontier, an "empty" land that their ancestors came to farm. The Russian claim to the northern oblasts was articulated with particular eloquence in 1990 by Alexander Solzhenitsyn in his widely distributed "How Are We to Rebuild Russia?"[3]

For all but a small minority of Kazakhstan's Russians, however, citizenship was the focus, not separatism. Many felt as much a part of Russia as of Kazakhstan, and they did not want their ethnicity or their citizenship to be fully distinct. All of Kazakhstan's residents received citizenship in the republic, and only citizens would be awarded a stake in the privatization process and the right to ownership of their residences. Still, Kazakhstan's Russians also felt that they were a part of Russia, and with the support of Moscow they sought to be citizens of Russia as well.

Not surprisingly, the Kazakh government refused to give in to escalating pressure on the question of citizenship in 1993 and 1994.[4] Nazarbayev consistently rejected the idea of dual citizenship. During those years, Russia's policies went from a quiet endorsement of the ethnic Russians' goals to a strong defense of the rights of all Russians living in what Moscow saw as its "near abroad."[5] They also tried to involve the international community in their protection, and the OSCE High Commissioner for National Minorities, Max van der Stoel, made several trips to Kazakhstan during this period, in April 1994 issuing a letter that expressed concern over the developing situation.[6]

President Nazarbayev, nevertheless, remained unshaken in his belief that Kazakhstan could not thrive as a nation if the loyalty of its citizens was constantly in question as it would be if they were simultaneously the citizens of two different and potentially competing states. Nazarbayev was not alone in this conviction: All the CIS leaders, except the presidents of Turkmenistan and Tajikistan, rejected the Russian demand for dual citizenship, and the Turkmen government eventually backed away from this position.[7]

Nazarbayev was not willing to let the matter simply rest because he recognized that an accommodation had to be made to the desires of his country's Russian population or risk that it might destabilize the country from within. He proposed that Russia and Kazakhstan simplify the procedure for exchanging citizenship in one state for that of the other, and Yeltsin agreed in principle. In January 1995, the two leaders signed agreements that defined the treatment of citizens of one state permanently residing in the other and made it easier for such people to switch their citizenships.[8] The Russian Duma (parliament), however, did not pass the necessary enabling legislation until 1998, when the local Russian population no longer felt as comfortable in Kazakhstan as it had earlier. Russians were leaving the country in increasing numbers, up to nearly a half million (483,000) a year by 1994, and then in a steady but decreasing stream until 1997, when the emigration of Russians began to increase again.[9]

Ethnic Russians often felt excluded from the country's public life. In the world of the Soviet Union, a Russian was usually standing behind every Kazakh. The pattern of the proverbial Russian second secretary exerting influence over the Kazakh first secretary was repeated through most Communist Party and government hierarchies and in the leading enterprises in the economy. In reality, the pattern of decision making was more complicated, and access to power was not neatly predetermined by ethnic origin. Almost all key decisions were made in Moscow and conveyed to the republic capitals, but those in the republics had a great deal of discretionary responsibility for implementing them.

In Kazakhstan, as in the other former Soviet republics, the ruling elite began to come disproportionately from the titular nationality. This has been true since the first big government shakeup in October 1994, when five of the six newly named vice-premiers were ethnic Kazakhs, and Kazakhs accounted for all but a handful of senior ministry posts. Complaints from local Russians that they were being eclipsed from political life initially seemed to have had some impact because Prime Minister Akezhan Kazhegeldin then brought in a number of prominent Russians to occupy key posts, especially in the areas of finance and economics.[10] Most of these Russians left after Kazhegeldin's departure in October 1997, and the new streamlined administration brought to power by Nurlan Balgimbayev was once again heavily Kazakh in makeup. By this time, though, deteriorating economic conditions made the ethnic makeup of the cabinet portfolios seem irrelevant to most Russians.

In a post-Soviet world in which images of interethnic violence are commonplace, it is important to maintain a sense of perspective when talking about the state of interethnic relations in Kazakhstan. Interethnic differences were an irritant in Kazakhstan, but they have not been a cause for an unbreachable rift in the social fabric. What is less clear is whether the policies of the Nazarbayev government have the capacity to ignite interethnic strife like dry timber should rising nationalist sentiments among small groups of Kazakhs and Russians be set off by a spark from within or even outside the country.

Kazakhs and Russians have been living near one another for more than three hundred years. For virtually all their shared history they have been able to accommodate themselves to one another peacefully. Until now, the rules of this accommodation have left the Russians in charge of the Kazakhs, who were allowed varying amounts of communal self-rule. Now the situation is reversed. For all the talk of a multi-ethnic Kazakhstan, it is the Kazakhs who now dominate in the republic. They are the country's most prominent political and economic leaders, and for the first time, it is the Russians who must take their cues from them. The former colonists find themselves in a difficult position, and the figures for outmigration eloquently speak to the difficulties that ethnic Russians are having accommodating themselves to the situation.

Decreeing Patriotism

Those living in Kazakhstan do not seem to be developing a strong sense of civic pride or loyalty to their new state. In late 1995, a slender 22.9 percent of respondents admitted in a newspaper poll that they were "proud to be Kazakhstanis," as opposed to the 40 percent who said that they were "satisfied" with their citizenship, and the 30.6 percent who characterized their feelings as "indifferent."[11]

It would be premature to expect them to have developed civic pride even now. However, patriotism should not be confused with ethnonational pride. The latter is something of which neither the Kazakhs, nor the other populations who live in the country, are short. Yet despite the recent rewriting of Kazakh history to stress the state-building agendas of their premodern ancestors, the country's titular nationality has not managed to translate its ethnic pride into a coherent and widely accepted ideological defense of its unique nation-state. Nor has the government managed to transcend ethnicity to give all the country's ethnic groups an equal or nearly equal stake in their new homeland. Such transcendence was certainly one of the goals of the authors of the 1995 constitution, which for the first time refers to the "people" of Kazakhstan, who are "united by a common history." It also omits all reference to ethnic Kazakhs and to their special rights, substituting for this a reference to the rights of individuals and their right to preserve their cultures.

The government would like to do both simultaneously: to make Kazakhstan special for the Kazakhs, while stimulating civic pride for all other nationalities. At times they have stressed one goal over the other, and as more Russians leave the country, the state ideology that is being fashioned has become more explicitly pro-Kazakh.

Most of the symbols of statehood are drawn from the Kazakhs' history or culture. The flag is blue, the color associated with the Turkic Khaganate that dominated the steppe before the Mongols and Kazakhs. It has a sun, an eagle, and a traditional Kazakh ornamentation at the side. The center of the state emblem is the view of the world as seen from the inside of a yurt, the traditional dwelling of the Kazakh nomad, and is surrounded by a stylized version of a shield. The state hymn as well is designed for a Kazakh audience, describing a homeland of the Kazakh steppe and speaking of the need to preserve the mother tongue, and it is difficult to find a Russian translation of it in the country's stores and kiosks.[12]

The government also wants the ideology that it is developing to have meaning for all the country's nationalities. Pressure for this is caused in part by the withdrawal of the state and the privatization of many of its previous functions. In the face of deteriorating economic and social conditions, the government has resorted to an age-old tactic for trying to gain support: if you cannot satisfy the material demands of a population, then try convincing them that their ideological or spiritual needs are being met instead. Kazakhstan's government officials recognize that they are no longer performing many of the tasks that the governed expect from their governors, and the elite hopes to fill this gap by arousing public support for a newly defined civic nationalism.

The country's leadership recognizes that there is an ideological void in the society, the space left by the discrediting of the omnipresent Soviet ideology. The citizens in every state need to possess a system of beliefs that tries to define public conduct; that explains why some behavior is forbidden, some frowned upon, and some favored; and that places the state in a favorable spot on that continuum. The vilification of a previously widely upheld belief system has created the risk that people will find their own ideological or moral signposts for organizing their lives and evaluating their actions. In their search they might make "unacceptable" choices that could lead to the formation of potentially powerful radical religious or nationalist movements.

The pervasiveness and universality of the communist ideology made the need for a replacement ideology seem even more pressing. Communism was invoked at every turn of Soviet public and private life, much like a law of nature. In that sense communism was akin to the state religion in a theocracy; it was understood to be a true and unarguable description of the nature of the universe. This made former Soviet citizens appear particularly susceptible to other all-encompassing ideologies. For others, disproving of the "truth" of the old ideology discredited the idea that an intellectual and spiritual framework governs human behavior and made following the law of the jungle seem the best strategy for survival.

There is evidence of both impulses in Kazakhstan. There has been an explosion of crime that is partly a manifestation of contempt for anything save personal enrichment, while the growth of nationalism, clanism, religious fervor, and other varieties of exclusivist social bonding is driven by the hunger for an intellectual construct that both assigns the blame for the discomforts of the present day and indicates the one true path by which these discomforts may surely be overcome. Their long years of experience under communism have made the inhabitants of the new republics particularly susceptible to the conviction that there is but one truth, and so it drives them to seek one and, when they feel they have found it, to impose this truth on those about them.

Those running Kazakhstan have been raised in the conditions of the Soviet Union and still believe in the capacity of the state to shape the worldview of those whom they govern. They do not believe that social engineering as such has been discredited, just the work of the Soviet-era social engineers. Thus, they continue to spew state doctrines and plans for creating state ideologies designed to bring together the country's various ethnic communities.

In the wake of the collapse of a universal communist ideology, the task of creating an inclusive national identity is a particularly difficult one, to which Kazakhstan's leaders have devoted considerable energies. Their position is best summed up in a 1996 official statement of Kazakhstan's state ideology, or, as it is formally termed, its state identity. According to this the goal of the state is:

To confirm in society the idea that Kazakhstan is our common Motherland. The duty of every citizen, no matter what his nationality, is to assist in the creation of an atmosphere of friendship, peace, and agreement. In many countries the spirit of patriotism cultivated there promotes: the strengthening of the state; the consolidation of a society ruled by pride for the state; the faith that the state is ready to defend the interests of the citizen at any time, no matter where he is; a tender flutter of feeling for the symbols of the state.[13]

This document, and the similar ones that have preceded it, acknowledge that these sensations do not yet exist, defining the present moment as one of transition, but it then goes on to elaborate a definition of the state that will warrant such patriotism in the future.

One important source of patriotism, of course, is the emotional tie of the Kazakh people to their land. As the 1996 statement puts it,

Kazakhstan is the ethnic center of Kazakhs; they have no other state in the world which has demonstrated concern about the preservation and development of the Kazakhs as an ethnic group, about their culture, way of life, language, and traditions. The definition of Kazakhstan as a national state must identify the state in this capacity first of all.

The reason such a definition is important, the document argues, is that "the logic of ethnic evolution defines the inevitability of the appearance of the state as an instrument to preserve the material and spiritual conditions for the existence and development of the nation." At the same time, Kazakhstan's government acknowledges that the needs of all the nationalities of the country must be met, which is why the statement of state identity affirms the goal of creating a democratic system. Citing the republic's second (1995) constitution, the document affirms that Kazakhstan is to be a "democratic, secular, social state of law, the highest values of which are man, his life, rights, and freedom."

An effort is to be made to transform the state into a rule-of-law society, where, as the document states, "in the event of a violation of their rights the citizens [will] appeal to the courts first of all, rather than to an executive body," because they will be secure in the belief that "all are equal before the law."

There are certain clauses of the statement, however, that reveal the conflicting tensions at play in the republic. Perhaps the most revealing passage is one elaborating the relation between the citizen and the state. In this official analysis, there are two world traditions: one in which the citizen is a part of the whole, whose personality and social identity are realized only through common traditions and institutions; and the other, in which the citizen is an individual set apart from the government, whose support for the government is based upon giving up liberties in return for certain services provided by the government. Tellingly, Kazakhstan's official ideology recommends that the optimal conception for the republic is a synthesis of these two positions, since in terms of history it is the state that is constant and the citizen who is contingent. A citizen may leave the state, after all, or may be removed by the natural processes of aging, while the state remains one of the common values of the people. The state is further defined as unitary and cannot contain within it other ethnonational or autonomous governmental structures. There is a single citizenship, legislative structure, and system of governmental power.

This view of the state also justifies Kazakhstan's choice of the presidential form of democracy, creating a president who is elevated above all the structures of power in order to serve as "the guarantor of the republic's unity and the constancy of the Constitution and of the citizens' rights and freedoms." Such an injunction takes for granted, of course, both that the interests of the state and people coincide, and that "the people" will share a single, and discernible, group of interests. It can easily be argued, however, that one of the most obvious changes in Kazakhstan since independence has been a rapid and pronounced differentiation in the interests of the citizens according to their ethnicity, their place of residence, their age, and their position in Kazakhstan's ever-more lopsided economy.

An invocation of claims to understand and speak for "the people" is in part a habit of Soviet-era thought. In both Kazakh and Russian, the word that we translate as "the people" is grammatically and intellectually singular, unlike the analogous English term, which clearly implies a plurality of individuals grouped together. Both the Russian and the Kazakh term for the citizens of the state make it easy to suppose them to be of a single mind, and the belief that they can be made to behave as though they were of a single mind is at the core of official efforts to create a state ideology.

Accordingly, this makes it easier to claim that the people's common interest is identical to that of the state, which allows Kazakh leaders to argue that the preservation of stability, guarding the current state from unwanted pressure to change, is the maximum common good. It is the responsibility of the citizen to support the state in its efforts to "preserve social stability, civil peace, [and] interethnic concord," while the state will intercede as guarantor for those who have neither the "material nor spiritual possibilities for existence and self-realization." In practice, according to the 1996 document, that means the state will guarantee its citizens a minimum wage, a certain level of free medical care, and free secondary education, while also mandating the length of the work day and work week, state holidays, and yearly vacations.

Kazakhstan's citizens are obligated "to prompt the state toward corrections in the policies it pursues." This must be done, however, without endangering social harmony and stability. While political parties are encouraged, the issues they take up are to be limited, in part by the requirement that they too have the interests of the state and people at the center of their programs. Political parties may not argue for a particular group of ideas or people, and there is a specific injunction against religiously based political parties. The need for social harmony is seen as paramount. Thus, while the 1996 statement does not repeat this rather open defense of politically based censorship, it does urge the strict regulation of the activities of foreign religious organizations on the grounds that these have been engaged in a kind of "spiritual intervention in the ideological vacuum of society."

In an earlier statement of ideology, Nazarbayev also reserved for the state the obligation to "regulate the information balance,"[14] restricting the flow of information into the republic, so as to minimize the influence of alien opinions within the state. In that 1994 statement Nazarbayev expressed the fear that "young independent states frequently find themselves under the strong pressure of opinions imposed from outside," which leads to "complex internal processes with their particular logic [being] evaluated by an outside view, frequently explained superficially and, at times, tendentiously."[15] Thus, Nazarbayev argued, the indigenous media must be protected and shaped, until they learn to "uphold the interests of the republic and create their own information space in the world's political arena."

State Ideology Formation in a Nationalist Age

The soft censorship that is increasingly more characteristic of the country's political climate makes it hard to gauge how well the government is doing in its efforts to evoke patriotism. Growing restrictions of free political discourse, marked in particular by growing pressure on the media, make it difficult to offer much more than anecdotal evidence because those who research public opinion in Kazakhstan must remain sensitive to the implicit constraints of the environment in which they are working.

The evidence that is available points to incomplete ideological transformation. It seems to have been far easier to get people to renounce the political ideology of the Soviet Union than to abandon the social contract that went with it. The Kazakh government is still being judged by what material benefits it provides its citizens. The younger generation appears to be less ideological and more cynical than their parents, but they seem to retain their parents' expectations that the state will meet its citizens' social welfare needs.

The Kazakh government's embrace of the vocabulary of postcolonialism has further divided the country into the colonized and the colonizers. Although this is not an explicit part of the ideology, it has become a more powerfully implicit one, especially since Russia has continued to weaken. This hastens the departure of ethnic Russians and other Slavs and also helps to alienate a Russified Kazakh elite from other Kazakhs. Many in Kazakhstan may see both things as positive, but their departure and alienation also have explicit consequences for the political and economic development of the state. In this regard, at least, the implementation of Kazakh government policy is completely at odds with its officially stated purpose of fostering interethnic harmony.

These efforts at ideological transformation are also creating a generational divide, one that might someday translate into mass support for a communist or socialist revival. For now at least, movements that advocate a return to the policies of the Soviet past draw support disproportionately from the older generation, which is decreasing in numbers each year.

More likely the state-sponsored ideological tenor of postcolonialism will continue to divide the population along ethnic lines and create the various ethnically rooted forms of radicalism that the state has identified as antithetical to its goals. This risk is easier to identify, though, than it is to control.

The emergence of nationalism as the most common replacement ideology for communism in most of the neighbor states has worsened the problem of identity for more multi-ethnic states like Kazakhstan, and even more so when the Kazakhs felt entirely vulnerable to Russian pressure. As already noted, Kazakh leaders no longer feel that the country must take cultural and political direction from Russia, but that Kazakhstan's own economic and security needs should be the driving force in the relationship.

The "Kazakhness" of the state was always a part of official ideology. Just as the 1993 constitution claimed its first political authority to arise from the "the Kazakh people,"[16] so the 1996 statement of ideology bases itself on the claim that: "The territory of the republic of Kazakhstan . . . has since the most ancient of times been settled by large empires and separate khanates of the Turkic peoples, the ancestors of the Kazakh people. Since the fifteenth century this was the territory of an independent government, the Kazakh khanate, the world's first state organization of Kazakhs." Thus, while making the necessary bows in the direction of multi-ethnicity, the various statements of state ideology also assert unambiguously that, as Nazarbayev's 1993 statement put it, "There is only one way of realizing national interests, which consists of a guarantee of the equality of all peoples with the integrating role of the Kazakh nation."[17]

It is difficult to be certain what is meant by "the integrating role of the Kazakh nation," in part because the same document also specifically rejects the political heritage of the Kazakh past "based on a resuscitation of archaic forms of social arrangement, tribal mentality, and a system of legal views characteristic of the territorial organization of Kazakh society in the eighteenth and nineteenth centuries."[18] This is a reference to the traditional division of the Kazakhs into three *zhuzes,* the Small, Middle, and Great Hordes. Largely because of the direction from which Russian conquest came and the speed with which it advanced, it was the Great Horde that managed both to preserve more of its subethnic identity and to take most of the government positions in the Soviet period, which means that it continues to constitute the greatest part of the republic's elite today.

The government also draws a strong line between clan and family. While many would claim that clan politics plays an important role in the country, this is officially denied. Family, though, is quite another thing. President Nazarbayev's 1993 statement urges support for "development of the national language, art, culture . . . and the family." In his public presence, the president is very much a family man, being frequently photographed with his wife, children, and grandchildren.

There is no escaping the central role of the official family in Kazakhstan's formal public life. His wife, Sara Alpysovna, is very much Kazakhstan's first lady, heading an active national children's charity called Bobek. Nazarbayev's oldest daughter, Dariga, was the head of the only independent national television channel, Khabar, and remains in the public eye. His youngest daughter, Aliya, became a public person, if only briefly, in July 1998 when she married the oldest son of Kyrgyzstan's President Askar Akayev. The marriage, which was celebrated in a highly public fashion, was put forward as an example of the closeness of the two nationalities and the symbolic joining of their two newly independent states. The two presidents are also distant cousins, or at least publicly claim to be, a fact that was also played up at the time of the marriage of their children. The marriage was treated as history in the making, and its seeming failure is rarely discussed. All this is in addition to the prominent economic and political roles played by Nazarbayev's two older sons-in-law, Timur Kulibayev and Rakhat Aliyev. In their cases, though, their formal ties to the president are generally not emphasized.

The increased importance of family is strengthened by the leadership's continuation of the Soviet practice of reinforcing the approved view of history by elaborately staged public ceremonies. The occasions chosen are all new ones that emphasize Kazakh cultural continuity and the strengthening of dynastic rule.

An example is Unity Day, declared on May 28, 1993, on Ordobasy Hill (outside Shymkent), chosen to memorialize a 1726 meeting of three Kazakh elders, or *biis,* who joined forces to oppose (unsuccessfully) the Jungar Mongols who were invading from the east. The celebration drew more than 50,000 people, including: official representatives from each of Kazakhstan's then nineteen oblasts; the presidents of Kyrgyzstan and Uzbekistan; a Kazakh *akyn,* or oral poet, who chanted the history of the first meeting; and flocks of people demonstrating traditional Kazakh dances, crafts, and sports. While such an event may have fostered feelings of unity among the participating Kazakhs, and even perhaps a certain solidarity with the Kyrgyz and Uzbeks who attended, it is hard to imagine that Kazakhstan's Russians, Germans, or Ukrainians identified with it. It is equally difficult to imagine that non-Kazakhs identified with similar events, such as the celebrations of Kazakh writer Muhtar Auezov's centenary and of the 1500th anniversary of the founding of the city of Turkestan. These celebrations cost several million dollars, which was charged to the 1997 state budget.

One gesture to the country's non-Kazakh population was the creation of a Eurasian University in May 1996 to serve a Russian-speaking population from all the neighboring states. To give life to President Nazarbayev's claim that Kazakhstan is a bridge between Europe and Asia, the government decided to name the university after Lev Gumilev.[19] An attractive symbol for the country's varied population, Gumilev was the son of Anna Akhmatova and the poet Nikolai Gumilev, who was shot by the Soviets in 1921. Incarcerated in Kazakhstan as a political prisoner during the Stalin-era,[20] Lev Gumilev went on to write books on the ancient history of the many peoples who inhabited the Kazakh steppe from antiquity to the present.[21] Although Gumilev was criticized by the Russians for exaggerating the role of Turkic peoples in Russian history and by the Kazakhs for underestimating it, the Kazakh and Russian versions of his pamphlet "I am a Eurasian" were both bestsellers in Kazakhstan.[22]

In general, though, Kazakhstan's effort to construct a new public history repeats some of the failings of Soviet-era attempts, when, to quote President Nazarbayev, "there was a discrepancy between the ideological symbols and people's real values."[23] Inflated and dubious claims to past glories usually do not convince skeptics, but rather incline them to greater cynicism. Similarly, equating oral works and written literature and maintaining that traditional Kazakh thought is somehow superior to European philosophy (with an utter disregard for the core religious heritages upon which each draws even though Kazakh writers have sometimes made just such claims)[24] will only make other ethnic groups view them with genial contempt.

Kazakhstan's government has not yet fully grasped that the development of a strong and Kazakh-centered national identity need not be a cause for interethnic antagonism. With the exception of a small group of extreme nationalists, the Kazakhs on the whole look on their shared history more benignly than do many other former colonial peoples. The difference between Kazakh and Uzbek attitudes toward Russian rule is striking in this regard. The Uzbeks have always seen their culture and civilization as not just equal to, but superior to that of the Russians. By contrast, even today most Kazakhs will grant that Russian culture was an appropriate vehicle for joining the Kazakhs to world culture. For example, compare the statements made on the questions of past ties to Russia by President Nazarbayev and his counterpart in Uzbekistan, President Islam Karimov. While both talk of the need for the two states to continue to cooperate with Russia, President Karimov refers to Uzbekistan's colonial past and the Soviet period in pejorative terms; he depicts those periods as times of cultural, economic, political, and spiritual suppression that have now been lifted.[25]

By contrast, President Nazarbayev continues to depict the shared history of the Kazakh and Russian peoples in substantially more positive terms.

The injustices of Soviet rule were the product of incompetent or venal rulers rather than a form of systematic ethnic discrimination foisted on a weaker community by a more powerful one. The Kazakhs recognize that the abuses of Soviet rule were applied to other cultures, and an effort is made to distinguish Russian culture from Soviet rule. Kazakh culture is praised for its inherently positive traditions, which were not compromised by the approaching world culture through the Russian language and culture.[26]

The Kazakhs, however, no longer need mediators to interact with the global culture. Indeed, most Kazakhs feel that the sufferings they have endured in roughly a century of colonial rule, followed by seventy years of Soviet domination, have more than balanced the scales for the benefits that they have gained during those years of Russian domination. Even the distorting mirror of the Soviet view of history did not depict the union of the two peoples as a wholly voluntary one. The conquest of Turkestan (which included the lands of the Great Horde) was always presented as a Russian military victory. Kazakhs and Russians, though, are both aware that they share a centuries-old preoccupation with security threats from the east. Both experienced defeats by the Mongols: the Russians with the imposition of the Tatar-Mongol Yoke in the thirteenth century, and the Kazakhs during their Great Retreat from advancing Kalmyk Mongols in the seventeenth and eighteenth centuries. It was this latter crisis that led those Kazakh *khans* whose pasturelands lay in the north to seek protection from the Russians, whom they saw as the lesser of the two evils.

The Kazakhs' first efforts to gain protection from the Russians in the seventeenth century gained them little. The Russian tsars' prime concern in the period was to secure trade routes eastward through Siberia—not southward expansion—and they believed that the fortress settlements of the Cossacks provided better protection than did alliances with "primitive" peoples. The first Russian fortresses were built by Cossacks along the Yaik (Ural) River in the 1630s and 1640s.

The next groups of forts were erected in the first half of the eighteenth century, stretching from present-day Orenburg to present-day Omsk. Former Russian prime minister Viktor Chernomyrdin is a descendant of the Cossacks who garrisoned those forts. Cossack descendants remain an important political force in both southern Siberia and northern Kazakhstan. In 1731 and 1740, respectively, the *khans* of the Small and Middle Hordes appealed for protection to the commanders of these forts, leading most of present-day western and northern Kazakhstan to come under Russian protection.

The resulting ties between the Russians and the Kazakhs were loose. The Kazakh *khans* paid tribute to the Russian tsar, who also held "captives" from the Kazakh royal families as security. The Kazakh *khans* generally found this arrangement agreeable, as it kept the Kalmyk Mongols at bay, and the Russians allowed the Kazakh rulers to manage their tribesmen as before. The Kazakh rulers of the Great Horde in southern Kazakhstan continued fighting against the Kalmyks, who were themselves soon defeated by the Chinese to their east. The eastern part of the Great Horde wound up paying tribute to the Chinese, while most of the other clans had to pay the Uzbek *khans* in the south.[27]

In the late eighteenth and early nineteenth centuries, during the reigns of Catherine II and Alexander I, Russia's priorities changed. Both rulers showed far more concern with governing the territories that were under the tsar's control, as well as a much greater interest in southern expansion. The rights of Kazakh self-government were sharply curtailed. The Russians were no longer willing to tolerate the increasingly less competent rule of the Kazakh nobles, whose authority was openly challenged by internal power struggles. Russia's growing presence in the steppe had created many new economic problems to replace the earlier security issues. Thus, from the mid-nineteenth century on, the Russians became both the Kazakhs' enemy and their "civilizer." When the Russians moved southward to conquer the lands of the Great Horde, they were met with armed resistance. These lands were eventually subdued with the help of Cossack irregulars who established a new line of forts in what is now southern Kazakhstan. Some of their descendants still live in Kazakhstan's Turgai oblast (near the Chinese border in what is now Almaty oblast).

The children of the Kazakh nobility (from the Small and Middle Hordes) for the most part fared well under Russian rule. Following the Tatar model, they functioned as cultural intermediaries. These intellectuals also determined that the Kazakhs should survive as a distinct people. In the second half of the nineteenth century, they created a modern Kazakh written language and sponsored schools that forced young Kazakhs to master Russian as well as Kazakh.[28] Like the Tatars, most Kazakhs were Muslim moderates, believing that Islam would survive only if it reconciled itself with the modernity of the Europeans. The fundamentalist Islam of the Turkestanis to the south was not much in evidence in the Kazakh steppe.

Even the most apparently assimilated of these intellectuals believed that pastoral nomadism was at the heart of Kazakh culture and national identity. This increasingly pitted them against a Russian government that was coming to see the interests of nomadic livestock breeders as being in conflict with those of the country's land-starved peasants. This came to a head under the reform-minded Stolypin government, which opted to solve Russia's land problem by sending out millions of Russian and Ukrainian homesteaders to work Kazakh lands that were declared to be surplus. Few Kazakhs saw this as a positive development. World War I and the Bolshevik Revolution intervened before Stolypin's project could be completed, but not before tens of thousands of Kazakhs were pushed out of northern Kazakhstan. Hundreds of thousands more were evicted from southern Kazakhstan after an anti-Russian and anticonscription uprising in 1916.[29]

The Bolshevik rulers showed an even greater lack of consideration for Kazakh sensibilities as they sought to achieve ideological goals as well as economic ones. They resettled "kulaks" in Kazakhstan and forcibly ended nomadic livestock breeding with the collectivization drive of the late 1920s and 1930s, which resulted in millions of deaths, and in the exodus of hundreds of thousands Kazakhs.[30] Khrushchev delivered the final insult in the 1950s when he sent thousands of Russian and Slavic "volunteers" to create a second USSR breadbasket from Kazakhstan's Virgin Lands, pushing most of the remaining Kazakh collective farmers out of northern Kazakhstan.

These policies left Kazakhs with complex feelings about the nature of the Soviet experience. Certainly, it ended the pastoral nomadism of their ancestors and thoroughly changed the defining relation of the Kazakh people to their land. The traditional foods and ceremonies of the nomadic past may be preserved and remembered on special occasions, but there is no serious talk of returning the Kazakhs to their pastoral nomadic past.

The largest single grievance that the Kazakhs have against Russian and Soviet rule is that they were left a minority in their newly independent state. Their feelings on this are by no means uniform across society. Unlike in the Baltic states, there is little talk of the Soviet period as one of "foreign occupation." The small and vocal group of nationalists who have made such arguments have lacked wide popularity. Most Kazakhs see their nation as young and lacking a history of juridical statehood as defined in the Western sense.

Kazakhs are proud to be descended from the traditional society that ruled the steppe and see this past as a fine symbolic foundation for modern Kazakhstan. Virtually all Kazakhs also feel a sense of debt to the Russians.

Some of this is socioeconomic; the Kazakhs credit the Russians with bringing them the advantages of modern technological society, and, most important, with developing the educational systems necessary for the Kazakhs to sustain their level of development without direct Russian assistance.

Kazakhs see the Russian people as neighbors with whom they have shared triumphs and tragedies. They fought World War II together, and the commemoration of the victory remains an important national holiday. The Kazakhs also recognize the shared suffering of the Stalin years. Hundreds of thousands of Soviet citizens were deported to Kazakhstan, including whole peoples, like the Volga Germans, the Crimean Tatars, and the Chechens, who were decreed genetically disloyal during World War II. The luckiest of these were given all but barren ground to cultivate in common; the most unfortunate were assigned to hard labor at one of Kazakhstan's prison camps, where many prominent Kazakh intellectuals and political figures died alongside their Russian and other fellow citizens.

Some of the Kazakhs' affinity for the Russians is cultural. The Kazakhs see themselves as a small people in a world in which small peoples are rarely granted the chance to stand alone. Most Kazakhs feel that history might have given them far crueler overlords, like the Chinese or the Mongols, or even a despotic Islamic ruler conquering them from the south. This probably helps to explain why various surveys in the country have confirmed that most Kazakhs continue to be willing to learn and use Russian, although they do not believe that Russian should be used to the exclusion of their own national language.[31]

A 1994 survey found that some 78 percent of the Kazakhs questioned thought that the Kazakhs should continue to learn Russian. This should not be particularly surprising since 51 percent of those Kazakhs surveyed still used Russian at work, and 55 percent identified it as the language that they use when speaking to friends and neighbors, while only 26 percent reported that they speak Russian at home.[32]

This imbalance between the languages of public and private life is changing, and Kazakh is replacing Russian in all spheres of public and private life as the generation educated since independence is coming of age. Younger Kazakhs already feel less strongly that Russian should be taught than do older ones because independence means they can choose the cultural mediators through which they approach the world. English is now enormously popular in Kazakhstan. Rich or intellectually gifted students may now dream of studying in the West, and Moscow is fading as a desirable destination.

For now, Russian remains the language of business, and most ordinary Kazakhs still orient themselves to the outside world largely through a Russian linguistic or cultural lens, preserving with it the complicated mix of gratitude for the advantages that the Kazakh peoples gained through their access to Russian civilization and the deep anger for the pain and suffering brought by Russian colonial, and later, Soviet rule.

Russian Objections to Decreeing a Kazakh Nation

Local Russians do not believe that dominance by the Kazakhs is in the natural order of things. It is hard to judge whether ethnic Kazakhs or the local Russians benefited more from the social and political arrangements of the Soviet period, although each group saw the other as the principal beneficiary. Kazakhs viewed themselves as a subject population; they became the near-equals of the dominant population only when they accepted the latter's political, economic, and cultural ground rules. Russians took their linguistic and cultural primacy for granted, but they felt victimized by a two-tiered system that, although controlled by a Russian-dominated Communist Party elite in faraway Moscow, was managed by local Kazakh-dominated representatives. Even in northern Kazakhstan, the Russian-dominated Communist Party *nomenklatura* was immediately subordinate to the Kazakh-dominated republic party structure. Many Russians felt taken advantage of by the Kazakhs, who they saw as reaping the benefits of the Soviet social welfare system by having large families without making a proportionate contribution to the state economy. They give little credence to Kazakh claims that Moscow had taken far more out of this resource-rich republic than it had reinvested in the very social services that the Russian residents bemoaned as being too generous.

The Kazakh national revival made local Russians uncomfortable from the start. Russian nationalist groups developed during the Gorbachev era alongside Kazakh ones, and both communities saw the control of linguistic space as critical to the defense of their cultures. The 1989 legislation that named Kazakh as the official language of the republic led to a marked increase in Russian nationalist activity in Kazakhstan. Much of this was organized by Yedinstvo (unity) and, after independence, by LAD as well.[33]

Although the language law specified that the affairs of government in the predominantly Russian regions would still be carried out in Russian for fifteen years, its passage made clear that the political and cultural life in Kazakhstan was changing in ways that ethnic Russians were almost powerless to influence. Most ethnic Russians did not know Kazakh; less than 1 percent of the Russians in the republic claimed fluency in Kazakh in the 1989 USSR census; and few had any interest in mastering the language. In a 1994 survey of local Russians, two-thirds of the respondents answered that they should not have to learn Kazakh,[34] and only those Russians who lived in southern Kazakhstan believed that they should be obliged to learn the language of the titular nationality.[35]

The debate surrounding the 1989 language law and the 1997 language legislation strengthened the Russians' perceptions of discrimination. They felt especially aggrieved at the 1997 law, for unlike with the earlier version, there was no turning to Moscow for intervention. Initially, the 1997 legislation made important distinctions between Kazakhs and all other nationalities; ethnic Kazakhs were expected to function in the Kazakh language several years earlier than non-Kazakhs were, as though to emphasize the different role to be accorded the two groups of people. This provision disappeared when the versions passed in the upper and the lower houses were reconciled, and the grace period for language mastery by all citizens was extended to January 1, 2006. The law purports to provide virtually equal status for the Russian and Kazakh languages, and it is designed to put Kazakh on the same footing as Russian, requiring that it too be a language of command in the armed forces and police and security services. Russian activists, though, have complained that the law effectively turns Kazakh into the sole state language since it requires that Kazakhstan's executive branch list managerial, administrative, and service-sector posts for which a knowledge of Kazakh is required and provides for language certification through proficiency exams. The legislation also mandated that a minimum of half of all television and radio broadcasts be in Kazakh, in both privately and publicly owned media outlets.[36]

The growing use of Kazakh in the media has added to the sense of alienation of ethnic Russians. Broadcasts from Russia have steadily declined over the past several years. Initially this was because the Russian stations refused to pay the asking price for access to Kazakh airways. Now many argue that the Kazakh government is using these payment requirements and the provisions of the language law to limit public access to the unfavorable Russian coverage of events in their country and to ensure full control of the airways by the Kazakh government.

Formerly, those living in Kazakhstan could subscribe to the major Moscow newspapers as easily and as cheaply as those living in the Soviet capital. Many of these publications were available after independence, especially while Kazakhstan was part of the ruble zone. Now it is so costly that few are interested in subscribing to the Moscow press. Those with access to the Internet, however, are finding some small relief. There is still a wide selection of books printed in Russian in Kazakhstan, and popular fiction from Russia reaches Kazakhstan, but with a market of some ten million Russian-language readers, the quality and scope of Russian-language publications are considerably limited. The economics of publishing creates greater problems than does political censorship but political volumes, published in Russia by Kazakh and Russian opposition figures alike, are subject to seizure.

The Russian-speaking population's lack of knowledge of Kazakh is an underlying cause of the strained interethnic relations in the country. What seems to anger the Russians most are the petty indignities of not understanding what is going on around them when they are addressed in public in Kazakh. Russians do not understand why some Kazakhs who know Russian still insist on addressing them in Kazakh, while the Kazakhs are angered by the presence of so many people living in their country who cannot exchange even polite greetings in the local language. This said, Russians who are able to receive Kazakh language instruction as a component of their working life are usually willing to do so.

Yet anecdotal evidence suggests that Russians do not believe that learning Kazakh will reverse their diminishing influence in the country. This is supported by Kazakh, Russian, and Western field research in Kazakhstan.[37] David D. Laitin, who has studied the responses of the Russian diaspora in a number of post-Soviet states, argues that the economic payoffs of learning Kazakh are unclear and that the incentives are further diminished by the colonial pattern of relations between the Kazakhs and the Russians. The Kazakhs were linguistically highly assimilated and were fairly isolated from positions of importance outside their own republic in the Soviet era. Laitin claims that this combination makes Russians unwilling to strive for even partial assimilation. He sharply contrasts the situation in Kazakhstan with that in Estonia, where ethnic Russians will often go to considerable lengths to learn the language and become integrated in Estonian society.[38]

The prospects for Russian influence began to decline at the same time that semicompetitive elections were introduced in the republic. Kazakhs were overrepresented in the Soviet-era Supreme Soviet of Kazakhstan. This did not bother the Russians when that body was politically impotent, but when the legislature gained some power, Kazakhstan's elite took care to shape the nomination and election process. Those favored were disproportionately, but not exclusively, ethnic Kazakhs. The Supreme Soviet elected in March 1990 was 54.2 percent Kazakh and 28.8 percent Russian in makeup, compared with 46.7 and 41.8 percent, respectively, in the predecessor body elected in 1985.[39] The Kazakh elite that dominated this last Soviet-era body no longer acted like the timid Communist Party functionaries they had once been, and the legislators forcefully advanced Kazakh interests on key questions.

Before independence, local Russians were for the most part tolerant of Kazakh nationalist aspirations, which echoed their own attempts to reclaim lost national rights. While Russians were not eager to learn Kazakh or pleased to see familiar place names replaced to commemorate Kazakh national heroes of whom they had no knowledge, most accepted this as part of the national revival. Russian cultural figures were being restored along with Kazakh ones, if not by the government in Almaty, then by the authorities in Moscow. After independence, however, a fear of the language laws and the cultural reversals that they represented eroded Russian support of the Kazakh national revival.

In 1991 the Russians were embarrassed by their almost total ignorance of the local language; by 1994 that sentiment was replaced by the conviction that the state should protect Russians and Kazakhs equally and should not relegate the Russian language or culture to second-class status.[40] Russians were beginning to see themselves as a minority fighting to define the nature of their state.

New Understandings of Boundaries

The past several years have seen a hardening of the boundaries between the newly independent states of the region, which has served as an added source of tension between the governments and the minority communities that live in them. The Russian government's decision in 1999 to begin demarcating and defending the Kazakh-Russian border is a good indication that it sees the current independent status of Kazakhstan as nonnegotiable and that they believe that only minor shifts in territory between the two states are likely to occur. This is good news for the Kazakh government, which is also introducing formal border controls and can now more easily prevent the penetration of its country by seditious groups or ideas.

There has never been strong evidence that Russian nationalist groups (including the Cossacks) pose a serious threat to the Kazakh state. While Russian nationalists within the Russian Federation are vocal on the need to support "compatriots" living in Kazakhstan and elsewhere and have formed institutes and committees to study their problems, the fate of these "stranded Russians" has never been a major campaign issue of mainstream political figures.

Yet it seems likely that a substantial part of Kazakhstan's Russian population would vote for reunification with Russia if it were offered. In a 1994 survey, some 27 percent of those surveyed said that they saw the northern territories of Kazakhstan as rightfully belonging to Russia, with an additional 14 percent saying that these territories should have autonomy within Kazakhstan. In East Kazakhstan oblast 42 percent of those surveyed said the northern territories should be part of Russia, as did 37 percent of those surveyed in North Kazakhstan oblast, with an additional 11 and 16 percent, respectively, supporting the idea of autonomy for those regions.[41] The lack of support for Kazakh statehood by the local Russian population could explain why these two oblasts fell victim to the administrative "rationalization" program in 1997 and were annexed to neighboring (and more loyal) territories.

To advocate changing Kazakhstan's current boundaries publicly risks violating laws on inciting ethnic violence, and this had forced most militant separatists in northern Kazakhstan underground, making it difficult to ascertain their numbers. Most support reunification passively, but there is a vocal minority of ethnic Russians living in northern Kazakhstan that is committed to redrawing Kazakhstan's boundaries. They believe that the northern half of most of the border oblasts belong in Russia, claiming that these lands were shifted to Kazakhstan in the aftermath of the Bolshevik Revolution when the Kazakh republic was still a part of the Russian Federation. These Russian complaints, however, have little grounding in historical fact. Although the Kazakh territory was enlarged from 1920 to 1924 to include Orenburg, the boundaries were reset in 1924 and 1925 to recreate the old colonial era ones.[42]

The Cossacks, in particular, have had an uneasy relationship with Kazakhstan's government since 1991 when their activities were legalized in

Russia. Banned from forming military detachments in Kazakhstan, the Cossacks simply cross the border and participate in the legally sanctioned paramilitary activities of the Orenburg and Omsk Cossacks, from whom most were descended, and many in both countries advocate the creation of a single autonomous Cossack Republic encompassing parts of northern Kazakhstan and southern Siberia.

The status of Kazakhstan's Cossacks is in sharp contrast with their privileged role in Russia, where Cossacks are enjoying a state-supported cultural revival. Russian authorities have used Cossack units to ensure law and order in parts of Chechnya and to patrol the Russian border with Kazakhstan. Courted by Russian presidential contenders in early 2000, the Cossacks have also become a new political force in Russia.[43]

The Cossacks see themselves as a distinct ethnic group and claim the same rights that Kazakhstan's other national communities enjoy. Kazakhstan's government classifies them as a sociopolitical grouping, invalidating Cossack claims to cultural self-preservation, not to mention to national self-determination. It is hard to know how great a threat the Cossacks are, or even to know how many of them still live in Kazakhstan. At the time of the Bolshevik Revolution there were nearly seven hundred thousand Cossack families living in the republic, but the Cossacks disappeared from the formal census count after their military formations were outlawed in the 1920s. Although persecuted, thousands of Cossacks preserved their culture and religion (Russian Orthodoxy) in secret closed communities and even transferred military rank from generation to generation. Most lived on state or collective farms near the Russian border, which has facilitated their joining Cossack military groups in Orenburg. Many of these Kazakh Cossack settlements simply flow into those in the neighboring Russian oblast, and the Russian government has granted that there will be nine Cossack settlements in Orenburg that will have no frontier guards.[44] A smaller group of descendants of Semirechie Cossacks lives in what used to be Turgai oblast (now Almaty oblast), and these people are kin to Kyrgyzstan's Cossacks. Tens of thousands of other Russians have attenuated ties to the Cossacks, often no more than a family memory that a grandparent was a descendant of this community.[45]

Like South Africa's Boers, the Cossacks acknowledge racial and cultural differences from the people among whom they live, while rejecting claims that they belong elsewhere. Just as the Boers assert that they are African, the Cossacks' demand for self-government is based upon continuous residence on a fixed territory for approximately three hundred years. This makes their paramilitary nature—which they defend as a cultural tradition that involved bearing only "cold" weapons (meaning no firearms)—troubling to the Kazakh government.

The political agenda of the Cossacks comes up for periodic consideration in northern Kazakhstan, although the government has prevented a national debate on their status. The one exception was in 1995 when the defense of a Semirechie Ataman, Nikolai Gunkin, was embraced by Kazakhstan's Cossacks, local Russian nationalists, and political groups in Russia. Gunkin was arrested on January 8, 1995, for holding an unauthorized march and meeting. Cossacks argued that the meeting, held at a cathedral, was devoted to prayer. Gunkin was detained, and in November 1995, he was given a three-month prison term.[46] The Russian government and Duma decried the incident. The publicity surrounding the arrest and detention led to an airing of Cossack and Russian nationalist claims. Russian television, for example, reported Gunkin's comments that Kazakhstan was a "fascist" state that endorsed "genocide of Russians."[47]

Still, despite some public outrage, Gunkin's cause never fully took fire. In part, this was because the public lacked the will to make this an enduring popular cause, and in part because a number of prominent Russian nationalists who might have agitated for the cause had earlier "coincidentally" fallen victim to street hooliganism and decided to relocate in Russia.

The legal status of the Cossacks has improved because Kazakhstan's leaders have become more confident that their country will survive. In 1996 they were allowed to wear their uniforms in public and to sponsor meetings and other organized activities. Yet they remain under suspicion and are banned from engaging in paramilitary training, which they are said to do clandestinely.

Although the Cossack threat may be exaggerated, the Kazakh government disquiet is understandable. Kazakh Cossack leaders show no formal recognition of Kazakhstan as a sovereign state and that as such it is free to award the Cossacks a status different from the one enjoyed by their kin in Russia. Kazakhstan's Cossacks believe that since they suffered the same persecution as those in Russia did during the Soviet period, they should now receive equal compensation. They seem unable to grasp the fact that the division of the Soviet Union into sovereign states left the Russians free to take up past grievances and the Kazakh government free to ignore them.

The various Russian media, however, give their cause good coverage, and Russian nationalists from Kazakhstan use that to their advantage.[48] Many are now active in political groups located and registered in Russia. These groups, of course, are free to defend the rights of Kazakhstan's Russians, while legally registered Russian national groups in Kazakhstan must be cautious about their political programs. At first, groups in Kazakhstan pushed for local autonomy for the northern regions, but the constitutional reforms of 1995 sharply reduced the prospects of democratically elected local governments being assigned a meaningful political role.

By this time ethnic Russian support for Nazarbayev was eroding as well. Local Russians had liked the Kazakh president's stance on preserving the USSR and his subsequent interest in restoring some form of union. Kazakhstan's Russians supported plans that would in some way turn back the clock; one 1994 survey found that a full 86 percent of Russian respondents were in favor of the reconstitution of the USSR.[49] This same poll found that only 45 percent of the Russian respondents expressed complete faith in the president. Sixty-seven percent of their Kazakh fellows did the same.[50] A 1995 study also found Kazakhs more supportive of Nazarbayev than were the Russians. When asked who might best lead the country out of crisis, 72 percent of the Kazakhs named Nazarbayev as opposed to only 55 percent of the Russians surveyed.[51] Russian identification with opposition nationalist groups such as Yedinstvo and LAD increased as Nazarbayev's popularity declined. The support for such organizations grew from a scant 6 percent of respondents in 1991 to 26 percent in 1994.[52]

Local Russians remain oriented toward Russia. A USIA-sponsored survey conducted by a local polling organization in September 1997 found that Russians were nearly twice as likely as Kazakhs to favor the idea of Kazakhstan entering into a close union with Russia such as that planned between Belarus and Russia.[53]

Talk of the secession of the northern territories, though, is heard with decreasing frequency in Kazakhstan. When it occurs, as it did with the arrest of a group of alleged secessionists in Ust-Kamenogorsk in November 1999, it arouses a great deal of suspicion. There is much controversy over what the group was and who was responsible for it. Of the twenty-two people arrested, twelve were Russian citizens. Their alleged leader was identified as Viktor Kazimirchuck (who calls himself Victor Pugachev[54]) of the *Rus* patriotic movement. The authorities in Kazakhstan charged that Kazimirchuck gathered fifteen people, mainly former military officers with combat experience in Chechnya and Tajikistan, to commit "terrorist acts" in Kazakhstan.[55] There is even speculation that the entire incident was actually a provocation of the Kazakh government, designed to demonstrate to the population that there was a Russian threat to Kazakhstan's sovereignty.[56]

The Ust-Kamenogorsk arrests did provoke a Russian response, but a measured one, in which locally based Russian diplomats sought to intercede to ensure that the rights of those arrested were not violated. Similarly, during their trial there were calls for the extradition of the prisoners to Russia, but there was little or no consequence when these calls were not heeded. Yet even these muted responses may represent enough hope to encourage fringe groups like the one in Ust-Kamenogorsk to form.

It is always hard to know whether an act is a provocation, and by whom. In the current political environment of Kazakhstan, however, it would be a waste of political capital to advocate secession because, in the absence of strong support from powerful political groupings within the Russian Federation, there is no likelihood that interstate border changes can occur.

Although the Russian government has recognized Kazakhstan's borders, there is always the possibility that the position of the Russian government will change. As long as this hope exists, many Russians in Kazakhstan still see reunification with Russia as inevitable, even after the move of the capital to the northern city of Akmola (now Astana) in late 1997 and the reorganization of several northern oblasts.

Accepting Citizenship

The nature of the Kazakh state, like its boundaries, is becoming more fixed with time. As in the Soviet era, the national identity is still shaping the political perceptions of Kazakhstan's population, stimulated by a state-building strategy that reinforces the idea that Kazakhs are finally the masters of their homeland. While Kazakhs may be critical of economic or political policies, they are at peace with their past and able to honor their ancestors. Kazakhs place great importance on historic continuity and the relation between people and their land (in a communal sense). Now for the first time in hundreds of years, this relation has been righted.

The same cannot be said for most of the country's other ethnic communities. The choices facing Kazakhstan's Russians, in particular, appear increasingly stark. They can either remain in a country where they have decreasing political loyalty in the hope of achieving some economic benefit, or they can move back to Russia and take their chances economically.

Ethnic Russians believe themselves to be more disadvantaged than Kazakhs. A study done in 1994 found that only 5 percent of the Russians questioned felt that they live better than the Kazakhs, down from 12 percent in 1991.[57] A full 88 percent of the Russians reported that life had been better for them under the old system.[58] Russian dissatisfaction is increasing, and the pace of emigration from Kazakhstan picked up in the last half of the 1990s, although property in Kazakhstan had become harder to sell and resettlement in Russia was complicated by that country's own economic difficulties. As I detail in chapter 6, although Kazakhstan has suffered a large numeric and proportional loss of Russians, that still leaves about three-fourths of Kazakhstan's Russians who are trying to accommodate themselves to life in a Kazakh-dominated republic.

To be fair, the Kazakhs also complain of the declining quality of their lives. Interestingly enough, their sense of discontent seems to be greatest when they live in more mono-ethnic or Kazakh-dominated regions, such as southern Kazakhstan. Admittedly, these are some of the poorest areas of the country, but it may be that those Kazakhs who live in more multinational areas have a greater sense of increased entitlement. In general, the Kazakhs seem less pessimistic than do the ethnic Russians. [59]

Ironically, it is unclear whether the government is as concerned over the consequences of Kazakh discontent as it is over Russian unhappiness, largely because the Kazakhs have no foreign power to take up their cause. For example, in late 1997 the ethnic Kazakh-dominated strike movement in Kentau was allowed to gain momentum for several weeks before the government agreed to pay back wages, even after there were reports of several deaths linked indirectly to the strikers' protest march on the capital. It is hard to imagine that the government would have dealt with Russian strikers as callously. The Russian media—and especially ORT, the second most frequently cited source of news in Kazakhstan[60] after Kazakhstan's own Khabar television station—did report on the Kentau strikes as well as the earlier labor unrest in Karaganda, albeit quite differently. The coverage of strikes by the predominantly Russian work force was designed to evoke sympathy for unpaid and unfairly treated employees, while footage from Kentau highlighted the incompetence—and even venality—of the Kazakh government, which was neglecting its own workers, not just the Russians.

However, unlike the Russian population, the Kazakhs do not perceive that their future economic prospects are shaped by nationality. Soviet-era educational advantages brought local Russians the very industrial jobs that are being eliminated. Politically well-connected Kazakh families dominate the new economy, placing the Russians at a disadvantage. Even those rare Russians who do know Kazakh still inevitably find themselves outside the family and the subethnic bonds that increasingly dominate Kazakhstan's economic culture.

Ethnic Kazakhs who were educated in Russian suffer from the same sense of a constricting cultural universe, but they do not feel politically disenfranchised. When surveyed, Russians tend to express confidence that the republic's ethnic problems are solvable and to characterize their attitudes toward their Kazakh fellow citizens as generally favorable, more frequently than the Kazakhs make similar claims of ethnic Russians. This willingness to share the republic, however, appears to be based upon the expectation that they will be able to live in the linguistic and cultural environment to which they are already accustomed.

To many of the Kazakhs, such parity too closely resembles the much-bruited "multinationalism" of the Soviet era, which disguised a genuine Russian dominance. Truly exclusionist nationalism is rare among the Kazakhs. Even the groups that are considered extremist, such as Alash and Azat, speak only of consolidating the primacy of Kazakh language and, in the case of Alash, of Islam. There has never been formal public pressure to push Russians out of the republic. At the same time, though, the country's leaders are quick to quash plans that might erode Kazakh dominance. The language question is one example of an issue on which even pro-Russian Kazakh leaders seem determined to bend but not break. Another such issue is the firm rejection of anything that smacks of federalism, which in the Kazakh political lexicon becomes a near synonym of eventual separatism.

From the beginning, Kazakhstan's leadership rejected the idea of introducing a federal system in the republic, opting immediately for a unitary state. Before independence Russia was a federation; Kazakhstan was not and had no autonomous republics or oblasts within its borders. Although there has been lengthy discussion of turning the country into a federative state, especially among the Russian political activists, the Nazarbayev government has rejected this, fearing that federalism would unnecessarily dilute central authority and foster secession. This decision, as we will see, was made by people who had little idea about the varieties of federalism or about the role that power-sharing relationships can play in creating political legitimacy.

The government has also quietly supported efforts to shift the republic's ethnic balances, with a goal of establishing Kazakh majorities in the northern oblasts. Efforts such as the repatriation of Kazakhs from Mongolia and China proved both expensive and unnecessarily inflammatory. Less obvious encouragement to native Kazakhs to move northward has led to pronounced shifts in local demographic balances throughout the country (see chapter 6).

It is probably this dynamic that most affects the varying perceptions of the two populations about the republic. When surveyed, both Russians and Kazakhs tended to say in equal numbers that their primary allegiances were to their places of immediate residence and to their jobs or occupations. Yet the two populations differed sharply in their expressions of allegiance to Kazakhstan as a state. In a 1995 survey nearly 40 percent of the Kazakhs listed the state as among their three primary loyalties, whereas only 25 percent of the Russians did so.[61]

The presence, and initial near parity, of the two huge populations in the republic usually obscures the fact that Kazakhstan is home to many other nationalities. Some of these groups, such as the Belarusans (1.1 percent of the population in 1992) and Ukrainians (5.3 percent), have much in common with the local Russians, including that they are leaving the country. The republic's Uzbeks (2.1 percent) and Azerbaijanis (about 1 percent) also have homelands elsewhere, but representatives of these two groups seem to be moving into the republic, not out, probably because of the better economic opportunities in Kazakhstan.[62]

The country's Uzbek population, located primarily in southern Kazakhstan and also in Zhambyl oblast, occupies an economic position that is far more prominent than their numerical proportion would suggest. In fact, many see them as dominating the private sector in this part of the country. The Uzbeks, however, are not pushing for political influence and are content to accept the linguistic and cultural domination of the Kazakhs. This population is largely trilingual (Uzbek, Kazakh, and Russian), and until 1999 it was quite easy for them to cross the border. Since then tensions between Uzbekistan and Kazakhstan have increased because the Uzbeks have been seizing territory purported to be Kazakh territory as they fortify their border, giving rise to protests and unease in southern Kazakhstan.[63] The interethnic tensions caused by these border disputes, which have turned violent at times, have been contained to the localities affected, and the two states are moving toward final delineation.

Kazakhstan's Jews are also a small but disproportionately influential group, composed of the descendants of wartime evacuees or of people who sought quieter backwaters in Soviet times. Jews are leaving for Israel and the United States and are moving to Russia and Ukraine, but the reinvestment of Jewish capital is sufficient for Kazakhstan to maintain formal and cordial relations with Israel.

Germans constituted 5.8 percent of Kazakhstan's population in 1989. [64] They are the descendants of settlers originally enticed to the Volga region in the eighteenth century by fellow German Catherine the Great. More recently their ancestors were exiled to Kazakhstan by Stalin during World War II. They began leaving the country for repatriation in Germany in the late 1980s, and by 1992 they accounted for only 4.7 percent of Kazakhstan's population. In the wake of German reunification, the Bonn government's enthusiasm for absorbing these distant relatives waned, and good ties between Kazakhstan and Germany led to economic assistance from the latter to fund projects of the local Germans. The Germans, however, have continued to leave, with the German government continuing to provide formal reabsorption assistance. The size of Kazakhstan's German population has dropped to roughly one-third the 1989 figure. [65] The country's senior German, then Akmola oblast *akim* (governor) Andrei Braun, the head of the region of Kazakhstan in which the Germans were densely concentrated, was interviewed to offer reassurance. [66] Instead of calming the situation, the interview led to some embarrassing admissions. It turned out that Braun's daughter and grandchildren were living in Germany, and when asked whether he himself had plans to relocate there, the Akmola governor joked that job prospects for former senior Kazakh political appointees were not reported to be very favorable.

There are large numbers of Chechens and Tatars (about 1 percent in 1992, including both Volga and Crimean Tatars) in Kazakhstan. Both the Crimean Tatars and the Chechens are the descendants of peoples expelled from their homelands by Stalin after World War II. Disputes between Russia and Ukraine over ownership of Crimea make it highly unlikely that these Tatars will be able to press a claim for their homeland any time soon, while Kazakhstan's Volga Tatars are often descendants of families who have lived on the Kazakh steppe for centuries.

The nature of Chechnya's political status remains a point of bloody contention, and fighting between the Chechens and Russians has been a cause for Kazakh nervousness. The Kazakh government has never endorsed the Chechen cause. At the time of the first war, 1994–1996, the Kazakhs were uncomfortable about the precedent that a successful secession would give to groups within their own country. By the time of the second conflict, 1999–2000, their opposition to the Chechen cause was stronger still. They were now very concerned about the potential contagion from armed or terrorist groups that had enjoyed safe haven in Chechnya.

Even more ticklish is the situation of the Uighurs, whose only homeland, if it exists, is in the (eponymous) autonomous region of China. Although not especially numerous in Kazakhstan (slightly under 1 percent in 1992), the Uighurs' presence is significant in Kazakhstan as well as in Kyrgyzstan and Uzbekistan. While better assimilated into their places of residence, the Uighurs nevertheless resemble the Kurds in that they see themselves as the heirs of a historical nation that now lies buried beneath several other states. Since the largest group of Uighurs lives in China, where they sporadically and violently press for greater autonomy, this population worries all the leaders of Central Asia. Kazakhstan has been particularly anxious to forestall any appearance of sympathy for Uighur nationalist aspirations because its border with China is Central Asia's longest, and the number of Chinese troops stationed near the Kazakh border is three times the size of Kazakhstan's entire army.[67] Each time that there has been ethnic-inspired unrest in neighboring Xinjiang province, local Uighurs have tried to find a forum in Kazakhstan to air their grievances and have regularly protested the presence of visiting Chinese dignitaries. The most severe Uighur protests occurred in February 1997 after a wave of riots left as many as one hundred dead. Since then there have been several demonstrations in Almaty against the Chinese repression of Uighur separatists.[68]

In short, Kazakhstan is going to face problems created by the multinational nature of its population far into the future. Long after the Kazakhs have emerged as the dominating majority in the country, Kazakhstan will remain the home of a huge and disparate minority community. Minority constituencies, though, will share little other than the common awareness that they are not Kazakh. Coping with the large Russian population has tended to present the discussion of multi-ethnicity in Kazakhstan as a kind of zero-sum problem: if there is no language law asserting the primacy of

Kazakh, then the Russian language will dominate; if better regional representation is permitted, then Russian separatism will develop in the north; if the Kazakhs do not promote their kin, fellow hordesmen, and co-nationals for jobs and places in the university, then the Russians will reassume their former economic and political control.

While Russians are likely to remain Kazakhstan's largest single minority for long into the future, the dynamics of demographic change seem certain to reduce their importance. The diminution of ethnic Russians' influence, however, and of the historically peculiar challenges and fears that they evoke among the Kazakhs, will still not automatically create a country in which ethnicity and patriotism are easily linked. While Kazakhstan is certain to become a state in which the Kazakh language and culture predominate, its leaders must still find ways to stimulate a sense of belonging and citizenship among the enormous minority of its people who are not Kazakh but who live and work in the republic. The government does not yet feel secure in its ability to meet this challenge, and this insecurity is making it more nervous about placing its fate in the hands of the people before whom it is supposed to be accountable.

4

Trying Pluralism and Abandoning It

President Nazarbayev quickly became frightened by the prospect of not being able to predict outcomes, which is an inescapable feature of a democratic system. As former Communists, he and his advisers were aware of how public opinion could be manipulated, but as they began to experiment with political reforms they quickly learned how difficult it was to shape public will. In a democracy, incumbents can be turned out of office, and Communist-leaders-turned-presidents have sometimes fared poorly when facing their newly independent electorate. President Nazarbayev found this risk unacceptable and was unwilling to accept the legislative rebuffs inherent in a democratically and popularly elected parliament.

After a few years of trying to keep pace with political changes in Russia, the Kazakhs began to back away from the idea of establishing even a quasi-pluralistic system. As a result, over the past ten years the arenas of political contestation in Kazakhstan have grown more limited in number and more restricted in scope. The parliament has been stripped of power; the media, although partially privatized, has come under tighter government control; local governments have been kept from becoming effective sources of political challenge; and it has become increasingly difficult for those who object to these changes to organize themselves into effective opposition parties.

Nazarbayev began a seemingly irreversible course in March 1995 when he dissolved the parliament, ruled by decree for nine months, and extended his rule to 2000 by use of referendum. The current constitution dates from August 1995, when it was also adopted by referendum. It further strengthened Kazakhstan's presidential system. The president gained the right to petition for delegated legislative powers for a term not exceeding one year, providing that two-thirds of the deputies at the joint session of parliament concurred. The current constitution reaffirmed the right of the president to appoint government and regional leaders and to dissolve parliament if it passed a vote of no-confidence in the government or twice rejected a president's nominee for prime minister. It provided for a weak bicameral legislature with an upper house (the Senate) dominated by presidential appointees. This remains the case today, even after the constitutional modifications of 1998.

The government is also a creation of the president. He appoints the prime minister, who presides over a cabinet that has been streamlined during the past few years. In the name of government efficiency, a goal pressed on Kazakhstan by international financial institutions, this streamlining has made the cabinet little more than a conduit for policies originating in the presidential administration. Although the administration has been trimmed, made more professional, and had its power enhanced, a glass ceiling keeps all save those in the president's immediate circle from rising to the very top. The president has the right to annul or suspend the decrees of government and the governors of oblasts and major cities. Further, the constitutional amendments of October 1998 freed the president from the requirement to submit international treaties to parliament for approval.

Interested in courting favor and investment from the West, the Kazakh president has been more concerned with explaining away his behavior than in modifying it. Thus, before the January 1999 presidential elections, a series of one-page advertisements were placed in prominent U.S. newspapers explaining the various accomplishments of independent Kazakhstan, including its political ones. These ads appeared at the very time the United States and the OSCE were having little success in pressuring Nazarbayev and his advisers to conduct the elections according to OSCE norms.

Nazarbayev and his family have a great deal to lose from a competitive political system. While the president has regularly engaged in well-publicized campaigns against corruption, they have never resulted in the dismissal or prosecution of family members or those in political favor. In fact, the economic influence of President Nazarbayev and his extended family is steadily growing. The family is said to hold millions—and possibly billions—of dollars of assets in foreign accounts, partially obtained from Western oil companies as signing bonuses. Nazarbayev has come under investigation in Switzerland and the United States, and his political opponents have made scores of purportedly official documents available to corroborate the charges.[1] Some even claim that Nursultan Nazarbayev is one of the ten richest men in the world.[2]

Kazakhstan's leader maintains that as Asians the Kazakhs are not disposed by history or culture to be democratic and that popular rule could empower nationalist demagogues, secessionists, communists, or Islamic radicals and put the future of the nation—not to mention economic reform—at risk. As the region has become manifestly more unstable, this argument is becoming deeply rooted among the Kazakh elite and has begun to appeal to Western audiences as well.

Kazakhstan's people have little experience with the responsibilities of citizenship in a democratic society, but it is hard to know how essential a population's historical consciousness is to a successful democratization effort. The desire to live in a democratic society is more important than the legacy of having done so. A number of Central European states that lack historical precedents are evolving in democratic ways. In 1989 and 1990, the Kazakhs participated in a process of popular empowerment triggered by Gorbachev's reforms. After gaining independence, however, the Kazakh ruling elite began to back away from those policies. Popular support for democratization efforts did not wither, but the defenders of the efforts were neither sufficiently numerous nor vocal to convince a reluctant elite to support democratic change.

Democratically inclined elites can move a more reluctant population toward political change, but an elite that is more conservative than its population will put the nation's stability at risk. In this period of nominal popular empowerment, Kazakhstan's elite must keep the public minimally satisfied, but it is also succumbing to the temptations of office, with few public safeguards in place. Having made it impossible to be voted out of office, Kazakhstan's leaders face the risk that the people will take to the streets instead.

Experimenting with Political Participation

During the last years of Soviet rule, the USSR became a veritable laboratory of political experimentation as Soviet party leader Mikhail Gorbachev tried to find ways to stimulate popular involvement in the country's political life to create the appearance of popular empowerment without subjecting the government to risks. A critical part of this effort was the 1988 decision to permit the formation of so-called informal groups to take the pressure off the Communist Party, which until that time was the sponsoring organization for all legally sanctioned political and social organizations in the USSR. Like so much else that was tried in the late Soviet years, this action had much the opposite effect. Environmental groups, language societies, and commemorative history groups—all acceptable categories for organizations in the Gorbachev scheme—became forums for nationalists and even pro-independence forces. Although Kazakhstan did not have any formal separatist or independence movements, several of the informal groups that were organized along ethnic or national lines were effectively nationalist proto-parties. Ethnic Kazakhs organized Alash, Azat (Freedom), and Zheltoksan (December),[3] while the Russians founded Yedinstvo (Unity) and Vozrozh-denie (Renaissance), a Cossack organization.

Yet none of these groups attracted nearly as much support as did Nevada-Semipalatinsk, a mass movement that genuinely cut across ethnic lines and distinguished Kazakhstan. The antinuclear movement Semipalatinsk, soon renamed Nevada-Semipalatinsk, was founded by Olzhas Suleimenov in 1989 in an attempt to halt Soviet nuclear testing in the northeastern region of Semipalatinsk.[4] Encouraged by this organization, more than a million people, both Russian and Kazakh, signed petitions demanding a test ban on Kazakhstan's territory, and huge crowds turned out for this group's rallies in protest of decades of ecological and human degradation.

After forty years of testing equal to the explosion of 20,000 Hiroshima bombs, the situation in the region was dire. According to the Kazakh Ministry of Health, human birth defect levels in the region were at least six and a half times the Soviet average, mental retardation and diseases of the nervous system were two and a half times greater, and cancer rates were significantly higher.[5] Local people described cases of deformed newborn livestock (such as sheep with three legs or only one eye), and stories circulated that babies were also being born grotesquely deformed.

While the tragedies inflicted on the Kazakhs by nuclear testing were real, the decision to channel the political energies of Kazakhstan's population toward this kind of activism was not the product of a grassroots initiative. The origins and financial support were murky. Even though Suleimenov liked to cast himself as an opposition figure—and he was clearly the *enfant terrible* of the Kunayev-era Communist Party—he was an establishment figure of the late Gorbachev period, an active Communist Party member who enjoyed Gorbachev's favor, and had the privileges usually accorded a Central Committee member.[6] Whether the formation of the movement was solely Suleimenov's idea—as he repeatedly claims in personal interviews—is hard to know, but in the long run, the existence of Nevada-Semipalatinsk worked to the benefit of both Mikhail Gorbachev and Nursultan Nazarbayev.

From Gorbachev's point of view, Nevada-Semipalatinsk was a potent instrument in his campaign against the further deployment of nuclear weapons and fit in well in his "nuclear free world by 2000" campaign. Gorbachev was also shopping for a potential successor for Nazarbayev, should the latter falter during what were very unpredictable times. Georgia, Azerbaijan, and Tajikistan all had violent disturbances directed against the Communist Party, in addition to politically crippling but peaceful demonstrations in the three Baltic republics. Nevada-Semipalatinsk transformed Suleimenov into a prominent political figure who would be acceptable to a broad spectrum of Kazakhs as well as be loyal to Moscow.

Nazarbayev had taken over for the unpopular Kolbin in June 1989 and needed little help in emerging as a strong and well-respected leader. This could not have been predicted, since the Kazakhs might easily have turned on him for being part of Kolbin's "team" and for his tacit support in ousting party boss Kunayev. Instead, a strong rivalry developed between Nazarbayev and Suleimenov, with the latter serving as a useful gadfly—the leader of the house opposition—for several years. When Suleimenov's lingering presidential ambitions became too burdensome in 1995, he was appointed as Kazakhstan's first ambassador to Italy,[7] but not before he had purportedly benefited handsomely, borrowing the membership dues of Nevada-Semipalatinsk to engage in commercial transactions.[8]

The Nevada-Semipalatinsk movement, though, was far less troublesome than its leader and came to personify the defense of the well-being of the Kazakh people and their homeland. Thus it was Nevada-Semipalatinsk, and not one of the less predictable informal groups, that was able to serve Nazarbayev in a hectic maneuvering to define and enlarge the republic's economic sovereignty. A kind of protoparty, it also absorbed popular energies that might have otherwise gone to forming alternative political parties.

Kolbin's purge of the Kazakh elite during his two and a half years in power also reduced the arena of political competition in Kazakhstan. During 1987 and 1988, when the intellectuals in other Soviet republics (which had experienced their purges three or four years earlier) were forging ahead to independence from the center, the Kazakh elite was preceding more cautiously because those with party backgrounds were often vulnerable to attack for prior associations with Kunayev. In 1990, therefore, when Kazakhstan elected its first Supreme Soviet on a semicompetitive basis since the mid-1920s, the Communist Party was still the republic's only functioning political party and Kazakhstan one of the few places where a quarter of the seats in the legislature were reserved for candidates chosen by the Communist Party or by its affiliated organizations.[9]

Those elections were part of Gorbachev's campaign to bolster the sagging political legitimacy of the Soviet system. In many republics they proved to be an enormous tactical blunder because independence-minded legislators swept Communists and unionists from their seats, creating new, republic-level parliaments whose agendas were to separate their republics from Moscow, or at best to sharply reduce Moscow's influence. By contrast, Kazakhstan's elections had few surprise outcomes and produced a fairly predictable legislature.[10] All but a handful of the deputies were Communist Party members, and none of the republic's informal organizations ran blocs of candidates, most likely because they did not want to put their legal status at risk. The parliament was also disproportionately Kazakh, reflecting the growing organizational strength of the Kazakh-dominated republic Communist Party. Kazakhstan's elite had begun to realize that Moscow's power was receding, but the masses were now expected to ratify their governors' choices.

The ruling elite and the legislators they helped to empower represented a single political universe. After independence was achieved, however, the legislature began to see itself as having a political mandate that was independent of the president and his government. The tension grew so great that Nazarbayev eventually suspended this body. The dissolution of the Communist Party added to the growing complexity of Kazakhstan's political scene. After the failed August 1991 coup, the governing class of Kazakhstan no longer had a single corporate interest. The privatization process, in particular, was creating substantial rifts within the elite and provided opportunities for unsanctioned individuals and groups to become political claimants.

The patronage of the Kazakh president was seemingly limitless, given the wealth of the country that was at his disposal, but those who lacked personal ties to the Kazakh leader were also freer to follow their own political instincts. Increasingly, the old *nomenklatura* elite—which was, after all, the group principally represented in the legislature—began to divide into those who felt advantaged by the new political and economic world and those who did not.

Initially the legislature was united, and one of its first actions was to name the Kazakh Communist Party first secretary to the newly created office of republic president, a title confirmed through popular election in December 1991 when Nazarbayev received 98 percent of the popular vote.[11] Although Nazarbayev ran unopposed in the 1991 race, that election introduced the principle that leaders derive their powers from the people they lead. Legislatures could reject their leaders, as the Kyrgyz had done in October 1990 when dark horse candidate Askar Akayev was chosen over party First Secretary Absamat Masaliyev. The specter of being unseated in a free and fair election has haunted Nursultan Nazarbayev for more than a decade.

As President Nazarbayev gained new powers, which he used in the legislative struggle to define Kazakhstan's sovereignty, the parliament's first experience with coalition politics and political consensus building began. In summer 1990 the Democratic Bloc, a group of 100 legislators, issued a more extreme statement of sovereignty than Nazarbayev wished to endorse, leading to the government sponsorship of a slightly larger bloc, the Communist Faction, to ensure passage of the preferred text.

The presidential control of parliament became more difficult after the August 1991 coup and the dissolution of the Communist Party. Nazarbayev therefore tried to create a presidential party to be the functional equivalent of the banned CPSU. Nazarbayev and his supporters, though, quickly lost control of the first two parties that were founded: the Socialist Party, created in August 1991 to inherit the property and membership of the Kazakhstan Communist Party, and the Congress Party, which followed in October 1991 and was headed by Kazakh poets Suleimenov and Mukhtar Shakhanov. In October 1992, when Suleimenov was becoming a potential political rival, Nazarbayev sponsored the creation of the Union of People's Unity (SNEK—later renamed the People's Unity Party, or PNEK), which proved more compliant but equally ineffective in mobilizing popular support. Although it occupied a diminishing role in public life, PNEK was not fully abandoned until March 1999 when former Prime Minister Tereshchenko formed the Otan (Fatherland) party to advance the presidential choices in the then-upcoming legislative elections.[12]

The stimulation of political party development is proving to be a slow process in even the most democratic of the postcommunist states. It is still less successful in places like Kazakhstan, where the playing field is not a level one, where legal roadblocks are placed before all but proregime groups, and where political participation does not really influence political outcomes.[13]

While Kazakh law provides for the creation of independent political parties, there is nothing in the political environment of Kazakhstan to stimulate their development. According to a 1997 poll, more than 40 percent of the population showed distrust of and apathy toward political parties.[14] Such polling results reflect the popular fatigue with living in the highly ideological environment of a single-party society, where the executive has used the vertically integrated nationwide party structure to link the government directly to the people.

From its formation, the presidential party has lacked an intellectual organizing principle. While the presidential apparat has drafted several concept statements on the nature of the new national ideology, it has never succeeded in making them sound like anything more than platitudes about such generally shared humanistic ideals as ethnic tolerance, the social and spiritual well-being of all citizens, combined with a vague endorsement of economic and political reform.

By contrast, the CPSU was an ideological party, and everyone knew what is stood for. Even after the support for the party's ideals began to diminish substantially, people of all ethnic backgrounds, including some Kazakhs of the younger generation, continued to support its program. There are more than fifty-five thousand members of the reconstituted Communist Party scattered throughout the country, drawn mainly from the scientific intelligentsia, civil servants, workers, and pensioners.[15] Most observers believe that if the votes in the 1999 parliamentary election had been tallied honestly, the Communists would have taken more seats on party-list balloting than any other group. As it was, they received 17.8 percent of the party-list vote, compared to 30.5 percent for the presidential party, Otan.[16]

Despite the massive amounts of money pumped into promoting their activities, the lack of popular interest has ensured that these parties will never became mass organizations. Aggravating the problem is the size of Kazakhstan's elite base. There were not enough talented people willing to work as bureaucrats to staff competently the senior administration in the ministries, oblasts, cities, and districts or to organize party branches in every locality, especially since talented young people were being drawn into the country's new economy.

These problems only magnified the difficulties encountered when the presidential apparatus sought to overcome the lack of public support for a single presidential party by stage-managing the creation of a multiparty system, sponsoring the creation of a variety of proregime parties, each designed to appeal to its own group of voters. These include the Civil Party, formed in November 1998, and the Agrarian party, formed in January 1999, to appeal to entrepreneurs in business and industry and to proponents of private property in agriculture, respectively.[17] These have little more support than the mass patriotic parties do. None of these parties is designed to serve as a civic training ground by identifying and nurturing potential elites, nor are they used to help the government deliver goods and services to the community.

Opposition parties have done little better in filling these roles. Certainly it is true that the current political system limits their ability to contest seats in the parliamentary election successfully,[18] and some of the nationalist parties are further hampered by their weak financial bases. Yet a lack of cadre and the low level of public interest are far more devastating to political party development in Kazakhstan than are the financial problems that the independent political parties often face. For even in cases where there seems to be ample money, such as was true of the RNPK (Republican People's Party of Kazakhstan) organized in 1999 by former prime minister Akezhan Kazhegeldin,[19] public apathy has proved hard to surmount, and it has been difficult to attract elite support. Political patronage is so fully controlled by the office of the president that those who seek to create an independent political power base have little to offer to attract support.

Even when political life in the country was at its freest, in the early 1990s, Kazakhstan was moving toward a kind of managed democracy, where the ruling elite set strict barriers on those engaged in independent political actions. Over time, President Nazarbayev and his close supporters have grown more fearful of the vagaries of political control that are associated with grassroots political parties and voluntary political organizations, not to mention those that result from a competitive political party system. This attitude has fostered structural obstacles—including restrictions on freedom of the press and speech as well as the reduced role of parliament—that ensure that antiregime groups will have trouble in mobilizing public support. The constraints make it impossible for independent local nongovernmental organizations (NGOs) to attract a broad membership. What little NGO pressure existed came from organizations with international support.[20] Nonetheless, formal institutional and informal individual pockets of opposition persist in the country, despite official efforts to define how Kazakhstan develops as a strong unitary state.

Defining the Unitary State

Kazakhstan's first constitution was adopted on January 28, 1993, and largely legitimated the continuation of the Soviet-era political arrangements. Although modified a number of times and completely replaced in 1995, the first constitution invested the greatest part of the republic's political power in the office of the president, where it remains. That power was strengthened by the declaration of Kazakhstan as a unitary state, with republic interests placed above regional ones. The constitution also established Kazakhstan as a secular state and forbade the president to be even a member of a "public organization," including any political party.

The first constitution formally divided the government into three branches: the executive, represented by the large presidential staff; the legislative, represented by the then-unicameral Majilis (Kazakh Supreme Council), whose representatives were elected on a territorial basis; and the judiciary. The president himself, while a part of the executive branch, was also assigned a supersystemic role, charged with ensuring the proper functioning of all three branches.

The president was also given decisive control over the local government, because although representatives were elected to the local councils mandated for each of the republic's (then) nineteen oblasts, the councils were made subordinate to the oblast governor (an *akim* or *glav*), who was a presidential appointee. These *akims* would name their subordinates as department heads. The oblasts are further subdivided into *raions,* most of which have several points of settlement. Each of the oblasts and *raions,* and most of the settlement points, including all the cities (many of which are further subdivided into urban *raions*), also have their own elected council, called a *maslikhat.* These are charged with administering local services, for which they are given budgeting powers, and very limited powers of local taxation.[21]

The 1993 constitution gave local governments a narrow range of activities in which they had independent authority. They were intended to be a conduit in a vertically integrated hierarchy, managing the economy in the days before privatization while supervising tax collection to the center, and paying social welfare benefits to the population. These functions were all those of the old Soviet oblast.[22] With time, the system of local administration was modified, and the oblasts have been given expanded rights of taxation and additional discretionary authority to pursue economic investments. In addition, the second (1995) constitution gave a more well-defined description of the duties of local government.

While the 1993 constitution stipulated that local authorities were responsible for "the resolution of all questions of local significance" and the "fulfillment of the constitution, laws, and acts of the President and his administration," the 1995 constitution listed a range of activities to be pursued by local authorities.[23] The powers of the *maslikhat*, however, may be terminated by the Senate.[24] The Kazakhs recognized, though, that the authority of the local governments could be better elaborated and their capacity to discharge their responsibilities could be improved—both goals that U.S. Agency for International Development (USAID) and UN Development Program (UNDP) assistance programs were working with the Kazakhs to address.

The growing professionalization of local government was not intended to shift the balance of power in the country since President Nazarbayev and his advisers remain concerned over the risks associated with regional differentiation.[25] From the beginning, Nazarbayev has been reluctant to take any measures that would increase local autonomy, recognizing that Kazakhstan is, after all, an enormous country, one whose constituent units, shaped by their varying ethnic and economic situations, are likely to understand their needs and potentials in distinct ways.

Nazarbayev's fear of local autonomy is deep-rooted. The early years of independence were a period in which the centrifugal forces that helped bring about the collapse of the Soviet Union seemed to be still very much in evidence, especially in neighboring Russia. Although none of Kazakhstan's regions gave any indication that it might really resist Kazakh central government authority, Nazarbayev felt that the Kazakh state had to develop institutions that would counter those forces rather than reinforce them. He believed that a federal system would make oblasts the implicit enemy of the state and would doom the center to be little more than an arbiter of competing regional interests.

The choice of a unitary state has left Kazakhstan's oblasts dependent on the center to respond to specific local economic and social conditions, but as we see in chapter 6, it did little to guarantee that the national authorities would be competent to deal with them. The hardships of the transition period, combined with the institutional decisions made, guarantee that the tension between center and periphery will certainly continue for the foreseeable future because the richest and the poorest regions alike feel thwarted in their desires to serve local residents well.

Kazakhstan could easily have evolved into a system, even a unitary one, in which there was great variation in how local power was exercised. At the time of independence, most of Kazakhstan's population lived in border oblasts, with which it typically enjoyed close economic and political ties.[26] The country's main regions, the north, the west, the south, the southeast, and the center of the country were all distinct and, usually at least, an overnight train ride away from one another. After independence, most oblasts tried to keep their cross-border ties and did so with the support of the center, which had limited resources to contribute to stimulating employment and ensuring access to food and communal services in the periphery. Except on a formal level, however, the center did not facilitate border ties.

The most-well-organized connections were along the Kazakh-Russian border. In 1993, the Interstate Association of Contiguous Territories of Russia and Kazakhstan was formed to maintain and manage cross-border economic and infrastructural ties.[27] The Kazakh government did not feel directly threatened by this, because for all the talk of Russia possibly imploding during those years, there was little evidence that the Siberian oblasts could organize themselves into an effective regional association, let alone form an independent state. There was also little prospect that the northern oblasts of Kazakhstan would unify.[28] The oblast administrators and Russian nationalist groups alike remained focused on their respective geographic areas, in large part the product of how the transport system was laid out. As I discuss later, although the Kazakh government has begun various highway and railroad bypass projects to connect the Kazakh oblasts better, these links continue to be through Russia.

When the broader regional initiative began to fail, a number of Russian oblasts sought to strengthen their bilateral ties with their Kazakh counterparts but found the unitary nature of the Kazakh state to be inhibiting. An example is the case of Orenburg, located just over the border, in Russia. Orenburg was the site of the gas-condensate plants that traditionally processed output from the Karachaganak field in western Kazakhstan. Orenburg firmly sought cross-border ties with its neighbors to the south, and in June 1997 the heads of Orenburg, West Kazakhstan, and Aktiubinsk signed an agreement on cooperation in protecting the environment and in combating common states of emergency. Little came of these efforts, however, and close cooperative relationships between officials in the two oblasts are more the exception than the rule.[29]

Cross-border ties have been difficult to maintain in southern Kazakhstan as well. In the early years strong informal relations persisted, bolstered by the creation of a Central Asian Economic Community in 1994. However, Kazakhstan, Kyrgyzstan, and Uzbekistan have all pursued protectionist policies that inhibit trade across borders, with the most profound disruptions resulting from Uzbekistan closing its borders in 1999.

Kazakhstan's oblasts nevertheless continue to press for a devolution of authority, and there has been regular talk of electing governors and mayors, partly in response to Kazakhstan's Russian-dominated provinces. Nazarbayev seriously considered this idea in 1993 when Boris Yeltsin introduced the election of local officials in the Russian Federation. By that time, Nazarbayev had replaced Moscow-era appointments with governors (and mayors) who were loyal to him. By transforming these offices into popularly elected ones, Nazarbayev would have created opportunities for mass political involvement at the local level, helping to appease Kazakhstan's Russian population without triggering an adverse response from most Kazakhs. It would, however, have diminished the president's personal authority and slowed the process of developing a unitary political culture in the country.

Talk of elected local officials shifted to a vague distant future after the 1995 constitution retained the presidential appointment of all government officials, adding only the proviso that local councils can express no-confidence in their *akims* by a two-thirds majority vote. The president, however, was under no obligation to honor such a vote, and he can also overturn decisions taken by the local councils. After Nazarbayev rejected an opposition proposal that regional governors be elected and not appointed as being a threat to social and economic stability,[30] in May 1999 the Kazakhs held "experimental" elections for the mayor of Chemolgan, Nazarbayev's native town in southern Kazakhstan.[31] Those elections led to the short-lived speculation that the popular election of local executives might be forthcoming, a speculation that was revived in April 2001 when the Nazarbayev government promised to hold competitive elections experimentally for one or two rural district *akims* in every *raion*. The restrictions on these elections—that every candidate must be over the age of twenty-five, have a higher education, and (most important) not use "regional connections or play the game by tribal, ethnic, or religious principles"—promise that there will be a great deal of official orchestration in these contests.[32]

Defining the power of local government in Kazakhstan is likely to remain highly contentious in Kazakhstan well into the future. As Pauline Jones Luong has persuasively argued, the *akims* in the resource-rich regions are managing to enhance their own personal power and discretionary authority largely by gaining concessions from foreign investors who seek to run successful projects in their regions.[33] Yet it is unclear that the incumbents would benefit from the introduction of direct elections. Even in the resource-rich regions, popular dissatisfaction is said to be high because of low government reinvestment rates, and dissatisfaction is even greater in those regions with a deteriorating industrial infrastructure and little or no foreign investment. Incumbent local governors might well be saddled with the blame, especially given the limitations of protest voting in the 1999 parliamentary and presidential elections.

President Nazarbayev is reluctant to limit his control of the regions but remains unsure of how to maximize it. Kazakhstan had its first major administrative reform in 1997 when five oblasts were fused with their neighbors. This was justified as an effort to advance economic efficiency by uniting natural resource deposits with potential refineries and eliminating the bloated bureaucracies of the country's least populated provinces.[34] These changes also increased the proportion of Kazakhs in Russian-dominated regions, a move designed to yield more Kazakh representatives in local as well as national legislatures. The reorganization conveniently erased some of Kazakhstan's debt since the central government claimed no liability for the money owed by juridical entities that no longer existed, as Russia's Roskontrakt learned when it sought to collect $50 million in undelivered grain elevators from Taldy Kurgan.[35]

In spring 2000 there was further talk of dividing Kazakhstan into five super regions, one for each of the major economic zones of the country. Nazarbayev may eventually move in this direction, especially if he can work out a power-sharing arrangement with the so-called donor oblasts—Atyrau, Mangistau, and Almaty—whose borders would change. Kazakhstan has a real need to curb government spending, but there was a hypocritical quality to the 1997 reorganization, which was done against the backdrop of creating the new national capital of Astana.

Independence spurred a discussion of moving the nation's capital from Almaty (in the extreme southeast) to Akmola (renamed Astana, which means "capital" in Kazakh), a city near the country's center. The legislature endorsed this in a July 1994 resolution that was backed by presidential decree in September 1995, and the move was formally executed in November 1997. The reasons for this move have been hotly debated. The decision was certainly in part a strategy to root the northern section of the country firmly under Kazakh control. When the decision was taken, Nazarbayev and the legislators had little idea of the real costs of such a move, but the president clearly understood the potential patronage tied to the construction of a new capital through the awarding of contracts for construction and the provision of goods and services. There are also rumors of how the Nazarbayev family solicited funds for erecting various public buildings and then shunted some of these corporate donations to off-shore accounts.[36] Despite pledges that taxpayers would not have to pay for building the new capital, they have had to pay the millions of dollars of annual expenses associated with moving legislators back and forth between the two cities and housing them while they are in Astana. Although legislators and public officials are under constant pressure by President Nazarbayev to move to the new city, few are willing to do so. It is also clear that the hundreds of millions of dollars collected for the construction of the capital, in a style designed to make it a worthy international centerpiece, could have been used for more direct public benefit.

The move to Astana is a good illustration of the current state of political life in Kazakhstan. It is a decision that few outside the senior ruling circles seem to have viewed as a good idea, yet a search of the country's press or examination of the record of its legislative debate turns up little critical discussion of it. Despite the enormous cost of the project and scanty popular support, the change of the capital went ahead because it was something that the president saw as necessary to demonstrate his authority and attract international attention to the new Kazakhstan he hopes to build.

The Rise of Legislative Politics and a Vocal Press

It seemed at first that public opinion and legislative politics might help to define Kazakhstan's political life. By late 1993, the legislature, whose members had political ambitions of their own, was beginning to serve as a magnet for growing popular disenchantment with a flailing economy that sported a 2,500 percent annual inflation rate. Somehow, this popular dissatisfaction had yet to stick to the still very popular Kazakh president. This was a major reason for Nazarbayev choosing to pressure compliant supporters into a "voluntary" dissolution of the parliament in December 1993, two years before its term ended. Claiming that the old parliament had been an impediment to economic reform, Nazarbayev had little to fear from international criticism, for in October 1993 Boris Yeltsin had eliminated his troublesome legislature by opening fire on it.

Designed to be a professional parliament that would sit in constant session, the new body was to have only 177 seats, forty of which were to be filled by candidates on a presidential list. In the run-up to the March 1994 Majilis election, the restrictions on party registration were made tighter still, and districts were reconfigured to guarantee Kazakh majorities wherever possible. Campaigning was strictly controlled, making it hard for voters to learn the party affiliations of candidates and often even their platforms. The voting process was also closely stage-managed, so much so that observers from the OSCE were initially reluctant to certify that the election had been free and fair, and the OSCE received much criticism for eventually certifying the election.

Nazarbayev had good reason to expect the 1994 legislature to be a pliant partner. A full 90 percent of the new legislators were senior officials in state or partially privatized organizations,[37] while more than 70 percent of them had never before held public office.[38] At the same time, the new parliament reflected a surprisingly broad political spectrum. The Communist Party was not permitted to compete, but its supporters were able to vote for candidates from two former Communist organizations, Profsoiuz (formerly the state-controlled trade union) and the Peasants Union, which together received 17 percent of the votes. The Socialist Party, which had become largely Russian in membership, won 15 percent of the vote. The soft opposition of the People's Congress, organized by Suleimenov, appealed equally to Russians and Kazakhs, most of those northerners, and won 13 percent of the vote. The more nationalist-inclined parties did not fare as well: several Kazakh groups joined under the umbrella name Azat, but these succeeded in electing only a single, shared delegate. Tight restrictions made it impossible for the Russian nationalist groups to run candidates openly, but four delegates with close ties to LAD were nevertheless elected.[39]

The largest single bloc of candidates came from SNEK, the presidential party, which received 40 percent of the vote. Obviously not a majority, this bloc, and the other approximately thirty legislators who were staunch president's men, quickly proved unable to ensure even the election of SNEK's party leader, former Komsomol head Kuanish Sultanov, to the post of parliamentary speaker, leading Nazarbayev to accept his second choice for this job.[40] Nazarbayev, a skilled political operator, had learned always to provide himself with a fallback position, but the Kazakh president did not forgive the loss. Gaziz Aldamzhanov, a rising critic of the Nazarbayev regime, robbed Sultanov of his majority and earned Nazarbayev's lingering displeasure.

The Kazakh president wanted the legislature to be a rubber stamp for the economic decisions taken by his government. Having just weathered the blows of attempting, first, to cling to a continued joint currency with Russia and, second, of having faced the inevitable necessity of abandoning that attempt, the country had now begun the complex process of privatizing the greater part of its small- and medium-sized enterprises. This process was turned over to a government headed by Sergei Tereshchenko, a Kazakh-speaking Ukrainian born in Russia who lived and worked for most of his life in Kazakhstan and who served in a cabinet dominated by ethnic Kazakhs.

Public opinion ran strongly against privatization. Many feared that it would favor privileged families, clans, and horde members and were angry that it would systematically shift economic advantage from the administrators—many of them Russian—to a new group of mostly Kazakh successors. Many Kazakh legislators also feared that they and their supporters would be disadvantaged by the process. A distrust of privatization, and of Prime Minister Tereshchenko's government, provided an immediate focus for the legislature. Soon after the opening of the parliament, a left-center opposition bloc announced itself under the name Respublika (Republic),[41] several of whose members formed a shadow cabinet and developed an alternative legislative program.

The opposition to Tereshchenko and his ministers came from across the political and ethnic spectrum and included many in the Socialist Party, members of the new Communist Party (made legal again in 1993), and Russian and Kazakh nationalists. In May 1994, joined by legislators from the Congress Party, they passed a vote of no-confidence in the prime minister, 111 to 28. Not constitutionally bound by this vote, Nazarbayev stated that Tereshchenko would remain prime minister until privatization was completed. This drew more members to the Respublika group and led to the formation of a nonconstructive opposition called Otan-Otechestvo (Fatherland, in Kazakh and Russian), whose members called for Nazarbayev's resignation as well.[42] By July 1994 this swollen opposition was able to override Nazarbayev's veto of two consumer protection bills. Finally, in mid-October, after a month-long scandal about the financial improprieties of two of Tereshchenko's ministers, Nazarbayev was forced to accept the resignation of the prime minister and his government.

As with so many other scandals in Kazakhstan, this one fizzled after initial attention. Mars Urkumbayev (the minister of economics) and Vladimir Shumov (the minister of the interior) were eventually charged with bribe taking, as was Shumov's son (Andrei) who worked for him as an investigator in the Main Department for the Struggle against Organized Crime. Urkumbayev's case was dropped at the end of 1996 by the prosecutor general's office owing to the "passage of time and change in circumstance." In fall 1997 he was chosen as head of the union of industrialists and entrepreneurs. Shumov returned to Russia and served with the Ministry of the Interior (MVD) in Chechnya. Ironically, no Kazakh government has ever come as close to being held accountable as this first one was, but even then, little headway was made in controlling an already pervasive pattern of official corruption.

By 1994 Kazakhstan had developed a relatively free and vigorous media, which provided the legislators with a venue through which their opinions could reach the wider public. Naturally, *Kazakhstanskaia pravda* and *Vesti Kazakhstana,* the two largest official newspapers, were strong supporters of the government's positions, but they felt compelled to report the speeches of opposition parliamentarians, whose activities were more fully reported in the major independent newspapers. The largest and most popular of these was *Karavan* (and its smaller companion paper, *Karavan-Blitz*), a tabloid-style newspaper that was attracted to scandals. The discussions in and around the parliament provided *Karavan's* publisher, Boris Giller, with a great deal of material. The republic's other major independent newspaper, *Panorama,* also gave coverage to parliamentary maneuvering, although the paper sought to be an arbiter of social and economic issues. Television and radio covered these issues as well. Kazakhstan had several independent radio stations and one large independent television company, KTK. Access to the airways was still tightly regulated, so radio and television had to treat political scandals more lightly, but nevertheless they too were able to air them.

Even in 1994 the Kazakh media was not as free as the then virtually untrammeled and decidedly raucous press in neighboring Kyrgyzstan. Kazakhstan already had laws that used vague but threatening terms to forbid the publication of materials "insulting the honor of the presidency," which have been invoked on several occasions since independence. An ethnic Kazakh historian was the first to be punished.[43]

In hindsight, this period was the heyday of free journalism in the country. Since the mid-1990s, the government has been exerting growing control over the media but in an indirect fashion. Of some twelve hundred media outlets in the country, more than 75 percent are in private hands.[44] Yet when pressure for self-censorship fails, the government resorts to more direct measures, such as ordering the dismissal of television journalists who have reported the activities of leading members of the opposition.[45]

The government went about reasserting control over electronic media in a clever fashion, using the stated goals of economic restructuring to work against those of political reform. As part of the privatization process, starting in 1997 all television and radio companies were required to "competitively bid" for their licenses to use broadcast frequencies. In 1993 the Ministry of Information granted licenses to 200 private applicants for a minimal fee, but during this next round, the starting bids for television stations were set at $150,000 and for radio stations at $50,000, forcing thirty-one stations that could not raise such high amounts to close.[46] By 1999 Kazakhstan had registered fifty electronic and more than three hundred active mass media organizations, but the nature of the broadcast industry was changing rapidly.

As noted, President Nazarbayev's daughter Dariga "won" the license to the nationwide independent television broadcast frequency and quickly emerged as a power in the broadcasting industry. The situation with regard to print media began to change as well. In 1998 Boris Giller received an offer for *Karavan* so generous that he thought it wise to retire from publishing entirely and devote himself to his film-producing activities.[47] *Karavan* and its printing press were then transferred by stages to the Nazarbayev family media empire,[48] leaving the country without a major independent printing operation. The publishers of *Panorama* also yielded to informal pressures. The major opposition paper became *XXI Vek*, which had been associated with former prime minister Akezhan Kazhegeldin. Their offices were extensively damaged by a firebomb in September 1998, and they were eventually forced to suspend their operations.[49] After international criticism of the incident, the paper was allowed to reopen the following year but has been unable to publish regularly because the authorities are pressuring its publishers not to print the newspaper.[50]

Some of the country's newspapers closed because they were not economically competitive, but the mass media were now being held to a tight Law on the Press that was invoked in some two hundred criminal investigations in 1998 alone. Members of the press were charged with "abuses of freedom of speech, incitement of national enmity . . . aimed at instigating disputes and controversy over the country's history and sovereignty" and for permitting "nonobjective, insulting statements directed at government organs, officials, and ordinary citizens." Official statements proclaimed: "It is the media that should shape the ideals of our state and patriotic feelings."[51]

The press was further manacled by the adoption of the June 1998 Law on National Security, which gave the procurator general the right to suspend the activity of the news media without providing for appeal. Foreign media was also subject to the provision of this law, and these provisions were used in October 1999 when the authorities briefly took Russian television channels that broadcasted the discovery of President Nazarbayev's Swiss bank account off the air.[52] Foreign media was subject to further restriction in a new media law passed in 2001.[53]

The most sustained complaints about abuses of press freedom occurred during the election campaigns of 1998 and 1999 when opposition newspapers complained that they were confronting serious administrative barriers for publication and distribution. As a result, some papers had to close before the elections, most notably *SolDat*. There were also complaints by election monitors about limited access of the opposition to the press.[54]

More recently, efforts to muzzle the press have severely hampered Kazakhstan's ability to pursue a serious anticorruption campaign, allowing the government to set whatever standards of corruption it wishes. Given the high level of public concern, the government must appear to be actively routing out those who abuse their official position. According to an April 2000 poll by the Association of Social and Political Scientists, 43.1 percent of the respondents deemed corruption to be the worst evil. The press is filled with accounts of corrupt officeholders being removed, and in 1998–1999, twenty-four judges in Kazakhstan were fired and eight were suspended, and 497 people were convicted on corruption charges.[55] There was also good coverage of the May 1999 blacklist of the names of civil servants dismissed on charges of crime or corruption who were to be banned from further civil service.

These actions did little to convince the population that the government is either honest or effective. According to the same April poll, only 5 percent of respondents believed that the Kazakh National Security Committee was effective in fighting corruption, 3 percent credited the prosecutor general's office with effectiveness, 2.1 percent the president, and the government and parliament scored no points. By contrast, 45.4 percent believed that *Nachnem s Ponedelnika* newspaper, which was subsequently closed by the government (supreme court) for publishing a series of articles on corruption, was the most effective in the fight against corruption.[56]

The government, however, will not allow the press to lead a campaign to achieve clean government. In July 2000, the government shut down two independent newspapers, *SolDat* and *Vremia Po,* for reprinting articles from foreign media about alleged corruption in the Kazakh government.[57] The government has also sought ways to regulate news services on the Internet, and access to sites that reprint allegations of financial malfeasance by President Nazarbayev or his family members has become restricted in Kazakhstan.[58] Kazakh authorities are also trying to establish a national subscription service that will coordinate all Internet access.

Despite increasing repression, Kazakhstan's various media have generally been the most professional in the Central Asian region. Partly this reflects the quality of journalism in Kazakhstan at the time of independence and partly the training offered to these journalists by U.S. and other international NGOs. Proximity to Russia and the willingness of Russian media to disseminate the views of Kazakhstan's opposition also stimulated the Kazakh press to play a watchdog role. The presentation of the news from Kazakhstan is sometimes skewed to support Russian agendas and although the changes in currency and intergovernmental squabbles about paying for the transmission of television programs have limited the access of those living in Kazakhstan to Russian media, the presence of this alternative source of news has served to keep the confines of political debate in Kazakhstan from contracting completely.

Parliament Flexes and Pluralism Delayed

President Nazarbayev quickly became unnerved by the workings of a partially unfettered media and a vocal parliament. By late 1994 and in early 1995, Kazakhstan was becoming a rapidly differentiated society. Privatization had created a small but visible layer of extremely wealthy people, while economic collapse was creating a much larger, and no less visible, group of newly impoverished ones. Added to this, Kazakhstan's various minority communities were beginning to feel increasingly disadvantaged.

Even so, public support for the president remained high, including among non-Kazakhs. In one poll in late 1995, 72.3 percent of Kazakh respondents and 55.1 percent of Russians named the president as the one factor doing the most to solve the republic's crises. In the same poll, only 14.7 percent of Kazakhs and 9.7 percent of Russians said that the government was trying to solve Kazakhstan's problems, while 8.5 percent and 9.2 percent, respectively, thought this of local administrators.[59]

The enormous institutional advantages that Nazarbayev had as president, combined with the symbolic ones he accrued as the "father of his country," would presumably have made him all but impossible to defeat. Yet Nazarbayev would have had to campaign hard to ensure victory in the presidential elections that were scheduled to be held in late 1995 or early 1996. By this time there was already talk that several legislative critics had presidential ambitions, most of whom had been involved in abortive efforts to create presidential parties, including Gaziz Aldamzhanov and Serikbolsyn Abdildin (both initially of the Socialist Party).[60] Of all these men, only Abdildin has remained an opposition figure. He heads the Communist Party of Kazakhstan and was Nazarbayev's principal opponent in the January 1999 presidential elections.[61]

Presidential criticisms of the parliament were not wholly unfair. Some of Nazarbayev's critics were rivals from the Soviet era, while others had their ambitions fed by the murky interrepublic politics of those years, and especially by Russian groups trying to retain an economic and political foothold in Kazakhstan. The lack of professionalism among many of the parliamentarians must have irked Nazarbayev, who faced the pressures of running the country and did not see himself as having the luxury of long-winded speeches from the floor of the Majilis.

Kazakhstan's parliament was surprisingly unproductive, passing only seven pieces of legislation in its single year of existence. Some of the assertiveness of parliament was clearly empire building. In late 1994 the legislature attempted to seize control of the republic's budgetary disbursement apparatus, and in early 1995 some of the most open anti-Nazarbayev factions talked of putting forward an alternative economic development plan that would have slowed privatization, changed the tax structure, and given a decided investment advantage to local producers over foreigners.

At the same time, however, for all the obvious growing pains it was exhibiting, the legislature was beginning to develop some of the fundamental characteristics of an institution capable of providing the checks and balances essential to the functioning of a pluralistic society. Even staunch supporters of Nazarbayev were beginning to understand that they had responsibilities as legislators if the parliament was to function as a legislative body.

The best illustration of this growth toward parliamentary responsibility came from Speaker Abish Kekilbayev. While remaining a strong supporter of the president, Kekilbayev tried to increase the competency of his fellow legislators and to defend the constitutionally defined rights and responsibilities of the Majilis. He encouraged parliamentarians to visit other legislatures and parliaments and began pushing the business of the Majilis away from long-winded floor debates to that of standing committees and commissions. Kekilbayev also began holding the government accountable for its actions and decrees, claiming that they must have a basis in law and that parliament had to propose and pass new legislation rather than leave the initiation of legislation to the executive branch. Indeed, by the beginning of 1995, Kekilbayev was calling on the Majilis to resurrect and defend a Kazakh parliamentary tradition stretching back to the councils of *biis* of the fifteenth to eighteenth centuries. To Kekilbayev, the parliament, not the president, embodied Kazakhstan's democracy, and the country's leaders must answer to the parliament, and not the other way around.[62]

A collision between Nazarbayev and the parliament seemed inevitable until a March 1995 decision of the constitutional court invalidated the 1994 parliamentary elections. This provided Nazarbayev with an opening to redefine the constitution of the country and to avoid presidential elections.

At the time, Kazakhstan's judiciary was the least transformed branch of the government. There was an acute shortage of trained jurists and real indecision about how much autonomy judges should have. The judicial branch was also chaotically organized with what amounted to three separate supreme courts with sixty-six judges, including a supreme court for criminal matters, an arbitrage court for economic ones, and a constitutional court. None of these courts had shown particular activism, but the constitutional court had been the least active of all, rendering only eight decisions since its formation in 1993, and no decisions from January to October 1994.

Thus it was wholly unexpected when the court suddenly ruled in favor of a complaint that an unsuccessful legislative candidate had brought to it ten months before. The plaintiff in the case was Tatyana Kvyatkovskaya, a journalist from the Abylaykhan electoral district of Almaty. She charged that the electoral districts for the 1994 election had been disproportionately drawn, so that legislators represented constituencies of vastly different sizes. She also claimed that the cross-out method of voting allowed vote counters to accept a single ballot as having been cast for many candidates if the voter marked his ballot improperly (indeed, in several districts more votes were recorded than there were voters). Although the complaint had been brought about a single voting district in Almaty, the constitutional court ruled that the entire 1994 parliamentary elections had been unconstitutional.[63]

In a rumor-prone political culture like that of Kazakhstan, there have been many theories advanced as to Nazarbayev's role in this court decision. As noted, the original complaint had merit, for the election had indeed been overtly stage-managed, so it is possible that the constitutional court acted without informal or official interference. The constitutional court may have been prompted to render a decision because its own existence was under attack. Complaints about the costs of maintaining overlapping jurisdictions had already prompted the previous legislature to reduce the powers of the court and transform it from a body able to initiate its own investigations to one that could render opinions only when asked by the other branches of government.

Minister of Justice Nagashbai Shaikenov wanted to create a U.S.-style single supreme court and to take away from the president the power to remove judges in order to encourage the growth of a genuine independent judiciary. The new parliament also targeted the court, seeking to reduce its funding and to prune its staff. The justices had much to explain: collectively they had taken thirty-five trips abroad at state expense; the deputy chief justice had spent a year in Moscow studying law at state expense; and two were facing recall attempts because as senior officials in the republic's law school they had disciplined students and faculty for participating in the Alma Ata Uprising (protesting Kunayev's dismissal).

At the same time, the fate of the plaintiff in the case, Kvyatkovskaya, suggests presidential collusion, for she went on to head the Otan party list in the 1999 parliamentary election and then to serve in the Majilis. The court decision also coincided with the strengthening of Kazakhstan's security organs. Many of the judges on the court had close ties to Kairbek

Suleimenov, at that time a first deputy minister of Internal Affairs and a strong critic of Shaikenov's proposed legal reforms.[64]

Although the president may not have directed Kairbek Suleimenov, Nazarbayev was certainly pleased by his behavior. In the two-year period following the dissolution of parliament, Suleimenov went from running the Committee on Fighting Crime and Corruption to being the minister of the interior, and then having the added responsibility of supervising all other internal security issues, a function that he discharged until December 2000.[65] During his tenure in office Suleimenov increased the reach of these security organizations. Members of Almaty's political establishment became keenly aware that their actions were being watched and that displeasing behavior was being duly noted. The same pattern was observed in regional centers, which had traditionally been under tighter control.

President Nazarbayev used the March 1995 court decision to his personal advantage. He appealed the decision one day after it was issued, on a national holiday. When the court reaffirmed its original decision, Nazarbayev went immediately before the parliament to inform them that they were being annulled as an improperly constituted body and that all their decisions were revoked. To make the point even clearer, Nazarbayev suspended the use of all government automobiles and other perquisites; had the power, water, and telephone for the parliament building turned off; and sent a swarm of workmen to begin what was called necessary remodeling. Using powers that he had been granted by the 1990 parliament right before its dissolution, Nazarbayev declared direct presidential rule and reinstated the government of Prime Minister Kazhegeldin, who had first been appointed prime minister in October.

President Nazarbayev quickly looked for ways to make his actions seem in accordance with democratic principles, but the strategy he chose showed contempt for the goals of genuine popular empowerment. Soon after imposing direct presidential rule, Nazarbayev created a People's Assembly to substitute for the parliament, and these handpicked delegates adopted a resolution requesting that presidential elections be postponed until December 2000. Claiming that he wanted to defer to "popular will," Nazarbayev then submitted the question to a nationwide referendum, which was held in April 1995. At that time 91.3 percent of the voters turned out, of whom 95.8 percent voiced their support for extending Nazarbayev's mandate. At the end of August, a second referendum was held to sanction the adoption of an entirely new constitution, which further strengthened the president's power. That referendum saw a 91 percent voter turnout, with 89.1 percent approving the new constitution, which was duly adopted. The opposition claimed these figures were dramatically inflated through electoral irregularities. Although there certainly is substance to the charges, independent polls in Kazakhstan during this period also make clear that an absolute majority supported Nazarbayev's proposed changes, so vote tampering was simply gratuitous and a further sign of the growing official contempt for democratic norms.

The new constitution expanded presidential power at the expense of the legislature, which became a largely consultative body, with legislation initiated by the president.[66] The new constitution created a bicameral legislature, composed of the Senate (upper house) and the Majilis (lower house). The latter had sixty-seven seats, based on districts with approximately equal numbers of voters; representatives were to be elected for four-year terms, with half the seats to be contested every two years. The Senate had two senators to represent each of the republic's oblasts plus Almaty (which has oblast status), to be chosen in joint sessions of the oblast councils, but the new constitution also gave the president the power to overturn actions of those same councils. An additional seven senators were appointed directly by the president, and ex-presidents were named senators for life. The composition of the Senate almost ensured that the parliament was unable to override a presidential veto, which required a two-thirds majority in both houses, as did a vote of no-confidence in a prime minister. In fact, the only check upon the president's power was a demonstration of infirmity or a charge of treason that is approved by a majority vote of both houses of parliament.

The Eclipse of Parliament and the Strengthening of Cabinet Government

This shift of more power to the president was a formal institutionalization of trends begun after the disbanding of the Soviet-era parliament in 1993 and the nine-month period of rule through presidential decree. Since that time official interest in building democratic institutions began to fade. In his major presidential message of 1997, *Kazakhstan 2030,* Nazarbayev did not even mention the development of a democracy in Kazakhstan as one of the eight principal goals of state building.[67]

In fact, democracy building was only tangentially mentioned in the goals for the period 1998–2000.[68] The statement paid little attention to the need for modifying Kazakhstan's political system. Political freedom was termed a good thing, but only as long as it did not interfere with the ability of the government to provide for the social welfare of the population. Similarly, maintaining ethnic tolerance was a goal, but those drafting the statement no longer saw the risk of ethnic conflict as an immediate threat to the state.

It was clear that the president was feeling more confident. The 1995 Majilis, and even more so the Senate, became an extension of the presidential court. The largest single bloc in the Majilis came from the president's own People's Unity Party, while another twenty-one seats came in ones and twos from such past or present elite organizations as the Youth Union, the Lawyers Union, the Union of Entrepreneurs, and the (new) Communist Party of Kazakhstan.[69] Yet even this legislature was unwilling to turn itself into a rubber stamp of presidential initiatives. While legislative rebellions were rare, their very existence demonstrated that pressures toward pluralism were continuing in Kazakhstan, especially with regard to social welfare issues.

Kazakhstan was slowly retreating from the unrealistic social benefit programs that it had originally enshrined in the constitution, a legacy of what the citizens of socialist states expected to receive from their governments. Among these benefits was the right, retained from the Soviet period, for men to begin receiving state pensions at age sixty and women at age fifty-five. In May 1996 a bill was brought before the lower house to raise those ages to sixty-three and sixty, respectively. Pensions, although miserly and irregularly paid, nevertheless constituted a major item in the republic's budget.[70] As then Prime Minister Kazhegeldin noted, Kazakhstan had 2.8 million pensioners, 16 percent of the entire population; more important, the republic had one pensioner for every two workers. With many others approaching the existing pension age,[71] the projected costs of state pensions threatened government efforts to reduce the state's budget deficit to 3 percent of the GDP, which was required for continued international financial support.

It came as a surprise when the parliament rejected the government's bill and created a full-blown government crisis. As the new constitution stated, if a government bill is twice rejected by the parliament, the president has to either dissolve parliament or dismiss his prime minister. After postponing the second vote for 48 hours, presumably to give all sides a chance to think through their positions, parliament faced a vote of confidence requested by Prime Minister Kazhegeldin, which passed 35 to 10 in the Senate and 41 to 19 in the Majilis. The pension bill was therefore resubmitted the following day, and it passed by the same margin.

The passage of this bill averted the possibility that Kazakhstan would face its third set of parliamentary elections in as many years. While the parliamentary about-face demonstrated a general inclination to defer to President Nazarbayev and his ministers, there remained a minority, even in the Senate, that cast an independent judgment. More remarkable is the shame-faced air evident in the accounts of the maneuvering that took place between the first and second votes. Although most of the legislators caved to governmental pressure, the speaker of the Majilis, Marat Ospanov, took pains to depict the parliamentary reversal as both principled and logical, arguing that the legislature had put the government on notice that future parliamentary support should not be taken for granted, especially on social issues.[72]

Of course, President Nazarbayev was usually able to nudge the legislature, given its makeup, in directions that he and his advisers considered necessary. Even so, the government faced heavy opposition in early 1997 when pushing for the passage of a bill requiring the universal use of the Kazakh language by ethnic Kazakhs by 2001 and by non-Kazakhs by 2006. Nazarbayev was able to get support from the Majilis but was rebuffed by the Senate, forcing the language bill back into the Majilis for modification. The final version, from July 1997, stated that Kazakh would be the language of state administration, legislation, legal proceedings, and record keeping in all spheres of social relations.[73] While mandating the advancement of Kazakh through education, the schools, and special training programs so that all residents would be fluent, it also reaffirmed Russian as an important language in the country and awarded it a status "on par with the Kazakh language in state organization and bodies of local self-government."[74]

With the muscle taken out of parliament, the cabinet and ministry system was becoming one of the few potential arenas for political contestation. Largely because of an effort sponsored by international financial institutions to downsize the overblown bureaucracy that Kazakhstan had inherited from Soviet times, an effort was made to eliminate redundancies at every level of administration—in the ministries, in the presidential apparatus, and in the oblasts.[75]

These changes too were handled in ways that increased Nazarbayev's personal authority or were otherwise convenient to the ruling elite. In March 1997 the cabinet system was sharply streamlined, with the number of ministries reduced from twenty-one to fourteen, and the number of subcabinet committees and commissions was curtailed as well. By the end of May one-third of the national government had been eliminated, creating a savings of nearly two billion *tenge* (the Kazakh currency since 1993) in annual salaries for 1997 alone, and freeing 200,000 square feet of government office space for commercial use, which provided a new source of kickbacks to the government officials who managed the ministries and agencies that were free to dispose of excess space.

However, while the streamlining of government may have led to budgetary savings, it did not make incumbents more competent or eliminate bureaucratic redundancies. For example, after the shakeup, the responsibility for economic planning was still divided among the newly created Strategic Planning Agency, the Supreme Economic Council, the Ministry of Economy and Trade, the Ministry of Finance, and the Customs Service.[76] If anything, the government reorganization led to a greater turnover at the top levels of government since President Nazarbayev wanted simultaneously to create government sinecures for loyal supporters and to build international confidence in his administration.

Nazarbayev's hand was freed by the departure of Kazhegeldin as prime minister in October 1997, initially claimed to be due to health problems. In fact, Kazhegeldin was removed because he was a potential rival to Nazarbayev and more popular with Western business people, since the Kazakh prime minister seemed knowledgeable about economics and was perceived to be less corrupt than were the president and his entourage. Kazhegeldin's critics would argue that the former prime minister was better only about hiding his malfeasances. Nazarbayev saw Kazhegeldin as posing a threat, largely because of the powerful economic interests to which the former prime minister was connected. Kazhegeldin, who is from northern Kazakhstan, spent most of his career developing ties to defense-related industries, and for at least part of this time he served as an employee of the KGB. Kazhegeldin rewarded some of his former colleagues when he presided over the privatization process, passing control of Kazakhstan's vast metal deposits, stockpiles, and refineries to Russian investors with purported ties to the old Soviet security establishment and exempting the stockpiles from payment of Kazakhstan's value added tax. Initially, Nazarbayev may have felt too weak to take on these powerful interests, but by 1997 he felt able to step in to forestall Kazhegeldin's developing an impregnable power base.

Kazhegeldin was replaced by Nurlan Balgimbayev, who had previously headed the Kazakh state oil company and who was a close associate of President Nazarbayev. Balgimbayev's ascendancy also marked Kazakhstan's growing preoccupation with the development of oil and gas reserves, which was the one area of the economy that showed signs of being able to sustain long-term foreign investment interest. Balgimbayev was eager to be rid of his predecessor's team but proved a less competent administrator and was more susceptible to presidential pressure. Several prominent reformers left, including most notably National Securities Commission Chairman Grigory Marchenko,[77] while a number of people with dubious pasts reappeared, such as Asygat Zhabagin, who was appointed to a new combined ministry as the minister of energy, industry, and trade,[78] and the controversial Sarybay Kalmurzayev, the former director of the State Property and Assets Committee, became *akim* of Zhambyl oblast.[79]

Balgimbayev tried to make the government more appealing to the international community by inviting some of the "young Turks" of the Kazakh business world into the government.[80] The young Turks were in their twenties and thirties and had managed to amass large personal fortunes during the late Soviet period and the first years of privatization, some because of ties to the Nazarbayev family and others because they had sufficiently ingratiated themselves.[81] For example, Bulat Abilov of Butya became one of the leading patrons of Kazakhstan's Children's Fund, which is headed by Mrs. Nursultan Nazarbayeva (Sara Alpysovna). At the same time, the young Turks were not permitted to compete with those in the inner circle, as Mukhtar Ablyazov found out when he positioned his company to compete in the sugar market with the firm run by Nazarbayev's son-in-law Rakhat Aliyev. The finances of Ablyazov's sugar operation were scrutinized, and taxes with penalties were assessed, although his other holdings went untouched.

This effort to broaden the base of the government, though, did little to deflect the criticism of Balgimbayev that was mounting within Kazakhstan's political establishment by people in business who were on the outs with the government, the remnants of the former Communist elite, and the opposition forces from the previous two parliaments. Nazarbayev may have dominated the country's political life, and even pilfered enough from the economy to allow all those close to him to live like royalty, but his control was not sufficient to make the elite speak with one voice.

Issues pertaining to the economy could still be debated. Particularly contentious was the fiscal conservatism of Balgimbayev, who was seeking to maintain Kazakhstan's credibility with the international financial institutions that were financing the country's economic recovery program. Parliament continued to be the locus of criticism on these questions.

Balgimbayev's popularity was not aided by Russia's financial crisis in August 1998, which produced rapid aftershocks for the Kazakh economy. Although Kazakhstan's economic downturn was not nearly as severe as that of Russia's, the Kazakh prime minister was criticized for not doing enough to insulate the Kazakhs from the influences of their powerful northern neighbor. Parliament initially focused its frustration on the minister of finance, Saut Mynbayev, and even brought an unsuccessful vote of impeachment against him in the fall of 1998: twenty-six for impeachment and twenty-eight against. This was the vote of a supposedly loyal legislature.[82]

In fact, the growing mutterings concerning Balgimbayev's performance may have been partly responsible for President Nazarbayev's decision to call for early elections for both the presidency and the parliament. Nazarbayev initially met with some resistance when he proposed the constitutional amendments necessary for these elections to be held, first from the legislature and then from the constitutional court. In the end, a joint session of Kazakhstan's parliament approved compromise legislation that cut Nazarbayev's presidential term by two years but gave a green light to the early elections.[83]

Yet Nazarbayev stuck with Balgimbayev, a career oilman with close ties to Russia, whose policies were still credible for the foreign investment and financial community. On January 21, 1999, the day after Nazarbayev's inauguration, the country's parliament once again endorsed Balgimbayev to the post of prime minister and kept most of the prominent figures in place.[84] In August 1999 Balgimbayev also managed to avoid ouster in the North Korean MiG sale, although the United States would have liked the Kazakhs to have done more official atoning for these events. Only Defense Minister Muhtar Altynbayev and Security Committee Chairman Nurtai Abykayev were dismissed "for grossly violating procedures for selling military equipment."[85] Altogether, forty MiG jets were sent to North Korea under the supervision of these top figures in the Kazakh government. In addition, in the spring of 1999, six Kazakh MiG–21 fighter jets on board a Russian Ruslan aircraft en route to Bratislava and destined for North Korea were seized at the Baku airport.

The parliamentary pressure on Balgimbayev began steadily mounting after the presidential elections, largely because of budgetary issues. The combined impact of the previous year's financial crisis and the low price of oil made maintaining a low budget deficit difficult. Ospanov went so far as to threaten that the Majilis would vote no-confidence in the government if it would not negotiate the terms of the proposed budget deficit.[86] In the summer of 1999 Ospanov again led a parliamentary tirade on budgetary issues, this time clashing with the president, who floated the idea of bypassing the old parliament entirely and ruling by decree until after the parliamentary elections scheduled for late 1999. Ospanov, who died in January 2000 after suffering a brain hemorrhage, was a rather enigmatic figure. A leader of Tereshchenko's Otan, he wanted to become prime minister and might have been trying to fashion himself as a democratic alternative to Nazarbayev given Ospanov's forceful defense of the idea of freedom of the press and the importance of competitive elections.[87]

Nazarbayev chose to move the government in a different direction. In early September, when the Kazakh president sharply criticized the cabinet at the opening session of the country's parliament, it became clear that the government was doomed. The Kazakh economy would have sustained much lighter damage, he said, had the cabinet not made numerous errors, including the choice of a floating exchange rate and of the National Bank's refinancing rate.[88] Balgimbayev's suggestion that Kazakhstan sell a 10 percent share in the Tengiz oil field (40 percent of its remaining holdings) in an effort to keep the budget deficit under control led to further criticism that Kazakhstan was sacrificing its long-term interests to short-term ones.[89]

Eager to hold parliamentary elections in a less hostile environment, Nazarbayev asked for Balgimbayev's resignation on October 1, 1999, naming Kasymzhomart Tokayev in his place, allowing the dismissed prime minister to return to his former post as the head of Kazakhoil.[90] Nazarbayev also used a presidential decree to reorganize the government, once more redefining the institutions that were charged with overseeing economic reform and many basic social services.[91] The Tokayev government brought back several reformers, most prominently Grigory Marchenko, who became the head of the National Bank, which was not a formal cabinet position. Although the capital was already awash with rumors about Tokayev's own alleged malfeasances, Nazarbayev stressed the clean records and moral purity of these nominees in an effort to breathe credibility into his failing anticorruption campaign.

The appointment of the Tokayev government put to rest the rumors that were circulating in Kazakhstan for close to a year that President Nazarbayev would simply eliminate the institution of the cabinet and rule by decrees issued through his presidential apparatus.[92] Cabinet reorganization seemed sufficient to meet the apparent goal of strengthening the economic hold of the official family. Most of the so-called young Turks were removed and replaced by people whose connections might be beneficial to Nazarbayev.[93] Uraz Dzhandosov, the former first deputy prime minister, managed to hang on as the minister of finance, but he eventually left his position in 1999, only to return in December 2000 as the deputy minister.

Manipulating the Electoral Process

The stage was now set for the 1999 presidential and parliamentary elections. Most observers view as disingenuous Nazarbayev's claim that he was not personally responsible for either the timing or the conduct of these elections. Certainly, he tried to make his actions seem acceptable to the international community. In these months the Kazakhs were reported to have paid large fees to Western law firms and public relation firms, including Akin, Gump, Strauss, Hauer, and Feld, the Carmen Group, and Mark A. Siegel and Associates.[94] The latter firm was hired to help the government reform its electoral system and to lobby Western experts on behalf of the government.[95] The Kazakh government tried to create an image of supporting democratic reforms; for example, in a September 30, 1998, address, less than two weeks before parliament moved for early election, Nazarbayev laid out a blueprint for the further democratization of the country, promising to increase the power of parliament, decrease that of the presidency, and pledging that all future elections would be free and fair.[96]

Nevertheless, parliamentary legislation introduced on October 7 was tailor-made to allow Nazarbayev to serve out the rest of his life as president. It brought forward the date of the elections, extended the president's term in office from five to seven years, and dropped age and term restrictions. Elections were set for January 19, 1999, too soon for any meaningful opposition to be launched since most potential contenders had oriented themselves to the idea of an election in December 2000.

The one presidential contender who seemed poised to move quickly was barred from seeking office because of his newly acquired criminal record. Former Prime Minister Akezhan Kazhegeldin, who had been heading the country's Union of Industrialists and Entrepreneurs since he left the government, was convicted of participating in an unsanctioned election rally, planned by the hastily organized Movement for Fair Elections.[97] Despite considerable U.S. and OSCE pressure to pardon Kazhegeldin, Nazarbayev, who disclaimed personal responsibility for Kazhegeldin's arrest, maintained that as president he was bound to enforce the country's laws and did not criticize the action of the Kazakh court.

In November 1998, while struggling to get on the presidential ballot, Kazhegeldin formed the RNPK political party, which quickly attracted many of the leaders and supporters of Azamat. Referring to a "citizens' movement," Azamat was organized in 1996 by Petr Svoik, Galym Abilseitov, and Murat Auezov. Svoik was a former legislator who had chaired the antimonopoly committee in Kazakhstan's first postindependence legislature, while Abilseitov served as the minister of science until August 1994, when he was named deputy prime minister. He remained in the government until 1995. The third co-chairman of Azamat, Murat Auezov, was a former ambassador to China. Auezov's status as the son of Kazakhstan's most celebrated Soviet-era writer, the late Muhtar Auezov (1897–1961), seems to have offered him some protection. In December 1997, Svoik, his wife, and two other party leaders were beaten up in a hotel room in Bishkek, Kyrgyzstan. In the same month, Abilseitov was sentenced to fifteen days in jail for organizing an unsanctioned demonstration.

Auezov initially announced his intention to oppose President Nazarbayev in the January 1999 presidential race but later dropped out. Nazarbayev did not seem concerned with the threat posed by Auezov or by any of the Kazakh and Russian nationalist leaders, and Communist Party leader Serikbolsyn Abdildin became Nazarbayev's principal opponent in the 1999 elections. The Communist's candidacy could have been foiled by legislation that restricted the activities of agents of foreign states, and in April 1996, Kazakh Procurator General Mahsut Narikbayev threatened to ban the Communist Party because its founding documents called for reinstating the Soviet Union. This, he said, violated Kazakhstan's constitution, which set down sovereignty, independence, and indivisibility as the core principles of the state.[98]

The opposition candidates had slightly longer than a month to register, collect the signatures of 170,000 supporters, pass a Kazakh language exam, and pay an election fee of $3,000.[99] This was something that those who were committed to a free and fair election in Kazakhstan found disturbing, but the OSCE was unsuccessful in its rigorous efforts to get the Kazakh government to postpone the elections so that Nazarbayev's opponents would have more time to campaign.[100]

Nazarbayev was obviously frightened that someone from the Kazakh political elite would decide to oppose him. For the first years of his presidency the figure he feared most was Olzhas Suleimenov, who by the 1999 election was in his sixties and seemingly had fully spent his political ambitions. Now Nazarbayev had two far more formidable figures, Kazhegeldin and the former mayor of Almaty city, Zamanbek Nurkadilov. Both men had powerful bases of support, Kazhegeldin because of his close links to Russia's military-industrial elite, and Nurkadilov through business and real estate interests around Almaty.

Nazarbayev was able to come to terms with Nurkadilov, who was allowed to shift his power base to Almaty oblast, which he was appointed to head. Given the nature of his contacts, Kazhegeldin could not be bought off, and Nazarbayev simply did not want to face him, despite the fact that most independent observers thought that the incumbent president would handily defeat the former prime minister. Maybe the Kazakh leader was fearful that his margin of victory would be an embarrassing one and thought that he was above potential embarrassment.

Nazarbayev was able to claim a resounding victory against the Communist Party leader and two political lightweights; he received 81 percent of the vote, with a reported voter turnout of 88 percent. Abdildin came in second with 12 percent, independent Gany Kasymov managed 5 percent; Engels Gabbasov of PNEK received 1 percent; and 2 percent of the voters cast their ballot against the standing candidates.[101] Stories of election-return falsification circulated throughout the country, and Nazarbayev was reported to have done particularly poorly in western Kazakhstan, where promises of oil and gas wealth have yet to be transformed into improved standards of living.

Claiming a new mandate and acting impervious to foreign criticism, the president and his supporters turned their attention to the parliamentary elections that were scheduled for the fall of 1999. Although the October 1998 constitutional amendments had raised the term of office for deputies in the Majilis from four to five years and that of deputies in the Senate from five to six years, these changes also opened up the electoral process slightly. Ten new seats were added to the Majilis, to be filled by proportional representation from political party lists. The size of the filing fee for candidates decreased from 100 to 50 times the minimum wage, the restrictions against those who had participated in unregistered public groups were lifted, and the requirement that a 50 percent voter turnout was necessary for a contest to be valid was eliminated. All these changes were incorporated in the May 1999 election law,[102] which did not set the conditions for the elections to be free and fair since the candidates were not guaranteed equal access to mass

media, and those, like Kazhegeldin, who had received "administrative pun-
ishments," were barred from running.

Elections to the Senate were held on September 17, 1999. International
observers found the conduct of the voting to have been generally fair, but
not without irregularities, such as the refusal of the chairman of the Almaty
election commission to accept guidance from the secretary of the Central
Election Commission. More troubling was that senators were elected by the
outgoing *maslikhats*, whose members would face election in less than a
month.

Another black mark was the treatment of Kazhegeldin, who was arrested
in Moscow on an outstanding Kazakh warrant the day after he was denied
registration as a parliamentary candidate. Although he was later released,
RNPK refused to participate in the Majilis elections as a party and recalled
its party list from the Central Election Commission. By this time, though,
party unity was at issue as some in Kazakhstan's opposition were becoming
uncomfortable with the hypocrisy of Kazhegeldin's people giving vast sums
of money to advance democratic ideals. Lira Bayseitova, a former leader,
explained why she opted to leave the RNPK: "They [the staff of the executive committee of the party] are both former Young Communist League
(Komsomol) and Soviet Communist Party members who care nothing for
the people. I decided that it was pointless to fight from within. You have to
start waging the fight from outside."[103]

The Majilis election campaign was marred by other irregularities. According to the RNPK members, thirteen state-controlled companies refused to
publish their party's election platform. In addition, the pro-regime Civil
Party was accused of buying votes with charitable gifts. *Panorama* published
an article accusing the party of distributing free home appliances, including
television sets and stereo systems, to Kazakhstan's border guards. The Central Election Commission took no action, however, citing the election law
provision that parties could spend campaign money for charitable purposes.

In the first round of elections to Majilis and local *maslikhats*, held on
October 10, 1999, the official voter turnout was 59.78 percent, low by
Kazakh standards, which suggested that public apathy was becoming more
of a problem. Four political parties crossed the stipulated threshold of 7 per-
cent of the popular vote and would occupy the ten seats. The opposition
Communists and Agrarians won two seats each, and the propresidential
Otan and the Civil Party received four and two seats, respectively.[104] Twenty
candidates received a majority and were elected in single-mandate districts.

The remaining thirty-seven seats were contested in the second round, held on October 24, 1999.[105] As a result of the elections, the progovernment parties received 57 percent of the vote and managed to secure 80 percent of the seats in the Majilis. According to the Central Election Commission, 60 percent of the newly elected Majilis members were either already deputies or were connected to state or local power structures.[106]

One hundred seventy international observers, including 150 from OSCE, monitored the voting, and most of the Westerners among them considered Kazakhstan's 1999 Majilis elections to be seriously flawed. Kazakhstan's neighbors offered little or no criticism, however, seemingly agreeing with Vladimir Yatsenko, a member of the Ukrainian parliament and the CIS inter-parliamentary assembly, who concluded that there were no major irregularities in the elections.[107]

The representatives of most of Kazakhstan's opposition parties disagreed. Azamat, the Socialists, Azat, Yedinstvo, and the RNPK all complained to the international observers about harassment, surveillance, denial of access to the state-run media, and arbitrary banning from registering candidates. One former Majilis candidate, Vladimir Chernyshev, even requested political asylum at the British embassy, citing the "impossibility of being able to exercise the right to be elected"; he maintained, "It is better to live in a monarchy than in secular, law-governed Kazakhstan."[108]

Is the Current System Workable?

The 1999 elections helped to transform Kazakhstan into the kind of country that President Nursultan Nazarbayev wants it to be, one with a strong president and an opposition that is sharply restricted in its freedom of action and range of activities. What is less clear, however, is whether this form of government is well suited to the tasks that Nazarbayev and his government face. The president is powerful and insulated from the population by a "court" of family and loyal supporters who surround him. While structural changes impede the potential success of opposition groups, these groups continue to exist and to challenge Nazarbayev. Nevertheless, they are denied the institutional setting necessary to do so in constructive ways.

The intimidation of leading opposition members has continued and even escalated. In September 2000 Lira Bayseitova was beaten up and nearly killed, while RNPK leader Gaziz Aldamzhanov formally resigned his party post in January 2001, citing his weariness with the official harassment of himself and his family members. The absence of an elective opposition is beginning to prove costly for Kazakhstan. While the level of professionalism of the presidential apparatus is increasing—and a new generation of bureaucrats who have international experience is beginning to replace the older, Moscow-trained ones—the legislation put forward lacks the kind of reflection that a vigorous debate in the press or the legislature would produce.

Thus, while individual pieces of legislation are often drafted in close consultation with international experts—and this includes some of the legislation redefining Kazakhstan's legal system as well as many of the major economic reform bills introduced since 1995—the resulting political system is founded on the idea of the rule of law but whose incumbents lack respect for the law itself. As I explain in the next chapter, the legal infrastructure does not offer predictable or consistent protection for either foreign or Kazakh property and contractholders.

While the president regularly delivers strident speeches on the need to stamp out corruption, there are few if any checks on his own personal power or the exercise of authority by those close to him. All the formal political institutions that could serve as centers of opposition have had their autonomy curtailed, while the strengthened presence of security organizations inhibits journalists and ordinary citizens from expressing their displeasure at the concentration of power in the hands of a privileged few.

The top leaders of the country are all reported to have used political position for their own economic advantage. Nazarbayev's efforts to uncover Kazhegeldin's hidden assets led to some of his own being divulged as well and have spurred investigations by Swiss and U.S. courts.[109] Well-paid international legal teams, retained by the members of the Kazakh ruling family as well as by the Western firms alleged to have provided money to them, may succeed in getting any future indictments quashed and making it more difficult to report on these developments. An atmosphere of official corruption continues to set the tone of public life in Kazakhstan.

In today's Kazakhstan, elite preferences are all that matter. A small and largely mono-ethnic elite has taken a disproportionate share of the benefits of economic transformation but has failed to provide basic services to a large and increasingly impoverished multi-ethnic majority. Even though the country's population has become more ethnically homogeneous (as I discuss in chapter 6), it has also become poorer and more dissatisfied.

Whatever the desires of its leadership or of any single constituency within the state, Kazakhstan will remain a heterogeneous society for some time to come, with enormous regional as well as ethnic diversity. It is impossible that the interests of all these many groups should coincide, and the pressures inherent in the country's makeup will need venting. This was precisely the justification for the liberalization campaign of the late Soviet period when Gorbachev, in an effort to allow popular grievances to be expressed, permitted the formation of informal groups.

Many of the agenda items of these first political groups have been addressed; the Kazakhs have had their language and culture restored to a place of prominence and can rewrite history to their own choosing. Although the ecological despoliation of Kazakhstan has not been reversed, both the government and the international community accept its redress as part of their burden. Moreover, the Kazakhs have, formally at least, become the masters of an independent country, something that its first political organizations, formed only twelve or thirteen years ago, never thought was a real possibility.

Independence is not a political solution; it is simply a change in juridical status, a critical one to be sure, especially for the ruling elite. But in the absence of institutional development, the only difference for the masses is psychological, and the benefits or hardships it provides are ephemeral. Ethnic Kazakhs may have believed initially that they had gained status from independence, just as ethnic Russians felt they had lost it, but the differences in perception of the two communities are narrowing and will continue to narrow with time. Those who live in a country should feel they have a stake in its future or, failing that, feel some hope for their own future or that of their children.

When the Kazakhs became independent, the government gained breathing room and various new symbolic weapons to use in its efforts to appease the population. Central to this was the idea that independence in and of itself would be the source of a better life for Kazakhstan's new citizens.

In the early years of independence people could still hold on to the old Soviet-era myth that things would be better in the not too distant future. Ten years later, however, the poor are growing poorer and recovery seems beyond their reach. The memory of the last years of the Soviet Union is still vivid for most of Kazakhstan's citizens; they know firsthand that governments are brought down when thousands of people take to the streets. To some extent, this has had a salutary effect: in Kazakhstan the old Soviet pessimism still prevails; people believe that things might get worse if one tampers with them. As long as there is no particularly attractive political figure on the horizon, President Nazarbayev is safe because the people of Kazakhstan are likely to continue to prefer the devil they know.

However, this will not make Kazakhstan's citizens happier about their fate. If the government continues to maintain institutions that are only nominally participatory and fail significantly to reflect public will, then Kazakhstan's social tensions could erupt when the population inevitably demands accountability from the country's leadership. The press may choose not to report the kinds of pressures that the regime is under, but the sources of social unrest will continue to well up and seek political expression. Nazarbayev realizes this and so has curtailed the independence of the press and the power of the legislature. For this same reason the Kazakh president has limited the authority of local governments and refused to allow local executives to be elected by their populations.

Nazarbayev's self-confidence has certainly increased in recent years, and he believes that he can get away with such actions. He has learned about the privileges accorded to the leaders of resource-rich states. Frequently feted in the national capitals that are home to the Western oil companies investing in Kazakhstan, he sees no reason to pretend to embrace political ideologies that are fully alien to him, and he is not shy about making it clear that democracy is one such ideology.

Nazarbayev's complacency is in part fed by the neighborhood where he lives. There are few success stories in the states carved out of the Soviet Union. Nazarbayev's support for macroeconomic reforms has made Kazakhstan a model in the region. It is easy for him to compare the conditions in neighboring Uzbekistan, where the regime is approaching Stalinist norms in its repression of the population, and feel self-congratulatory about how good things are in Kazakhstan. When he looks at Russia, he sees a regime trying with real difficulty to reassert control over a fractious political system that some see as weakened in the name of democracy or local autonomy.

Yet a tour of these countries does not give a full accounting of the political options available to the rulers of newly independent states, nor does it speak to the likely political and social outcomes of their choices. Nazarbayev is ignoring his population, and those living in Kazakhstan are still being fed a diet of future gratification, with promises that when the country begins to realize profits from its oil and gas sector, the National Oil Fund will ensure that the whole population benefits.

Portioning out small shares of future income will not substitute for political reform. The Kazakh government must either embrace the diversity of interests in Kazakhstan or close off all avenues for the expression of its nation's diversity by imposing an unabashedly autocratic form of government. After some cautious exploration of the former, Kazakhstan's leadership has increasingly tended to move toward the latter. Whether such autocracy might be imposed, and whether it will prove stable if imposed, depends to a great extent upon the republic's economy, the subject of the following chapter.

5

Economic Development or Stealing the State?

The process of economic transformation in Kazakhstan gives striking testimony to the difficulties of moving to a market economy, even in the most resource-rich of newly independent states. Kazakhstan's leaders inherited a situation that gave them a real reason for optimism. The country's economy was diverse, with sufficiently well-developed manufacturing and agricultural sectors to allow a smooth transition to an independence in which public satisfaction was kept high enough to maintain political stability.

In the postcommunist world, Kazakhstan is second only to Russia in the variety and abundance of its natural resources. At independence, Kazakhstan was nearly as rich in human resources as it was in natural ones. With a relatively small, well-educated, and reasonably well-disciplined population, the quality of the state's human development—a UNDP-devised measure based on a combination of life expectancy, basic living conditions, education level, and gross domestic product (GDP)—put Kazakhstan in a similar position to Mexico and Poland.[1]

There was thus every reason to expect that Kazakhstan was poised to become an economic success story, a new "snow leopard" to sit alongside the Asian tigers. To succeed, Kazakhstan's leaders had to confront a fourfold challenge: they had to disentangle their country's economy from Russia and also from the economies of the other post-Soviet states; they had to privatize the country's resources and economic enterprises but leave the state capable of meeting its own payroll and social welfare burdens; they had to stimulate foreign investment; and finally, government officials had to find the political will to discipline themselves and their relatives to ensure that the level of corruption would not cripple the functioning of the economy.

The first three problems were partially interconnected. Though diverse, the economy was far from self-sufficient. Virtually every enterprise—whether a mine, a factory, or a business—was a link in a production cycle that stretched outside the republic. Most of the economy of northern Kazakhstan was directly connected to that of southern Siberia, while enterprises in southern Kazakhstan were almost entirely dependent on energy sources in Uzbekistan.

The same was true of Kazakhstan's transportation and communication system. Although designed to integrate Kazakhstan into the larger Soviet Union rather than to serve the needs of the republic as a unit, the infrastructure of the republic was nevertheless well established, with roads, bridges, railroads, telecommunication, and other structures that most newly created countries could only envy. As a landlocked nation, however, Kazakhstan could reach the outside world only by sending its goods through neighboring states. This has created enormous complications for investors in Kazakhstan. While the country has attracted more FDI per capita than any other post-Soviet state, the money coming into the country has been slow to contribute to an overall improvement in the standard of living.

Despite its promise, the reality of the republic's economy since independence has been one of sharp decline followed by partial recovery. Although the shift to market conditions (and world prices) has led to an increase in the per capita income in Kazakhstan, this comes chiefly from the sale of natural resource stockpiles. The profits obtained from these sales went largely into a small number of private hands and were not reinvested in the country's economy. So while the per capita GDP increased fourfold from 1991, up to $1,317 per capita in 1995, the share of both industry and agriculture declined, from 30.1 to 23.5 percent and from 16.2 to 11.7 percent, respectively, in these sectors that accounted for most of the country's employment. Kazakhstan's industrial crisis left the country with an unresolved debt crisis with Russia and bankrupted many of its municipalities. By late 1996 the situation was dire. That winter (1996–1997), many of the republic's cities were without heat or power for long periods, and even in Almaty frequent power shortages forced some residents to cook over open fires in the courtyards outside their apartment buildings.

According to Kazakhstan's Ministry of Finance, 44 percent of businesses lost money in 1996 (these statistics include only those firms that were still operating). Industry had all but collapsed, while unemployment had risen sharply, its true extent masked by the widespread practice of keeping workers on their jobs only nominally, producing little, and withholding their pay for months at a time. While workers in the Russian-dominated northern part of the country had been demonstrating periodically since the early 1990s, by 1997, the workers in the Kazakh-dominated southern part of the country had also begun to organize and sustain strikes on their own.

Increased foreign investment and higher oil prices have brought some improvement, but the per capita GDP peaked at $1,423 in 1998 and then went into a steep decline in 1999 (down to $1,058), reflecting the downward trend in the global economy. In 2000, the per capita GDP managed a slight comeback.[2]

The process of economic development has yet to create a flourishing new entrepreneurial class. Instead, it has led to the formation of a narrow and extremely wealthy elite that has enormous resources concentrated in its hands. The elite has been reluctant to reinvest its resources at home, even when offered a tax amnesty. While the country is becoming increasingly oligarchical, the government has adopted a formal posture designed to develop public confidence. A well-publicized anticorruption campaign was launched in 1997, and measures were taken to strip corrupt investors of lucrative management contracts that had been given during the privatization of certain large enterprises. The bureaucracy charged with overseeing private investment was overhauled and put on notice that corrupt and wasteful practices had to end after there was a nearly tenfold increase in "budget evaporation" in 1996. A few dismissals have occurred, but the effort to "root out and punish" prominent figures is at best symbolic. The favorites of one prime minister were simply replaced by the industrial entrepreneurs championed by his successor.

At the same time, the living standards of the population have been steadily eroding, so that by 1996 Kazakhstan stood just below the Philippines in the United Nations' Human Development Index ranking. By 2000 Kazakhstan had climbed back to seventy-fifth place, a level that is still fourteen places below its original rank at the time of independence.[3]

While there is still great hope for the next phase of foreign investment, which is to include increased rates of exploitation of the nation's oil and gas reserves, and the government promises that these profits will be invested in the National Oil Fund, this stage is still several years away. For now, though, while the size of Kazakhstan's economy continues to increase, the decline in both the agricultural and the industrial sectors has continued (see appendix 5), meaning that Kazakhstan's economy is increasingly based on the export of raw materials. This creates a series of problems for Kazakhstan, including whether the economic policy that the government began in 1995, with full privatization and heavy foreign investment as its backbone, will succeed in creating enough jobs and state revenue to tide the country over until its long-range development plans can mature.

Interdependence with Russia

In the final years of the Soviet Union, Kazakhstan was the third largest Soviet republic in terms of net material product (NMP) produced and the fourth in industrial output.[4] Kazakhstan was a major supplier of raw materials, agricultural products, and manufactured goods for the entire Soviet Union. The World Bank has estimated the republic's 1991 gross national product (GNP) to have been $25.1 billion. This figure reflects Kazakhstan's contribution to the Soviet economy and does not readily translate into what the GNP of Kazakhstan would be as a standalone economy. Approximately 40 percent of the republic's GDP was derived from manufacturing, extraction, and processing. Kazakhstan was a major producer of iron ore, aluminum, heavy equipment, and rolling stock, and in 1989 Kazakhstan produced about one-fifth of the USSR's gold and coal. Because of the contribution of its natural resource exports to the Soviet economy, Kazakhstan provided implicit trade subsidies for other Soviet states. In 1990, implicit transfers as a share of the GDP were measured at 7.4 percent for Kazakhstan.[5]

In the Soviet period, the local elite rarely controlled facilities located within a republic; only 8 percent of Kazakhstan's economy was under direct republic control, while Almaty shared control of 48 percent of the economy with Moscow, and 43 percent of it was controlled directly by Moscow. The latter included more than fifty factories belonging to the USSR's military industrial complex, which accounted for more than 11 percent of total Soviet military production. The push for republic sovereignty brought Kazakhstan's party leadership into partial control of virtually all aspects of the republic's economy. Nearly two years after independence, however,

President Nazarbayev admitted that there were two closed cities in the country that he learned about only after Russian Defense Department officials had shut down their factories and their workers had gone home to Russia.

Soviet planners had little interest in developing the economy of Kazakhstan as an end in itself, so the economic potential of some regions was exploited while that of others was totally ignored. As already noted, most of the republic's manufacturing, mines, and processing facilities were concentrated in the north and northeast and were interdependent with those of southern Siberia. Kazakh coal helped to power Russia's electric grid, and its oil and gas went to Russia to be refined, while Kazakhstan's own refineries processed oil and gas from neighboring republics. Agriculture was split between the north-central and southern regions, with grain concentrated in the former and the lucrative cotton and rice crops in the latter. Again, economic integration made the grain growers reliant on elevators and flour mills in Russia, while the southerners depended upon Uzbekistan's roads to transport their goods and service their economy.

At independence only 21 percent of the republic's GNP derived from intraregional trade, which accounted for nearly 90 percent of its total foreign trade, most of which was with Russia. As important as that trade was in the aggregate, it was even more important in certain sectors, so that Russia was Kazakhstan's sole customer for such commodities as iron ore, lead, phosphate fertilizer, and heavy equipment, while Russia was the republic's sole or major supplier for such things as paper, timber, tires, most agricultural equipment, and—even more important—oil, gasoline, and other refined-petroleum products. While each could inflict damage on the other, Russia had a far greater capacity to punish Kazakhstan than the reverse, hence the Kazakh president's strong interest in integration.

Russia's special relation with Kazakhstan was transformed by the demise of the ruble zone in November 1993. The new Kazakh currency, the *tenge*, was formally launched on November 15, 1993. Kyrgyzstan, another important trading partner, introduced its currency, the *som*, in May 1993, and the Uzbek *som* came into use in June 1994. Russia's leaders had hoped to bind the CIS countries together with a single currency, which would have allowed Russia to dictate economic terms.[6] As the proponents of more radical economic reform gained the upper hand in Kremlin decision making, these calculations began to change, and the continuation of a single currency zone was seen as a major cause of Russia's hyperinflation.[7]

The collapse of the ruble zone created the first major economic crisis in Kazakhstan, leading to the rapid and nearly complete collapse of cross-border trade, crippling hundreds of interconnected industrial enterprises and making thousands of workers redundant in the process. It also allowed Kazakhstan to devise its own economic policy and gradually to substitute cash transactions for barter trade. This also served the interests of Russian reformers, who sought to establish economic domination over an integrated economic space consisting of other reforming economies. In spite of the wide fluctuations across the CIS in the value of the ruble, Kazakhstan's government had been reluctant to introduce a national currency, despite the fact that it was being pushed to do so by foreign advisers as well as its own young Western-trained economists. The Kazakhs stayed with the ruble after Russia freed prices on January 1, 1993, and even after Moscow withdrew Soviet-era rubles from circulation in late July. The first action obligated Kazakhstan to follow suit, to avoid a run on differentially priced products (which would worsen existing shortages), while the second removed currency emission entirely from the republic's control. Kazakhstan bargained with Russia for either the right of emission or a reliable supply of the new rubles, in return for coordinating its export policy, foreign borrowing, and even its budgeting with Russia. In November 1993, Russia imposed the further condition that Kazakhstan turn over its gold reserves, at which point President Nazarbayev felt impelled to establish the tenge. Kazakhstan, though, paid a price for its tardiness in leaving the ruble zone, as the country was flooded with rubles from CIS states that were preparing to launch their national currencies,[8] leading to an inflation rate of 2,500 percent in 1993.

The IMF-supported stabilization program, which was introduced with the tenge, made controlling inflation a priority, and the government of Kazakhstan has done well in meeting this obligation. Although during the first year of the currency's existence the dollar-tenge exchange rate depreciated from the initial $1 for 5 tenge to $1 for 56 tenge a year later, the currency's value gradually stabilized. The average exchange rate for 1995 was $1 for 61 tenge, and the rate in mid-1996 was $1 for 67.2 tenge. The currency continued to depreciate over the next two years, dropping sharply following the Russian crisis of mid-1998, when it fell to $1 for 81 tenge,[9] in large part because trade with Russia still accounted for 31.5 percent of Kazakhstan's exports and 42.5 percent of Kazakhstan's imports.

In April 1999 the Kazakh authorities introduced a free-floating exchange rate regime. As a result, the tenge depreciated by more than one-third by the end of September 1999. President Nazarbayev was critical of this measure. This was probably one of the reasons for the government shakeup in early October. Many believe, however, that the tenge float helped to end the economic recession and contributed to an economic growth rate of 1.7 percent in 1999.[10] Rising world commodity prices and favorable weather conditions also played a part. Before the Russian crisis, Kazakhstan had been able to maintain a steadily dropping inflation rate. Average consumer price inflation was 1,880.1 percent for 1994, falling to 176.3 percent for 1995. Inflation for 1997 was 17.4 percent, below initial IMF projections, and fell even further to 7.3 percent in 1998.[11] The sharp drop in the country's inflation rate was a direct result of the increased fiscal responsibility being exercised by Kazakhstan's government. The planned 1997 budget called for a spending deficit of only 3.2 percent of the GDP and a sharp cutback in the size of the state administration when the government saw that these goals were unlikely to be met. However, in 1999 inflation increased to 17.8 percent.[12] The 1998 budget called for a consolidated fiscal budget deficit of 5.5 percent of the GDP, but the decrease in government revenues caused by the falling prices of Kazakhstan's major exports, such as oil, made this target virtually unattainable. The government was slow to react to this state of affairs, finally announcing an austerity program on July 13 after much pressure from Nazarbayev.[13] Kazakhstan's 1999 budget set the deficit ceiling at 3.7 percent of the GDP.[14] The country's 1999 budget deficit was 4 percent of the GDP.[15] By January 2001 the tenge traded at $1 for 145.4 tenge, and since the August 1998 crisis Kazakhstan's currency has depreciated only about half as much as the Russian ruble.

Russia's share of Kazakhstan's trade is steadily diminishing. According to the Kazakh Statistical Agency, trade turnover between Kazakhstan and Russia amounted to $2.46 billion in 1999, falling $82 million against the amount in 1998.[16] Yet by the end of the first quarter of 2000, Russia remained the country's most important trade partner, with a share in total trade turnover of 28 percent (32 percent of imports and 25 percent of exports).[17]

Russia's withdrawal from Kazakhstan has been welcomed much more than mourned, especially by a local elite that has gained a clear economic advantage. By 1989–1990 the decay of central control and the attenuation of intra-union economic ties created strong incentives for republic elites and senior management with access to valuable commodities to bypass Moscow and market their goods directly. The flood of money fell into private hands when changes in Soviet legislation allowed commodities to be traded through cooperatives and then through privately owned companies. Initially this was done semiclandestinely, but after independence Kazakhstan's leaders were largely free to award the management of the country's resources to whomever they chose, making it even easier for people to turn political privilege into private fortunes, which were then put to use during the country's privatization campaign.

Public debt, however, continued to increase at a rapid pace in these first years. No longer directly tied to the neighboring economies, Moscow was free to charge escalating prices for its various sources of energy, which had previously been supplied at fantastically steep discounts. The newly independent states thus acquired ballooning bills that they were unable to pay. By mid-1995, for example, Kazakhstan was importing about $1 million a day of energy products, about 65 percent of it on credit from Russia. At the same time it began to accumulate debt to Uzbekistan, which was the major energy supplier for the southern part of the country.

At several points, Kazakhstan has had to swap equity in some of its state-owned enterprises to meet this debt. In the case of the national power grid, for example, half of the $663 million that Kazakhstan's consumers owed to the state power supplier in 1997 was in turn owed to Russia for payment arrears. Kazakhstan cleared this debt with a $370 million debt-equity swap, giving Russia ownership of one of the high-voltage lines running through northern Kazakhstan and some equity in one of the republic's generating stations.[18] This fragmentation of ownership of the national grid complicated later efforts to interest foreign investors in taking over other parts of Kazakhstan's major utilities. Kazakhstan's energy interdependence with Russia has remained a problem, as has the accumulation of Kazakh debt. With time, the focus has shifted from political actors to economic ones, as in January 2000 when it was the Russian energy giant RAO–UES (Russia's Unified Energy Systems), and not the Russian government, that acquired a piece of the national Kazakhstan energy network in return for the forgiveness of $239 million in debt to the Russian company.

A similar debt-equity swap occurred in the case of the spaceport of Baikonur, which was the subject of protracted negotiations with Russia. While Kazakhstan gained considerable foreign policy advantages from the process, the final agreement reached for the space-launch facility passed full control of Baikonur and Leninsk, the support town, to Russia, including legal extraterritoriality, in exchange for an annual rent of $115 million (on a twenty-year lease). While Russia has offered Kazakhstan a greater role in future commercial launches, the facility remains under nearly exclusive Russian control, and the relationship has never been a very satisfactory one. Until 1999 the Russian payment was offset by Kazakhstan's debts, and the Kazakhs prohibited Russian launches after major accidents. The crash of a Russian Proton rocket booster in October 1999, scattering harmful debris over the Kazakh steppe, sparked acute resentment. The Kazakh ban was lifted only after Russia investigated the cause of the crash and paid compensation.

The Privatization of Industry

Kazakhstan's liquidity crisis created strong pressure for the government to accept the advice of international experts and to privatize the economy. While more tentative steps were taken previously, Kazakhstan's current program of privatization dates from 1995 when the government introduced a staged policy to turn nearly all the country's public assets into private ones, a move that was designed to attract foreign investment, stimulate production, and rid the state of responsibility for debt-ridden enterprises.

In the context of the breakup of the Soviet Union, Kazakhstan's economic collapse was neither unique nor especially severe. Industrial output throughout the Soviet Union, including Kazakhstan, had been in persistent decline (in real terms) since the early 1980s, providing one of the engines driving first Yuri Andropov's[19] and then Mikhail Gorbachev's attempts to revitalize the socialist system. Beginning in 1990, however, and continuing through the first years of independence, Kazakhstan's industries went into precipitous decline. Industrial production shrank by 25 percent in 1994, and Kazakhstan's GDP in 1995 was 31 percent below the 1991 figure.[20]

The desire to privatize the economy was an important complicating factor. Not surprisingly, given their economic inexperience with all but the Soviet system, Kazakhstan's leadership embarked upon privatization rather gingerly. Privatization in Kazakhstan was done in several stages: the privatization of housing using flat coupons (1991–1992), mass privatization using investment privatization coupons (1993–1995), and finally, after the government adopted a new full privatization program, the privatization of individual projects (1996–1998). As a result, by 1999 the private sector employed about 60 percent of the labor force.[21] As of July 1999, 75.6 percent of the economy was privatized, including 80.2 percent of small enterprises, 40.8 percent of medium enterprises, and 52 percent of large enterprises.[22] The process was not as equitable or as fair as had been hoped. In fact, the *Financial Times* labeled the latest stage of privatization "the Kazakh sale of the century."[23]

The first stage of privatization passed with little public objection because it consisted largely of turning state-provided apartments into the private property of the occupants. Inevitably, there were inequities, most of them the result of demography. The legacy of Soviet-era hiring and promotion practices meant that a disproportionate number of the better apartments, especially those in the capital, now belonged to Russians. Cultural differences also played an important role in job selection during the Soviet era, resulting in what most observers noted as a disproportionate number of stores and kiosks becoming the property of Slavs or Uzbeks and Uighurs, all of whom had a stronger mercantile tradition than did the Kazakhs.

The second stage of privatization began in 1993 with the launching of a government coupon privatization program for medium-sized firms and factories with more than 200 employees.[24] It was then that the real stresses of economic transition began to appear in Kazakhstan. A kind of "spontaneous privatization" (essentially a form of legalized theft) of salable commodities had begun even before the collapse of the USSR. This too favored Russians, who were more likely than Kazakhs to be the managers of factories, mines, and warehouses. Now the Kazakh government would have to ensure that the economic advantage shifted.

The Kazakhs chose a voucher system, which had been pioneered by the Czechs and later also used in Russia. Vouchers representing a set value were distributed to all the citizens of Kazakhstan, which they could deposit in one of the many investment privatization funds (IPFs) established for the purpose. The various fund managers would then bid for up to 20 percent of the shares in the mid-sized enterprises that were offered at privatization auctions, using their vouchers as initial capital. Fifty-one percent of shares were to be auctioned, 10 percent were to be given to workers and staff, and 39 percent went to the government.[25]

The various IPFs were intended to function like a combination of governing board and mutual fund, protecting their members' investments while helping to encourage greater efficiency and probity in the various enterprises. When the first 3,500 enterprises were put up for privatization in April 1994, 170 investment funds were already registered, which should have given Kazakhstan's citizens a wide choice. In fact, more than three-fourths of the vouchers were in one-fourth of the funds, while half the funds had a total of 4 percent of the vouchers.[26] More remarkable, perhaps, is that one fund, Butya-Kapital, received nearly 10 percent of the republic's vouchers, making it by far the largest single actor in the second stage of privatization.

This second stage strengthened the personal fortunes of the leading fund managers, who went on to form Kazakhstan's new economic elite. The overwhelming majority of these men, such as Mukhtar Ablyazov of Astana Holding, who in 1998 was appointed the minister of energy, industry, and trade, and Bulat Abilov of Butya Kapital, were ethnic Kazakhs.

Ordinary Kazakhs, though, were nearly as suspicious of privatization as the Russians were, particularly as the rumors grew of closed auctions at which state properties with deflated assessments were being sold and as a new affluent elite began driving expensive new foreign cars and building vast houses in and around Almaty. Many of the Communist-era legislators who were still serving in Kazakhstan's parliament began voicing public outrage, especially those who had not directly benefited from the privatization process. This pressure led to Prime Minister Tereshchenko's dismissal in the fall of 1994, but the new prime minister, Akezhan Kazhegeldin, was charged with pressing forward with full privatization even more rapidly. He was also given the task of improving the foreign investment climate, something the country's legislature had been reluctant to do. The Kazhegeldin government used the nine-month gap between parliaments (1993–1994) to introduce laws through presidential decree designed to make the privatization process more transparent and to protect the rights of property owners, as well as to stimulate the development of small- and medium-sized businesses. These decrees, in many cases prepared in close consultation with international financial institutions, were all reaffirmed by the new legislature.[27] In March 1996, the government declared that small-scale privatization in Kazakhstan was complete, with 93 percent of small enterprises in industry and agriculture in private hands. By that time, the shares of 1,600 larger enterprises had been put up for sale at twenty-two auctions. The shares represented the charter capital with a nominal value of 1,261,500,000 tenge.[28] According to then Economics Minister Umirzak Shukeyev, in early 1997 there were 90,000 small- and medium-sized businesses in Kazakhstan that, along with small traders, employed 20 percent of the labor force, or 1.65 million people. Their economic impact, though, was limited because small- and medium-sized businesses produced only 160 billion tenge worth of products, or some 10 percent of the GDP in 1996, accounting for 5 percent of exports and 15 percent of imports.[29]

The third tier of privatization, which was designed to privatize the largest factories, was scheduled for 1995, postponed until 1996, and was still not yet complete in late 2001. The republic's mineral and petroleum wealth, as well as industries deemed to be of national significance, were originally intended to remain public property, but as the country's financial crisis deepened, some of these have been sold. This third phase has been termed privatization through individual projects and case-by-case privatization.[30] The companies were sold (or put under the management) of individual investors, under an individually negotiated arrangement, making this the most corrupt stage of the three tiers, in part because the enterprises on offer were the republic's largest and potentially most profitable. There were a limited number of sources for the kind of capital required since most of the enterprises had extensive debts and many also had unproductive attached assets—such as day-care centers, hospitals, and apartment buildings for their workers. Thus the government was willing to envision a kind of concession—called a management contract—in which the government, or government-controlled companies, would find foreign partners to update or renovate existing factories and to market the enterprise's assets without fully assuming its debts. This foreign partner would have first rights to purchase shares from the government-controlled packets, and it was hoped that they might do so if these enterprises were divested of their various social welfare responsibilities and became profitable.

The use of management contracts began during the second stage of privatization, and between December 1994 and August 1996, the government offered forty-two of these contracts. Many of them were suspect, but tens of millions of dollars were invested in Kazakhstan that might otherwise have been withheld. This included several contracts that went to the subsidiaries of the Trans-World Metal Corporation (and its sister companies, Japan Chrome, Ivedon International, and White Swan of England), which was a group of largely Russian metal traders that took major positions in some of Kazakhstan's largest metal plants, including a giant aluminum smelter in Pavlodar and a ferro-alloy smelter in Aksu.[31]

The Trans-World Group was headed by David Reuben, an Israeli, who was in business with the Chernoy brothers; the latter were reportedly tied to organized crime.[32] Trans-World was also said to enjoy the support of Oleg Soskovets, former first deputy prime minister of Kazakhstan and then of Russia, and he in turn was reputed to be on good terms with Akezhan Kazhegeldin.[33] Certainly, after Kazhegeldin's departure, the fortunes of Trans-World began to falter. One of the original partners, Aleksandr Mashkevich, left Trans-World in a grab for company assets, in which he was said to have brought in the Nazarbayev family as a silent partner.

The Kazakh government was able to declare the leases in default and used this to political advantage after Nurlan Balgimbayev replaced Kazhegeldin as prime minister. Trans-World Metals became a particular target and brawled with the Kazakh government in the courts of several nations. The government's endgame seemed clear, albeit unspoken, that those close to the president should now benefit from these transactions, although this has never been formally demonstrated. These management contracts also had an impact on center-periphery relations since the oblasts inherited many of the social obligations that were dropped by large enterprises.

The management contract for Karaganda Metallurgical Combine (Karmet) was also controversial. This giant steel mill was declared bankrupt and was then offered to Ispat, a largely unknown Indian steel producer.[34] Rumors that this transaction directly benefited Nazarbayev, who worked in Karmet for five years (from 1965 to 1969), make the rounds regularly, fed by the fact that the mill was set to be privatized after a $50 million payment by Ispat for a plant that had a $1 billion replacement cost. Karmet was the sixty-seventh largest steel mill in the world at the time of its privatization, with a capacity to be the twenty-fifth largest.[35] Even working at half capacity, the plant accounted for 10 percent of Kazakhstan's GDP in 1995.[36]

The privatization of Kazakhstan's most valuable assets remains both slow and corrupt. While Nazarbayev instructed the cabinet to complete privatization by July 1997, only 62 of the 194 enterprises listed for privatization in 1996–1997 were actually offered for sale,[37] in large part because the enterprises continued to depreciate in value and few would pay the asking price. In December 1998, for example, the Ust-Kamenogorsk Titanium and Magnesium Plant was withdrawn from offer because its share price had dropped to one-tenth the August 1997 value.

Still, the government's intention throughout has been to complete the sale of the country's principal assets by gradually transforming them into open stock companies. In 1997 the Kazakh government reorganized the country's stock market to facilitate the privatization of the country's largest utility companies, its principal bank, and some of its natural resources. This action has yet to have the desired effect.[38] The Law on Securities, the Law on Investment Funds, and the Law on the Registration of Security Transactions, all passed in 1996–1997, were designed to replicate the U.S. securities exchange legislation of 1933. The shares of thirteen large companies were to be traded on the stock exchange by the end of the first year; but only three companies were fully tradable by June 1998.[39] The slow start-up of the stock market was partly the result of Kazakhstan's failure to create investment banks. As of the third quarter of 1998, less than 5 percent of the country's large enterprises had been privatized, as had 11 percent of its medium-sized enterprises. By comparison, nearly 85 percent of all small enterprises were in private hands.[40] To compensate for the sluggish start, the Kazakh National Securities Commission drafted another program for the development of the securities market for 1999–2000, which reevaluated the role of portfolio investments, attempted to create conditions favorable to the demand and supply of securities, and tried to develop an oversight system. This program also envisioned tax incentives for securities issuers and assumed a high investment potential within Kazakhstan itself since the government estimated the population's hidden assets at $3 billion.

The final stage of privatization was designed to achieve yet another goal of the state, the privatization of the country's pension system. Since 1998, workers were to have the choice of investing their pension money, still to be based largely on employer contributions, in the state pension fund or in private funds. The institutional structure of the new fund system includes accumulative pension funds, asset management companies, custodian banks, and state regulatory bodies. Kazakh pension funds are divided into private (PPF) and state (SPF) funds, and all are closed joint stock companies. According to the law, PPFs are allowed to organize as investment funds, accepting clients regardless of their workplace, or as corporate PPFs serving only the employees of shareholder companies. According to Prime Minister Tokayev, during 1998 and 1999 the country's fifteen private funds and a state accumulative pension fund gained about $400 million in investments.[41] The new accumulative pension fund system (APFS) has helped to support state borrowing, but it has done little to stimulate effective saving.

Guidelines for the use of pension funds are still confusing, and an announcement by the Ministry of Labor and Welfare that pension funds would be used to modernize the Atyrau-Samara pipeline created a stir early in 2000. The National Security Commission then issued a ruling that pension funds would not be invested in industry. Legislation requires that at least 50 percent of a fund be invested in state securities, and currently 96 percent of the funds are in state securities.[42]

Many in Kazakhstan still view the new pension system with skepticism, and most ordinary Kazakhs find it difficult to function in the private sector. Anecdotal evidence suggests that those with medium-sized and even small enterprises who lack official connections are at a disadvantage from the start because of the difficulties of getting capital and the need to purchase protection. In a recent survey by a high-level commission on corruption, 60 percent of the 250 managers of small- to medium-sized firms surveyed admitted to having encountered extortion and bribery.[43] Many shy away from going into the private sector because they see the economy as corrupt and believe that organized crime plays too great a role. In a study done by *Karavan* in 1994, 64.5 percent said that the mafia exerted considerable influence on the government, and more than 60 percent said that the mafia either completely controls business or does so to a considerable extent (21.0 and 39.1 percent, respectively).[44] It is interesting that organized crime is so pervasive in Kazakhstan that the newspaper felt no need to offer any explanation of who the mafia was, and the perceptions of its pervasiveness may have limited participation in the private pension program. Only 18 percent of the Kazakh work force signed up with private pension funds one year after pension reform was introduced.[45]

Although further along than many other post-Soviet states, Kazakhstan's privatization process has been slowed by the government's vacillation on the question of what to do with the country's natural monopolies. In February 1998 the privatization of Kazakhstan's oil sector was suspended when the government claimed that it could not find a suitable strategic partner for the national oil company, largely because of the oil sector's lingering transport problem. Then, in December 1998, Nazarbayev announced that railways, power transmission lines, and oil and gas pipelines must remain in the hands of the government, and that the government had suspended the sale of state-owned shares in Aktiubemunaigaz and Mangistaumunaigaz, two state-held gas companies.

The government, though, continues its exhortations, and despite the instruction that privatization be completed by the end of the year (mid-December 1999), Kazakhstan's total privatization earnings in 1999 (local and national budgets) came to 35.8 billion tenge (approximately $250 million), compared with a target of 61.2 billion tenge (approximately $430 million). This included the sale of a 16.7 percent stake in one of the blue chip companies, Halyk Bank (the national savings bank), to a local financial sector consortium, Asia-Invest, which was priced at 1.38 billion tenge ($10 million). Once again, the Nazarbayev family is reported to be involved in this group.

Privatization plans for 2000–2001 are not likely to open the economy much. Although Prime Minister Tokayev stated early in 2000 that privatization would be completed in 2000, Finance Minister Mazhit Yesenbayev claimed that only 31 of the 215 companies slated for sale in 2000 were actually ready for privatization. Kazakhoil, KazTransOil (pipelines),[46] Kazakhstan Electricity Grid Operating Company (KEGOC), Kazakhstan Temir Zholy (railways), and Kazaeronavigatsia are still not eligible for privatization, and only two of the ten blue chip companies initially earmarked for privatization (Mangistaumunaigaz and Kazakhtelekom) had any real chance of being privatized in 2000,[47] and even they were not privatized. It is also unclear whether these companies will be stripped of their assets before sale, which has already happened in several instances. While the state oil company remains a powerful economic force, in 1998 the government sold Kazakhoil's most promising asset, a 14.28 percent stake in the Offshore Kazakhstan International Operating Company (OKIOC, now known as AgipKCO),[48] which will develop Kazakhstan's sector of the northern Caspian Sea.

Still, even with its scale-downed effort, Kazakhstan planned on earnings of more than $400 million from privatization in 2000. The blue chip government program for privatization intended for 2000 seems certain to be extended to 2001, including the sale of state shares (once again) in the Aktiubemunaigaz and Mangistaumunaigaz oil companies, Kazakhmys (Kazakhstan's largest copper producer), Kazakhstan Chromium, Kazakhstan Zinc, the Ust-Kamenogorsk titanium and magnesium enterprise, the Sokolov-Sarbai mining corporation, the Kazakhstan Aluminum Company, and also Kazakhtelekom and Halyk Bank.

Foreign Direct Investment

Foreign investment goes hand in hand with privatization, and Kazakh officials plan for their country to receive about $70 billion in foreign investment
over a forty-year period, overwhelmingly in the oil and gas sector. But a considerable portion of the country's enterprises will never be profitable enough
to attract interest, something that troubles the country's leaders, who would
like Kazakhstan to avoid the trap of becoming solely a producer of raw
materials. Yet it is not clear that they have the knowledge or the discipline
necessary to do this. Nazarbayev's strategy plan, *Kazakhstan 2030,* sets the
goal of transforming the country into "a technologically advanced society
with well-developed information and telecommunication systems that support scientific and technological personnel."[49] The plan provides little direction, however, as to how this might be accomplished.

The Kazakhs had thought that the task of restructuring their diversified
economy would be easier than it has turned out to be. They knew that agricultural reform would be contentious, but they erroneously expected the old
industrial framework to make way automatically for a new one. Kazakhstan's
leaders had little understanding of how technologically obsolete their economy was, a situation that was aggravated by the departure of Russian (and
other) specialists. The emigration of these specialists had an impact on all
sectors of the economy. This left the country's policy makers more eager than
ever to attract foreign investment, a task that was given over to the new
prime minister, Akezhan Kazhegeldin.

President Nazarbayev remained the standard bearer of the effort, outlin-
ing the areas of the economy that had the highest priority for foreign investment: energy, especially oil and gas; food processing (reflecting the fact that
Kazakhstan was a major food producer but had almost no capacity to process
its yield); gold mining and refining; and other nonferrous mining and processing. The bulk of its attention was directed toward the United States and
Europe, casting itself as a Europeanized, quasi-democratic secular society that
afforded ready access to the markets of Central Asia and beyond. When
appealing to Korean, Japanese, and other Asian investors, Kazakhstan
stressed its Asianness, and its willingness to combine capitalism with authoritarianism as some Asian tigers had. Kazakhstan courted Turkey and, to a
lesser extent, the oil states of the Middle East, reminding them of its shared
ethnic identity (with Turkey) and religious identity (with the other Muslim
states), without raising the specter of Pan-Turkism or Pan-Islam.

The policy of attracting investments in key spheres of production has been relatively successful. From 1993 to 1999, Kazakhstan received $9.29 billion in FDI, about 53 percent of which went to the oil and gas industry; most of the rest went to the steel, nonferrous metallurgy, energy, and other industries. FDI totaled $1.36 billion in 1999, 84 percent going to the oil and gas sector and 4 percent to metallurgy.[50] The country hoped to attract $1 billion to $1.5 billion in 2000,[51] and in the first quarter of 2000 FDI increased by 30 percent over the first quarter of the previous year. In 2001, the EBRD projected FDI will total $1.8 billion for the year.

The greatest number of foreign investment projects has been in the area of import-export. Their average value has been small because they include the so-called shuttlers, or petty traders, who provide a steady flow of consumer goods into the republic. Others were substantial, especially in the early years, when fortunes were made by selling down existing stocks of metal, ore, or other commodities. A second type of joint venture has involved the purchase and refitting of existing facilities. Kazakhstan has attracted some of the world's best-known companies, such as Samsung and Philip Morris.[52] Philip Morris now controls 80 percent of Kazakhstan's tobacco market and has been in the country since 1993. It opened a $340 million factory in 2000. Samsung has a 40-percent share of Kazakhmys (Kazakh copper), a vertically integrated metals company. Another reported success story is Glencore International's takeover of KazZinc, a joint venture created in 1997 out of Ust-Kamenogorsk Lead-Zinc Combine, the Zyryznovsk Lead Plant, and the Leninogorsk Polymetallic Combine. The Kazakh government retained 15 percent and gave Glencore 62.4 percent of the project.[53] Glencore is privately held by global commodities trader Marc Rich, who is no stranger to the murky ways of the metals business in the post-Soviet world. The project reported a net profit of $11.3 million in 1999, after which Glencore announced plans to invest $191.5 million over the next five years, to be added to $110 million spent in 1997–1999.

Yet the number of success stories involving global actors is limited. "Green field" projects comprise the third type of joint venture, involving extensive retooling or, more often, establishing entirely new production facilities. Many of the largest energy projects are in this category, and the Kazakhs have had considerable difficulty attracting other types of projects.

The potential of the republic was recognized by foreign investors even before the collapse of the USSR. Chevron Oil began negotiating for the rights to develop Kazakhstan's Tengiz oil field in 1990, although its agreement was not made final until 1993, a year when the country had $1.3 billion in foreign investment. The firming up of plans for the development of the Tengiz field stimulated further interest in the country, but 82.5 percent of the $660 million that Kazakhstan attracted in foreign investment in 1994 went to the oil and gas sector.

The government was concerned that the pace of investment was far too slow to stem the country's economic collapse. By 1994 more than half of the republic's enterprises had sharply reduced the length of their workweek. Workers throughout the country were put on furlough; and workers were often handed scrip, given a part of what they produced to sell as they could, or most commonly, simply not paid at all for months at a time. Such maneuvers kept the official figures for unemployment low—under 7 percent in 1995—but hidden unemployment was widespread. The ethnic Russian-dominated northern and eastern parts of the country were the worst hit. In 1994, for example, in the northeastern oblast of Pavlodar, 11 percent of the industry was shut down entirely, while 10 percent made no profit, and another 44 percent survived only by selling off their assets.

This collapse, and the fear that it would grow worse before it got better, led Kazakhstan's government to accept the IMF stabilization program that was designed to support the introduction of the national currency.[54] The government also followed the guidance of economic experts from multilateral organizations more generally,[55] with the twin goals of speeding up privatization and establishing a more attractive climate for international investment. In fact, almost every piece of economic legislation offered during the second half of the 1990s reflected consultation with experts from one or more of the multilateral financial institutions, who nonetheless rarely felt that the Kazakhs were taking all their advice.[56]

Over the next several years the government tried a number of approaches to improve Kazakhstan's international image for potential investors so that the country could reach beyond the oil and gas sector. The law on land, passed in December 1995, reintroduced private land ownership, which was not fully extended to agriculture until 2000, and even then important restrictions remained, including that foreigners could not own land, which limits their ability to recover capital after a failed investment.

A government contract with Mobil Kazakhstan Ventures Inc., confirmed in May 1996, provided a preview of upcoming legislation designed to spur investment, and in February 1997, the State Support for Direct Investment law was passed. Among the law's provisions were legal guarantees and certain benefits and preferences for investors. During these years, the

Kazakh government also began awarding development rights to strategic natural resources through tenders that were organized by international financial experts, another action that was pursuant to the advice that the Kazakhs had been receiving.

While the legal environment in Kazakhstan was certainly more supportive of foreign investment than that in Russia, there was still a critical need to increase investor confidence. Kazakhstan's government tried to address this through a "one-stop shopping" program for foreign investors, creating the State Investment Committee in November 1996. The committee took over the task of organizing tenders and supervising the negotiation of investment terms (taxes, tax relief, and royalty payments) with foreign companies. The streamlining of the investment process was strongly supported by most international experts monitoring or advising Kazakhstan. This procedural change substantially reduced the number of bureaucratic logjams that foreign investors faced. It did little, however, to create an atmosphere of transparency, especially after Akhmetzhan Yesimov, a confidant and reputed relative of Nazarbayev, was named the first head of the State Investment Committee and the first deputy prime minister. It seemed as though the process of influence peddling was being streamlined as well. Yesimov lasted until February 1998, when he was appointed the head of the presidential administration.[57]

Kazakhstan was also modifying the ownership terms available to foreigners. The necessity to meet its rising budgetary debt led the leadership to sanction investment deals that provided immediate liquidity, even at the cost of giving full ownership of a project to foreign developers. The result, as Aman Tuleyev, then Russia's minister for CIS Affairs, observed in 1996, was that nearly all Kazakhstan's industry had been handed over in whole or in large part to investors from other countries.[58] By 1998, mineral deposits were being turned over in full as well.

The government continued to increase the incentives to foreign investors even after economic conditions began to improve, in early 2000 offering expanded concessions to those investing in priority economic sectors. In addition to its well-publicized activities in the oil sector, the Kazakh government has made a strong effort to attract foreign investors to large mining projects. In February 2000, Ispat-Karmet acquired the Lisakovsky mining combine, and six months later the Kazakh government found a foreign buyer for its Vasilkovskoe gold deposit, which was turned over to Israeli diamond dealer Lev Leviev. As always, the air was rife with rumors of how those close to the president were benefiting from these transactions.

While the changes in government strategy and tactics have led to increased investor confidence, neither foreign nor flight capital is rushing into the country. Most foreign investment projects have yet to yield substantial income (or new jobs) for Kazakhstan. This places the government under continued pressure to sell off its resources to any available buyers, transferring valuable reserves to exclusively foreign control and leaving the treasury dependent on taxes and royalties not immediately forthcoming because of the incentive packages offered to stimulate investment. All this causes a disproportionate amount of official attention to the oil and gas industry, where investors will pay big cash bonuses and signing fees at the expense of planning for a more balanced form of development.

Oil and Gas Development

Foreign interest in Kazakh reserves was inevitable. The country has 70.52 trillion cubic feet of gas reserves and at least 16.4 billion barrels of oil reserves. This latter figure might even triple when Kazakhstan's offshore reserves are fully proved.[59] Many of these deposits will not come on line for many years, and the reserves will not be transformed into production for 40 years. Kazakhstan's goal is to produce 170 million metric tons of oil per year by 2020, by which time the oil and gas industry are to be completely privatized.[60]

Kazakhstan's oil reserves have been the subject of grand geopolitics as well as local political infighting. While the United States, Russia, Iran, Turkey, and China have all lined up, trying to influence the shipment of Kazakh oil, many actors within Kazakhstan have been struggling to benefit from the country's wealth as well. Many of these people have had connections with American businessman James Giffen, who served as an intermediary for Kazakhstan in many multinational oil transactions.[61] Rumors of large bribes being paid to Kazakh government officials have circulated for years. These went a long way toward substantiation when the U.S. Department of Justice issued a request to the Swiss government to report on the bank accounts of President Nazarbayev and two former prime ministers, Akezhan Kazhegeldin and Nurlan Balgimbayev. The Swiss report charges that these men took signing bonuses of $115 million offered by Mobil, Amoco, and Phillips Petroleum and diverted them to personal accounts.[62]

For U.S. officials, the critical question is whether American businesses knew these funds were being diverted. That the Kazakhs would try to profit from the foreign development of their oil should not be surprising, given the pervasive environment of official corruption. Kazakhstan's decision to seek the foreign development of its oil resources through the creation of international consortia involved most of the world's largest oil companies.[63] The strategy created numerous foreign stakeholders in the country's government as well as in its companies and many seeking ways to befriend the regime.

The foreign development of the oil sector was facilitated by a June 28, 1995, law on oil and gas. While there is talk of Kazakhstan someday becoming another Kuwait or even Saudi Arabia, for now Kazakhstan is just beginning to exceed the late Soviet-era production figures in the oil and gas sector and is a producer more on the scale of Yemen.

Whereas the republic extracted 25,823,000 tons of crude oil in 1990, Kazakhstan produced only 22,990,000 tons in 1996 and first approximated Soviet-era production in 1997, when 25,780,000 tons were extracted. Similarly 7.11 billion cubic meters of gas were produced in 1990, compared with 6.40 billion in 1996 and 2.72 billion in 1997.[64] Oil production rose to 25,776,000 tons in 1997, and gas production rose to 8.115 billion cubic meters.[65] In 1997, the oil industry contributed about $400 million to the country's budget from income, royalties, and taxes. From 1997 to 2000, crude oil production in Kazakhstan rose from 495,000 to 569,000 barrels a day.[66] Rising world oil prices made it more profitable to sell rather than to refine the product, especially for those who were able to obtain existing export contracts and resell the oil at world prices outside the country. This left most of Kazakhstan's refineries operating well below capacity, forcing the government to ensure that Kazakhstan had an adequate supply of diesel and other refined oil products by banning the export of lubricants until March 2000 and by setting an export quota for oil for 2000 at 22 million tons, or 440,000 barrels a day.

The greatest challenge confronting Kazakhstan's oil and gas industry is transporting the country's resources to market. While Kazakhstan projects six pipelines to be constructed by 2015,[67] to date only one new pipeline route has been agreed upon, that controlled by the Caspian Pipeline Consortium (CPC), which did not begin even limited operation until 2001. CPC is building a 1,580-kilometer pipeline, with an initial capacity of 28 million tons a year, or 560,000 barrels a day, from the Tengiz field in western Kazakhstan to the port of Novorossiisk on Russia's Black Sea. The total cost of the pipeline is set at $2.6 billion. The CPC project dates from 1993, and the pipeline was originally expected to be operational in September 2000. The first shipment of oil was sent along the route in March 2001, with the pipeline expected to be fully operational in October 2001.[68] The Russians began blocking shipments of Kazakh oil almost immediately after the first section was opened, however, allegedly because of a customs dispute. Informed observers maintain that the real reason that shipments through CPC were cut off was that the segregation of the higher quality Tengiz oil from that flowing through the rest of the Russian pipeline reduces the value of what the Russians are themselves marketing.[69] Before CPC was operational, Tengiz's production—7.5 million tons in 1997, 8.5 million in 1998, and 9.5 million in 1999, and 10.5 million in 2000—was transported through Duybendi and Ali-Bayramly, where it was loaded onto rail cars and shipped through Khashuri to the Georgian port of Batumi on the Black Sea.[70] The transit costs were much higher before the opening of the CPC route.

Despite the difficulties, the Tengiz venture attracted $700 million of the $1.5 billion that U.S. companies invested in Kazakhstan from 1993 to 1998.[71] The high demand for the Tengiz light crude and favorable financial projections led Chevron to boost the amount that will be invested in production and have kept the company bullish on the project. In spring 2000, Chevron bought an additional 5-percent stake in Tengiz from Kazakhstan, bringing its ownership share to 50 percent, although the structure of ownership is such that Kazakhstan still retains effective control.

The difficulties that Chevron encountered in negotiations to get a pipeline route to export Tengiz oil, though, helped to sour U.S. firms and the U.S. government on the idea of Russia as a partner in Caspian development. The original Soviet-era proposal for the development of Tengiz did not grant rights for the transport of oil to Chevron. After independence, in June 1992, these rights were awarded to CPC, which consisted of Russia's Transneft (the Soviet-era pipeline operator), Kazakhstan's government, and an Omani group.[72]

CPC seemed in no hurry to set attractive terms for the construction of this pipeline. It initially asked Chevron to finance the construction of what was then budgeted as a $2 billion pipeline, offering the American company only 20 percent of the pipeline profits.[73] By now, Russia's leaders had realized that they were losing control of resources in the newly independent states, which were further becoming competitors for Russia's own oil, gas, gold, and other commodity markets. As the legal heir to the Soviet Union, Moscow, in 1994, made a formal claim to part ownership of all the oil and gas sites in the former USSR. Although Russia lacked a strong legal precedent, it had numerous pressure points for advancing these claims.[74]

As a result of Russia's efforts, the then-leading Russian oil company, Lukoil, together with its U.S. partner, ARCO, purchased 5 percent of the Tengiz project from Chevron for a seemingly discount price of $200 million.[75] At the same time, cash-strapped local officials from Atyrau (previously Mangyshlak) fought for another piece of Chevron's investment, arguing that the oil lay beneath their sands, thus making them entitled to a portion of the proceeds to meet the region's own pressing needs. Chevron was forced to renegotiate several times, reducing its share of the eventual profits with each rewriting. The transit issue was not resolved until 1996 when Mobil was brought into the Tengiz project to interject the capital necessary to reduce the share of the Omani stakeholder.

During these years of negotiations, Russia tried to restrict oil and gas development by invoking Soviet-Iranian treaties which Moscow held required that Caspian reserves be developed through common consent.[76] Teheran concurred. Azerbaijan, Turkmenistan, and Kazakhstan said that they did not need Russia's permission to explore on- or offshore deposits and demanded that the Caspian be divided into national sectors that extended out to the middle of the sea.[77]

Rising international interest in Caspian resources increased the confidence of each of the Caspian states, and all three began to sell off parcels of their offshore reserves to foreign investors. Azerbaijan was the first to aggressively market its resources and presumed that a suitable pipeline route would inevitably follow if enough foreign investment was forthcoming. This helped the Kazakhs to develop the confidence to sell their self-declared national sector of the Caspian. The Kazakhs set up the multinational OKIOC—including Italy's Agip, British Gas International (including BP and Statoil), Mobil, Shell, and Total—to explore ten of the two hundred blocks that make up Kazakhstan's Caspian Sea shelf. In August 2001, OKIOC was renamed AgipKCO (Agip Kazakhstan North Caspian Operating Company) to reflect Agip's status as sole operator. Faced with an effective fait accompli from neighboring states, Russia gradually modified its position from the common development of national zones extending 45 miles from the shore, to the idea that there would be national sectors reaching to the middle of the sea with wide, 31-mile corridors of shared development.[78] The latter formed the basis of a 1998 bilateral agreement with Kazakhstan on the joint development of their shared Caspian reserves, which Russia hoped would serve as the basis of an agreement for all five states.[79]

This has yet to occur, and the bilateral agreement does not solve all Kazakhstan's problems since Moscow is still committed to the general use of the sea's water and undersea surfaces, meaning that all five states would have to consent to any Transcaspian pipeline project. Moreover, Russia remains opposed to the proposed oil and gas pipelines and is able to cloak its position in environmental terms. Although no one would dispute that the Caspian is a fragile ecological zone, Russia's position is to its economic benefit, reinforcing the need to ship fuels across Russia. By contrast, the U.S. government is a strong advocate of Transcaspian oil and gas pipelines as a way to make the Baku-Ceyhan pipeline from Azerbaijan to Turkey's Mediterranean coast (through Georgia) more commercially feasible. The gas pipeline is designed to benefit Ashgabat, while the oil pipeline would move Kazakh oil (particularly that belonging to AgipKCO) through Kazakh and Azerbaijani national waters.

The U.S. government has therefore been trying to push Kazakhstan into committing oil export volumes to Baku-Ceyhan, without complete success. Kazakhstan is a signatory of the four-state agreement of November 1999 endorsing the construction of the Baku-Ceyhan pipeline, signed before President Bill Clinton during the OSCE Istanbul summit. Unlike the Azeris, however, who are looking to market their oil safely and if possible earn further transit fees, the construction of the Baku-Ceyhan pipeline is not a priority for the Kazakhs. There has been much speculation about the kind of oil commitment that Kazakhstan would offer, especially since it is not clear whether the proposed pipeline is economically possible without a major commitment by the Kazakhs. The *Financial Times* claimed that Kazakhstan had earmarked 400,000 barrels a day of throughput, only to have Nazarbayev deny the statement a few days later.[80]

The Kazakh position is that no firm commitment will be made until the offshore blocks are proved and exploitation planned. The United States continues to try to entice the Kazakhs into supporting a Transcaspian pipeline and the larger pipeline project, which is now referred to as Aktau-Baku-Ceyhan, after the Kazakh city. It has asked KazTransOil, Kazakhstan's state pipeline company, which is headed by Nazarbayev's son-in-law Timur Kulibayev, to be the operator of the Transcaspian leg to Baku. While Kaz-

TransOil, now a part of TransNefteGaz, had to be included in the scheme since it is Kazakhstan's designated agent for oil exports, the company is reported to serve Nazarbayev family interests. Naming it project operator might have been a subtle inducement for the Kazakhs to support the Baku-Ceyhan route. U.S. administration officials have justified the decision as a way to make TransNefteGaz more transparent.

Kazakhstan continues to hope that a new pipeline can go through Iran, an easy and inexpensive routing for Caspian and western Kazakhstani oil. The Kazakhs say that they will use any route made available to them, including across Iran, but they are too dependent on U.S. goodwill to push hard for such an option.[81] Although the United States counsels Kazakhstan not to ship through competing oil-producing states (both Russia and Iran are in this category), the Kazakhs' priority is to get their oil to market quickly, which means that they are intent on maintaining good relations with Iran and accepting attractive transit offers from Russia. The Iranian interest in Kazakhstan heightened as the Clinton administration drew to a close, raising the prospect that a new U.S. administration might be more receptive to a diplomatic opening with Iran, which is a virtual prerequisite for the international financing of a new Iranian pipeline. A large Iranian delegation attended the April 2000 Eurasian Summit in Almaty that the World Economic Forum organized, including First Deputy President Hossein Kazempour Ardebili. At the very end of the year, the visit of Iranian Deputy Foreign Minister Sadyk Kharrazi led to rumors that the Kazakh and Iranian governments had signed a pipeline agreement for a 50–50 split ownership between them and a number of European oil companies.[82]

The Kazakhs have also been receptive to overtures from the Russian government. In December 1999, Vladimir Putin, then the Russian prime minister, supported the CPC export pipeline as being of "exceptional significance for Russia both from an economic and from a geopolitical point of view."[83] Transneft also agreed to increase the volume of Kazakh oil exported through Russia's pipelines in 2000, to ship 8.5 million tons (170,000 barrels a day) of Kazakh crude to markets outside the former Soviet Union, up from a 1999 total of 7.5 million tons (150,000 barrels a day). The Atyrau-Samara pipeline, Kazakhstan's largest, has a maximum annual capacity of 11 million tons, but there are plans to increase that to 15 million tons. The Russian government is eager to have Kazakh oil mixed with the lower-quality Ural crude. If part of the AgipKCO oil is shipped through the existing Russian pipeline system, then conditions for CPC and Tengizoil are likely to improve as well.

The Russian position is sure to evolve as more is learned about the size and quality of the AgipKCO reserves from the exploration wells being dug. There is often a lot of sulfur in Kazakhstan's oil, which is difficult to eliminate in offshore deposits, but if the deposit proves economical to work, AgipKCO may need to commit to the Baku-Ceyhan route for at least part of its oil, even if it is required to barge its oil across the Caspian. The development of the AgipKCO deposit, however, is fraught with technical difficulties. The project cannot be up and running until 2004–2005,[84] and probably not until 2006–2007 or even later, although by then the Western firms will feel considerable pressure since the period for the tax concessions negotiated as part of their production-sharing agreement will already be lapsing.[85]

Geopolitical concerns combined with the slowness with which the proposed pipelines were becoming operational led Kazakhstan to make plans to ship its oil to market through China. In 1997, when the Chinese government promised that a $9.6 billion pipeline would be erected over a span of eight years, the Kazakhs sold the China National Petroleum Corporation (CNPC) a 60-percent stake in the lucrative Uzen field, an onshore deposit second in size only to Tengiz, which Western oil firms had thought they would be able to develop.[86] The Uzen field (in Aktobe oblast) is some three thousand kilometers from the Chinese border. In addition, CNPC promised to build a 250-kilometer pipeline to the Iranian border.[87]

The China-Kazakhstan connection was reaffirmed in April 1999 when President Nazarbayev and Turkmen President Saparmurat Niyazov promised jointly to give priority to energy export lines through China in the next century.[88] Yet this statement was made in part to address rumors that the Chinese would withdraw, as CNPC had raised Kazakh government ire by laying off 2,000 workers. Finding business operations in Kazakhstan costly, CNPC contributed only about 60 percent of the planned investment in 1999,[89] in what the Chinese have viewed as a project with long-term rather than short-term potential. The Chinese government clearly did not want to be excluded from Kazakhstan's oil rush, but it is not interested enough in this western neighbor to make the development of the Kazakh field a priority. Increasingly this project is coming under the domination of the U.S.-based Access Industries, founded by Russian émigré (and naturalized U.S. citizen) Len Blavatnik. Access is one of the owners of the Tiumen

Oil Company, just across the border with Kazakhstan, and is eager to rationalize these Russian holdings with the Kazakh ones.[90]

There has never been a shortage of interested investors in Kazakhstan's energy sector, and President Nazarbayev's choice of former Kazakhoil head Nurlan Balgimbayev as prime minister in 1997 was designed to capitalize on this. Balgimbayev was a professional oil man who had worked in the USSR Ministry of Oil and Gas before independence. While the development of oil has been plagued by well-reported chronic transport problems, the development of Kazakhstan's gas sector has received less attention but has had no less difficulty. The biggest gas project, the realization of the Karachaganak field in northwest Kazakhstan, has been slow, again because Russian interests have had to be accommodated. The field is estimated to have reserves of 300 million tons of oil and gas condensate and 500 billion cubic meters of natural gas.

Here, too, a large part of the problem has been difficulties involving negotiations with Russia, in this case with Gazprom, which controls the Orenburg condensate facilities to which Karachaganak traditionally is shipped. Still, negotiations with the Kazakhs were also difficult, and the foreign partners—Texaco, Agip, British Gas, and Lukoil—did not complete the negotiation of their production-sharing agreement with Kazakhstan until 1998, a task they had begun five years earlier. The consortium also plans to open a gas processing plant (with a yearly processing capacity of 10 billion cubic meters of gas) by 2005. Kazakhstan now imports more than half of the gas it uses. Without a new pipeline system, southern Kazakhstan remains dependent on Uzbek gas. For now, the Kazakhs are seeking ways to manage these relationships better. In December 2000, KazTransGaz, run by Nazarbayev son-in-law Timur Kulibayev, signed a major agreement with Russia's Itera,[91] setting high transit fees across Kazakhstan for the shipment of Russian as well as Uzbek and Turkmen gas. The two will share the fees, although the precise division has not been revealed. The partnership, however, offers sufficient promise that the two companies have agreed to the reopening of a stretch of Soviet-era pipeline to provide extra capacity. The foreign development of Karachaganak's oil and gas fields was jump-started by a December 1999 decision to build a pipeline linking the Karachaganak to CPC. The 650-kilometer link will cost $440 million and have a capacity of 140,000 barrels a day. Progress in developing Karachaganak can now be expected, and production is set to reach nearly 200,000 barrels a day in 2002, with the total investment in 2000–2002 set at $2.1 billion.

The reorganization of KazTransGaz in May 2001 further strengthened the prospects of cooperation between Kazakhstan and Russia since all the forms of transport for Kazakhstan's oil and gas are now controlled by one company and by the Nazarbayev family, although these assets have never been formally privatized.[92]

Although control of the oil and gas industry remains a political plum in Kazakhstan, it has yet to be transformed into a source of profit for the Kazakh population. In 1998, the oil and gas sector accounted for less than 40 percent of the country's exports. The oil sector itself was in a partial state of collapse, with nearly a third of all workers in the oil sector unpaid for the first half of 1998. Two of Kazakhstan's major refineries (in Pavlodar and Shymkent) were at a virtual standstill because they could not cope with the high cost of processing local oil.[93]

The government has regularly promised to turn this situation around and is now promising that the country's oil wealth will be shared with the population through the creation of a Norwegian-style national oil fund. Part of the proceeds from the sale of the additional 5 percent of the shares of Tengizchevroil to Chevron went to this fund.[94] Even earlier, in its short-term program for the development of the energy sector adopted in 2000, the government called for energy independence for the republic, stable power tariffs, the completion of restructuring of the sector, and the creation of economic conditions for energy conservation.[95] Meeting these goals will be difficult, especially in the current atmosphere of perceived corruption and increasing domination of the oil industry by leading political families.

Major Western oil companies investing in Kazakhstan's giant fields have little interest in engaging in the restructuring of the oil sector, but they want to create new facilities and start-up projects. Smaller companies can be eaten alive by the conditions of doing business in Kazakhstan. Take, for example, the case of Hurricane Hydrocarbons, an Alberta-based company that bought the rights to Kazakhstan's Yuzhneftegaz in 1996 and with it the rights to develop Kazakhstan's Kumkol Munai, with its estimated 450 million barrels of reserve, at a bargain price of $120 million. Three years later Hurricane Hydrocarbons was on the verge of collapse, its chief executive officer had been dismissed, and the company was forced to accept a Kazakh bank as a partner in order to remain in business. This is partly because the management of Hurricane Hydrocarbons did not fully understand that it was buying an oil company with substantial community obligations that operated in a fixed market.[96] Kumkol Munai oil went to the neighboring Shymkent refinery (known as ShNOS for the Shymkent Kumkolneftetorgsintez refinery), which purchased the oil at a discount price for distribution in southern Kazakhstan and Uzbekistan. This relationship, compounded by the decreasing price of oil at the time, led the company into debt, and Kazkommertsbank, one of the country's leading banks and industrial conglomerates, which by then owned the Shymkent refinery, offered the company a $7 million loan. When the company could not repay it, as well as its considerable additional debt, it was forced to buy the Shymkent refinery for a third of the shares of Hurricane Hydrocarbons and $54 million in cash.

Kazkommertsbank acquired the Shymkent refinery as part of a shakeup in the oil industry that occurred after Prime Minister Akezhan Kazhegeldin was removed from office. The refinery had originally been controlled by Vitol SA, a Houston-based trading company, which lost control of the project (then known as Vitol-Munai) for nonpayment of disputed taxes. The local Vitol chief was fined $5.6 million and was even jailed briefly by the Kazakhs.[97] Vitol had bought the refinery in 1996 for a proposed $150 million investment and sold its shares in early 1998 for $60 million, the sum of the original down payment.[98] In fact, Vitol was not the original victor in the tender but got the project when the Kazakh government and tender winner Sampson Oil could not come to an agreement. Kazkommertsbank, which had supervised the original tender, took over ShNOS at that time. It was rumored that Kazkommertsbank had been participating in the venture alongside Vitol from the start.[99]

This move was all part of a fight to create a role for Kazakh investment in the oil industry, something that was strongly advocated by Nurlan Balgimbayev, who was appointed head of Kazakhoil in early 1997. At the same time, Kazakhstan's Ministry of Oil and Gas, which Balgimbayev had headed since October 1994, was dissolved. Ironically, Balgimbayev would be given the task of promoting Western oil interests when he was prime minister in October 1997. In 1992–1993, Balgimbayev, who had been associated with the Tengiz project since its inception, spent time studying at the Massachusetts Institute of Technology and then did a training stint at Chevron's U.S. headquarters.

Balgimbayev's term in office was of limited success from the point of view of the Western energy community, although the Kazakh oilman, said to be from a family who had worked in Kazakhstan's oil industry for several generations, seems to have used the time for his own benefit. Claims of his pocketing signing bonuses may never be substantiated, but there is no question that under his stewardship the Kazakhoil company diversified its assets with a Ukrainian subsidiary (Ukrnefteprodukt) that owns 60 percent of the Kherson refinery (in partnership with Russia's Alliance Oil). It hopes to use the Kherson refinery to form a Ukraine-wide dealer network. Kazakhoil also owns 86 percent of the Atyrau oil refinery, which it is refurbishing in partnership with Marubeni of Japan. Its subsidiaries include Uzenmunaigas and Kazakhoil-Emba. In addition, it has stakes of varying sizes in nine oil production companies.[100]

Balgimbayev succeeded in making Kazakhoil strong enough to be viewed as a threat to Nazarbayev family interests. Nazarbayev's son-in law Timur Kulibayev, who left Kazakhoil to head KazTransOil, now part of TransNefteGaz, has tried to undermine his former firm to make it little more than a large, self-governing state-owned oil company that manages a packet of government of shares, at least until the firm is returned to direct family control. In June 2000, Nazarbayev's nephew, Kairat Saltybaldy, became the first vice-president of Kazakhoil as a step in this direction, and Balgimbayev encountered stiff resistance over the acquisition of the Kherson refinery. Although the deal stood, Kazakhoil had the range of its foreign activities restricted.[101]

The Kulibayev group has also developed a cooperative relationship with Russia's Gazprom and is strengthening connections with Lukoil as well. The group has also worked closely with Kazkommertsbank in recent years, although the relationship has had its ups and downs. Kazkommertsbank was originally organized to serve the interests of those close to Kazhegeldin, but through partial reorganization it was able to accommodate itself successfully to his departure. The chairman of the board of Kazkommertsbank is Daulet Sembayev, the former head of the National Bank of Kazakhstan and a Nazarbayev intimate. In the spring of 2000 Kazkommertsbank took control of the Pavlodar refinery, after the local government defaulted on a $10 million loan. The fight over the Pavlodar refinery was a lengthy one, and the oblast unsuccessfully appealed to the central government to block the takeover of the refinery, which had reverted to state control after a Western investor, CCL Oil Ltd., was forced out.[102]

The clashing interest groups within Kazakhstan's oil industry, which in part mirror Kazakhstan's clan divisions, add to Prime Minister Kasymzhomart Tokayev's task of trying to maintain a favorable investment climate. Despite the oil industry's need for capital infusion and technological assistance, there is still a wariness among Kazakh officials toward foreign investment in the oil industry. Foreign investors need to feel that they are being treated fairly and not being forced into unprofitable relationships with Kazakhstan's rising oil oligarchs.[103]

Many of the challenges to foreign investment are not of Kazakhstan's making. Local policy makers cannot break the transportation deadlock on their own. Even major changes in the international climate, which might make Russia a more amenable partner or Iran a more acceptable one, may not make it sufficiently profitable to develop some of Kazakhstan's more costly projects; only higher energy prices could do this. Low energy prices will scare off diffident investors like Saudi Arabia's Nimir Petroleum Company Ltd., which sold its share of the Buzachi deposit in 1998, but most of Kazakhstan's foreign partners are there for the long haul.

Problems for Foreign Investors

Kazakhstan will continue to have difficulty in securing and sustaining foreign investment, especially outside the oil and gas sector, until there is the will at the top to regulate corrupt practices. In a 1999 poll conducted by the Washington-based International Center for Taxes and Investment, 60 percent of the businesses operating in Kazakhstan described the country's investment environment as negative.[104]

Kazakhstan's government has not always kept to the contractual terms initially offered to foreign investors, although there is more transparency in business transactions than in many other countries in the region. Some of the difficulties that foreign investors encountered reflect the learning curve of policy makers in a newly independent state, when the government decided it had somehow been "had" in the privatization process. In the early years, a foreign investor might have found its contract pulled; today the Kazakh government is careful to make its behavior consistent with the provisions of Kazakh law and may offer the distressed investor redress in the court system. This does little, however, to stimulate investment confidence, given the growing environment of official corruption, which permeates the courts and Kazakhstan's legal system. The situation is said to be so bad that foreign companies unwilling to bribe judges ask the representatives of their embassies to sit in on court proceedings in the hope that a diplomatic presence might prompt a Kazakhstani judge to render a fair and unbiased decision.

While the international press has highlighted a series of privatization reversals in recent years, the Nazarbayev government is taking great pains to retain an international image of being "investor friendly," using Western public relations firms to try to lay blame for the reversals on the Kazhegeldin government. Stories of payoffs to Kazhegeldin circulated frequently in Kazakhstan during his years in office.[105] Aspersions on his character escalated on the eve of his dismissal, when it was revealed that he had served as a KGB officer for at least part of his career, until he was dropped in 1987 for financial malfeasance.[106] If anything, the problem of official corruption seems to have grown worse after Kazhegeldin's departure.

Kazakhstan's corruption problem has been staggering. Kazakhstan is said to have lost $500 million in 1996 alone in a transaction in the oil sector.[107] Stories of bribes and insider deals involving Nazarbayev and his family abound, giving an element of farce to President Nazarbayev's very public anticorruption campaign and his claims that corruption "threatens the existence of the state."[108] The "court" around Nazarbayev seems to thrive on money skimmed from the foreign investment process, and when his circle becomes too ostentatious in its spending, bad press must be contained, such as after a January 1996 presidential visit to Israel when some of the official entourage spent $250,000 on a shopping spree.[109] In the aftermath, in a very public effort to find a scapegoat, Chief Justice Mikhail Malakhov was dismissed for taking more than $100,000 in bribes.[110]

By November 1997, things were so out of control that Nazarbayev ordered high-ranking officials to declare all personal income and then reportedly told them to return a third of what they had stolen. Little effort was made to obtain compliance, however, and the tales of luxurious shopping sprees remain common during Nazarbayev's official travel. The November 2000 United Kingdom summit meeting was said to have been a bonanza for several prominent London boutiques, some of which were commissioned to make hundreds of thousands of dollars' worth of items for Nazarbayev to give to visitors.

It is hard to know how serious a problem insider trading is for those trying to gain access to Kazakhstan's key assets and whether government officials line their pockets as they make these decisions. Certainly, Almaty usually buzzes with rumors of outstretched hands, and of businessmen from countries with lax foreign anticorruption laws who are willing to fill them. The pressure on foreign investors certainly increased in 1997 and early 1998 when the Nazarbayev government pressed for donations to the building fund for the new capital at Astana. The money collected was rumored to far exceed the cost of the buildings erected.

Anticorruption campaigns have had a minimal effect on the conditions that trouble foreign investors. High-level officials have periodically come under attack for bribe taking but with little consequence. A case in point was that of Vice-Premier K. Abdullayev, who was dismissed in mid-1992, purportedly for having accepted a bribe of $1 million to block the advance of negotiations with Chevron. After a short period in apparent disgrace, Abdullayev returned to the public arena as the head of an entrepreneurial group.

Deputy Prime Minister Asygat Zhabagin left office in 1993 because of claims of official favoritism toward his family firm, Ansat, which was trading in Kazakh metals.[111] Nothing was ever done to follow up on these charges, and after several years of very successful business activity, Zhabagin returned to government as the minister of industry in 1998. At that time he was even entrusted with the supervision of the privatization process. But the high and mighty do occasionally fall. The general director of Balkhashmed (Balkhash Aluminum), for example, was charged with embezzling $7 million of copper from his company, and two years later, in 1995, the chairman of the Central Bank and then financial adviser to Prime Minister Kazhegeldin, Galym Bainazarov, was arrested for offering a bribe to the interior minister, the country's senior law enforcement official.[112]

Political infighting, though, plays a much greater role in the fall of senior public figures than does serious government attention to the problem of official corruption. Those on the outs politically are quick to have their finances scrutinized. Communist Party presidential candidate Serikbolsyn Abdildin has had his finances examined, as has Akezhan Kazhegeldin.

Although Kazhegeldin has certainly been hounded by the Nazarbayev government, the former Kazakh prime minister may not be the innocent he has claimed to be. Kazhegeldin appears to have accumulated a considerable personal fortune, in part through contacts in the Soviet-era military industrial establishment, including contacts in the security forces. Many of the decisions made by Kazhegeldin were of questionable economic wisdom. The case of the Trans-World Group already cited rapidly ballooned into a major player in the world aluminum business with annual sales of $5–$7 billion.

Trans-World's profit margins were helped by the extremely low prices at which it purchased the Pavlodar and Aksu sites. Within months of taking on management contracts for Pavlodar and Aksu, the Trans-World Group exercised its contract option to buy majority stakes in both for a total of just $143 million.[113] This price was markedly deflated, allegedly because the government officials responsible for negotiating the sale of this state asset were silent partners in Trans-World subcorporations. This rumor was fed by the fact that among the top figures in Trans-World was Vladimir Lesin, a former engineer from Kazakhstan who in the late 1980s was Oleg Soskovets' deputy at Karmet.[114] Soskovets became the first deputy prime minister of Kazakhstan, serving until October 1992, when he moved back to Russia to take the post of deputy prime minister for industry, charged especially with overseeing issues involving resource exploitation in the former Soviet republics. Russian interior ministry officials later charged that Soskovets was working on Trans-World's behalf while working for the government.[115] There has been much speculation about Soskovets' relation to Nazarbayev. The two knew each other for decades, since Nazarbayev's days at Karmet, and the Kazakh president may have helped Soskovets make his leap to Moscow in 1991, when he was accused of stealing state and cooperative property while the head of Karmet. The criminal case disappeared when Soskovets was made the minister for metallurgy in the last cabinet of the USSR.[116]

The Trans-World Group had little difficulty in creating a dominant position for itself even after Soskovets left Kazakhstan, causing speculation that Kazhegeldin took over as the protector of its interests. It is also hard to believe that Nazarbayev or those close to him did not benefit from the Trans-World relationship, possibly in the transport of metals because a Nazarbayev family member was charged with issuing export licenses for much of this period. Yet when the initial contracts with Trans-World were drawn up, Nazarbayev perceived himself as dependent upon the goodwill of the powerful Soviet-era military and industrial elite that dominated Russian and Kazakhstani metallurgy. By the mid-1990s, Nazarbayev felt much more in control and demonstrated this by seeking to isolate Akezhan Kazhegeldin, who if not Russia's creature, was at least someone who allowed certain Russian interests easy access to Kazakhstan's market. As Kazhegeldin's influence waned, the Kazakh government began withdrawing some of the Trans-World management contracts, most prominently the one for Sokolov-Sarbai mining corporation. The metallurgical conglomerate began to fight back, bringing suits in Kazakhstan as well as in U.S., British, and French courts.

Management splintered, and the group favored by Nazarbayev reentered Kazakhstan's market as Kazakhstan Mineral Resources Corporation (KMRC) registered in Switzerland. KMRC was dominated by three men, Aleksandr Mashkevich, Fatakh Shodiev, and Almaz Ibragimov, who used their Eurasian Bank as a holding company.[117] Mashkevich, in particular, was known to be close to the president and often travels abroad with him. He is said to be close enough to go clothes shopping for the Kazakh leader at Versace's in London.[118] So when 1997–1998 reorganizations turned the management of the Trans-World empire over to KMRC, the perception that Kazakhstan's metallurgy industry was structured to serve the personal needs of the regime was further strengthened. It came as no surprise when Kazakhstan's supreme court found on KMRC's behalf in January 1999, and then again in July 1999, when it allowed KMRC to disregard a court order from the British Virgin Islands that required that management of the disputed companies be turned over to an independent manager. In February 2000, Trans-World settled with Kazakhstan after the company received a significant payment to terminate the litigation of an $800 million claim.[119]

Kazakhstan had much more difficulty casting itself as the wronged party in its clash with Colorado's World Wide Minerals, which lost its management contract for the Tselinnyy Mining Chemicals Plant, a uranium processing plant, in August 1997 and then filed a suit against the government of Kazakhstan in a U.S. federal district court. Given the conditions that the company encountered in Kazakhstan, it would have been hard for the Denver firm not to be in at least partial default of its contract. Those trying to run mineral extraction, processing, or other heavy industrial projects have had to confront higher-than-budgeted labor costs, rising energy costs that are often combined with simultaneous energy shortages, and some responsibility for the social welfare obligations (the running of schools and hospitals and the maintenance of housing) of the firm they have taken over. Any default, however, usually gives the Kazakh government an opportunity to renationalize a project. In the case of Tselinnyy, renationalization may well have been the government's goal from the beginning, because the Kazakh government reversed itself and in early 1999 gave control of the project to Lev Leviev of Sabton (now renamed KazSabton), whose growing activities in Kazakhstan are detailed below. Leviev promised increased investment in the project but effectively bought the rights to Tselinnyy for about $300,000 and roughly $3 million in debts and back wages.[120]

Even murkier are the relations between Kazakhstan and Tractebel, the Belgian energy group, which sold all its holdings to KazTransGaz, the state gas company, for $100 million in 2000, $10 million down, the rest payable over ten years. Tractebel had acquired a twenty-year concession for Almaty Energy (Almatyenergo) in August 1996. The latter, formed to supply heat and lights to Kazakhstan's capital and surrounding area, sold its assets and some debt to Tractebel for $5 million, plus a pledge to invest $270 million. All told, Tractebel is reported to have paid $55 million to the Kazakh government through the Eurasian Bank, leading to rumors that these were bribes for top-ranking Kazakh officials.[121] Bank chairman Mashkevich maintains that this was a fee for services that his Albeli group provided in checking and repairing gas pipelines.[122]

Tractebel got into trouble immediately after taking control. It frequently operated in Kazakhstan at a loss and certainly never realized the 25-percent profit guaranteed by its agreement. That first year, with winter approaching, the Belgian firm discovered that it possessed antiquated generators and had virtually no stocks of coal or fuel oil with which to run them. The mines from which they had planned to buy coal had been privatized in the interim, and even when a new price was finally agreed upon, delivery proved almost impossible. It also proved difficult to substitute fuel oil, and Uzbekistan, the major supplier of natural gas for the region, had cut off shipments because of Kazakhstan's nonpayment of outstanding debt. Tractebel was further hampered by Kazakhstan's widespread shortage of electricity. Even when found, additional generating capacity was impossible to purchase because the transmissions in southern Kazakhstan pass through western Kyrgyzstan, which refused to cooperate with the arrangement.

The company became deeply unpopular in Kazakhstan. When Tractebel took over, government figures put the total unpaid debt for the energy used by domestic customers at about $663 million, or about 80 percent of the total for all outstanding loans carried on the books of the republic's banks. The Kazakhs were used to getting energy almost for free and balked at paying market prices. A campaign to force the payment of past-due bills by shutting off the power to debtors backfired when the company demonstrated itself incapable of supplying energy even to those few who did pay on time. When the first frosts began, Tractebel's electricity was 36 percent below peak demand, resulting in a pattern of brownouts and blackouts that led many Almaty residents to live without electricity and fuel. Trying to introduce Western management practices also proved disastrous. Exercising its right to hire and fire, Tractebel sacked 500 employees, only to have one of these commit suicide by setting himself on fire in front of the company's headquarters.

The relationship between the Kazakhstan government and Tractebel became so tense that the company threatened to withdraw from Kazakhstan in the first quarter of 1998 when it was effectively barred from introducing even modest rate hikes. To forestall this, President Nazarbayev had the Balgimbayev government issue a public apology, but two years later Tractebel had had enough. In early 2000, it announced that it was withdrawing from Kazakhstan, and a week later a municipal court authorized the seizure of Tractebel's property and six bank accounts belonging to its subsidiary, Intergas Central Asia (ICA). Finally, in May 2000, a buyout agreement was reached.

Almaty Energy was turned over to Access Industries, headed by Len Blavatnik. As already noted, Access is another of the companies that has enjoyed a privileged position in Kazakhstan as well as in Russia. It has strong ties to Mikhail Fridman and Peter Aven of Russia's Alfa Group, sharing ownership with them of the Tiumen Oil Company (TNK). Access Industries has been developing the Bogatyr coal pit in Pavlodar since 1996, and in the fall of 1999 it received the rights to the Severny pit, which is owned by RAO–UES. Access, which has periodically clashed with the local government in Pavlodar over taxation and social obligations, is part of the new breed of companies that manages to be on good terms with any government. Len Blavatnik has been rumored to enjoy a privileged relationship with President Nazarbayev. Blavatnik has also managed to learn how to make the U.S. system work for him as well. He and his family have been regular contributors to the election campaign of U.S. House of Representatives International Affairs Committee Chair Benjamin Gilman.[123] Access and TNK were also the beneficiaries of a controversial $500 million loan from the Export-Import Bank of the United States (Ex-Im Bank) in which Halliburton, Inc., received payment for services, and this at the time when Vice President Richard Cheney was working as Halliburton's chief executive officer.[124]

Other energy companies have tried to find ways to benefit from Tractebel's problems, including a U.S. firm, the AES Corporation, that has held on to its investments in northern Kazakhstan, and AES-Ekibastuz, whose local tax arrangements have had to be renegotiated to "adhere more closely" to local laws.[125] It is not uncommon for foreign investors to discover that agreements negotiated under one legal regime must be renegotiated when the laws change without warning.

Kazakhstan's gold industry has been particularly hurt by the loss of investment confidence, which was compounded by the dropping value of gold, the increased cost of energy and even of labor in the country, and for the high cost and difficulty of transport into and out of Kazakhstan. The result is that the major players in the gold industry have shunned permanent involvement in Kazakhstan, and the country's two major gold deposits, Vasilkovskoe and Bakyrchik, are being developed by so-called industry juniors of uncertain reputation.[126] The country's gold industry has been in serious decline over the past decade. In 1997, Kazakhstan's export of gold and other precious metals was valued at $133.1 million and accounted for only 2.1 percent of the country's total exports.[127] There was a partial recovery in 1999 and 2000,[128] but the increase in production came in part through the rapid and inefficient working of the country's biggest deposits in ways that could reduce their ultimate profitability.

Vasilkovskoe, which is the most attractive project of Kazakhstan's gold industry, has been abandoned by foreign investors on at least three occasions. First Australia's Dominion Mining, a junior in the industry, was given the mine but failed to meet the terms necessary to develop it. Then, in 1995, Kazakhstan unexpectedly cancelled a tender for the mine that had been organized by the European Bank for Reconstruction and Development (EBRD), instead letting the site to the Canadian firm Placer Dome. This action sent a considerable chill through the international investment community since it suggested that the republic might no longer be playing by the rules of international business. After paying a substantial deposit for the rights to Vasilkovskoe, Placer Dome had second thoughts about the details of the arrangement and withdrew. It was about this time that stories began to surface about Grigori Loutchansky, the reputed Russian Jewish organized crime figure with operations in Russia and Ukraine. Loutchansky was reportedly close to the Nazarbayev family and had been promised a piece of the country's gold industry.[129] In the next year, the mine appeared to have been let again, to the Teck Corporation, which then withdrew when it could not reach an agreement on securing a reliable power supply. The mine was then turned over to a Kazakh gold company, Altynalmaz, which lacked the resources to expand the area under exploitation substantially.

In September 2000, 60 percent of the shares in Vasilkovskoe were transferred to the Leviev group, controlled by Lev Leviev. Eighteen months earlier, in the spring of 1999, Leviev had taken control of the Tselinnyy Mining and Chemical Combine in Stepnogorsk, the second largest uranium-processing facility in the former Soviet Union. Leviev is a Russian Jewish émigré from Tashkent with considerable business ties in Russia.[130] He has considerable business interests in the former states of the Soviet Union and is one of the world's leading diamond cutters. His Kazakh projects were initially carried out in partnership with Arkady Gaidamak,[131] who has been tied to the arms trade in the post-Soviet states. It is still too soon to know who will actually develop Vasilkovskoe, or how fast. Leviev associates were awarded 60 percent of the project, but subsequent to the transfer, articles appeared in the Russian press claiming that Vasilkovskoe was really held by a firm from the Dutch West Indies.[132]

The history of the privatization of Bakyrchik is equally murky. In 1993 a joint venture of MinProc and Chilewich briefly took control of the project and then in 1995 made way for Bakyrchik Ltd., a venture incorporated in London that was put together to develop the project. The latter group was bought out in stages by Robert Friedland, of both Ivanhoe Investments and Indochina Goldfields, a U.S.-born venture capitalist who eventually took Canadian citizenship and became infamous in the Canadian press for going into the copper business with Burma's military government. Friedland, who has always maintained that he is an environmentally conscious investor, took full control of the Bakyrchik project in 1996,[133] agreeing to a 70–30 split with the Kazakh government and 100 percent of the profits until his investment (which by 2001 reached $50 million) is returned.[134] When this will be is hard to know, for the project was effectively frozen from 1998 to 2001, in large part because of the high cost of refining Bakyrchik gold because of the high content of arsenic and carbon in the deposit. In total, Kazakhstan's government has reported receiving fees and signing bonuses worth $35 million in connection with Friedland's payment for the government's 60 percent stake in the Bakyrchik deposit.[135]

Current Situation

Nevertheless, the government has reason for some optimism. For all the murkiness of doing business in Kazakhstan, foreign investment is still up compared to that in other newly independent states.[136] The economy seems to have bottomed out, inflation is largely in check, and economic productivity is increasing. Moreover, unlike most of its neighbors, Kazakhstan has for the most part remained on good terms with the World Bank and other international financial institutions.

Kazakhstan's economy began to show signs of recovery in 1996 and early 1997; the GDP grew by 2.1 percent in 1997 and was projected to grow by 3.5 percent in 1998.[137] Largely as a result of the Russian financial meltdown in August 1998, Kazakhstan's GDP declined by 2.5 percent in 1998. It grew by 1.7 percent in 1999, however, and increased by 9.6 percent in 2000—higher than anticipated in earlier forecasts. In 2001, GDP was expected to grow by approximately 9–10 percent.

Some argue that part of this increase in the GDP was an artificial product of changing the actual economic indicators that were being used to measure productivity,[138] as well as the result of unexpected gains in the oil sector. Given the declines that Kazakhstan experienced in the past decade, a rapid increase in the value of its production creates the appearance of a sharp upswing in productivity. The real test will be whether Kazakhstan is able to sustain the increase in the GDP over time.

Economic recovery is not distributed evenly across the economy, either geographically or by sector, and industry's and agriculture's share of Kazakhstan's GDP have both declined. Agriculture's performance has been particularly disappointing, and this sector still awaits fundamental restructuring. Although formally privatized, agricultural remains organized around former state and collective farms, which are increasingly inefficient. The 1998 grain harvest was about a third smaller than that of the previous year, and climatic conditions explain only part of this decline.[139] The harvest of 2000 exceeded government expectations, but some have cast doubt on the accuracy of the official statistics and point to the growing indebtedness of Kazakhstan's private farmers as an indicator of the long-term problems that lie ahead. Debt is turning many into tenant farmers.[140] Foreign investors still lack sufficient legal protection to invest in Kazakh agriculture, and they cannot yet own land, only harvests, which leaves agribusiness as an area ripe for investment by rapacious Kazakhs.

Kazakh livestock breeding is also in a continuing state of decline. It is estimated that livestock numbers in 1999 were just 50 percent of their 1995 levels.[141] Most of the decline appears to have been the product of an overall lack of capital available for investment in agricultural technology, as well as of poor management and an overall lack of good feed and medicine. By the end of the decade the situation had changed somewhat. A bumper crop in 1999 that provided plenty of good feed, as well as a general rise in demand, increased Kazakhstan's sheep and cattle population by 1 percent and the swine population by 10 percent in that year. Although lamb and beef production continued to drop, small private farms, responsible for 97 percent of the pork production in 1999, produced 24 percent more pork that year than in 1998.[142]

The situation in industry is mixed. Talk of developing Kazakhstan's light industrial potential remains just that—talk—and heavy industry still accounts for about 85 percent of Kazakhstan's industrial output.[143] Still, recovery in heavy industrial sectors has been very uneven, and in the late 1990s the government was still vacillating between fully freeing the market and introducing greater state controls in an effort to jump-start the sluggish sectors. In 1998 and 1999 the economic crisis grew so severe that the government began talking about a state plan for industrial development in which many of the large heavy industrial enterprises would be kept under government control and operated at a loss to keep the labor force employed. By 2000 industrial production increased by 15 percent during the first nine months. Given the previous level of collapse, however, this constitutes only a very tentative recovery.

The consequences of the economic collapse that the country experienced from 1993 through 1995 when the combination of hyperinflation and cash starvation led enterprises to extensive bartering are proving long-lasting, as has the interenterprise indebtedness that was in excess of $11 billion in late 1996.[144] At that time, unpaid wages and pensions had reached 40 percent of the GDP (about $1 billion), and it took until January 1, 2000, for the government to pay all government arrears in pensions and state social payments. While the state debt has been formally discharged, it was done in part by privatizing some of the debtor companies, complete with debt.

Kazakhstan's leaders recognize that increasing foreign investment is the key to industrial recovery. To this end, with strong support from the World Bank, Kazakhstan is developing a leveraged insurance facility for trade and investment to insure foreign investors against corruption. The World Bank has promised to lend Kazakhstan $50 million to cover future payouts, which would be used to leverage as much as a further $200 million in additional coverage from commercial insurers. This step alone will not significantly raise investor confidence and is costly to companies since they will have to pay between 1 and 5 percent of the value of their projects in premiums.[145]

The performance of Kazakhstan's financial sector is more encouraging, although it suffered during Russia's financial crisis. Kazakhstan has been doing a good job of managing its foreign debt and has been cautious about additional borrowing. Official government figures put Kazakhstan's international debt at $1.94 billion in August 1998, and its internal debt at $1.04 billion.[146] In December 1999, Kazakhstan secured a renewal of the IMF three-year $453 million Extended Fund Facility (EFF) loan that was suspended after the July devaluation of the tenge. The increase in world oil prices, however, gave the Kazakhs unexpected income, and in May 2000, the National Bank of Kazakhstan made an early repurchase of all outstanding balances owed to the IMF drawn between 1993 and 1998. Kazakhstan's existing economic program, supported by the three-year EFF obtained in December, remained in place, but Kazakhstan did not need to draw funds under this arrangement, treating the EFF as a precautionary source of capital.[147] Kazakhstan's external debt payments in 2000 will total an estimated $473.3 million, including $267 million in sovereign debt payments. Thanks to high oil prices during this year, the government currently has no problem generating sufficient revenue to make these payments.[148] The republic is still vulnerable to a trade imbalance with Russia, and the import side is driven in particular by Kazakhstan's dependence on foreign gas. The trade imbalance with Russia was $345 million in 1998, a figure that dropped to $78 million in 1999.[149] Kazakhstan is always seeking a balance between a debt crisis and an acute energy shortage. Gas shortages are a perennial problem. To have enough fuel for the new capital city of Astana, supplies to the rest of Akmola oblast were sharply cut in the winter of 1997. In 1998 a number of cities in northern Kazakhstan had their power cut, and it was only in the last days of 2000 that officials in Uralsk made an arrangement with Russia's RAO–UES for a partial debt payment, ending several months of brownouts. The Kazakh debt to Uzbekistan is equally burdensome. In autumn 1998 the regions in southern Kazakhstan were paying their Uzbek suppliers 42 cents on the dollar,[150] and in 2000 Kazakhstan preordered only half the gas it needed, citing high prices ($50 per thousand cubic meters, up from $35 the previous year).

Overall, conditions have not yet improved to the point where capital is returning to the country, and even the official family is reinvesting on only a limited basis. In addition to the billions of dollars that are rumored to have left the country, the volume of shadow capital in Kazakhstan is estimated at $1.5 billion to $3 billion, and President Nazarbayev has publicly claimed that there is close to $2 billion in hidden savings within Kazakhstan.[151] He has asked for legislation to allow this money to be legalized without question, stating, "Maybe we will be criticized [by the West], but in the end it is our internal affair."[152]

Kazakhstan today is an economic paradox, a place of great potential wealth, that still has trouble meeting many of its immediate obligations, in part because of the scale of corruption of those in and near power. By November 2001 the situation with regard to corruption had grown so serious that a group of prominent young business people, including the head of Kazkommertsbank, Mukhtar Ablyazov, and Bulat Abilov joined together to form a new lobbying group called Democratic Choice of Kazakhstan to try and press for greater transparency.

The republic's leadership has taken great pains to attract foreign investment and support and has sporadically tried to be responsive to the needs and interests of the international business community. The apparent resolution of the pipeline question seems particularly likely to stimulate the inflow of revenue that the republic desperately needs. At the same time, however, the distribution of that income within the republic is going to remain a pressing issue. If the republic's economic recovery is distributed across a wide enough cross section of the republic's population, the economic difficulties of the first years of independence are likely to become no more than a memory, one of the inevitable birth pangs of a new state. However, if the republic continues to solidify the oligarchical pattern of income distribution that has emerged in this period of transition, then the economic and political outlook for Kazakhstan will remain clouded.

The Kazakh government decision to move to a market economy has had political consequences, which in turn created new actors. The new generation of political elite is likely to come from the economic sector, a pattern already developing. Ministry appointments are now made with an eye to making sure that key economic groups are represented, largely because of the forceful lobbying of powerful economic groups, such as Kazkommertsbank. The same pattern is found at the oblast level, where powerful enterprises are often able to capture posts in the local administration to protect their own interests. The political and economic ambitions of these people must be accommodated, but so too must those of the vast majority of the Kazakh population, which has been left almost completely out of the country's economic reform.

6

A Divided Society

Kazakhstan's population has been surprisingly patient during a time of extraordinary political and economic stress. There have been no armed conflicts or violent demonstrations, and only limited public protests. In 1997 it seemed the country would develop a massive strike movement, but that potential challenge faded. Since then the government has managed to quell public discontent with a minimal use of public threats and virtually no overt displays of force.

At the same time, Kazakhstan's social problems have grown faster than the government's ability to solve them. Social differentiation is proceeding rapidly along a number of fault lines: rural versus urban, old versus young, north versus south, and Kazakh versus non-Kazakh, to name some of the most prominent. This has created much larger numbers and classes of people than ever before who perceive themselves to be poorly served by their political leaders.

While the government places increasing stress on the need for a national consensus and social stability, the actions of the governing elite often stimulate social and even ethnic discord. They make no effort to draw the population into a meaningful debate on how the country should be governed, let alone involve them in the governing process. The ambitions of elite aspirants are being handled little better than those of the masses. Instead, there appears to be a growing separation between the governors and the governed.

For now the population seems little inclined to test the government's power, even though for most people independence has brought steadily declining standards of living. Many still expect things to get worse before they get better. The impact of the rising GDP has not been readily felt by most of Kazakhstan's citizens, and the government is growing better able to control the illegal barter trading and off-the-books employment that many Kazakhs depend on to make ends meet. The anticorruption effort also seems to be targeting the less affluent, who lack political connections, rather than the big offenders. In 1998 alone the "taxation police" filed 1,943 tax violation lawsuits, and 387 people were jailed for tax evasion.[1] In 1999 the pace of arrests increased, but during the first five months of 1999 Kazakhstan's courts convicted only forty high-ranking officials,[2] and none of these arrests or trials involved those close to the president. In 1999, Kazakhstan's prosecutor general claimed that corrupt practices have cost the economy some 1 billion tenge.[3] This excludes the hundreds of millions of dollars of flight capital, much of which is held by the Nazarbayev family.[4]

So while the government formally registers the proper level of concern, its actions often belie the image such concern is intended to create. Accounts of bribe taking by government officials are commonplace in Kazakhstan, and the seeming futility of doing anything about it is underscored by signs of the growing role of the Nazarbayev family in the activity. All this contributed to the June 2000 Transparency International ranking of Kazakhstan eighty-sixth of the ninety-nine nations listed in the Corruption Perceptions Index.[5]

Anecdotal evidence suggests growing public apathy about the government. The divisions in society seem to be deepening as a feeling of powerlessness spreads. Administrative redistricting has done little to smooth the country's geographic divisions. The north and south are still distinct, as are western and central Kazakhstan. To some extent, these geographic divisions are reinforced by clan differences; the west and center belong to the Small Horde, the north to the Middle Horde and to the Russians (termed by some as the Fourth Horde), and the south to the Great Horde. Clan membership in Kazakhstan, however, is not as powerful an indicator of behavior as is ethnicity, which is seen as the most important determinant of future success. The rise in the importance of religion has further accentuated ethnic differences. By contrast, economic factors have had a mitigating effect. The state's increasing withdrawal from the social service sector has led to greater differentiation in the standards of living between urban and rural Kazakhs. The chasm between rich and poor is even more prominent and is beginning to transcend ethnic and regional lines, although it has not offset the radicalization of the population along ethnic lines.

The Kazakhification of Kazakhstan

Changing Demography

Kazakhstan is becoming increasingly more stratified along ethnic lines, yet the society is becoming less multicultural and less European over time. In large part, this trend toward homogeneity is because the demographic makeup of the population is changing.[6] Outmigration and the natural processes of aging have tipped the demographic balance incontrovertibly in the direction of the Kazakhs, who began claiming to be an absolute majority of the republic's population in 1997.[7]

Russian settlement in Kazakhstan was mostly the product of Soviet policies, although there has been a Russian population in Kazakhstan since the sixteenth century. In 1926, at the time of the first full Soviet census, Russians accounted for 20 percent of Kazakhstan's population. By 1939 they constituted 40 percent of the population, largely because of the disproportionately massive losses that the Kazakhs suffered during collectivization. The high birthrate of the Kazakhs (their families are traditionally about twice the size of Russian ones) kept them from losing too much more ground against the Russians, but in the 1959 and 1970 censuses the Russians continued to account for 42.7 and 42.4 percent of the population, respectively. The Virgin Lands drive led to part of this increase, when the Kazakhs were pushed into the southern and western parts of the republic to make way for incoming Europeans. The rest of the Russians came with the expansion of Kazakhstan's industrial and resource extraction base in the late 1960s and the early 1970s. Beginning in the mid-1970s, the Russians began to leave Kazakhstan at a faster rate than they were moving into the republic, a trend that further accelerated with independence.

In the 1979 census the Russians still accounted for 40.8 percent of the population. It was not until the 1989 census that the Kazakhs constituted a greater percentage of the republic population than did the Russians—39.7 percent as opposed to 37.8 percent. The Kazakh share had grown from 30.0 percent in 1959 to 32.6 percent in 1970 and to 36.0 percent in 1979. Even with this growth, relative and absolute, at the time of independence the Kazakhs still made up only about 40 percent of the population in seven of the country's nineteen oblasts and were outnumbered by the Russians nearly three to one in their new nation's capital and in three other oblasts (North Kazakhstan, East Kazakhstan, and Karaganda).[8]

The population makeup has continued to change since independence, with the Kazakhs accounting for a growing percentage of the population, both in the country as a whole and in the oblasts where they were most underrepresented. There has been a substantial movement of ethnic Kazakhs back to their ancestral regions, especially in the northern and northeastern parts of the country, which has occurred with strong but unstated government support. The Kazakhs, for example, accounted for 73.5 percent of those who migrated within the country in the first quarter of 1998.[9] The administrative reorganization of 1997 increased Kazakh representation in several oblasts. In 1999 there were still eight oblasts in Kazakhstan, in which the Kazakhs were a minority of the population, as compared with ten such oblasts in 1989 (using current boundaries).[10] Ethnic Russians, though, still dominate most of Kazakhstan's principal cities, and in Karaganda, Kostanai, and Pavlodar, the Kazakhs still account for less than a quarter of the population.[11]

The Kazakhs are reproducing faster than the Russians, although the country's birthrate has declined since independence, this in spite of officially sanctioned efforts to encourage the Kazakhs to have large families.[12] The Demography Fund, for example, created by a group of Kazakh businessmen in March 1999, offered the parents of the first 2,000 babies born after the new year a 100,000 tenge (about $1,500) bonus. The donor companies, which include Kazkommertsbank, claim to have the backing of Kazakhstan's first lady, Sara Nazarbayeva.[13] The bonuses were offered to everyone in the country, but the public relations effort attached to the campaign made it clear that the focus was on strengthening the Kazakh family.

Everyone living in the country knows that many Russians see themselves as having no future in Kazakhstan, and the departure of nearly a quarter of Kazakhstan's Russian population, mostly back to the Russian Federation, is the single biggest factor in the country's shifting demography. Russian sources claim that 1.1 million Russians left the country from 1988 to 1998.[14] Kazakh sources offer an even higher figure and a somewhat different timetable for the Russians' departure. According to Kazakhstan's official statistical agency, a fairly steady outmigration took place until 1994, when it rose sharply and then began to drop again, with a total of 1.5 million Russians leaving the country from 1992 to 2000.[15]

The departure of this Russian population contributed to a decline of 44.2 percent in the number of skilled workers from 1985 to 1993. The losses were far greater in some oblasts than in others. Karaganda, for example, succeeded in keeping its labor loss to only 35.1 percent, while in Almaty oblast the loss was 65.4 percent, in Akmola 59.8 percent, and in Zhambyl 50.5 percent.

The Russians are still coming into the country as well. From 1991 to 1998, some 375,378 people arrived in the country beyond the government quota, of which about 250,000 were Russians.[16] About half of these are said to be people who moved to Russia and then back to Kazakhstan, and the remainder have come from neighboring Central Asian countries.[17] This Russian population does not qualify for government assistance, but it does bring expertise back into the economy.

By contrast ethnic Kazakhs are being encouraged to return to Kazakhstan and are initially supported by a state fund that provides money for the resettling of Kazakhs returning to their motherland. The in-migration of Kazakhs has been more of an irritant to interethnic relations than it has been a source of demographic change. Between December 1991 and December 1998, approximately 170,000 Kazakhs migrated to the country,[18] with the numbers dropping off sharply thereafter.[19] This number includes those Kazakhs returning from other CIS states who are not eligible for assistance programs for which other Kazakhs (referred to as *oralman*) returning from Mongolia or China do qualify. This is but a small part of the Kazakh diaspora. One Kazakh social scientist estimates that there are 4.1 million ethnic Kazakhs currently still living abroad, including 1.5 million in Uzbekistan, 740,000 in Russia, 70,000 in Turkmenistan, 1.5 million in China, 80,000 in Mongolia, 30,000 in Afghanistan, and 25,000 in Turkey.[20] Moreover, some sources report that more Kazakhs have left Kazakhstan since independence than have returned, that 210,000 left the country from 1992 to 1998, while others place the figure at about a third that number.[21]

The Kazakhs were initially enthusiastic about resettling their kin from Mongolia and displacing local Russians in the process. The efforts to absorb Kazakhs from Mongolia, China, and Iran, however, showed to all but the most intransigent nationalists how much the Kazakh culture has been shaped by decades of living in a Russian-dominated society. While the introduction of sixty thousand nomads from Mongolia has helped to tip the demographic balance in a few largely ethnic Russian enclaves such as East Kazakhstan oblast (formerly Ust-Kamenogorsk), the local Kazakh authorities found that large cultural and linguistic differences made the assimilation of these returnees almost prohibitively expensive.

Seventy years of Soviet rule left Kazakhstan's Kazakhs closer to the European-dominated global culture than to their own nomadic past. This observation has not escaped the country's Russian population and leaves them troubled by what they see as Kazakh efforts to turn Kazakhstan into an ethnonational state. While the country's elite is 80–90 percent Kazakh, the Russians are still the backbone of the country's middle class, although this is changing. The Russian population is older on average than the Kazakh and has a lower birthrate. The natural decline of the Russian population will only continue over time since younger Russians, and especially those with families, are leaving the country in disproportionate numbers.

The outmigration of other ethnic groups has also made Kazakhstan more mono-ethnic. About two-thirds of Kazakhstan's German community have left the country over the past decade, some six hundred thousand people, and about a third of the Ukrainian population (three hundred thousand people) have left Kazakhstan as well.[22] The departure of the Germans is really something of a special case since the relocation support provided by the Federal Republic of Germany creates strong economic incentives for seeking the "restoration" of citizenship. The decision to leave for Ukraine is much like that of choosing to go to Russia and carries no certainty of economic benefit.

Many of Kazakhstan's Slavic population seem to feel that they have sharply diminished economic prospects if they remain. A recent study of Kazakhstan's Russian population, by Galina Vitkovskaya for the Carnegie Moscow Center, found that roughly a third of those interviewed would like to leave Kazakhstan permanently; of those, 40 percent had concrete plans to leave the country over the next five years.[23] Most people who were planning to leave wanted to do so because of a fear for their economic future (29 percent) or from a concern for the future of their children (48 percent). Explicitly ethnic motives were cited in only 29 percent of the cases,[24] but in the context of Kazakhstan, most people always see ethnicity as linked to their prospects of employment.

Language Matters

Russians and other non-Kazakhs feel discriminated against by the government's language policy, which forces their children to master Kazakh and limits their own participation in the public sector if they are not fluent in the language.[25] While Kazakh nationalists feel that the government should do more to bar those who do not speak Kazakh from public life, including prevent them from serving in the legislature, most of Kazakhstan's citizens seem willing to accept a continued public role for the Russian language, greater even than what the government is willing to grant. According to a public opinion poll in the mid-1990s, 56 percent of the country's citizens believed that Kazakhstan should have both Russian and English as the state's languages; 29 percent believed that Kazakh should be the only state language and that Russian should have legal status as the language of interethnic communication; only 4 percent believed that Kazakh should be the only state language; 4 percent believed that Russian should be the state language; and 7 percent believed that there should be no state language.[26]

No one expects Russian to disappear from public life, and according to the 1999 census, more people are still fluent in Russian than in any other language, 75 percent of the population in all, including 67.4 percent in the rural areas.[27] Russians, though, fear that their language will be degraded by the emphasis on developing proficiency in Kazakh. Some of that fear is warranted. The number of Kazakh language schools is on the rise, while the number of Russian language schools is declining. In 1991, there were only 2,768 Kazakh schools (34 percent of the total), but by September 1999 they numbered 3,357. Over the same period, the number of Russian schools declined from 3,641 to 2,412.[28]

The language policy has created real dislocations in the education system. It is already burdened by the requirement to translate or write textbooks, technical manuals, and other materials in Kazakh. Much of the responsibility for compliance with the language laws falls on local authorities, who struggle with the demands of finding people competent to teach technical subjects in Kazakh, as the curriculum now requires. Teacher training is expensive, and the profession is low paying, making it difficult to attract young people. The curriculum requirements—such as the October 1, 1999, order that those schoolteachers in West Kazakhstan oblast not proficient in Kazakh enroll in language classes—may serve as formal compliance, but they do not produce competent bilingual faculty. Local school officials also find it tempting to assign Kazakh speakers to teach in fields beyond their expertise, simply in order to offer the mandated courses. Even those fluent in Kazakh often lack the technical vocabulary necessary to change their language of instruction, as most Kazakhs received their higher education in Russian.

Russian still remains the dominant language of higher education, and in 1999, 72 percent of college students pursued a course of study taught in Russian, 27 percent in Kazakh, and 1 percent each in Uzbek, English, and German.[29] Many people, however, have difficulty in finding instruction in their preferred language, both in primary and secondary schools. According to a 1997 poll, three-quarters of the population throughout northern Kazakhstan and nearly one-half in the ethnically Kazakh-dominated west and south wanted to be educated in Russian. By contrast, under 25 percent of the Russian-dominated population of northern and eastern Kazakhstan wanted to be educated in Kazakh.[30]

As already pointed out, Russians often say that they there is no real reason to learn Kazakh, because even if they master the language, they will still have no real future in the country. The pervasiveness of this kind of sentiment is probably why the percentage of Russians with Kazakh language ability effectively remained steady in the mid-1990s, dropping slightly from 8.5 percent in 1994 to 7.7 percent in 1996.

Kazakhstan's Russians are finding it difficult to build strong emotional ties to their new country. According to a 1998 poll by Kazakhstan's Parliament Information Analysis Center, around 46 percent of the country's Russian population still considered the former Soviet Union, and not Kazakhstan, to be their motherland, and less than 15 percent believed that adaptation to life in independent Kazakhstan was possible.[31] The authors of another 1998 study, this time of university students in Almaty and Astana, found that, respectively, only 33 percent and 39 percent of the Russians sampled planned to stay in Kazakhstan,[32] while just under 15 percent of the young Kazakhs surveyed said that they planned to leave the country.[33]

Although the emphasis on Kazakh language education may be ensuring the future of the language, it is also creating a new kind of generation gap. By some estimates, as many as 40 percent of the adult Kazakh population have not fully mastered the language. Such a generation gap has the potential to cause rifts within the ruling elite.[34]

Much depends upon the definition of language mastery offered, and Kazakh parliamentarians have been struggling with the problem of choosing an appropriate standard. According to a 1996 commission on language, if *mastery* is defined as the ability to make oneself understood in spoken Kazakh, then 96.3 percent of ethnic Kazakhs could be said to speak Kazakh; however, if *mastery* is defined as the ability to read, write, and speak fluently, only 74.7 percent could be considered to have mastered Kazakh.[35] Many prominent Kazakhs do not read and write Kazakh well and so are unable to edit Kazakh texts properly. In August 2000, the politically ambitious Kazakh deputy Serik Abdrakhmanov took the government to task for the Kazakh-language text of a bilateral agreement with Iran on combating crime that was signed by Prime Minister Tokayev. According to Abdrakhmanov, who branded Tokayev and his co-signer, Foreign Minister Erlan Idrisov, as "illiterate," the agreement contained no fewer than 150 spelling and grammatical errors.[36] Even at the highest levels, it seems, true mastery of the Kazakh language is rarer than the statistics show.

The requirement of demonstrating language proficiency is a ready tool for political exclusion. The emphasis on Kazakh language proficiency works to the benefit of those from the Great Horde who are more likely to be fluent in Kazakh, and it places not only Russians but also many Middle Horde and Small Horde Kazakhs at a competitive disadvantage.

The language laws have yet to be invoked in high-stakes political games, as they were in the 2000 presidential election in neighboring Kyrgyzstan when President Akayev's principal political opponent, former Vice President Feliks Kulov (an ethnic Kyrgyz) was barred from running for president because of a rigorous and arbitrary Kyrgyz language test that was required of all candidates. In fact, President Nazarbayev has taken pains to demonstrate sensitivity on the language issue, delaying or slowing down implementation of portions of the law. On a number of occasions he has taken care to point out both that the republic specifically forbids discrimination based upon language and that Russian will remain for most people in the republic what he calls in his 1993 statement "a channel of introduction" for the flow of information into the republic. On at least one occasion, shortly after independence, Nazarbayev even went so far as to suggest that there was no need for Russian-speaking adults to learn Kazakh, a stance from which he quickly retreated.

But while President Nazarbayev has taken pains to reassure the local Russian population on the matter, he has done little to slow the trend toward Kazakh linguistic domination. While Nazarbayev promises that the introduction of Kazakh will take at least a generation to be completed and must be done through the education system rather than by excluding people from public life, the present leaders seem committed to making Kazakh the republic's only public language. In 1993 Nazarbayev called the Kazakh language "an additional factor of the consolidation of all citizens of Kazakhstan" and the 1996 official statement called it "a consolidating medium of communication for the free development of the languages of the representatives of nationalities living in Kazakhstan." Such statements offer little encouragement to most of the country's non-Kazakh populations, who are unable to function effectively in the Kazakh language in work situations. Many Kazakhs cannot either.

The scale of difficulty inherent in making Kazakh the language of the work environment was illustrated by a December 1996 parliamentary study that found that only 9.5 percent of the respondents worked in exclusively Kazakh-language environments, while 39 percent worked in exclusively Russian-language environments, and another 19.7 percent worked in environments that were predominantly Russian-language, with some translation into Kazakh. Although the proportion of Kazakh and mixed-language environments is increasing steadily, they are still more characteristic of cultural milieus and rural settings than they are of urban and especially modern economic ones.

The use of scarce resources to enlarge the Kazakh-language work environment at a time when the republic has so many other pressing needs seems of questionable wisdom and remains a contentious issue. The Kazakhs themselves spar over whether their language can be made to serve as a modern technical language, at least without the adoption of considerable numbers of non-Kazakh words and phrases, since Soviet-era discrimination against Kazakh kept the language essentially a "kitchen tongue," in which there are still, as Kazakh political scientist Nurbulat Masanov put it, "dozens of words to describe a camel . . . [but] no words for modern technology or science."[37]

Yet languages can be adaptive if state resources are invested to that end, and Kazakh nationalists are quick to suggest how this can be done. In September 1998, the leaders of the Azat civic movement made a series of proposals on expanding the sphere of the Kazakh language, including forcing commercial, private, and foreign organizations to emphasize it, and the introduction of a special tax on non-Kazakh speakers to pay for the cost of Russian-Kazakh interpreters employed by the government. They also demanded that prospective applicants who did not speak Kazakh should be granted employment only on condition that they will learn the language. Starting in 1999, Azat wants college entrance and high school exit exams to be conducted in Kazakh only.[38] Such suggestions, although insupportable in Kazakhstan's current political climate, still leave non-Kazakhs feeling much alienated from their new state.[39] Adding to this is that they are being cut off from the Russian media. Kazakh officials lament that an enthusiastic audience for Kazakh-language media has still not been created, yet by 1998 Russian-language radio broadcasting accounted for less than 10 percent of the total, a topic that then Prime Minister Vladimir Putin took up during his September 1999 official visit, with little evidence of success.[40]

The Russians in particular look to their ethnic origin as the explanation of why things go wrong, and when surveyed, non-Kazakhs are more likely than Kazakhs to claim that ethnic relations have worsened.[41] The Russians believe that they have been subjected to more than their fair share of downsizing in the government and even in private enterprise, where there are no formal legislative restrictions on Russian language usage. More than half the young Russian university students surveyed in Astana and Almaty said that ethnic origin would determine their career chances, whereas only a quarter of the young Kazakhs gave a similar answer.[42] The atmosphere of suspicion is growing so great that Kazakhstan's Russians sometimes claim that the government is finding secret ways to aid the Kazakhs; for example, when pensions were not paid for three months in North Kazakhstan oblast, rumors circulated that the Kazakhs were on special rosters and were receiving their pensions at local mosques.

The local Russian population does not trust the Kazakh-dominated government. According to a 1997 poll, only 14 percent of the Russian respondents trusted Kazakhstan's local authorities and 13.6 percent trusted the country's republican ones. For the Kazakhs, these numbers are significantly higher: 23.5 and 35.3 percent, respectively, said that they trusted the government, which was also far from resounding support.[43] The Kazakhs were also more likely to endorse the government's treatment of minorities and cultural policies. In a 1999 poll funded by the U.S. Department of State, 51 percent of the Kazakhs thought that their government was doing a good job in protecting minorities, while only 31 percent of the Russians agreed; 67 percent of the Kazakhs and 50 percent of the Russians thought that the government was doing a good job in maintaining national unity; 74 percent of the Russians believed that the government was doing a good job developing Kazakh language and culture, as did 67 percent of the Kazakhs, which speaks to how large a constituency exists for a Kazakh nationalist lobby. The rifts within the Kazakh community on these questions, however, are also clear. A minority of the Kazakhs did not feel that the government was providing enough support for the Russian language; 72 percent of the Kazakhs believed the government was doing a good job of developing Russian language and culture, and only 38 percent of the Russians shared that belief. For all the complaints about discrimination, however, only 23 percent of the Russians surveyed (and 9 percent of the Kazakhs) believed that they had been discriminated against in the past three years because of their ethnicity.[44]

One thing that seems to frustrate Kazakhstan's Russians is that there is no one to champion their cause. The freedom of action afforded most NGOs in Kazakhstan is steadily diminishing, particularly those that are genuinely independent of ties to the government. Most Russian nationalist politicians have left the country; some have accepted government sinecures and others have been frightened into inactivity. Equally important is the sharp diminution of Russia's interest in "offshore" ethnic Russians. While support for the "25 million Russians of the near abroad" was something that played well in the Russia of the early 1990s, the issue has slowly faded with time when it became clear how difficult Russia's own transition would be.

There is still a core elite group in Russia, including politicians, nationalists, and human rights activists, that remains concerned with the fate of Kazakhstan's Russians. They continue to hold out hope that Russian President Putin may embrace their cause. Putin appears to have other priorities, and most ordinary Russians are too preoccupied with their own lives and problems in their own country to worry much about ethnic kin who live beyond their borders.

Thus, absent a strong foreign sponsor, the Russians of Kazakhstan are growing more stoic in the face of their steadily eroding political and economic status. Partly this is because the most discontent have been able, and sometimes even forced, to leave the country, leaving the Russian population older, poorer, and without strong political leadership. With time, the country's remaining Russian population seems to be reluctantly accepting its second-class status and the inevitability of the state's transition from multi- to mono-ethnicity.

Intra-Ethnic Relations

The increasingly more mononational nature of Kazakhstan is creating intra-ethnic tensions. Many in Kazakhstan, regardless of nationality, are becoming more nervous about the rise of another type of ethnic problem, clanism, which they see as exaggerated by the country's economic problems and the current level of corruption. While the role of clans in Kazakhstan can be overstated, [45] clans (or a subethnic identity) have become an ever more important source of patronage in Kazakhstan, since a person's clan identity has gone from something people sought to conceal to a source of public pride.

This is partly the result of a deliberate campaign by the government to reinvigorate clan identity as a building block of Kazakh statehood. About 35 percent of Kazakhstan's population belong to the Great Horde, 40 percent to the Middle Horde, and 25 percent to the Small Horde. These Hordes, or *zhuzes,* are further divided into *taip* and *ru* (tribe and clan), although the distinction sometimes proves to be a vague one. [46] The Kazakh clan system is patrilineally based, and not every Kazakh knows his or her clan identity. A Kazakh proverb states: "He is a fool who has forgotten what became of his ancestry seven generations before him and who does not care what will become of his progeny seven generations after him."[47] Yet many are unable to name their seven fathers (going back seven generations) as Kazakh tradition holds they should. Collectivization and the purges of the 1930s dealt a critical blow to the Kazakh patrilineal system; a state-induced famine and the arrests that followed left many Kazakhs with no family to continue their ancestry, while others were often deliberately left in ignorance of their family ties for their own protection by concerned family members who assumed the responsibility of raising them after the arrest of their parents.

The traditional function of clans, to regulate the pastoral nomadic economy of the Kazakh community, was long ago lost. After a period of steady decline during Russian colonial rule, it was effectively dealt a death knell by collectivization. In rural Kazakhstan, especially where local communities live on or near their traditional pastoral lands in ethnically consolidated enclaves, clans had a continuing regulative social function, especially when collective farms were successfully organized along clan lines. Although the latter was more the exception than the rule, since Soviet economic policy was designed to prevent the overlap of clan and collective farm membership, clans continued to play an important role, especially in the agricultural communities of southeast Kazakhstan, such as the one in which Nursultan Nazarbayev was raised. Even in northern and western Kazakhstan, where the population had been forced to move a great deal and clan identity is usually more attenuated, extended-family networks were commonplace and offered their members protection and access to scarce goods and services. In these parts of Kazakhstan the family structure at its base may have been smaller, dozens of people rather than hundreds, but in the case of those families with access to the privileges of the Soviet economic and political system, the family structures were no less powerful.

The career of Nazarbayev was given a boost by his marrying into a politically prominent Middle Horde family. His future wife, Sara Alpysovna, was a cafeteria worker at Karmet, the giant metallurgical plant in Karaganda where the future Kazakh president began his career. The job (and it is not clear whether the future first lady actually spent any time waiting on customers or simply had this job registered in her passport as proof of employment) was a plum. It meant ready access to meat and other foodstuffs, which would provide for a family's needs and could be sold at a handsome profit to friends and family. Sara Alpysovna undoubtedly got the job because her uncle, Syzdyk Abishev, was in charge of the local meat and dairy trading association. While Nazarbayev would eventually rise well beyond the status of his wife's uncle, the career of the two remained fully intertwined until Abishev's death in 1997.[48]

These networks took on increasing importance after independence. According to a 1995 poll, 39 percent of the respondents believed that belonging to a particular *zhuz* was important in getting a job or a promotion.[49] Clan politics plays the greatest role in southern Kazakhstan, which is the territory of the Great Horde. This part of the Kazakh nation was territorially the least displaced by Russian and Soviet economic policy, and the extended family structure of the people is usually the most intact. The Great Horde was organized around a dozen subethnic units, making it less hierarchical than the Small and Middle Hordes, which had well-developed systems of nobility (known as the white bone) dating back to Mongol times. There is also a certain amount of rivalry between the clans, which in the first half of the nineteenth century regularly turned violent.

These tensions were transformed during Russian colonial and then Soviet rule. The nobles of the Small and Middle Hordes better accommodated themselves to Russian rule than did those of the Great Horde, and the sons of many of the noble families from both the Small and Middle Hordes were often educated in leading Russian schools and participated in the political life of the empire's two capital cities. The Kazakh contribution must have seemed marginal to the Russians, but from the vantage point of the Kazakhs it was significant. It led to a nascent nationalist movement, the Alash Orda, which seized power during the chaotic years of the Russian Revolution and was defeated by the Bolsheviks during the Civil War. Most educated Kazakhs (at least those from the Small and Middle Hordes) supported the

Alash Orda to some extent, and because of this loyalty nearly all the northern elite was questioned during the years of the Great Terror, regardless of how active in the Communist Party or the Soviet government some of these people were in the intervening years.

Conversely, largely untainted by the support of the nationalist cause during the revolutionary period, the leading families of the Great Horde did not suffer as badly as those from the north did, and the Kazakh Communist Party that was built in 1938 after the purges depended heavily on the political elite that had been nurtured in the southern part of the country. Over the next fifty years many families from the Small and Middle Hordes rose to positions of prominence in all sectors of Kazakhstan's economy, with Small Horde families predominating in the oil sector and Middle Horde families in metallurgy. For all this time, however, the leadership of the Communist Party of Kazakhstan was always in the hands of the Great Horde, which was obviously under Moscow's tutelage.[50] Yet the Russians always had an incomplete understanding of how the Kazakhs had divided power between themselves. Especially during the long Brezhnev years, Moscow was content to remain in ignorance, as long as the Kazakhs were able to produce a paper trail to demonstrate that the Central Committee's directives were being fulfilled, and if they provided the necessary payoffs to their superiors.

Moscow tolerated the perpetuation of patronage networks that were based in part on clans as long as the division of power between the clans was done quietly. Although inter-*zhuz* rivalries were subdued in the Soviet period, they have gained a new vigor since independence. Given their dominance in the Communist Party, the politicians from the Great Horde were for the most part more supportive of independence than those from the other two hordes. They realized that it would fall to them to apportion the property of the new state. They also worked fairly aggressively to build alliances with politicians from the Small Horde, especially those who came from regions with oil and gas, in their efforts to gain effective control of those assets. The politicians from the Middle Horde, whose members have lived much longer among Russians and who often worked in Russian-dominated sectors of the economy, were relatively more interested in cooperation with Russia.

Still, it is easy to offer an oversimplified view of clans as strongly deterministic of success in today's Kazakhstan. President Nazarbayev is from the Shaprashty clan of the Great Horde, and the former prime minister, Nurlan Balgimbayev, is from the Small Horde. Both men were able to work comfortably together for several years, and each has appointed or shown favor to people who are close and distant kin, as well as to people from their home regions. For the past several years the president has also managed to exclude Akezhan Kazhegeldin, who is of the Middle Horde, from playing an active political role in the country. He sparred with Olzhas Suleimenov, also of the Middle Horde. If Kazhegeldin were ever to be victorious, many people from the Middle Horde and northern Kazakhstan would push out some of those now holding powerful posts who come from the south and west of the country.

Yet it would be a mistake to conclude that clan drives any of the country's major political rivalries. For many reasons Nazarbayev would not consider Kazhegeldin *svoi chelovek* ("his man"), as those from the Soviet-era used to put it. Far more important than clan differences was that Kazhegeldin belonged to a different set of Soviet-era patron-client networks than did Nazarbayev; that he had powerful connections in Russia at a time when Nazarbayev felt ready to distance himself from Moscow; and that he was siphoning resources that might have gone to the president and those close to him.

Politics in Kazakhstan has always involved coalition building, and successful political unions are frequently made across clan lines. As already noted, Nazarbayev's wife comes from the Middle Horde, and their marriage has been a source of important alliances with people from the north. Family is as important as clan, but in the end, most important of all is to be part of a well-established patron-client network. Non-Kazakhs, people of mixed ancestry, Kazakhs who do not know their family history, and those from the "wrong" horde can all work their way into successful patron-client relations. These networks depend heavily on the loyalty of their members, who repay that loyalty with protection of various sorts. The issue of loyalty is closely intertwined with the role of family, for there are strong cultural norms among the Kazakhs that set up obligations to help one's relatives. When Amalbek Tshanov became *akim* of Zhambyl oblast in 1995, for example, he replaced 140 bureaucrats with people predominantly from his clan.[51]

The presence of these patron-client networks helps to sustain a pattern of official corruption and to put all who lack good connections at a considerable disadvantage.[52] This in turn fuels criticism of the power of clans in public life and increases the number of people who feel disadvantaged by their own ethnic or family circumstances. While much has been written about the rise in clan and horde rivalries,[53] even more dangerous is the countervailing tendency of a consolidation of power by Kazakhstan's first family.

It is natural in a nomadic society to want to profit from the riches of one's ancestral lands, and prominent Middle Horde families are used to drawing benefits from the various ores in their lands, just as those in the Small Horde have benefited from the oil industry. The first years of independence were good to some of these families, allowing them to accumulate considerable fortunes, some of which have gone offshore. In the past few years, however, President Nazarbayev and his various relatives have been working hard to ensure that the family group will be by far the most powerful of all families, holding controlling interests in every major sector of the country's economy. In addition to his daughters and sons-in-law, who control most of Kazakhstan's media, dominate Kazakhstan's security forces, are involved in the trade of alcohol, tobacco, and sugar, and have a growing role in the oil industry and the various mining and metallurgy sectors, Nazarbayev has made good use of his wife's relatives as well as his more distant kin. Some of these people, like Akhmetzhan Yesimov and Nurtai Abykayev, have held a series of key posts in the government and the presidential administration.[54] The president's brother-in-law, Saginbek Tursunov, served briefly as the head of the presidential administration. More important, his wife's relative, Syzdyk Abishev, Kazakhstan's first minister of foreign economic relations, is said to have played a key role in establishing the family's first foreign-held assets.[55] More recently, Kairat Saltybaldy Nazarbayev, the son of the president's younger brother, has come into official prominence. Saltybaldy (he has now legally dropped the name Nazarbayev), who was born in 1970, spent several years working as the deputy head of Astana and then worked as the first vice-president of Kazakhoil. Before that he spent several years working for the National Security Committee (KNB), as the deputy head of the division for the fight against corruption among high-ranking officials. Presumably he had the job of protecting Nazarbayev family interests.

The importance of clan and family ties certainly contributes to the problem of corruption in Kazakhstan, but while family connections may help to grease a person's way, those without blood ties can buy their way into official favor. Many people rumored to be in business with the Nazarbayev family, such as the Eurasia Bank Group or the Leviev group, are not relatives and often are not even ethnic Kazakhs.

Although the government has begun to set up a national agency to fight organized crime and corruption,[56] the problems inherent in Kazakhstan's campaign against corruption were underscored by Nazarbayev's son-in-law Rakhat Aliyev's being named to lead this effort as deputy head of Kazakh national security, a post that he held until November 2001. In a nationally televised interview on his wife's Khabar television, Rakhat Aliyev called corruption in law enforcement bodies the most dangerous evil facing the country.[57] Yet the first family has fought corruption by shifting blame from itself and the central government to the officials serving in the country's oblasts and regions.

Regional Differentiation

Discussions of clan and ethnic differentiation mask another sort of differentiation, the division of the country into more distinct regions. This differentiation is occurring despite aggressive state efforts to eliminate regional loyalties through the creation of a unitary state, by the presidential appointment of local governors, and by emphasis on an ideology of national consolidation.

Despite these policies, regional differences remain profound and are growing even more dramatic as the country's economic transition moves forward. Despite the changes in the budgeting processes designed to rationalize the tax base of oblasts and regions, local governments often lack the competence and financial resources to handle many of the tasks with which they have been saddled. Nor does the national government have the money to develop a new transportation and communication system to bind the country together in a reasonable time span. Several billion dollars for public works could have been put toward these goals but were diverted to building the new capital city of Astana. In addition, each of Kazakhstan's beleaguered oblasts was expected to build a high-rise building in the new capital.

Regional identities still dominate national ones in the northern and eastern parts of the country, especially among ethnic Russians. In a 1997 poll only 68.3 percent of Russians considered themselves citizens of Kazakhstan, including every fourth person living in North Kazakhstan and East Kazakhstan oblasts. In 1997 most people from Kazakhstan were still traveling with their old USSR passports. As the passports expired they had to be exchanged for new Kazakh ones, making the question of citizenship more than just one of psychological predisposition. Ethnicity remains highly politicized in northern Kazakhstan, and surveys have shown those living in these two regions have been found to place the most emphasis on the nationalities of prospective sons-in-law, neighbors, and co-workers.[58]

At the same time, the growing mobility of Kazakhstan's population is making it more difficult for regional identities to harden and is also changing the demography of the country's urban population. There is a constant inflow of rural Kazakhs into the country's cities, and some estimate that more than two million people moved into urban areas during the 1990s. Yet because many of these Kazakhs did not meet the criteria for legal registration (a job and a fixed place of residence), the magnitude of this population wave is not reflected in the recent census.[59] This migration is largely contributing to the growing decay of Kazakhstan's cities, where the number of applicants for jobs far outstrips the number of new jobs—in the most extreme cases by as much as seventy to one. Most people therefore content themselves to work off the books, drawing communal services from strapped municipalities while contributing no taxes. Most also live in overcrowded substandard housing, for despite the constant influx of new people to cities that were already suffering from a deteriorating housing stock, Kazakhstan has recorded an increase in new housing starts of only 8.6 percent for 2000, again attesting to the troubled nature of the economies of most cities.[60]

A few cities, however, are changing for the better. Most prominent of these is Almaty, largely because of the amount of foreign investment that city has received and the substantial foreign community that such investment has attracted. The new capital of Astana is also serving as a magnet and should quickly develop a Kazakh majority since a disproportionate share of the government officials, bureaucrats, and clerical staff who are coming to the city are from the Kazakh population.[61] The boom in Kazakhstan's oil industry has brought the creation of new urban centers in western Kazakhstan, and more than a third of all urban growth has occurred in Atyrau and Mangistau oblasts, where Kazakhs are moving.[62] The residence patterns within northern Kazakhstan have been changing as well, as whole industrial cities shut down in the wake of the collapse of their enterprises. Things got so bad in Saran, where there had been a large industrial rubber plant, that people were offering to sell their apartments for 1,000 tenge and even to trade them for a bottle of vodka.[63] People have also been fleeing

Soviet-era environmental despoliation, particularly in East Kazakhstan.[64] This has led to a shortage of qualified workers in East Kazakhstan, West Kazakhstan, North Kazakhstan, Karaganda, and Kostanai oblasts. If the pace of investment were ever to pick up dramatically, this shortage could create severe problems for the country.[65]

The rumor of jobs is enough to get people to go from failing farms in the countryside to their relatives' couches in the cities. In Almaty, where signs of economic recovery are visible in the new buildings and well-stocked stores that are cropping up throughout the city, the constant wave of migrants keeps unemployment relatively high. In 1997, before the impact of the Russian financial crisis, unemployment was reported to have been about 7 percent. Unemployment statistics, however, tell only part of the story. While unemployment decreased by roughly the same amount, by 7–8 percent, in both Karaganda and South Kazakhstan oblasts, the nature of the economic revival in the two cities was quite different. In a 1990 nationwide survey, 50 percent of the respondents in Shymkent said that they had opportunities to make additional income. Almost 80 percent of those living in Karaganda did not have such an opportunity. In the latter region the drop in unemployment was fueled as much by the outmigration of those seeking jobs as it was by the improved performance of the giant Karmet steelworks.[66] About 30 percent of the population in Shymkent and Almaty said that they thought that the quality of life has improved since 1991, while only 20 percent of residents of Karaganda think so. In 1997 the per capita GDP in Karaganda oblast was $1,711, just above the national average of $1,451, while in South Kazakhstan (where Shymkent is found) it was only $711. Those in Shymkent were on the whole more optimistic about their future, 50 percent of the respondents believing that they could rely on the government and official organs for help, compared with 14 percent in Karaganda.[67]

There are substantial differences in standards of living across the country, and in 1997 the per capita GDP varied from a low of $488 in East Kazakhstan oblast to a high of $4,654 in Almaty city. The economic situation in Almaty is in sharp contrast with that of the rest of the country since its GDP is nearly twice that of the next most prosperous oblast, Atyrau ($2,925); Kostanai and Kyzylorda oblasts and Astana city, which has the same legal status as an oblast (still officially referred to as Akmola oblast), all cluster around this same range. On the other end of the scale, six oblasts have a per capita GDP of under $1,000 a year.[68]

Not surprisingly, there is also enormous variation in the tax base of the various oblasts, although each is faced with the same set of tasks and each has the same sources of income. The oblasts, which are further divided into regions and cities of oblast significance, must pay for preprimary, primary, secondary, and specialized secondary (including vocational-technical) education, provide guaranteed health care assistance, and pay unemployment and other work-related benefits, as well as the cost of local law enforcement.[69] The uniform budget system adopted in 1999 provides local governments with the proceeds of half the corporate taxes collected, plus all the personal income tax, property tax, and local land tax. Oblasts are also responsible for collecting the value added tax (VAT),[70] which goes to the national government, although they can keep part of the excise tax on alcohol. This replaces the previous system in which the oblasts ran up considerable arrears, which were then partially covered by financial transfers from the national government.

Obviously, those parts of the country that have been most successful at attracting foreign investment have considerably more income than those that have not. The figures from the revised budget of 1999 tell us that Atyrau oblast (the site of the Tengiz project) collects 441 percent more corporate income tax per capita than the national average; Mangistau oblast, 230 percent; and Almaty city, 378 percent. Kostanai oblast in contrast collects 8 percent less than the national average; North Kazakhstan oblast, 12 percent less; and Almaty oblast, 13.8 percent less. There are similar disparities in the personal income tax collected on a per capita basis as well. The Atyrau and Mangistau oblasts and Almaty city all do considerably better than the national average (by 299, 276, and 317 percent, respectively), while the Akmola, Almaty, North Kazakhstan, and South Kazakhstan oblasts all do considerably worse (34.9, 27.5, 41.8, and 32.0 percent, respectively).[71]

That there are far more "loser" oblasts, where there is substantially less income generated on the part of the population than is the national average, probably helps to explain the low expectation level of government performance. Overall, the Kazakh residents do not have much confidence that they can expect help from the local governments. If a 1996 survey by Kazakhstan's Institute of Strategic Studies is at all representative of public opinion, then 48 percent of those who live in Kazakhstan think that the failings of local government are the result of corrupt administrators, while 44 percent blame incompetent administrators.[72] This adds up to most Kazakh residents having no confidence in local government.

The focus of the national anticorruption campaign has increased the public perception that those who live in Kazakhstan cannot trust their local officials. Over the past few years, for example, twenty-one members of the law enforcement bodies of South Kazakhstan have been prosecuted, and the local prosecutor's office has been charged with poor supervision because only 1,497 cases were tried in courts out of 4,244 criminal cases referred.[73] Law enforcement officers were implicated in several nasty corruption cases in Pavlodar, and in 1999 six officers were convicted of extortion and two of bribery. Four top law enforcement officials in the Mangistau and Zhambyl regions and two judges in Ust-Kamenogorsk were also fired in connection with corruption cases.[74]

Local officials are likely to remain the target of the anticorruption campaign since this helps to keep the public's attention away from the malfeasance being committed by Kazakhstan's leading officials or members of their families. In fact, in the past two years there has been a rather theatrical quality to the president's anticorruption campaign, given the leading role that Aliyev was assigned to play in it. In April 2000, the Special Commission for the Fight against Corruption was dissolved by presidential decree, and its powers were delegated to the president's administration. At the same time the heads of administration of the country's regions and the cities of Astana and Almaty were made personally responsible for law and order in their respective regions and cities, which made them even more directly accountable to the president.

Corruption is certainly pervasive at every level of society in Kazakhstan, but at least some oblast officials have been striving to meet their responsibilities. There have not been wide fluctuations in the expenditures of Kazakhstan's oblasts on both education and health care, which means that officials in the poorer oblasts are making an enormous effort to provide services to their constituents. The uniform budgetary system adopted in 1999 seems to have been met with displeasure in rich and poor oblasts alike. It certainly increased the power of the national government at the expense of the local authorities since it placed oblast income and expenditure levels in the hands of the central authorities.[75]

The current system has left the wealthier oblasts very frustrated.[76] Those living in resource-rich oblasts, especially those in western Kazakhstan, would like greater financial autonomy from the center and believe that the local elites would be better able to ensure that resource development works to the benefit of the region rather than entrust the task to the national elite.

There is also an important sector-specific elite especially coming from the oil and gas industry (which is disproportionately from the Small Horde), and this makes some of Kazakhstan's major political cleavages cross-cutting ones. These elites may press Astana and may even manage to gain concessions from the oil and gas companies working in their oblasts, but there are few formal instruments available to the oblasts to use in pressing their case. The Kazakhstan constitution (both the constitution of 1993 and the one of 1995) provides the oblasts with only statutory rights and gives the central powers the right to abolish oblasts and to name their heads.

The move of the capital to Astana in the center of the country has improved the government's reach and made the day-to-day supervision of the northern and western oblasts of the country much easier. The Kazakh government would eventually like to create more uniform and governable oblasts with the consolidation of sparsely populated oblasts. The process of doing this would create lucrative new sources of patronage as well as eliminate older ones over which the president's control has been incomplete.

Consolidation has eliminated what were some of the least populous oblasts (such as Turgay, which had only 315,000 people in 1992). Yet there are still marked differences in size. South Kazakhstan oblast, the most populous, contains nearly two million people, or nearly 12 percent of the nation's population, while Mangistau, now the least populous oblast, contains only 436,000, or just 2 percent of Kazakhstan's population. Seven of the oblasts now contain more than one million people, while two of them still hold less than a half million each (Atyrau and Mangistau).

The character of the oblasts is much different as well. Several of the oblasts are dominated either by single cities or by urban clusters, meaning that the bulk of the population in those regions is urban. Almaty city is, of course, 100 percent urban, but other predominantly urban oblasts include Karaganda (84.8 percent before Zhezkazgan, 79.1 percent, was joined to it), Mangistau (79.6 percent), and Pavlodar (61.2 percent). In contrast, South Kazakhstan oblast has only a single city (Shymkent, population about 400,000 in 1992, when it was the republic's third largest city), meaning that 61.1 percent of the population is rural or village-based. Almaty oblast (distinct from Almaty city) is the most rural of Kazakhstan's oblasts, at just 22.2 percent urban. In general, 55 percent of Kazakhstan's population lived in urban areas and 44 percent in rural areas.[77] The per capita income in rural areas is estimated to be 60 percent lower than it is in urban areas, with a far greater percentage of the population confined to the bottom one-fifth of average income than is true of the urban population.[78]

The ethnic balance in these oblasts also varies widely; Atyrau and Kyzylorda oblasts are each about 90 percent Kazakh, while Karaganda, Kostanai, and North Kazakhstan oblasts remain mostly Russian, despite recent administrative moves to reduce the Slavic majority. The old Soviet transport system reinforces these ethnic divides. There are no major highways directly connecting the various cities of the republic; the three major roads in the republic (M–32, M–36, and M–38) all tend northwest-to-southeast, while the most convenient true east-west highway (M–51) lies almost entirely within Russia. Tellingly, in an April 1997 interview, presidential spokesman Yermukhamet Yertysbayev listed the need to build a highway connecting Almaty, Karaganda, Akmola (now Astana), and Borovoe (in Kokchetau oblast) as second in national priority only to the need to construct a pipeline to transport oil from the Caspian Basin.[79] Upgrading the road and rail system will be a slow and costly proposition. The first major rail project begun by the Kazakh government, a 184-kilometer stretch from Aksu (near Kokchetau) to Konechnaya (outside Semipalatinsk) was begun in May 1998 and was planned as a two-year project costing about $20 million. The challenges of working in this terrain stalled the project, but it was completed in June 2001.[80] With this new stretch of road finished, the Kazakhs are able to ship freight across the country between China and Europe without going through Russia.

The present arrangement of the national infrastructure leaves Kazakhstan susceptible to economic pressure from Russia and reinforces the disposition of many citizens in the northern industrial cities to understand themselves as arbitrarily attached to Kazakhstan. These overwhelmingly ethnic Russian cities are closer to Russia than they are to Almaty or even to Astana.[81] The difficulties of linking Almaty to these cities is certainly one of the reasons President Nazarbayev moved the capital to Astana, but when Astana was first inaugurated, it was a twenty-two-hour rail journey between the two capitals, and there were only a few daily flights between them. The latter has changed, and rail service has been improved, but a major infrastructural overhaul is still decades away.

East Kazakhstan oblast and its capital, Ust-Kamenogorsk, are typical of the northern, largely Russian regions that present challenges for the government. The predominantly Russian cities of Kazakhstan's north are littered with the industrial relics of the Soviet past. Built to exploit deposits of beryllium, uranium, and other defense-related minerals, Ust-Kamenogorsk has been particularly hard hit by the economic changes of the past decade. The Ulba metallurgical plant, which was the city's largest employer, was forced to shut down a number of its operations, while other important economic functions of the oblast, such as mining, are under continual threat because of chronic wage and pension arrears.[82]

Industrial workers in the southern part of the country are no better off than their colleagues in the north. In late November 1996 there were mass demonstrations and disturbances in Shymkent, occasioned by Uzbekistan's failure to deliver electricity and natural gas as had been agreed; these disturbances were nearly identical to ones in Ust-Kamenogorsk and other northern cities that took place at about the same time because Russia had also stopped shipping energy to Kazakhstan.

Kazakhstan's poorest regions are in the south of the country, where more than half (55.5 percent) of the population lives below the established subsistence minimum.[83] Deteriorating economic conditions have caused real unhappiness for all the population and have left local ethnic Russians, about 15 percent of the population in South Kazakhstan oblast, feeling totally stranded because they lack typical Kazakh extended family networks to get them through tough times. A series of surveys from 1993 to 1996 found that 80 percent of the Russians living in South Kazakhstan wanted to leave, but only 10 percent expected to be able to.[84] The situation is little better in Zhambyl, where people are leaving such dying industrial cities as Kentau, Zhanatas, Tekeli, and Karatau. The most extreme case is the city of Zhanatas, which at one time had a population of more than fifty thousand people. Once the capital of Kazakhstan's phosphorus industry, this city is reported to have virtually become a ghost town by 1994, the population reduced by at least 30 percent, with more than three thousand abandoned apartments and no municipal electric or gas supply.[85] The factory continues to serve as the main employer for the town and in 1997 was the site of a major strike.

Despite Kazakhstan's serious industrial problems, the situation in the countryside is often seen as more dire than in the cities. In one year alone, 1997, nearly a hundred thousand people moved to cities and towns, including 14,000 who moved to Almaty.[86] This was before the August 1998 crisis! As a result, the long-term recovery of Kazakhstan's southern oblasts could be even more problematic than that of the industrial centers in the north. Kazakh-dominated South Kazakhstan and Kyzylorda oblasts have experienced higher than average rates of unemployment, and Kyzylorda has one of the worst ecological situations in the country.[87] Such cities as Pavlodar or Aktiubinsk, while far from thriving, are beginning to show signs of recovery since their basic industries (aluminum in Pavlodar, chrome in Aktiubinsk) have attracted foreign investors.

Such disparities suggest that Kazakhstan is likely to develop significant regional imbalances, with some areas becoming more affluent and others, perhaps the majority, mired in continuing poverty. The same imbalance should hold between urban areas and rural ones. These differences will continue to have ethnic overtones because most of the moribund industry will be predominantly Russian, while the new winners of economic recovery seem certain to be well-connected Kazakhs.

The Growing Gap between Rich and Poor

Growing poverty is a national problem, and severely depressed economic regions are found in every part of the country. Moreover, even where there are particularly densely Kazakh regions, such as in southern or western Kazakhstan, the national government is seen as to blame, given the unitary nature of the Kazakh state.

Regardless of where they are located, ordinary citizens in Kazakhstan feel ever more economically disadvantaged and powerless because of it. Much of the fault for this, they feel, lies with the government in Kazakhstan. According to a recent USIA-funded poll, 90 percent of those surveyed in Kazakhstan thought government was doing a poor job in providing social protection for unemployed, homeless, and needy; 71 percent believe that it is doing a bad job in guaranteeing the timely payment of wages, salaries, and pensions. Those surveyed felt that the old Soviet values were more equitable and better served their interests than do the new market-oriented ones, and 68 percent of those surveyed said that the situation would be improved by the renationalization of former state assets (68 percent) and by nationalizing private banks and companies (57 percent).

Employment

While it is clear that the economic situation in Kazakhstan is a major source of popular discontent, it is difficult to gauge how badly off most people are. Documenting unemployment is challenging since one encounters the twin problems of hidden unemployment and hidden employment. The government does not want to disclose how many people are unemployed. To record a high figure of unemployment puts both international and national confidence at risk. It also makes the government liable for the payment of social welfare benefits. Similarly, most people will go to great lengths to avoid recording their employment in order to avoid paying taxes on their earnings.

The figures for the employed and unemployed populations are hard to reconcile. Official figures show unemployment growing from 0.4 percent in 1992 to a "high" of 4.1 percent in 1996 and then dropping to 3.9 percent in 1997, 3.7 percent in 1998, and back up to 3.9 percent in 1999.[88] Even the Kazakh government does not consider these figures to be good indicators. The Kazakh labor minister considered the actual unemployment figure for this period to be 13.5 percent.[89] Informal estimates set the percentage of unemployed much higher. A 1998 article in *Novaia gazeta* criticizing Nazarbayev's performance listed the unemployment rate as 20 percent.[90] None of these statistics includes people on indefinite furloughs or those who are employed and not being paid because neither group is eligible for unemployment benefits. In mid-1996, about 80 percent of the industrial work force in North Kazakhstan, Karaganda, Semipalatinsk, and Kostanai were idle or not receiving salary, but official unemployment statistics for these oblasts ranged from a low of 7.0 to a high of 9.6 percent.[91]

At the same time, Kazakh government statistics on the number of people employed in the economy show a decline of 5.8 percent from 1995 to 1996 and of 20.2 percent from 1996 to 1997. Only a small percentage of this can be explained by outmigration and the natural aging of the population.[92] In fact, throughout this period the size of the working age population of the country continued to rise.[93] Those just entering the work force seem to be having the toughest time, the only exception being the graduates of new market-oriented training programs, still a privileged few. The Kazakh government unemployment service reported in December 1998 that 35.4 percent of those registered with the public employment service were between sixteen and twenty-nine years old.[94]

Being employed was no guarantee of security either. Government employees were not always paid in a timely fashion. Workers at Kazakh Air had not been paid for several months in 1998, when a scandal broke over tens of thousands of dollars of free trips that had been given to government officials.[95] The decision was then made to restructure and privatize the airline. The government has frequently tried to divest itself of unprofitable enterprises that cannot meet their payrolls, even if they lack feasible privatization plans.

The government attempted such a divestiture at the phosphorus plant at Zhanatas, outside Taras. Workers there responded with a series of protests and strikes that crippled the city and surrounding areas in 1997 and early 1998. Two hundred workers began to strike in mid-December 1997, and by January their numbers had swelled to 3,000. Fifty of them marched to Almaty, demanding $5–$6 million in back wages from 1996 and 1997, but the police prevented them from entering the city. This strike attracted negative press coverage throughout the CIS because the strikers included pregnant women and women with young children. Some of these staged hunger strikes to bring attention to their plight. The hunger strikes resulted in two deaths. Eventually, the government sent a detachment of approximately one thousand police to break up the strikers when they successfully blocked the railroad tracks and paralyzed the principal Moscow-Bishkek-Almaty train route. Not only were the strike organizers arrested, they were also made liable for the costs of the rail disruption.[96]

The government's harsh response in Zhanatas prohibitively raised the stakes for those interested in developing an independent trade union movement in the country. Independent groups in the north of the country were already being coopted, but support for independent unions was still growing in the south. In October 1997 some thousand workers from the Achpolimetal plant at Kentau in South Kazakhstan (Shymkent) set out to march to Almaty, protesting ten months of unpaid wages totaling about $1.6 million. Authorities stopped the protesters before they had gone very far, but the workers set up a tent camp and stayed there for almost a month. Many launched hunger strikes, and disease spread through the camp. The protests finally ended in early November when the government paid the workers through August, but they continued to demand the outstanding two months' wages, as well as guarantees of future payments.

Five union leaders were accused of organizing the march in Kentau, but they denied the charges.[97] For a while, in the mid-1990s, it looked as though the Kentau workers would link up with the independent labor movement in northern Kazakhstan,[98] but the two independent unions at Kentau were dissolved in 1998 because of their "illegal activities." Through the judicious use of arrest and intimidation, the government has succeeded in leaving the leadership of this independent union movement in disarray.

Kazakhstan initially had a powerful independent labor movement, which developed around the Karaganda coal miners' strikes in 1989–1991 and helped make Leonid Solomin, the head of the so-called Confederation of Free Trade Unions, a national political figure. Following that, there were periodic strikes in the north,[99] and in early 1995 some hundred thousand strikers protested in Karaganda.[100] Less than two years later, however, in October 1996, an effort to organize a nationwide day of protest largely fizzled. From then on the strike movement was characterized by much smaller actions, like the protest at Akmola oblast's Stepanogorsk Uranium Producing Plant on July 15, 1997, to protest five months of unpaid wages, or the demonstration by a thousand people in Kokchetau that protested the nonpayment of wages.[101]

The government concentrated less on satisfying workers' demands than on wooing the independent union leaders, pressuring them to support various government "national reconciliation" efforts. Prominent figures who proved unyielding were jailed. Most notable was the case of Madel Ismailov, of the independent Worker's Movement, who was sentenced to a year in prison for "insulting the honor and dignity of the president" at a November 7, 1997, rally. Even the seemingly coopted continued to be at risk. Leonid Solomin's wife, Valentina Sevryukova, for example, was named the deputy minister of labor, a post she held until 1999. Yet Solomin did not stay silent even in the face of his wife's success, and in 1997 he was tried on charges of illegal financial activity. Although Solomin was acquitted, the strong-arm tactics of the Kazakh security service were revealed by the case, with abuses including the intense intimidation of Solomin and other union leaders, often running along anti-Semitic lines.[102]

Although severely weakened, Solomin's organization still exists, but it is difficult to gauge how much support it, or other independent trade unions, still enjoys. In late 1999 the Confederation of Free Trade Unions claimed a membership of 250,000, while the state-sponsored Federation of Trade Unions claimed four million members. Informed observers, however, say that both figures are unrealistically high.[103] The independent union movement is able to organize small strikes, providing they are held in accordance with legal requirements, that required negotiations have failed, and that fifteen days' advance notice is provided, but everyone is well aware that the government would react quickly to quell any strike that showed signs of becoming a mass protest.

Employment is little protection against the risk of living in reduced circumstances. In fact, in early 1998 the government suspended its own minimum payment regulations until 2004 because it was paying base salaries of only $40 per month, or two-thirds of what the guidelines called for.[104]

The plight of Kazakhstan's farmers is even worse than that of the workers. In addition to having to struggle with the rising cost of living, those who previously lived on state farms are often also encumbered with personal debt acquired when their farms were privatized into individual household economies. In 1999 the per capita cash income was 2.2 times higher in the cities than in the rural areas.[105]

Living Standards

What percentage of the population is poverty-stricken depends on the standard employed. A 1998 UNDP study reported that 90 percent of Kazakhstan's population lived on under $100 per month, but based on a measure of the relative purchasing power of the local currency, only 30 percent of the population was considered poverty-stricken.[106] A UNDP report published in 2000 found that 65 percent of the population lives below the poverty line of $4 a day calculated in 1990 U.S. dollars at "purchasing power parity."[107] This corresponds roughly to an earlier International Committee of the Red Cross claim that 70 percent of Kazakhs are living in poverty.[108] According to the UNDP's *Human Development Report 2000*, the poorest 20 percent receive 6.7 percent of the country's income, while the richest 20 percent receive 42.3 percent.

One measure of the declining standard of living in Kazakhstan is the changes in diet, because while income has been rising, the prices of food have been going up even faster. While in 1990 the Kazakhs ate 71 kilos of meat, in 1995 they consumed only 43 kilos; per capita milk consumption dropped from 307 kilos to 208 kilos, and the number of eggs consumed dropped from 222 to 104 per person.[109] At the same time, the percentage of total expenditures that went for food increased from 38.6 percent in 1990 to 52.8 percent in 1997.[110] In some parts of the country this is creating a social crisis. In a 1999 study done by the Kazakh Association of Sociologists and Political Sciences, more than one-third of those interviewed said that they were unable to feed their family satisfactorily; the situation was reported to be most dire in western Kazakhstan, where 63.6 percent of urban residents and 43.2 percent of rural residents cited their inability to provide adequate food. The same study reported that 15.9 percent of all rural respondents and 13.9 percent of all urban respondents were suffering from famine.[111]

Health Care and Life Expectancy

The health care available to most Kazakhs is deteriorating as well. The state remains committed to providing some limited public health care, yet ordinary Kazakhs have less access to quality medical care than they did previously. The Soviet health care infrastructure that the nation inherited remains poorly maintained, and funding for improvement remains difficult to find. Although the government has made steps toward reform by introducing pilot projects that offer experimental new provider payment methods, the large-scale reform that is needed has not yet been undertaken.[112]

Like all other post-Soviet states, Kazakhstan now has to depend upon its own resources to meet the health care needs of its citizens. Although each of the republics had some specialist care, there was always the option of being sent to specialized treatment facilities in Russia. That still exists, but like all foreign medical care, it is exclusively fee-based. Much of the better medical care in the country is also on a fee-for-service basis. Kazakhstan introduced mandatory health insurance in 1996, which was designated as a 90–10 percent government–private subscriber co-pay.[113] Public expenditure on health care has declined since 1990 from 3.2 percent to 2.1 percent of the GDP, not taking into account the decline in the country's GDP over the same period.

As this shift from public to private medicine occurs, the country's medical establishment is contracting. Many rural and remote urban areas have lost doctors and nurses and seen their hospitals and clinics shut down in an effort to rationalize expenditure by closing marginal and ill-equipped facilities. The total number of hospital beds is decreasing as well, including the beds in maternity hospitals and pediatric wards. The number of beds devoted to the latter two categories decreased by almost a third between 1995 and 1998.[114] The number of doctors practicing in the republic has continued to drop, declining by more than 10 percent between 1995 and 1998 (down to 53,200). At the same time, in 1998, the UNDP reported that the doctor-patient ratio improved, suggesting that many in Kazakhstan are simply not using the health care system, especially those in rural areas, who now must make costly trips to more distant facilities. The UNDP, though, did report that the government is keeping up with previous performance records for most kinds of early childhood inoculations. The one exception is measles, where the percentage of vaccinated children declined by a little more than 20 percent from 1989 to 1994–1995.[115]

There is reason to call these official statistics into question since Kazakhstan's press has reported a marked rise in the incidence of several infectious diseases in a successive number of localities.[116] In the case of at least one disease, the government admits to a major problem: the incidence of tuberculosis is at epidemic proportions in parts of Kazakhstan, and mortality from the disease has increased by 50 percent in the past three years alone.[117] The government also admits that venereal disease has reached epidemic proportions, costing the country $15 million in lost labor time in 1997.[118] AIDS is a growing problem as well, and the health care system is doing a poor job of managing the growing drug problem among Kazakhstan's youth. The number of teenagers registered at Kazakh drug treatment centers rose fourfold from 1997 to 2000, and the bigger problem is that most addicts do not seek treatment. In fact, one Kazakh social service official estimated that about 40 percent of the country's youth are drug users.[119]

Official statistics show a two-year decline in life expectancy from 1980 to 1996, reporting a drop from sixty-seven to sixty-five years,[120] as well as an increased death rate for the same period, from eight to ten per thousand.[121] Some of this growth is explained by the overall aging of the country's population, but nongovernmental sources claim that life expectancy in Kazakhstan declined by four and a half years from 1990 to 1995.[122] The author of that report argued that environmental degradation was an important source of the problem, which was only compounded by declining health care in the country.[123]

Environmental Issues

The environment continues to be a cause of real concern, and some of Kazakhstan's poorest people live in the country's areas of greatest environmental despoliation. Environmental problems are contributing to the country's declining birthrate.[124] Kazakhstan's population is expected to grow by less than 1 percent a year until 2025. While independence has made more international funding available to clean up the various environmental problems that date from the Soviet era, these funds are sufficient to touch only the surface of the problems. The list of environmental challenges is seemingly endless, including the pollution of the Caspian Sea, as well as air and water pollution caused by Soviet-era industrial operations.[125] Oil leaks, the excessive use of pesticides, and the improper disposal of industrial chemicals all threaten the nation's ecology. Obsolete cotton-harvesting machinery led to the excessive use of chemical herbicides and pesticides, which averaged 20–25 kilos per hectare throughout Central Asia, as compared with the average for the former USSR as a whole of no more than 3 kilos.[126] Pesticide contamination has led to a general shortage of drinking water and a high rate of illness among women working in the fields.[127]

The Aral Sea crisis could be Kazakhstan's gravest environmental problem. Once the center of the world's most fertile regions and the fourth largest lake on earth, the Aral Sea has shrunk over the past 30 years to just a small part of its former size. Soviet planners, who made Kazakhstan the USSR's main producer of cotton, diverted local rivers away from the Aral Sea, causing not only a 16-meter drop in the level of the sea, but also a climate change when salt and dust from exposed mud beds blow across the region.[128] In addition, the pesticides and fertilizers used to feed the cotton fields have found their way into water and irrigation channels, poisoning the drinking water and food.[129]

Current and future generations will continue to suffer the aftereffects of the Soviet nuclear and chemical weapon testing programs in Kazakhstan, most particularly in and around Semipalatinsk. From the 1950s to 1990, 468 nuclear tests were carried out at the Semipalatinsk nuclear testing range, including twenty-six above-ground tests. Because of the high levels of radiation in the area that have resulted from nuclear testing, the number of stillbirths in the Semipalatinsk region rose from 6.1 for every 1,000 of the population in 1960 to 12.2 in 1988. In addition, the rates of neurological and psychiatric disorders in the region grew rapidly, as did cases of mental and physical retardation among children.[130] The country's tainted water, especially around the Aral Sea, and the legacy of nuclear testing are partly responsible for deteriorating maternal and child health. Between 1994 and 1997 alone, maternal mortality rates rose from 48.4 to 59.0 for every 100,000 deliveries.[131] Infant mortality rates increased in Kazakhstan from 26.0 to 27.4 per thousand between 1989 and 1995 and then to 36 per 1,000 live births in 1997.[132] According to a recent U.S. government–supported poll, 74 percent of the population think that their government is performing poorly in cleaning up environmental pollution.[133]

Education

Kazakhstan's citizens continue to have expectations of government performance that are not being met in other areas as well. In a U.S. government study similar to the one on environment above, 83 percent of respondents thought the government should be the main underwriter of the country's higher education.[134] Higher education is being partially privatized as well, although the state still provides free primary and secondary education. There is reason, however, to call official education statistics into question. Figures provided by the government to the UNDP admit a drop in the percentage of the preschool population attending school, from 54.7 percent in 1989 to 23.5 percent in 1995, but a drop of only 4 percent in the share of the eligible population attending primary school to 90 percent in 1996.[135] Unofficial sources report a much more serious problem and claim that up to 20 percent of the school age population remains at home.[136]

This, combined with a reduction in the number of state-funded preschool institutions, means that women of child-rearing age are more likely to be forced to remain at home than they were during the Soviet period. Similarly, if there is a choice to be made as to who will receive the necessary shoes and warm clothing to attend school, girls are more likely to have to forgo education than are their brothers. The current situation contributes to the further erosion of the position of women in independent Kazakhstan. In 1996 women made up 43 percent of the work force in the sciences, 55 percent in social management, 47 percent in industry, and 73 percent in culture.[137] However, in 1998 women held a bit over 11 percent of the seats in the Majilis, a percentage that remained almost unchanged in 2000 when women held eight seats out of seventy-seven in the Majilis, or a little more than 11 percent. The growing suicide rate among women in Kazakhstan is another indication of the hardship they face in a turbulent society.[138]

Reading between the lines of official statements gives more of a sense of the crisis in the education system than the government likes to admit. The state education committee asserts that it has taken pains to restore instruction in nursery, kindergarten, and primary schools that had been shut down. In 1998, 162 primary and secondary schools, 17 preschools, 29 vocational and technical schools, 20 night schools, and 4 boarding schools were reopened. The press release giving these figures did not, however, release any information on how many schools remained closed.[139] Far more could be done. When the Ministry of Internal Affairs sought to crack down on official shortfalls and thefts from within the Kazakh government, the biggest culprit was found to be the Ministry of Health, Education, and Social Welfare.[140]

Kazakhstan puts forward a misleading picture to the outside world. The new Kazakh elite, especially the young business people and lawyers with whom most foreigners deal, are able to function in a global environment. The kinds of skills that they demonstrate—fluency in English and a knowledge of market economics—are not representative of the population as a whole. These skills can be acquired only in a few elite schools and institutions, which are accessed through connections or by extraordinary merit. Almost all these schools are in Almaty. The practice of bribing admission committees and paying for diplomas is becoming more common as well, and respondents in a 1998 survey of students listed dishonest practices in schools as a major concern.[141]

The Elderly and the Disabled

The country's elderly are also suffering. Pensioners have been increasingly more disadvantaged since independence than any other group. As already discussed, the country began an ambitious new pension program on January 1, 1998. While this may better protect a future generation, it has not helped the government deal with the problems of the growing number of elderly who live in Kazakhstan. Their numbers were artificially reduced through the adoption of this legislation, when the retirement age went to sixty-five for both men and women (from sixty-three for men and fifty-eight for women), a change that substantially added to the number of hidden unemployed.[142] Yet the government has been tough on those who try and organize the country's pensioners.[143] Kazakhstan's disabled population has fared poorly as well, and helping them seems to be of no particular priority. In 1997 the government budgeted 413 million tenge to celebrate the anniversaries of Auezov and Turkestan.[144] At the same time, it allocated only 8 million tenge for people disabled by or who have lost a breadwinner to an ecological calamity.[145]

The Division between Believers and Nonbelievers

As the population becomes poorer, the potential appeal of extremist ideologies becomes greater, especially that of radical Islam, which generally cloaks its appeals in terms of righting socially inequitable situations. President Nazarbayev and his senior political advisers have always seen the management of religion as an important part of state building.

In many post-Soviet states the return to observance of a traditional and customary faith was taken as a sign of recovery. In Kazakhstan, religion has always been viewed as a potential source of opposition and a force that might stimulate interethnic conflict. The state has always closely monitored the activities of foreign religious organizations, fearing their seditious influence. Homegrown groups were usually viewed as acceptable; it was thought that their leaders understood the country's precarious interethnic situation and historical and cultural peculiarities. Initially the government took a relatively hands-off attitude toward Islam. Kazakhstan's security organs were more concerned with the activities of the various Protestant Pentecostal missionaries, those of Reverend Moon, and such groups as the Deva Maria cult since their activities seemed alien and at odds with Kazakhstan's "traditional" faiths, Islam and Russian Orthodoxy. Eventually Judaism was added to this list as well, when the trickling in of Russian capital from Israel turned into a flood.

Since the late 1990s Kazakhstan's leaders have become much more focused on the activities of Muslim missionaries. While hundreds of mosques and religious schools have been built in Kazakhstan over the past dozen years with funds from foreign countries (mostly from Turkey and Saudi Arabia), any foreigner not part of an official delegation who is caught "propagating" Islam is subject to rapid expulsion. Moreover, the Kazakh leaders seem to be offering a broader interpretation of what is included in missionary activities and have deported many people with little cause, including some who have come to visit relatives in Kazakhstan. In 2000 the government also began to recall students studying abroad in various Islamic academies and universities that were considered to be of a questionable nature.

The claims that religion makes upon adherents, particularly the insistence that true believers should not distinguish between private and public behavior, seems to unsettle the Kazakh government profoundly. In Kazakhstan the dictates of conscience cannot take precedence over those of the state, and religion is considered to be a private matter that cannot influence education or politics.

The Kazakh leaders fear Islam far more than they do Russian Orthodoxy. Islam remains the most visible religion in Kazakhstan. Ninety percent of the country's self-proclaimed religious believers profess Islam, and 1,150 of the country's 2,299 religious institutions are in some way associated with Kazakhstan's Muslim Ecclesiastic Administration.[146] Kazakhstan's officials often take great pains to put Russian Orthodoxy on at least near equal footing, and the country has 220 parishes and monasteries. In fact, President Nazarbayev was awarded the Order of Dmitri Donskoi by Patriarch Aleksei II (of all Russia) for the Kazakh leader's support of the restitution of Russian Orthodox institutions and practices in his countries. Other Christian groups periodically complain that they find it difficult to get state registration. By contrast, given the official desire to please some of Kazakhstan's industrial magnates, in recent years it has become easy for Jewish organizations to register in Kazakhstan. Although Kazakhstan has only 15,000 Jews left in the country and many of these plan to emigrate to Israel or the United States, the country has two active Jewish organizations, one sponsored by Aleksandr Mashkevich of the Eurasia Group and the other by Lev Leviev. The latter organization, associated with the world Lubavitcher movement, even has branches in eighteen cities in the country.[147]

The growing role of these Jewish figures serves as yet another reminder of the secular nature of the Kazakh state. So too do Kazakhstan's close ties to Israel, illustrated by Nazarbayev's well-publicized trip there in April 2000 that included meetings with potential large investors as well as leading Israeli officials. By this time it was already clear that there was not much investment capital forthcoming from Israel's Arab rivals, but Nazarbayev was careful to meet with Arafat as well.

Now Russian Jewish capital occupies such a prominent position in the country that it would be difficult to reorient Kazakhstan's foreign policy in the absence of a substantial redistribution of currently privately held assets. The prominence of Jewish investors is a constant irritant to Kazakhstan's small but more radical Muslim population and gives them a classic anti-Semitic formula around which to rally support.

There are many other reasons for the Kazakhstan government's nervousness about Islam. Initially the government feared that a surge in the public practice of Islam would intensify problems with the Russian and Cossack populations. With time, the risk of this has grown fainter, but a concern over the potential consequences of an Islamic revival for Kazakhstan's foreign image has grown as terrorist acts by extremists have become a major focus of international attention. Kazakhstan, for example, has pursued a relatively independent stance toward Iran, a posture that would have had a real impact on United States–Kazakh relations had the secular credentials of the nation's leadership been in doubt.

The greatest concern of Kazakhstan's leadership is with its perceived fitness to rule in the face of a major religious revival among the population it governs. The current ruling elite, most of whom are highly secularized and Europeanized, would clearly be unacceptable to a population that is strongly influenced by devout Islamic believers. Nursultan Nazarbayev even used to boast of being an atheist, and although he no longer makes such statements, he could never transform himself into a credible spiritual guide for a devout population.

There seems to be no danger that he will be called upon to do so anytime soon. Kazakhstan is the only Central Asian state that can truly call itself secular since it is the only state in the region that has not accorded Islam a special legal role. Still, it is hard to imagine that Kazakhstan will be able to maintain this position indefinitely, given the greater visibility of Islam in its neighboring states. At the same time, the specter of Islamic radicalism in the region is real, making the Kazakh rulers' defense of the secular nature of their society potentially more divisive.

The government has tried to deal with this by maintaining the Soviet-era distinction between religion as tradition and religion as faith, emphasizing the former while trying to restrict the latter to a matter of individual conscience. Muslim names, beliefs, and practices (often corrupted by or combined with pre-Islamic practices) are an integral part of Kazakh identity. Traditional Kazakh Islam retained many more pre-Muslim features than did the practice of the faith in the cities of Uzbekistan and southern Kyrgyzstan since the conversion of the Kazakh people was not completed until the eighteenth century. Further, the Kazakh nomadic life led worship to be more ritualistic than doctrinal. The Kazakhs lacked the elaborate systems of religious schools, shrines, and quartal (Muslim quarter) organizations that characterized the community of believers farther south. For this reason, the Nazarbayev government was optimistic that it could shape the development of Islam in independent Kazakhstan, and it hoped that official attempts to strengthen and encourage Kazakh identity would blend rather naturally to support "good" Islam, which it defined as traditional Kazakh culture and family practice.[148]

For nearly a decade of independence, Kazakhstan's rulers were able to proceed with a policy toward Islam that largely equated it with a locally based cultural system that had only rather tangential ties to global Islam.

These were to be orchestrated as much as possible by Kazakhstan's state-appointed religious authorities. The management of Kazakhstan's Islamic establishment was turned over to Ratbek-kazi Nysynbaiuly, who had changed his name from Nysanbayev in January 1990 when Kazakhstan's Muslim Ecclesiastic Administration began to function as an independent body. He held this post until June 2000, when he was replaced by Absattar Derbisaliyev, who had previously served as a diplomat at Kazakhstan's embassy in Saudi Arabia. Although he was trained as an orientalist, he lacks formal religious education. Mufti Derbisaliyev was appointed to keep a firm hold over the country's religious believers, and there is no way that they can think of him as one of theirs.

Throughout his tenure in office, Mufti Nysanbayev allowed his understanding of Islam and its needs to be more shaped by the government than by the congregation he was appointed to serve. He was no friend of Islamic radicals, and in 1991 he was attacked in his office near an Almaty mosque by a group of dissident Muslim activists who were members of the nationalist Alash party.[149]

Yet, perhaps surprisingly, the decade following this attack was peaceful in its civil-religious relations, this in a part of the world where there has been much religious-inspired violence. Still, although Islamic radicalism poses no direct threat in Kazakhstan, in the past few years the government has begun to think that it may pose an indirect one. In 1998 so-called Wahhabi missionaries (the usual term for Islamic activists) were arrested in Kazakhstan. These included a group of six missionaries from Pakistan.[150] Missionaries from Egypt, Sudan, and Jordan have been charged with crimes, a Turkish citizen was reprimanded for teaching Wahhabism, and an Uzbek citizen was deported for religious activities.[151]

Kazakhstan's persecution of religious believers increased after the February 1999 bombings in Tashkent and the siege in Kyrgyzstan's Osh oblast in the summer and fall of 2000.[152] These events have also led the Kazakh government to increase its spending on defense and internal security.[153] Kazakhstan has taken a firm position against Islamic extremism. When Russia was considering air strikes against Afghanistan in May 2000, Kazakhstan announced that it might allow overflights for Russian aircraft.[154] Kazakhstan has also advocated CIS security directives aimed at eradicating Islamic extremists in Central Asia and supported strengthening the CIS Collective Security Treaty in 2001 by creating a multinational force designed to help contain extremist-inspired terrorist threats. Nazarbayev also quickly offered support for U.S. George Bush's war against terrorism.

The government has visibly expanded the role of security forces in Kazakhstan society since the rise of the Islamic threat in the region, and in June 2001 former Minister of the Interior Kairbek Suleimenov was appointed as the commander of the country's expanding internal security force. Before that the government had closed what it claims to be training camps of Islamic militants in the mountains outside Almaty, and in January 2001 it set up a new special antiterrorism force. Some observers claim that these arrests were the too-convenient actions of a government determined to prove that a threat existed.[155]

There is no question, however, that Islamic missionaries have been active in all parts of the country, and mosques and religious schools have been opened in even the most Russified of Kazakh communities. Still, missionary activity is not the same as the propagation of militant Islam. That most Kazakhs had little knowledge of Islam at independence makes all the more significant the growth of religious observance. A July 1996 survey and analysis at the Institute of Development speaks of a growth in the number of Islamic institutions in the republic from forty-four in 1989 to more than six hundred in 1996,[156] and as already noted, the number of formally registered institutions has doubled since then.

Nearly all observers agree that Kazakhstan's Islamic revival has had the greatest societal impact in the southern part of the country, especially in the areas that border Uzbekistan and where Kazakhstan's Uzbek population is concentrated. Local Uzbeks seem to have served as a catalyst. The same 1996 survey found that Uzbeks were the most religious group in Kazakhstan, with 75.8 percent of respondents denoting themselves as believers, compared with 39.7 percent for the entire population and 47.1 percent for Kazakhs. The term *believer* is a vague one and may connote little more than a self-identification with Islam or adherence to a fundamentalist sect. This makes it even more interesting that the largest group of Kazakhs that identified themselves as believers were those who were in the age bracket 18 to 29. That argues for something more than cultural continuity and is evidence of Kazakhstan's religious revival. In addition, the greatest proportion of believers was those with secondary, technical, or incomplete secondary education. Only 15.8 percent of those claiming to be believers were people with higher education.

It is possible to read too much into such figures. Nevertheless, they do suggest the pressures that are very much in evidence elsewhere in the Muslim world. The attraction of Islam, and particularly of the strict observance of the faith, has been strongest in those societies that have large, poor, and very young populations. As noted above, the course of economic and social differentiation since independence has brought conditions in Kazakhstan to resemble those in other societies where the tug of Islam is strong—particularly in the southern oblasts that are the republic's poorest, most populous, and most heavily Kazakh. More recent studies have drawn similar conclusions. A 1998 survey of university students in Shymkent reported that 80 percent of the sample claimed to be believers. Yet more than half of these (44 percent) said that they went to the mosque only once a year. This shows that the extent to which identification with Islam is seen simply as an aspect of national culture. The understanding of Islam, and of its role in the national culture, can change over time, and since 11 percent of those surveyed said that they believed that the development of religious fundamentalism in Kazakhstan was inevitable, there is certainly an important constituency that believes that religion is likely to play a much greater role in the life of the country over time.[157]

A nationwide study of nearly two thousand adults commissioned by the USIA in August and September 1997 had similar findings.[158] Here the question was posed in terms of whether the government should be based on Muslim Shari'a law. Thirty percent of the Muslims surveyed said that it should, while 55 percent preferred to be ruled by secular laws.[159] Seventy-seven percent of the Muslims surveyed said that they were believers, but fewer than half (48 percent) could name a single pillar, or obligation, of Islam. Still, an overwhelming majority of the Muslims interviewed (61 percent) said that Islamic religious leaders should play a large role in Kazakhstan's public life. In this study the term *Muslim* was used to denote anyone of Muslim background, and not only a religious believer or practitioner.

This is not to suggest that Kazakhstan is in danger of "going Muslim" in the near future. The Kazakhs of tomorrow are likely to be much more differentiated one from the other than they are today. In the specific case of religion, this differentiation in faith could easily acquire overtones of political and economic competition. The orientation of the winners of Kazakhstan's economic transformation is overwhelmingly toward Europe and the West. Many, like President Nazarbayev himself, are still Soviet-era bureaucrats who tend to equate religion, and especially Islam, with backwardness or ignorance, while others, especially the younger members of the elite, tend to characterize Islam by the restrictions it places on public behavior, the way women must dress, and what people can eat and drink.

As the differences between the educational and economic levels of young Kazakhs grow, it will be more and more tempting for the large group of those without luxuries, benefits, or hopes to attack the much smaller group of the privileged on the grounds of the latter's alleged religious impiety. It will be equally easy for those lucky few to interpret the challenge to their position at the top of Kazakhstan's society as springing from religious dem-agoguery, rather than from a predictable response of a dispossessed people in a society that has rapidly become inequitable.

7

Can Kazakhstan Regain Its Promise?

Kazakhstan, just as most of the other states born of the collapsed USSR, is still something of an international novelty. Its existence is recent enough that analysts tend to concentrate much of their attention on forecasting the country's future, trying to determine from the nation's inventory of actual and potential assets and liabilities what kind of country Kazakhstan will be in another decade and beyond. Suggestions have naturally varied widely, depending on whether one chooses to emphasize Kazakhstan's enormous wealth that could be shared among a small population, or whether one underscores Kazakhstan's demographically riven society and its venal ruling elite.

Generally underlying both the negative and positive scenarios is the assumption that the United States is able to do something about shaping the course of political and economic developments in Kazakhstan. The country's relative newness creates a perception that the state of Kazakhstan is rather like a figurine that has been sculpted out of clay but not yet fired, so that it can still be shaped and reshaped for a while. Although foreign actors may still have some input, the time of their maximum potential effectiveness may well have passed.

Ten years into statehood Kazakhstan's political and economic structures are growing more fixed, even if there is some elasticity left in the system. Much can happen in a decade. Kazakhstan has been independent longer than Mikhail Gorbachev's entire tenure as head of the Soviet Union or the whole of World War II. This period is sufficiently long to allow us to at least observe a pattern in the way that issues are addressed and responses are framed. Each decision taken or ignored, each policy promulgated or abandoned, reduces the potential choices available for Kazakhstan's unrealized future, just as each step taken by degrees becomes a path, along which future options inevitably grow fewer, even as they grow defined.

This is not to suggest, however, that Kazakhstan has passed, or indeed is even approaching, any sort of Rubicon. One of the most striking features of the post-Soviet period, and especially of recent years, is the way that the tempo of history in the former Soviet republics appears to have slowed, certainly in comparison with the frenzy of the years from 1989 to 1991. The first catastrophes of economic collapse, currency creation, population transfer, and intra-elite competition are over, leaving political environments that, in most of the new states at least, seem relatively stable for the indefinite future, at least in comparison to many other states.

Yet the seeds of the country's future problems have already been sown. The formal collapse of the Soviet Union was brought about by a sharp series of crises, but only because the system was made vulnerable by the slow accumulation of problems unsolved or ignored during long decades of apparent stability.

The state-building process in Kazakhstan can be considered either a failure or a success, depending on the criteria adopted. The country still exists and seems in no danger of disappearing from the international community any time soon. Russia, now under two presidents, has accepted the idea of Kazakhstan's statehood, and with every passing year it seems less likely that some future Russian regime will challenge this status quo. Prospects for improved Russian cooperation with the United States and Western Europe should add to Kazakhstan's growing sense of security.

The Kazakhs will always remain wary. Nationalism is a powerful mobilizing tool in Russia, and it seems certain to stay so for a while, until that state becomes competent to meet its social obligations and the country's economy has been restored. The armed forces of Kazakhstan are no match for those of Russia, and the Astana government must hope that international pressure will keep a potentially belligerent Russian government from behaving aggressively, if reform in Russia were to be derailed. This is one reason that Kazakhstan has tried to create so many foreign stakeholders in its natural resource development projects; powerful Western energy companies bring with them the enhanced possibility of important diplomatic support.

Leaders in Moscow or maverick elements in a weakened Russian security apparatus are still capable of creating complex provocations that could push restive elements in the local Russian population into using force to convey their displeasure. To date, though, they have declined to do so in any significant way, and the Russian government seems to be accepting the preference of Kazakhstan's own Russian community to leave the country rather than to protest its exclusion from Kazakhstan's political life. The sense of resignation that prevails in the Russian community has contributed to the virtual absence of bloodshed in the country. From the point of view of the Kazakh elite, this is already a great victory and is more than most Kazakhs expected several years ago.

Independence has also led to an unexpected accumulation of economic power by a small elite that believed it could translate political power into economic wealth but never envisioned the scale on which this was possible. There has been an economic revolution of sorts in Kazakhstan, and privatization has gone further here than in most post-Soviet states, as has the introduction of a legal infrastructure necessary to support foreign investment. At the same time, the majority of citizens are living in more strained circumstances than they were before independence; official statistics claim that roughly half the population lives below the poverty line. This creates new political risks for the regime because economic power has not been dispersed equally throughout Kazakhstan's society.

Initially, the government had a simplistic view of how the transition would occur and hoped that it could translate the country's considerable natural resources into an ample state treasury. The idea was that if there was enough to go around, no one would care too much that a small elite had amassed a vast amount of political and economic control. The new National Oil Fund may well serve its stated function of using oil revenues to stimulate economic development and to help the government meet its social obligations. Nearly a billion dollars had been deposited in it by July 1, 2001, and the government plans the fund to reach $1.5 billion by the end of 2001. The transition to a market economy, however, has proved far more difficult than anticipated, and the perquisites associated with it far grander than anyone dreamed at first. Frightened that it will lose power, the elite has been trying to shape new political institutions that will maximize its control. This creates a potentially dangerous situation for the future, especially as efforts to inculcate patriotism in people are proving far more challenging than the leaders anticipated.

The Nazarbayev family has become the dominant economic force in the country, with tentacles that reach into every part of the economy. They are not just interested in stripping Kazakhstan of its wealth. While some of the money it skims from the economy is clearly going offshore, the ruling family is also committed to keeping part of its assets as working capital. The family recognizes that to do this it needs to encourage foreign investment, which in turn means that there must be some level of transparency in the way that the country's new companies do business. As a result, Kazakhstan is developing a small class of independent entrepreneurs whose activities are sometimes hampered but who retain the hope that the conditions under which they do business might still improve. Yet in many important respects, economic power is more restricted today than it was before, although it is a local elite that dominates—not one sent from Moscow.

This is somehow intended to be reassuring to Kazakhstan's citizens, as though moral superiority is somehow accrued through the transfer of power. To try to convince people of this, the government has developed an official ideology that stresses the importance of the Kazakhs' being in charge in their own home. This is being done with a certain amount of sleight of hand since the same person who was to protect Moscow's interests, Nursultan Nazarbayev, is now alleged to be the recipient of the national trust. The emphasis is on developing a sense of symbolic control rather than on empowering the population. This strategy has pushed the ruling elite to embrace policies that stimulate ethnonationalism rather than multiculturalism because that best serves their ends.

Nazarbayev and his close allies have used their accumulated power for personal advantage and have given relatively little thought to creating political institutions that will facilitate an orderly transfer of authority. Instead, their actions have made the inevitable transfer of authority more difficult. The opportunities for expressing political displeasure have grown limited over time, as the country has gone from a fledgling democracy to a state that is more interested in imitating democratic institutions than in implementing them.

President Nazarbayev has successfully manipulated the country's electoral system so that it should enable him to rule for life, but he has not yet satisfactorily addressed what will happen when he must inevitably pass from the political scene. Unlike the president of Turkmenistan, the Kazakh president seems to suffer no illusions of immortality, and there is mounting evidence that he would like to transfer power to another member of his family, preferably in his lifetime, so that he can orchestrate a successful transition. Since Nazarbayev has no sons, this complicates the prospects for a dynastic succession but does not eliminate the possibility. Even if Nazarbayev succeeds in passing power to a relative or in-law, eventually Kazakhstan will have to confront the limitations of contest and competition in the political system that Kazakhstan's first president has created.

The current elite structure resembles that of a society at risk of a messy succession struggle. There are several potential successors and no institutions in place to regulate their claims. No one would claim that Kazakhstan is currently on the brink of a civil war, but it is clearly a state in stress.

Violent crime has risen during the past decade, and the murder and suicide rates have risen substantially. Greater government attention to crime fighting has had some effect, although the manipulation of official statistics may exaggerate the impact of such improvements.[1] Criminal gangs have become deeply rooted in Kazakh society. The narcotics trade is flourishing throughout Central Asia, and Kazakhstan is an important conduit, further corrupting the country's security organizations.[2] At their worst Kazakhstan's security organizations are like semi-autonomous agencies, openly seeking bribes from all who traverse their territory. This atmosphere of lawlessness has caused rivalries, and the police and security forces have sometimes openly and violently clashed.[3] Police brutality is also said to be a serious problem.[4]

As earlier noted, the security forces have been reorganized to address these problems, and the recentralization of authority that has been introduced substantially lessens the prospect that the country can split into competing armed camps, especially given the expanded control exerted by Rakhat Aliyev and other members of the Nazarbayev family. Still, these efforts do little to address corruption at the grassroots level and nothing to eliminate the underlying societal malaise that caused such incidents.

The Kazakhs are developing a new legal system, and Kazakh lawyers and judges are receiving Western training. There is no real rule of law in the country, however, since no one really expects the legal system to afford any protection. Corruption remains pervasive, and influence can be purchased at all levels of government. In Kazakhstan it is often difficult to distinguish between law-abiding citizens and criminal offenders because even the best-intentioned must resort to bribery to protect property and family. With time, criminal and noncriminal behavior has begun to blend in Kazakhstan. Those who do not find ways to bend the rules are simply unable to function in Kazakh society or to provide for their families.

Societies that have such flawed legal systems and that lack well-established political parties, independent trade unions, and other political and social organizations often have difficult transition struggles. In the absence of political institutions to regulate the process, President Nazarbayev is simply hoping that his recommendation of a political successor will suffice. If Nazarbayev is to succeed in transferring power in this fashion, he must increase public confidence in his judgment by demonstrating that his priority lies with the people formally entrusted to his protection.

The population's expectations of the government obviously have to be reshaped from what they were during the Soviet period. The burden of social welfare has shifted from being exclusively a responsibility of the government to a burden shared with the individual. This shift may have been necessary to allow Kazakhstan to reduce public spending and stimulate economic growth, but such a change in expectations is easier when the government enjoys public confidence.

Kazakhstan's government has devoted considerable resources, especially in its early years, to various patriotism-building efforts, but political socialization does not exist in a vacuum. The credibility of the Nazarbayev government is affected by how much people's lives have deteriorated since the government came to power and whether it is seen as responsible for it.

The words of rulers are often at odds with their actions. It is hard to imagine that Kazakhstan's ordinary citizens are not disturbed by the behavior of Kazakhstan's governing elite. The typical Kazakh family includes people who are unemployed, on a pension, or in some way dependent on social welfare payments. In 1996, for example, when pension arrears were still commonplace, 2.5 billion tenge went astray, presumably siphoned by corrupt officials for their personal use. Ordinary citizens may not have known about it, but they were certainly aware of such common practices as diverting electrical and heating lines intended for factories to the private homes of officials; giving automobiles intended as prizes for top workers to factory officials; and using credits to factories for the purchase of homes and trips abroad and for private investment by state and industry officials. These practices are well established and are known through rumor, partially corroborated by press accounts.

The behavior of many of Kazakhstan's public figures so flagrantly violates the spirit of state building expounded by the government in solemn-sounding ideological pronouncements that only the most ardent patriots can be moved by the official rhetoric. Even their fervor is likely to be dampened by the spectacle of prominent nationalists who have been bought with comfortable government sinecures. Kazakhstan's leaders have not demonstrated civic responsibility. Rather, the model of public behavior ascendant in Kazakhstan is one of self-aggrandizement and self-enrichment, no matter the cost to the state, to its further development, or to one's fellow citizens. In such an atmosphere, the creation of "Kazakhstanis," a population who view themselves as sharing interests and duties with the millions of others with whom they share the territory of the republic, is a difficult, if not impossible, process.

Looking Ahead

State building is a complicated business. Nazarbayev's willingness to advance personal gain over public good has made it more difficult in Kazakhstan. Kazakhstan had a real chance to carve for itself a separate national identity—not simply one that stressed the distinctiveness of Kazakh history and culture from that of the history and culture of other peoples in the region. Kazakhstan could have become a secular multi-ethnic democratic state with a thriving market economy. Many of the preconditions for this existed when the country received independence, including a diverse and well-developed economy, a highly skilled and educated population, and the beginnings of independent media and independent political groups.

Although Kazakhstan could never have achieved the twin goals of democratization and market reform in the space of a decade, it wasted the opportunity to make genuine strides in that direction. While the government may not have done irreversible harm—and it is certainly too early to talk about the squandering of Kazakhstan's statehood—the country's rulers have not made the most of the opportunities that fate and good fortune gave to the Kazakh people for the public's benefit. Instead, they have judged themselves by the yardstick of what rulers were doing in neighboring states and found the comparisons to be in their favor.

The political economy literature is filled with articles about whether resource-poor nations do better than resource-rich nations. Poorer nations are said to avoid the perils of a resource-dependent and export-driven economy.[5] Still, it would be a gross oversimplification to argue that had Kazakhstan been poorer, its leaders would have been more honest. The patterns of official corruption that have developed in Kazakhstan are replicated throughout the former Soviet Union and are found in other parts of the post-Communist world as well. Even in resource-poor states, leaders find ways to extract "rents" from the economy and use their political power to create economic resources—such as profiting on the difference between official and unofficial exchange rates and skimming money from the drug trade—when few are naturally available.

Kazakhstan's economic diversity remains a source of future national strength, and while its potential has not been realized, nor has it been squandered. The opportunity for maximizing popular involvement in the economic transition has been missed, while the threshold that independent entrepreneurs have to surmount is continually being raised. Lost political opportunities seem greater still. The aspirations for representative government that were stimulated in the late Gorbachev years are steadily diminishing. With them the hopes that Kazakhstan can become a culturally diverse society in which citizenship and not ethnicity confers political status have also grown dimmer.

Kazakhstan is becoming more mononational, and ethnic Kazakhs are serving as the source of the country's new national identity. Simply designating a group of political winners gives little substance to a national identity. Kazakh history is being mined for suitable lessons. It can serve as a basic code of morality, but it cannot serve as a handbook for state building. Other sources need to be found to fill the gaps. Kazakh leaders must do more than create a new national identity. They must also undo the old one. The old hybrid Soviet identity, which was simultaneously part ethnonational and part supra-ethnic, is dying out, without anything particularly concrete taking its place. Russians, and even some ethnic Kazakhs, may still be nostalgic about the Soviet past, but they are realizing that there is no recapturing it.

The slow collapse of Soviet mass information networks may have made the process of political reidentification longer than might originally have been expected but no less inevitable. The young people of tomorrow—who will no longer share army service, university dormitories, or even, in many states, common television programs—will know much less about one another than did the generation before. Human nature being what it is, it seems probable that this ignorance may also make people less tolerant of one another. The way history is being taught will heighten this intolerance. The Kazakhs are now free to define their history as they please. Like most new nations, they are doing so in ways that irritate their neighbors and even one another. Each of the region's major peoples can claim historic roots that go well beyond current borders and groups in power. Each country can rewrite the past to emphasize its own special role.

Had it been redefined deliberately to emphasize common core values, the shared Soviet experience might have been a building block for a multi-ethnic form of national identity in Kazakhstan. Instead, that identity is fading. Knowledge of the Russian language will provide a cultural affinity for all Kazakhstan's peoples, especially since Russians and other Slavs will continue to make up about between a fifth and a quarter, respectively, of Kazakhstan's population well into the future. The role of Russian culture is certain to be continually redefined, in part because the old Soviet-era institutions necessary to maintain Russia's central cultural role are disappearing.

The Kazakh culture will continue to assert itself, but the collapse of shared institutions across the former territory of the Soviet Union has also meant the collapse of those institutions within each new state. The old Soviet-era museums, libraries, and cultural centers are gone. As these have vanished, little has emerged to replace them, even in Kazakhstan, where the local governments are not as financially limited as in many other countries. Some showplace museums have been built and new monuments erected to commemorate Kazakh statehood, but the kind of cultural penetration to the remotest parts of the country that was a defining feature of the Soviet Union is a thing of the past. At the same time, many in Kazakhstan are more closely integrated in the global culture than at any time before. These people have new tools at their disposal. Those who can afford it are free to study and travel abroad, and even ordinary people living in the country's leading cities often enjoy access to a wider world through the Internet.

Today the experiences, worldviews, and, ultimately, future prospects of the young people within Kazakhstan are also diverging in ways that were never true in the Soviet past. The gap between rich and poor is growing, as is the difference in the life experiences of urban and rural populations. The state has mandated a uniform education system, but not the funds to pay for it, and educational standards vary greatly today, far more than in the past. The children of the elite go to private schools, while many in the countryside do not have the money for the clothing necessary for year-round school attendance. The old state transportation system is being replaced by a far more costly private one, and most of Kazakhstan's citizens can no longer afford to travel freely across the country, an ability they used to enjoy. National media now dominate the airwaves, but many communities provide electricity sporadically, or with interruptions, and few Kazakhs in the countryside have the money to replace old Soviet-era televisions and radios when they inevitably break. Thus the Kazakh youth of the future will be more ignorant not only of their neighbors in Russia and elsewhere, but are equally likely to be ignorant of one another, their own compatriots.

The old Soviet identity was shaped by three generations of shared experiences, shared curriculum, and the pan-Soviet entertainment and information industry, which reached to the most distant localities. The elements of this shared Soviet identity linger, even if the state itself has disappeared, and have helped to keep the post-Soviet environment mostly free of ethnic tension, given the number of points of potential conflict that exist. The elite of the various states, for all that they disagree on fundamental issues, share a common language not only in the literal sense, since they are all still most comfortable speaking Russian (at least in their official interstate capacities), but also in the broader sense of knowing the same songs and jokes, recalling the same slogans of the past, and, in general, sharing similar assumptions and worldviews, whatever their ethnic heritage.

An attempt has been made to transform the Kazakh cultural identity into a national ideology, in part to serve as a substitute for those integrating experiences and institutions. Yet this ideology remains formless and inchoate and could devolve into more elemental forms of identity. A state ideology based on Kazakh history and culture will not appeal to Russians and most other non-Kazakhs, although there will be fewer young Russians and other Europeans in Kazakhstan in fifteen to twenty years than there are today.

It is far from clear whether the current environment can facilitate the creation of a shared identity among the Kazakhs themselves, one sufficient to serve as an ideological glue to keep together a stable polity. The Kazakhs have no modern history of independent statehood. They were a loosely defined ethnonational group whose elites were grappling with the question of shared identity when Stalin decreed them to be a "nation" fit for republic status.[6] Their fundament of loyalty was families and clans, people linked to each other directly by blood, even though the horde structure became more attenuated during the half century of Russian colonial rule. This is precisely why the Kazakh intellectuals who took up the question of their identity in the years before the Bolshevik Revolution differed about how—and whether—they were to be differentiated from the other peoples of the steppe region. Since that question was unresolved by the Kazakhs themselves, a sense of allegiance to smaller subunits continued beneath the surface of Soviet life and has reemerged since independence.

The interaction of Russian and Kazakh history has given the three hordes different fates, both during the period of colonial rule and that of Soviet power. It has left the families of the Great Horde in a position of political and economic dominance in the republic. Independence is once again reshaping the relationship between economic and political power and may be laying the foundation for the community to divide along subethnic lines, as has occurred in many parts of Africa.

In Soviet days the control of the Communist Party was key. Patronage and the pilferage of state assets had the value of economic goods and were a perquisite of power. Independence has meant that the control of these assets is up for grabs, except that now there is no one at the top watching how the assets are managed or who is awarded ownership. As a result, the control of Kazakhstan's natural wealth has gone disproportionately to those who began independence in charge of the state. These people have managed to turn much of that wealth into their own personal property precisely because of mechanisms afforded them by turning Kazakhstan into a quasi-market economy.

The current economic structure is intrinsically an unstable one. In a real market economy the relation between state power and economic power is inevitably a dynamic one. Assets that are judged to have been illegally acquired can be renationalized by successor regimes. Money sent abroad is much harder to trace and reclaim. The ruling family has asserted control over numerous valuable assets. If rumors are to be credited, they have a dominant position in most sectors of the economy and are growing more proficient at skimming profits from state-owned assets through the control of their management.[7]

What will the family do with their dominant position? Will they try to turn their wealth into transparent privately owned assets, in which case they will have to continue to work toward the development of a legal system in which others can also blatantly acquire and maintain assets? What seems more probable is that they will use their continued control of the legal system to introduce transparency only where necessary to meet unrelenting foreign pressure and will seek to expand family control (both kin and "court") of the economy wherever possible.

As the oligarchical group's share of Kazakhstan's economy grows even more, it is likely that its determination to continue the existing political arrangements will grow apace, since it will have more to lose. The most likely scenario for Kazakhstan's immediate future is therefore continued emphasis on stability, ensured either by not having elections at all or, if these somehow need to be held, by holding them under conditions that will reduce any uncertainty about their outcome to the smallest amount possible.

It is difficult to predict how long the Kazakh population will tolerate the current situation. There has been an enormous redistribution of wealth in Kazakhstan since independence. The gap in the incomes of the richest 10 percent and the poorest 10 percent was fourfold in the pretransition years; by 1998, it was more than elevenfold. The richest 10 percent received 27 percent of the national income, while the poorest 10 percent received 2.3 percent.[8] The current pattern of how the costs and benefits of economic transformation are distributed across the republic could create widening gulfs between the various populations in Kazakhstan, without providing many institutions capable of bridging the gaps between the haves and have-nots, or of ameliorating the hostilities that these gaps provoke. Disadvantaged people frequently seek an explanation for their failure to flourish. It is probable that Kazakhs will notice, for example, that the economically and educationally advantaged youth and young adults of the next century are most likely to be members of the Great Horde, while the poor and ignorant of the countryside, or of the dead factory and mining towns of the north, are more likely to be from one of the Small or Middle Hordes.

One should not exaggerate the amount of intra-Kazakh dissension that already exists, or too strongly suggest that horde rivalries are the sole basis of such intra-Kazakh tension. Nevertheless, many of the most heated political battles in the republic to date have been between President Nazarbayev and other Kazakhs. This tendency will increase over time.

It is natural for the focus of tension to be turned within the Kazakh elite, for the Nazarbayev regime has made the reward for state capture enormous, and the members of the elite are the ones who feel empowered by independence to seize such opportunities. Hypnotized by the apparent threat of the large Russian population and convinced that stability means, in the words of a presidential spokesman, "no protest against the system," it has become easier for Kazakhstan's elite to see the state's interests as synonymous with its own. This has led the elite effectively to sabotage from within whatever formal efforts have been made at political reform, and it may have made the opposition elite and the general population alike doubtful of the ability of Western institutions to serve as a basis for meaningful political reforms.

President Nazarbayev has spoken frequently of the need for each nation to develop its own brand of democracy and political culture. Yet the institutional arrangements available for power sharing are limited. This scuttling of reform from within will make it more difficult to modify the political system in an orderly or peaceful fashion in the near future. The people of Kazakhstan seem to be aware of the pitfalls of the growing concentration of power in the hands of a small elite and of a continued insistence that Kazakhstan remain an undifferentiated "unitary republic." A 1996 study conducted by the president's Institute for Strategic Studies found that 74 percent of respondents felt that there were too few political actors in the republic, and 62 percent felt that there were too few economic actors. More telling is that only 12 percent of the respondents felt that the entire spectrum of political ideas was being represented in an organized way in the republic.[9]

Political power is becoming synonymous with economic power, as the Kazakh state comes to resemble that of the world's other raw material suppliers, with a small native elite with enormous and growing personal wealth, a chronically underfinanced state apparatus that relies on foreign borrowing or the sale of natural resources to function, and a general populace that grows poorer and more ignorant as it grows larger.

For better or for worse, Kazakhstan will probably move toward further consolidation of the present system, which appears to lie somewhere between autocracy and oligarchy. As noted earlier, the tendency in political life in Kazakhstan, just as across much of the former Soviet Union, has been toward the preservation of the existing elites, who grow ever more entrenched as their finances improve. This is certainly the predominant pattern throughout Central Asia. In Russia, at least, this preservation has been maintained through elections that have been acknowledged, even by those who have lost, to have been essentially fair. While conceding that the electoral playing field is far from level because of the near monopoly on information maintained by the ruling elite, experts on Russian politics point out that this drive to control the media is itself a testament to the new importance of elections, which have become the way that power gains legitimacy in Russia.

Even this limited respect for elections seems unlikely in Kazakhstan. Following the lead of the region's other presidents, Nazarbayev has extended his own term of office into the new millennium and has rewritten the constitution to reduce parliament to little more than a cheering section, which he can suspend at will if the cheering fades. Although continuing to work through the formal structure of a government, Nazarbayev has also increasingly resorted to rule by fiat. The cabinet reflects his will, and all the local administrators must do his bidding. Political censorship may have tightened since the first days of independence, and the republic's security forces have been more in evidence, but Nazarbayev has been able to accomplish a consolidation of his power without recourse to overtly despotic means.

He very much enjoys the trappings of power that come with being the head of state of a potentially wealthy nation, which appears to shape his political judgment. He is a proud man, and one who does not seem to take criticism well. After being repeatedly humbled as a Soviet-era leader, this latter trait has become more pronounced with time. This means that he is certainly turning a deaf ear to any who seek to warn him of the dangers implicit in his consolidation of economic and political power by the members of his family. As this power grows, those willing even to contemplate discussing the matter with the president are sure to diminish.

There is little reason for ordinary Kazakhs to support the establishment of a Nazarbayev political dynasty, which would go against Kazakh cultural norms and the political and economic interests of most ordinary citizens. Similarly, other authoritarian or semi-authoritarian rulers have tried building dynasties, frequently leading to civil war after the death of the political incumbent, when the designated heir fails to consolidate power successfully.

Kazakhs may be publicly loath to criticize Nazarbayev's consolidation of power in the hands of his family because every good Kazakh is expected to take care of his relatives. So Nazarbayev's favoring of his various in-laws is culturally reinforced behavior that has survived the decades of Soviet rule with little modification. It would be wrong, however, to argue that dynastic rule would somehow be a natural one given the Kazakhs' history or their socioeconomic and cultural evolution in the past two hundred years. It is true that the Kazakhs were ruled by *khans* from the sixteenth through part of the eighteenth century, but the system of noble rule deteriorated steadily from that time until the mid-nineteenth century, when Russian colonial officials abolished it. Kazakhstan's three hordes managed to survive seventy years of Soviet rule, albeit being transformed in the process. Prominent families from the Small and Middle Hordes will not be willing to sit quietly by if power and wealth were to become almost exclusively associated with a Great Horde family. Nazarbayev has rivals within his own horde as well. Of course, this leaves aside the fact that ethnic Kazakhs make up just slightly more than 50 percent of the population and that key sectors of the economy are controlled by other groups.

This said, Nazarbayev's hold on power remains great. He might well be capable of appointing a successor (from either within or outside of his family) and have that choice confirmed by a majority of the Kazakh population. This could be accomplished through popular referendum, because Kazakhstan's constitution has proved itself to be an elastic document. Nazarbayev, though, lacks a natural heir. Much will depend on who Nazarbayev chooses and whether the family is united in that choice. Some have speculated that Nazarbayev may choose his younger brother's son, Kairat Saltybaldy, who to date has been an invisible figure in the country. This would be a choice that would be closest to Kazakh dynastic tradition. He could also choose a daughter. There are strong women in Kazakh history, but no female rulers. The choice of a daughter would seem less fraught with problems than that of a son-in-law. Nazarbayev's daughter Dariga is seen as doing well in her public appearances. She is said to have intuitive political skill and could manage to reach out to leading elite groups in Kazakhstan in an effort at constituent building that includes power sharing. Dariga has the liability, however, of not being Nazarbayev's biological daughter but Sara Alpysovna's child from her first marriage.

Nazarbayev could choose a son-in-law, but picking one over the other could spark heated competition between the separate elite groups that are close to each of these men. The two already show signs of behaving more like rivals than allies, and each is garnering supporters and assets to use in rewarding them. Competition between the two heightened in November 2001, when Dariga's husband, Rakhat Aliyev, was pushed out as deputy head of the country's national security forces by maneuverings of Nazarbayev's security chief, Marat Tazhin, a close friend of Timur Kulibayev. Until then Aliyev controlled the country's atomic energy industry, with its uranium and uranium-processing plants, and he may even have been the facilitator for some of the country's burgeoning illicit arms trade.[10] Timur Kulibayev, the president of TransNefteGaz, is married to Dinara, who is much less of a public figure.[11] The son of a former Communist Party first secretary from what is now oil-rich Atyrau, the youthful Kulibayev has a powerful commercial empire under his direct control, including, most prominently, exclusive oversight for the transport of all Kazakhstan's oil and gas reserves as well as shares in various other firms through his reported stake in Kazkommertsbank. Kulibayev, though, still faces the challenge of fully consolidating his position in Kazakhstan's oil industry. Former Prime Minister and Kazakhoil President Nurlan Balgimbayev is still a formidable actor who would know how to use the Russia card to his own advantage. Kulibayev has also been currying favor with some of the younger players in Russia's labyrinthine energy industry, and Russia's competing elite groupings are certain to be drawn into any succession struggle that might develop.

Elite politics in Kazakhstan are fluid, and blood ties are only one factor among many. Much will depend upon whether Nazarbayev attempts to transfer power during his lifetime or dies while in office.[12] If the latter occurs, the elite is sure to demonstrate its capacity to reorganize itself along new lines. Family-based oligarchies, young entrepreneurs with Western skills and contacts, those with ties to Russia and its economic elites, and critics of the president who have been grouped around the parliament, as well as Nazarbayev's vocal opponents living in exile, will all vie to improve their positions. We have already seen some of the fluidity of Kazakhstan's elite politics after each change of prime minister. A fight for control within the Nazarbayev political dynasty, even during Nazarbayev's lifetime, would have interesting and unpredictable outcomes as Nazarbayev's two eldest sons-in-law seek to enlist allies at home and abroad. This is not to say that the country's neighbors will be drawn in or that Kazakhstan will turn into another Congo, but the potential for a rift within the Kazakh elite is strong. Different factions could look for foreign patrons.

A Role for Foreign Patrons?

Any sign that succession is growing nearer will pique the interest of foreign actors. A succession struggle gives new levers to powerful neighbors able to provide security guarantees. All nations are dependent upon the goodwill of their neighbors, but the situation with Kazakhstan, which shares one of the longest open international borders in the world, makes the country's relation with Russia a defining one.

The passing of political authority to President Nazarbayev's successor will be a period of real risk to the country and might even contribute to the country's dismemberment if things should go horribly wrong. Nationalism might surge again in Russia in a particularly aggressive form at a time when Kazakhstan's Russians seem intent on demonstrating that the plight of these "Sudeten Russians" was beyond endurance. If all this were to occur, then

Russia might consider supporting a Russian Cossack–driven effort to declare northern Kazakhstan autonomous in actions reminiscent of those that led to the formation of the Transdniester Republic within Moldova.

This is highly improbable, however, given both the current international climate and, what is perhaps more important, Russia's own strategic priorities as well as its military and economic fragility. Even in the unlikely event that Russia were single-mindedly to encourage Russian separatist sentiment with an eye to engineering the splitting of the republic along ethnic lines, only a portion of Kazakhstan's richest natural resources would pass to it. Along with it would come the responsibility for feeding, housing, and employing several million additional Russians, but leaving the most valuable commodity—the Caspian oil—mostly in Kazakh hands. Even more daunting would be the international censure that Russia would certainly have to endure; no matter how well staged, the annexation of any part of Kazakhstan would be viewed as a Russian act of aggression. Unlike in the case of Chechnya, such an act could not be explained away as an internal problem. Added to this are the sheer technical problems of intervening, for unlike Moldova in 1991, there are no Russian troops in place within Kazakhstan to help orchestrate an insurrection. In fact, the trend in recent years has been for Russia to try to expand the use of Kazakh forces rather than Russian ones in situations that would provide for their mutual defense. Thus, by behaving aggressively in Kazakhstan, Russia would be losing a highly valuable potential ally and international surrogate.

There is also no reason to expect that the prospects of a leadership change will lead to a major change in Kazakhstan's current close relationship with Russia. There is only so much that Kazakhstan can do to overcome the problems presented by its geographic location, regardless of who heads the country. As the world's largest landlocked nation, Kazakhstan would find it difficult to survive if Russia should ever choose to close its borders to the passage of goods and materials in and out of Kazakhstan. Even today, Russia could easily cripple Kazakhstan economically and undermine any Kazakh leader it disapproved of by introducing prohibitive rail tariffs and transit fees and by turning border crossings into veritable bureaucratic choke points.

All this would change if both Russia and Kazakhstan were to become World Trade Organization (WTO) members. Even before this, the various attempts to lessen the republic's dependence on its northern neighbor are slowly yielding results. Kazakhstan has engaged in oil swaps with Iran in anticipation of future pipelines through that country; rail spurs have been built, linking Kazakhstan through Turkmenistan to the south; a truck route is being overhauled through western China to connect with roads in Pakistan, thus giving access to ports on the Indian Ocean; and there are oil pipelines planned across China to feed the energy needs of the Far East. For now, however, not one of these routes, is capable of moving anything like the volume of goods and materials that Kazakhstan requires to survive.

Although the ties are weakening, Russia still has Kazakhstan bound at both ends. Russia is Kazakhstan's major or sole supplier of several necessary commodities, but Russia is also Kazakhstan's major customer for a variety of finished goods and raw materials. Russia remains Kazakhstan's primary trading partner, responsible (in 2000) for 20 percent of the republic's total exports and for 49 percent of its imports.[13] This relationship is changing, but far more slowly than many may wish. No other state comes even remotely near Russia's significance as a trading partner for Kazakhstan. Indeed, both Kazakhstan's imports from and its exports to Russia alone roughly equal the total volume of import-export trade with all of the other former Soviet republics.

A reliance on trade with Russia has had a cumulative and negative effect, especially given the large trade imbalance that Kazakhstan has inevitably developed. In the short run, the cost of continued energy imports held back Kazakhstan's economic development and caused inefficient state enterprises to fail that might have otherwise been successfully restructured. It added incentives for enterprise managers to sell valuable stockpiles for personal gain. Although Kazakhstan's economic development will eventually be served by its rising domestic energy prices—and the reconstruction of industry is sounder for this—its accumulated debts have sometimes been difficult to discharge.

Its debt for equity swaps brought powerful Russian industrial interests ownership and management positions in Kazakhstan's large factories, processing plants, and even in primary resources, including some of the coalfields that feed Russian electrical generators in the Siberian rust belt. Russian firms will probably remain stakeholders in Kazakhstan, although they have begun to serve their own commercial interests rather than the more abstract geopolitical ones of the Russian government. It is already difficult to know the extent to which the Russian foreign policy establishment determines the moves of partially privatized Russian companies like Lukoil and Gazprom or whether these companies are now able to pursue their interests independently, dragging Russian policy in their wake. The result for Kazakhstan is the same; Russian companies have been able to stall negotiations, force the redrawing of completed contracts, and insert themselves as partners—increasingly with the introduction of capital—into deals already agreed upon with other foreign investors.

With time such practices are growing less frequent. The Nazarbayev government, however, gets high marks for Kazakhstan's growing level of economic independence from Russia. This is a trend that any successor will try to sustain. The country avoided becoming a puppet state, and it is becoming more distinct from Russia and Russia's economy with each passing year. Even in the early years, the republic has stood firm on certain issues. It was Kazakhstan's refusal to pass its gold reserves to Russia that led to the collapse of a shared ruble, just as its refusal to hand over the 1,360 nuclear warheads that were stranded in Kazakhstan upon the demise of the USSR led to a significant elevation in Kazakhstan's international profile as well as a considerable infusion of foreign aid from the United States. During a period of unusual political pressure Russia attempted to enlist international opinion against Kazakhstan as well as the new republics (especially the Baltic states, which were said to be discriminating against the Russians left there). Nonetheless, Kazakhstan refused to permit the introduction of dual citizenship for ethnic Russians.

It must be asked, however, what further recourse Kazakhstan might have had, if Russia had wished to push any of these issues harder than it did. At its birth the republic had virtually no military capacity, inheriting a piece of the Soviet army that was ill suited to the country's needs. In the early days of the republic, it was even assumed that Kazakhstan would not need anything other than a small national guard, whose duties would be primarily ceremonial since any true security needs would be met through combined CIS forces. It was presumed these would essentially be a continuation of the Soviet army. When it became clear that Russia intended to concentrate its resources on the creation of a Russian army, assuming control of all the troops on Russian territory, Kazakhstan was forced to follow suit, creating at least the formal basis for Kazakhstan's military.

The Kazakhs recognize that their defensive capacity will always be a limited one. Their tendency has been to reduce the size of the armed forces but increase their specialization. This decision was made partly because of costs and partly because since its birth the Kazakh army has been plagued with problems. Since most of the Soviet officer corps was Slavic, the nationalization of the army caused an immediate and massive hemorrhage of personnel since more than two-thirds of the company and battalion commanders left for other republics.[14] Kazakhstan had virtually no native officers with whom to replace them, leaving the armed forces staffed at 50 percent of readiness levels or less.[15] The preparedness and reliability of those who remained were uncertain at best. When Kazakhstan was able, after long political delays, to send a token number of troops to serve in the joint CIS forces in Tajikistan, Kazakh soldiers reportedly raped and robbed the villagers they were meant to protect.[16] Corruption and malfeasance in the higher echelons of the military remain a perennial problem.

Formal statements of national security doctrines may pose more comprehensive goals, including the lessening of the country's dependence on the Russian military, especially its air defense. For now, however, Kazakhstan must hope that Russia's understanding of its security needs coincides with Kazakhstan's own. Similarly, Kazakhstan's armed forces are slowly being completely reorganized. They now number sixty-five thousand people with the army numbering under fifty thousand and the air force nearly twenty thousand.[17] While Kazakhstan's military gets some training from NATO nations, most of its equipment still comes from Russia, partly paid for in cash and partly in exchange for debt forgiveness.

Russia's military superiority, coupled with its ability to cripple Kazakhstan's economy, explains why Nazarbayev worked harder than anyone else to keep the USSR alive. He then worked hard to make a reality the various postcollapse bodies such as the CIS, common ruble zone spaces, the Euro-Asian Union, and the five-nation customs union. The Kazakhs have been strong advocates of Putin's effort to redefine the customs union as a Eurasian economic community. This stance is unlikely to change should there be a transfer of power in Kazakhstan.

In fact, players in a succession struggle might promise closer ties to Russia than currently exist through deeper forms of integration, making Russia the kind of de facto ruler of the constituent states that the Soviet Union was for the nominally independent states of the old Warsaw Pact. Yet any major change in the current juridical relation between the two countries seems highly improbable. Russia is eager to limit the costs of its military engagements and refuses additional social responsibility. The Kazakhs would more likely trade economic concessions for protection than give away formal sovereignty, which would put the ruling elite's personal holdings at greater risk.

Kazakhstan's other neighbors will certainly be interested in the outcome of any future transfer of power. Most interested of all could be China, as a strongly nationalist leader in Kazakhstan could have an impact on China's internal security and might lead to a further deterioration of control in Xinjiang and western China. Still, there are no major political figures currently active in Kazakhstan's political scene who seem apt to upset the current state of Kazakh-Chinese relations, and it is hard to envision China playing an active role in an upcoming succession struggle. Any future Kazakh government will strive to remain on good terms with China. The Shanghai Cooperation Organization, formed as the Shanghai Five in April 1996 and renamed when Uzbekistan joined it in June 2001, has been a successful confidence-building effort. Eventually, this organization could serve as a vehicle for enhancing China's role in resolving regional security problems. Today, though, Russia remains Kazakhstan's most important security partner, and while China is sure to play a growing role in Kazakhstan, the pace with which this will occur is uncertain. For now Beijing seems content simply to mark its place at the table of great powers to which the Kazakhs recognize a sense of obligation.

If Russia were to grow so weak that China would regard that influence as withdrawn, it seems inevitable that China would move to replace Russia. It might do this militarily or by economic means, which would be determined by the nature of the vacuum China perceived to exist. The nearness of China also places an upper limit on how much Kazakhstan might prosper as an independent state, especially as it grows more self-consciously ethnic Kazakh. The Han who rule China have no interest in letting their millions of Turkic Muslims in what is historically Eastern Turkestan live alongside a strong independent state of other Turkic Muslims.

For now and for the foreseeable future, talk of Chinese expansion into Kazakhstan seems remote. In fact, the territorial integrity of Kazakhstan seems more ensured than that of any state in Central Asia or in the former Soviet Union more generally. Kazakhs have always feared the prospect of Uzbek expansion from the south, but the economic and political choices made by Islam Karimov initially doomed Uzbekistan to be no more than a neighborhood bully. Bullies like troubling their weakest not their strongest neighbors, making Kyrgyzstan and Tajikistan far easier targets than larger and more powerful Kazakhstan. The Uzbeks are likely to pay little attention to any transfer of power in Kazakhstan since it is expected to have little consequence for them. The southern border, however, could cause Kazakhstan problems in the more distant future.

Historically, the Kazakhs arose from the Uzbeks, making the latter a sort of senior people who might credibly assert a claim on the territories and population of Kazakhstan's south. More important, southern Kazakhstan is ethnically the most Kazakh, the most densely populated, the least developed, the poorest, and the youngest part of the republic. This combination of factors suggests fertile conditions for the spread of Islam, which the present elite views as a tangible threat to stability.

Uzbekistan is a traditional rival of Kazakhstan, and over the past decade the presidents of the two states have vied for preeminence in Central Asia. Long-term U.S.-Uzbek military assistance would change the strategic balance in Central Asia to Kazakhstan's detriment, and unless the growing U.S. presence is coupled with a successful effort at economic reform it will do little to increase the inherent stability of the Uzbek regime.

The Kazakh leadership is concerned about the political situation in Uzbekistan. There is an active tradition in Uzbekistan of fundamentalist Islam that threatens to change the nature of the Uzbek state and—failing that—the present political incumbent. Either way, Uzbekistan will continue to be a source of religious contagion for the Kazakhs. A deteriorating political situation could complicate the process of succession in Kazakhstan, adding to the atomization of the distant regions of the country. It also has the potential to drive Kazakhstan to closer security cooperation with Russia. Kazakhstan is thus likely to face a growing differentiation between its more secular, richer north and its poorer, more religious south. If the Kazakhs of the south were to become convinced that their leaders in Astana were both venal and godless, the political culture of Kazakhstan could become even more fractured.

Kazakhstan after Nazarbayev

It is hard to know when Kazakhstan will begin its succession frenzy. The Nazarbayev regime would like to concentrate its efforts on economic reform and draw attention away from its stagnating political system. Thus, the most likely scenario for the immediate future of Kazakhstan is continued emphasis upon stability and with it a deemphasis on the electoral process.

Political systems are not static, however, no matter how much their leaders may will them to be. President Nazarbayev may have the health and longevity that those closest to him wish and be around to govern his society for the next decade or even two. In that time, however, with or without Nazarbayev at the helm, Kazakhstan is certain to change, even if only in subtle ways, as a result of the political decisions that are being made, or not made, now. As with lever poles, the consequences of present actions and conditions will become more pronounced the farther away we move, resulting in very different sorts of futures in accordance with how immediate problems are resolved, both in Kazakhstan and elsewhere.

No Kazakh government will ever be able to take the preservation of the country's territorial integrity for granted. Kazakhstan will always be at risk from the prospects of Russia's fragmentation. If the Russian Federation were ever to dissolve, parts of northern Kazakhstan might try to join with parts of Russia, especially if Kazakhstan were experiencing a difficult succession struggle at the time.

Survival would be more certain if Kazakhstan were to succeed in establishing a credible monopoly of force in the republic by creating a workable military, making the police more reliable and less corrupt and reducing sharply the power of the various criminal and quasi-criminal groups that currently flourish. Assuming that the world continues its present trend toward economic globalization, however, the single strongest determinant of whether Kazakhstan is dismembered will probably be the attitude of the world community to the fragmentation of existing states. As may be seen in the international reaction to the events in Zaire (now the Democratic Republic of the Congo) and elsewhere in Africa over the past decade, the global economy's primary interest in states that are the producers of raw materials is continued access on reasonable terms. This is a goal that the proliferation of subauthorities makes more difficult. It thus seems most likely that there will be strong international pressure to resist any further redrawing of state boundaries in Central Asia and elsewhere.

In the years since the collapse of the Soviet Union the international community has taken little interest in the political conditions within existing states as long as the diamonds, chrome, oil, and other commodities produced by such states continue to reach the world's markets. If states want to become more democratic, the United States in particular is willing to devote resources to help them to do so, but no one seems willing to risk being cut off from a dependable source of raw materials in the service of a political goal. That international indifference gives Kazakhstan wide latitude in defining its future political nature. The option that would give the republic the greatest long-term stability would be the evolution and strengthening of some form of democracy. As noted above, the leadership of Kazakhstan has been fearful of democratization in part because of the republic's demography.

Making Kazakhstan more Kazakh is not, however, going to make the republic less divided. If however, most of the country's population felt an interest in the continued existence of the state, if others believed that they, or members of their group, might move into positions of leadership, make economic headway, or share in the future of the state in some way, such a Kazakhstan, for all its current problems, would likely be able to continue to depend on the loyalty of its citizens.

As noted earlier, the differences between old and young, rich and poor, and urban and rural Kazakhs are growing, as are the differences between northerners and southerners and between the secular and the religious. The consequences of these processes are that Kazakhstan is going to continue to be a heterogeneous society, even if it manages to become ethnically more uniform. The best way to ensure that the various constituencies of the state have an interest in the continuation of the status quo is to broaden participation in the processes of governance, regularizing elite replacement and reducing the appeal of groups that advocate catastrophic change.

Unfortunately, a survey of the present environment makes the strengthening of democracy seem unlikely. Indeed, if Kazakhstan does not become more democratic soon, it will be more difficult to do so in the distant future. If the population acquiesces to President Nazarbayev's transferring power to a handpicked successor, the prospect that democratic reform will soon be embraced seems remote. This is all the more true if the new president is a member of the Nazarbayev family. In either case, Kazakhstan's second president will probably lack the same level of political legitimacy that Nazarbayev has enjoyed and may lack his political skills, especially given the atmosphere of sycophancy that dominates Kazakhstan's political environment.

Democratic development in Kazakhstan is linked in part to developments in Russia. A strong democracy next door would not by itself be enough to convince the Kazakh elite to share political power, but an expanding and prospering Russian middle class would almost certainly stimulate the growth of a middle class in Kazakhstan as well. They in turn could push for the election process to become more open, so that the various regions and interests in the republic would get better and more responsive representation. Only then will Kazakhstan begin to move away from government by personalities, to government by institutions and laws. This scenario would become considerably more probable if Kazakhstan were able to distance itself from the emerging ethnonational basis of political entitlement and to move toward an understanding of citizenship that makes a positive use of Kazakhstan's multiple traditions and cultures.

The growth of a genuine democracy in Russia is no guarantee of a similar growth in Kazakhstan, but its absence is a detriment, at least for now. Russia's political influence on Kazakhstan, for better or worse, is apt to fade with time. When there are fewer Russians living in the republic, Russian opinion and Russian politics will be of less significance.

Realistically, it seems that in both Russia and Kazakhstan the same forces may be at work, militating against democratization in either state. The temptations and rewards of the enormous natural wealth in both countries make political control far too valuable to entrust to a mere democracy. The problem that this presents—for Kazakhstan at least—is that its natural resources, while vast, are nevertheless finite. If the profits from its oil and other resources are reinvested in the republic to at least a limited extent, then it is probable that the state will be able to continue to survive indefinitely in some version of its present autocratic-oligarchic nature. The regularization of tax structures, improved handling of the terms for and proceeds from international investment, and a check on the greed of the elite would probably allow Kazakhstan to continue to perpetuate the present system, and President Nazarbayev then might even be able to arrange his own succession.

Such a state would be characterized by relatively low levels of public education and public health; a pronounced rural-urban imbalance with a few cities becoming swollen magnets for the impoverished unemployed and underemployed from the countryside; and great disparities in wealth, with most of the country's income held by 5–10 percent of the population.

On the other hand, if Kazakhstan manages to waste most of the proceeds of its natural resources, as such states as Nigeria and the Congo have done, then the long-term outlook for Kazakhstan becomes much dimmer. Clasping the spent wealth of the past to themselves and having no promise of future wealth to hold out to the many poor, the elite would be forced to seek the support of regional protectors, thus turning Kazakhstan into a vassal state. Presuming that the United States would not make itself available to play this role, the master of next choice would be Russia, but if Russia itself is too weak or, less likely, has become too democratic, then Kazakhstan's elite would even feel pressed to seek the protection of China since the alternative would be the loss of its own position.

The people of Kazakhstan have exhibited extraordinary patience in enduring the effects of simultaneous political and economic transformation. As noted, most Kazakhs see the quality of their lives as sharply diminished since the collapse of the Soviet Union, but they find hope in the removal of the ideological encumbrances under which they once toiled. While the local Russians have difficulty in defining their relation to the state in which they now find themselves living, the Kazakhs at least can find a certain solace and consolation in their status as members of the international community.

In addition to the challenges Kazakhstan still faces in nation building and economic restructuring, the republic has a daunting list of environmental repairs. The continued desiccation of the Aral Sea and the ecological consequences that this brings have made large portions of Kyzylorda oblast toxic, fatal to infants and dangerous to adults. The Caspian shore faces a challenge of another sort (in addition to those posed by industrial pollution from oil development). For reasons that no one can explain, the Caspian Sea is rising, threatening to flood villages and many of the new oil wells on which Kazakhstan is depending for future prosperity. Environmental pollution is a huge problem in places like Karaganda, Pavlodar, and Semipalatinsk as well because of the legacy of Soviet-era industrial giants.

To its credit, the Kazakh leadership has made many efforts to grapple with the problems it faces. Given no choice but to become independent, Kazakhstan has attempted to create a framework for a market economy and initially sought at least the trappings of a participatory democracy and a society based on the rule of law.

Yet a variety of circumstances—some avoidable, some not—has diminished the Kazakh leadership's commitment to these goals, while the continued deterioration of Kazakhstan's quality of life is magnifying ever larger the consequences of the leadership's more venal, self-serving, and self-interested actions. As I have suggested, the nature of what Kazakhstan will be tomorrow is still open to definition. The state is blessed with huge natural resources, an educated population, and a civic fabric that, even if badly frayed, is still strong. An intelligent and patriotic use of those blessings would allow Kazakhstan to take a place as a vital member of the international community. If, however, those blessings are misused and wasted, then Kazakhstan could, unfortunately, taste the fate of several wealthy post-colonial societies where the masses live in misery as the price for the inordinate greed and stupidity of their rulers.

What Messages Should the United States Give the Kazakhs?

In a bipolar political environment, such as the one that predominated for most of the last half century, incompetent and kleptocratic elites who enjoyed little popular support were often able to find foreign patrons to help them remain in power. This was particularly true of those who ran resource-rich states.

It is harder to predict the longevity of such regimes in the new post–Cold War international environment. Because of its dependence on raw materials, the United States may continue to befriend resource-rich states with corrupt and undemocratic regimes, but the pressures of globalization may prove very unkind to such states. The need to become competitive or face ouster from emboldened masses who reject their disenfranchisement could force these rulers to sponsor economic and political reforms.

In a world in which people everywhere are becoming increasingly more interconnected, the cost of systematically excluding large portions of the population on the grounds of ethnicity, religion, or place of birth; the cost of stunting the development of one part of the nation for fear that it may eclipse the power of another part; and the cost of consigning the majority of a nation's citizens, especially its young citizens, to lives of poverty and ignorance to enable a privileged few to live in luxury may be harder to facilitate over long periods of time.

The leadership in Kazakhstan is not immune to such pressures. As this book went to press, challenges to Nazarbayev's power were growing. Rifts within the Kazakh ruling family were becoming public, and son-in-law Rakhat Aliyev was dropped from his posts after public accusations of his corruption. Several young reformers have left the government to lobby for more rapid economic and political change.

Now is the time for the United States to press the Nazarbayev regime to develop more participatory political institutions and to take seriously the need for economic transparency. To do so would produce clear advantages for Kazakhstan's population and a more reliable strategic partner for Washington in the process.

There is little to lose from such a strategy. Pressure from the United States will not push Kazakhstan into Russia's arms, nor will it endanger Western development of Kazakhstan's energy resources. In fact, improvements in the legal environment in Kazakhstan would provide new guarantees for U.S. and other Western firms and make their position in Kazakhstan more secure. Absent such changes, Western firms will always be subject to pressure to redefine contracts or risk renationalization.

Over the past several years Nursultan Nazarbayev has proved an ever-more competent manager of his relationships with both Russia and the United States. For all the trials and tribulations of Nazarbayev's relations with Russian leaders who have periodically threatened and bullied him over the past decade, the Kazakh leader has managed to carve out a relationship with Moscow that well serves both parties. At the same time, he has leveraged the U.S. relationship to his advantage, making the United States appear to be a guarantor of his sovereignty without actually getting it to offer any formal guarantees, and he has done this *without* endorsing key principles of U.S. foreign policy such as the isolation of Iran or the introduction of a democratic system of rule.

The Kazakh manipulation of its oil card has often been masterful. The publicity generated around the giant AgipKCO deposit has kept Kazakhstan regularly in the news and left everyone guessing about the final export route or routes, despite the fact that much of U.S. policy in Kazakhstan has been driven by an interest in securing access to its oil reserves without dependency on either Russia or Iran.

For all its vast reserves, however, Kazakhstan is not yet a major producer of oil and may never become one if the price of oil drops too low to make developing these landlocked offshore reserves profitable. Russia, right next door, has much vaster reserves that would be easier to develop technically, should their ownership finally be settled. Moreover, improved relations between the United States and Russia could lead to a rethinking of pipeline issues and the whole timing of Caspian development.

Western oil companies working in Kazakhstan will certainly be concerned parties to any succession struggle that develops, but they are more likely to have to accept an outcome than to determine the order in which the players arrange themselves. The sanctity of their current contracts is already being called into question by the same president who signed them; in early 2001 the Nazarbayev government began to complain that some of the tax arrangements to which it had agreed were not in the national interest and should be redefined. A new president, especially one chosen in a nondemocratic fashion, could make new demands on these Western firms, hoping to produce funds for either the national treasury or his personal coffers.

Given its geographic isolation, Kazakhstan will also always be dependent on the cooperation of neighboring countries to move its oil and gas to market. For this reason, the United States' interest in security cooperation in the region has been a repeated theme. It took on new importance after the September 11, 2001, terrorist attacks in New York and Washington, when the United States was able to transform the previous limited level of military cooperation to a much expanded U.S. military presence in Uzbekistan, Tajikistan, and Kyrgyzstan. But the newly opened bases are intended to help Washington meet U.S. strategic needs, not to address the security demands of the states themselves.

Further, the discovery that the nations of Central Asia can serve as strategic assets for the United States could compound the difficulty in defining a winning formula for engaging in the transition economies of the post-Soviet states. For the past decade, the United States has been sending these states, including Kazakhstan, conflicting messages, without making any one message a real priority.

Washington's stated preference—and it is a strong and clear one—is that the Central Asian states should remain independent and not become the puppet states of any current or potential enemy of the United States. Certainly the West would like the Central Asian states to succeed, and U.S. foreign assistance to Kazakhstan and the other newly independent states has focused on helping them to reform their economic, political, and social welfare systems so they can become sustainable market-oriented democracies.[18]

Yet the resources devoted to this have been truly limited, only about $50 million a year in the case of Kazakhstan, which had been getting more money than any of its other Central Asian neighbors. Given the monumental nature of the tasks these countries face, this level of support could hardly be considered to give the United States anything resembling a veto power in their affairs. All it has qualified Washington to do is to nudge them along in the direction that it wanted them to go.

In the wake of the bombings of September 11, U.S. spending in the region may well increase, but it is unlikely to rise meteorically. It is also unclear how much leverage the United States would have in Kazakhstan even if it were to spend five, ten, or even twenty times the amount budgeted in recent years. Moreover, given the earning power of its economy, the Kazakh government will always be capable of refusing assistance if the strings attached are not to its liking.

Kazakhstan's geographic vulnerability, however, is quite another matter—one that both puts its economy at risk and creates an opportunity for the United States to press the Kazakhs harder. As mentioned earlier, the United States has little to lose in Kazakhstan. The Kazakhs need the global energy leaders to invest in their country even more than the major energy firms need Kazakhstan. The Russians do not have the technical expertise necessary to exploit the deposits on their own, nor will the necessary technology be sold to them. So while Kazakhstan can play the Western firms off against one another, in the end the United States should have continued access to these reserves.

This means that Washington could have pressed Kazakh leaders to take the commitment to democracy building more seriously from the beginning. Had the United States adopted a more interventionist stance early on, Kazakhstan might have developed a different kind of political system, but this would have required the United States to spend more money and exert more pressure. Had the United States increased its pressure at the time of President Nazarbayev's bad behavior in 1994 and 1995, when he began reneging on his earlier willingness to engage in political reforms, Kazakhstan might not have as corrupt a political system as it has today. It also might have moved more rapidly toward economic reform. Some of the legislation necessary for macroeconomic reform might have been put in place more slowly, but this delay might have contributed to its ultimate effectiveness. Instead, Kazakhstan has many good laws, but no one in authority particularly interested in enforcing them. It also lacks an independent parliament, an independent judiciary, and popularly accountable local governments.

U.S. leaders should press the Kazakhs toward the creation of these institutions and, wherever possible, should tie continued U.S. assistance, political risk insurance, and loan guarantees to the requirement of transaction transparency. U.S. policy makers should be prepared to do this even in the energy sector, suffering no illusions that the Kazakhs will listen to them.

In the end, the argument for democracy building has to be grounded in a belief that it is in the long-term interest of Kazakhstan and its people. As a global leader, the United States must press the Kazakh leaders to take seriously the responsibilities of governing. Kazakhstan may be turning into a family-owned country, but it is an implicitly pluralistic society. Its ethnic diversity, vast territory, varied economy, and well-educated population all make it possible to sustain a democratic form of government if the country's leaders would allow one to develop.

The alternative is that the United States would engage itself in the country only as long as it views Kazakhstan's oil as valuable. The life of most of the production-sharing agreements that form the basis of Kazakhstan's energy developments is twenty years. After that, the United States and American companies alike can walk away and simply leave the Kazakh people to their own devices. If, however, the United States takes this attitude, it can rest assured that the next generation of analysts will be writing about who lost Kazakhstan and a number of other Caspian states, in much the same way that many are now writing about Africa's problems.

Appendices

Appendix 1
The Oblasts of Kazakhstan

Oblast	Total Population	Ethnic Kazakh Population (%)	Ethnic Russian Population (%)
Akmola: Located in north-central Kazakhstan, surrounding but not including Astana city; agriculture and light industry predominant. Capital: Kokchetau	836,000	37.5	39.4
Aktiubinsk: Located in northwestern Kazakhstan; produces chromium compounds and machinery. Capital: Aktobe	682,600	70.7	16.8
Almaty (oblast): Located in southeastern Kazakhstan, surrounding but not including Almaty city; agricultural region.	1,558,500	59.4	21.8
Atyrau: Located in western Kazakhstan on the Caspian Sea; major industries are fishing and oil, mainly from the Tengiz deposit. Capital: Atyrau	440,300	89.0	8.6
East Kazakhstan: Located at the eastern extreme of Kazakhstan; center of nonferrous metallurgy and site of Soviet-era nuclear testing. Capital: Ust-Kamenogorsk	153,100	48.5	45.4
Zhambyl: Located in south-central Kazakhstan on the border with Kyrgyzstan; contains several natural gas deposits. Capital: Taraz	988,800	64.8	18.1
West Kazakhstan: Located in northwest Kazakhstan on the border with Russia; contains several oil and gas deposits. Capital: Uralsk	616,800	64.7	28.2
Karaganda: Located in central Kazakhstan; center of coal mining industry. Capital: Karaganda	1,410,200	37.5	43.6
Kostanai: Located in northern Kazakhstan; specializes in agriculture and light industry. Capital: Kostanai	1,017,700	30.9	42.3
Kyzylorda: Located in south-central Kazakhstan; specializes in food and light industry. Capital: Kyzylorda	596,200	94.2	2.9
Mangistau: Located in southwest Kazakhstan on the Caspian Sea; livestock and light industry predominant. Capital: Aktau	314,700	78.7	14.8
Pavlodar: Located in northeast Kazakhstan; major industrial center. Capital: Pavlodar	807,000	38.6	41.9

Appendix 1 (continued)
The Oblasts of Kazakhstan

Oblast	Total Population	Ethnic Kazakh Population (%)	Ethnic Russian Population (%)
North Kazakhstan: Located in north-central Kazakhstan on the Russian border; junction of the Trans-Siberian and Trans-Kazakhstan railroads. Capital: Petropavlovsk	726,000	29.6	49.8
South Kazakhstan: Located in south-central Kazakhstan; agriculture and light industry predominant. Capital: Shymkent	1,978,300	67.8	8.2
Astana (city): New capital of Kazakhstan.	319,300	41.8	40.5
Almaty (city): Business and financial center of Kazakhstan.	1,129,400	38.5	45.2
Total population	14,953,100	53.4	30.0

Appendix 2
Population of Kazakhstan by Nationality, 1989 and 1999

Nationality	Population (thousands) 1989	Population (thousands) 1999	Population Change (thousands)	Population Change (%)	Percentage of Total Population, 1989	Percentage of Total Population, 1999
Kazakh	6,496.9	7,985.0	1,488.2	22.9	40.1	53.4
Russian	6,062.0	4,479.6	−1,582.4	−26.1	37.4	30.0
Ukrainian	875.7	547.1	−328.6	−37.5	5.4	3.7
Uzbek	331.0	370.7	39.6	12.0	2.0	2.5
German	946.9	353.4	−593.4	−62.7	5.8	2.4
Tatar	320.7	249.0	−71.8	−22.4	2.0	1.7
Uighur	181.5	210.3	28.8	15.9	1.1	1.4

Source: *Pervaia perepis' naseleniia Respubliki Kazakhstan,* 1999.

Appendix 3
Ethnic Composition of Major Cities in Kazakhstan

City	Total Population, 1999	Total Population, 1989	Percentage of Ethnic Kazakh, 1999	Percentage of Ethnic Kazakh, 1989
Astana	313,100	276,000	40.9	17.5
Almaty	1,130,000	1,071,900	38.5	23.8
Aktau	144,700	160,700	55.6	23.0
Aktobe	253,000	253,000	53.0	31.6
Atyrau	141,800	147,300	72.8	59.5
Ekibastuz	127,300	135,000	37.4	19.8
Karaganda	437,700	507,300	24.2	12.6
Kokchetau	123,300	135,400	36.0	18.5
Kostanai	222,500	229,800	18.8	9.1
Kyzylorda	157,300	150,400	84.9	71.3
Pavlodar	299,700	329,700	24.0	14.4
Petropavlovsk	203,400	239,600	13.9	8.6
Rudny	108,600	125,200	7.5	4.0
Semipalatinsk (Semey)	269,700	317,100	48.8	26.5
Shymkent	357,900	380,100	48.7	29.2
Taraz	325,500	306,300	52.1	28.7
Temirtau	171,200	213,500	11.8	5.9
Uralsk	196,100	199,600	35.5	22.1
Ust-Kamenogorsk	310,900	322,800	18.5	10.5

Appendix 4
Political Parties and Parliamentary Elections in Kazakhstan

On March 7, 1994, elections were held for the unicameral legislature, the Supreme Council, composed of 177 seats, 40 of which were to be filled by candidates on a presidential list.

Table A4-1. Distribution of Seats Won as a Result of Elections *

Affiliation	Seats
Union of People's Unity (SNEK, propresidential)	39
Trade Union Federation	12
People's Congress (NKK)	13
Socialist Party	14
Peasants Union	4
LAD Republican Movement	4
Other	10
Total	96

*Shows seats won in elections, not the composition of parliament.
Note: SNEK was a propresidential party, and received the support of the regime. The Trade Union Federation was formerly the state-controlled trade union organization. The NKK is a soft opposition party led by Olzhas Suleimenov, which appealed equally to Russians and Kazakhs, most of these being northerners. The Socialist Party and the Peasants Union are left-leaning parties and for the most part ethnically Russian in membership. The LAD Republican Movement is an ethnic Slavic opposition party.

On December 9, 1995, Parliamentary elections were held for a new bicameral legislature, established by the new constitution of August 30, 1995. The bicameral legislature was comprised of the Majilis, which had 67 seats, and the Senate, which had 47 seats.

(See table on next page.)

A4-2. Distribution of Seats in the Majilis Won as a Result of Elections

Affiliation	Seats
People's Unity Party (PNEK, propresidential)	24
Democratic Party (propresidential)	12
Peasants Union	5
Trade Union Federation	5
Communist Party	2
Independents (other)	19
Total	67

Note: SNEK was renamed PNEK and continued to be compliant with the president. The Democratic Party was a propresidential party that was created before the election and received the support of the regime. The Communist Party, legalized in 1993, was not permitted to compete in 1994 elections but was reconstituted and participated in 1995 elections, led by Serikbolsyn Abdildin.

On October 10, 1999, and October 24, 1999 elections were held for Majilis. Under the new system 10 seats of the 77-seat Majilis were elected from party lists, on the basis of proportional representation and the remaining 67 were elected in single-mandate constituencies.

Table A4-3. Distribution of Seats Won as a Result of Elections

Affiliation	Seats
Otan (propresidential)	24
Civil Party	11
Communist Party	3
Agrarian Party	3
Republican People's Party (RNPK)	1
People's Cooperative Party	1
Business	10
Independents (government associated)	20
Independents (other)	4
Total	77

Note: Otan is a propresidential party formed when the People's Unity Party (PNEK) and the Democratic Party, along with several other smaller propresidential parties and movements, merged after supporting Nursultan Nazarbayev's candidacy for president in 1999. The party is led by former Prime Minister Sergei Tereshchenko. The Civil Party, led by Azat Peruashev, cooperates with the regime and seeks to increase the welfare of Kazakhstan's citizens and protect domestic producers. The Agrarian Party, headed by Romin Madinov, seeks the introduction of private ownership of land, improvement of agricultural infrastructure, and changes in the taxation of the agrarian sector. The RNPK is an opposition party headed by exiled former Prime Minister Akezhan Kazhegeldin. The People's Cooperative Party, led by the chairman of Kazakhstan's Consumer Union, Umirzak Sarsenov, is a left-leaning party supporting agricultural producers and promoting a socially oriented economy.

Appendix 5
Gross Domestic Product of Kazakhstan, 1991–2000

	1991	1992	1993	1994	1995	1996	1997	1998	1999	2000 (estimate)	2001 (projection)
GDP (in billions of tenge)	–	3.4	29.4	423.5	1,014.3	1,415.8	1,672.1	1,733.3	2,016.5	2,596.0	2,992.2
GDP per capita (in USD millions)	357	357	328	721	1,040	1,333	1,429	1,452	1,123	1,225	–
Share of industry in GDP (%)	38.0	30.1	28.5	23.6	23.5	23.5	24.0	23.9	23.9	–	–
Share of agriculture in GDP (%)	29.0	16.2	16.6	15.0	12.3	11.7	11.4	9.4	11.2	–	–

Source: European Bank for Reconstruction and Development, *Transition Report 2000* (London: EBRD, 2000, p. 177); European Bank for Reconstruction and Development, *Transition Report Update*, April 2001 (London: EBRD, 2001).

Appendix 6
Trade Statistics for Kazakhstan, 1993–2000

Table A6-1. Export Statistics for Kazakhstan (USD millions)

Country/Region	Exports							
	1993	1994	1995	1996	1997	1998	1999	2000
Russia	–	1,438	2,366	2,484	2,288	1,611	1,139	1,784
Ukraine	–	128	122	213	304	263	115	269
Uzbekistan	–	177	153	202	148	119	66	139
Kyrgyzstan	88	60	75	112	66	63	60	59
Turkmenistan	–	25	48	39	50	12	14	7
FSU*, total	–	2,028	2,933	3,202	2,912	2,331	1,768	2,482
Germany	89	73	171	183	353	282	333	567
China	239	149	297	459	442	382	473	670
United Kingdom	76	65	112	231	549	484	189	231
United States	37	75	44	60	139	76	81	211
Turkey	39	49	70	52	102	94	36	64
Korea	43	60	92	178	130	40	36	34
Israel	–	–	–	1	1	3	6	7
Iran	–	12	49	63	83	67	100	204
World total	3,277	3,231	5,250	5,911	6,497	5,436	5,598	9,140

*Former Soviet Union

Source: International Monetary Fund, *Direction of Trade Statistics Yearbook 2001* (Washington, D.C.: IMF, 2001), pp. 281–82.

Table A6-2. Import Statistics for Kazakhstan, 1993–2000 (USD millions)

Country/Region	Imports							
	1993	1994	1995	1996	1997	1998	1999	2000
Russia	–	1,293	1,900	2,325	1,969	1,712	1,351	2,460
Ukraine	–	120	86	92	93	93	59	80
Uzbekistan	–	–	270	89	66	96	87	73
Kyrgyzstan	79	104	31	91	64	53	31	32
Turkmenistan	–	278	241	176	46	24	20	44
FSU* total	–	2,188	2,670	2,964	2,342	2,014	1,679	2,775
Germany	488	294	197	198	368	366	288	334
China	189	70	35	36	47	51	82	154
United Kingdom	25	66	84	77	141	219	233	219
United States	74	109	65	66	202	271	349	277
Turkey	74	87	124	151	177	209	112	143
Korea	45	67	43	88	130	101	49	83
Israel	–	–	–	1	1	3	6	16
Iran	–	12	49	63	83	67	100	13
World total	3,887	3,561	3,807	4,241	4,301	4,350	3,687	5,052

*Former Soviet Union
Source: International Monetary Fund, *Direction of Trade Statistics Yearbook 2001* (Washington, D.C.: IMF, 2001), pp. 281–82.

Appendix 7
Major U.S. and International Investment and Assistance Projects in Kazakhstan

Organization	Description	Amount
United States Agency for International Development (USAID)	Promotes economic reform and private-sector development, NGO development, the fight against corruption, the reform of health care and energy-industry	A total of $354.2 million in technical assistance since 1993, with $48.3 million requested for FY2001
Overseas Private Investment Corporation (OPIC): AIG Silk Road Fund	Provides equity financing to small- and medium-sized private-sector enterprises and joint ventures operating in Central Asia	Target size of $100 million, jointly funded with European Bank for Reconstruction and Development (EBRD). OPIC provides loans, loan guarantees, and investment insurance for the funds it supports.
OPIC: New Century Fund	Invests in diversified manufacturing, consumer products, and financial and service industries in the newly independent states, including Kazakhstan	$250 million fully invested
Central and Eastern Europe–Newly Independent States (NIS) Property Fund	Invests in light manufacturing and projects to develop office, warehousing, and the distribution of property in Central Europe and the newly independent states, including Kazakhstan	Up to $240 million invested
OPIC: First NIS Regional Fund	Seeks equity investments in companies involved with natural resources, telecommunications, light manufacturing, and consumer products in the NIS, including Kazakhstan	$200 million invested
OPIC: Agribusiness Partners International Fund	Invests in agriculture, food production companies, infrastructure projects, food storage, and distribution facilities in the NIS, including Kazakhstan	$95 million fully invested
OPIC: Russian Partners Fund	Invests in companies involved with natural resources, telecommunications, light manufacturing, and consumer products in the NIS, including Kazakhstan	$155 million fully invested
Central Asian–American Enterprise Fund	Promotes the development of emerging private sectors in Central Asia. Managed by a private board of directors, the fund makes debt and equity investments and offers technical assistance, focusing on projects in infrastructural sectors	Capitalized by the U.S. government at $150 million for 2000–2004

Global Partner Ventures (formerly the Defense Enterprise Fund)	Venture capital fund focusing on converting the human and technological potential of the former Soviet Union's military industry. Invests in joint ventures between Soviet military plants and Western partners in Kazakhstan, as well as in Russia, Ukraine, and Belarus	Received more than $50 million from the U.S. Defense Department, and $20 million from the U.S. State Department
Nunn–Lugar Cooperative Threat Reduction Program	Aided in the removal of all Soviet strategic nuclear weapons from Kazakhstan. In November 1994, funded Project Sapphire, a project to airlift nuclear materials from Kazakhstan	Inaugurated in 1991, the program cost less than $3 billion over seven years.
United States Trade and Development Agency (TDA)	Funded feasibility studies for U.S. firms in Kazakhstan for coal mine development, bank automation, gold mine development, gas pipelines, dairy modernization, customs automation, and oil field development	$3.9 million for nine feasibility studies
Export-Import Bank of the United States	Grants short- and medium-term credit insurance, medium- and long-term loan guarantees, and direct loans to U.S. firms trading in Kazakhstan	Not available
U.S. Military Assistance	Provides military education and training programs, as well as foreign military financing. Also includes U.S. support for NATO's Partnership for Peace Program	$8.6 million from 1993 through 2000
International Monetary Fund	Promotes structural reforms through loan packages for Kazakhstan's government	$538.3 million provided in loans since 1993
World Bank	Promotes development through five adjustment operations, three technical assistance loans, and thirteen investment loans, including loans for agricultural privatization, road transport improvement, health and legal reform, water and sanitation projects, and energy-sector reform	$1.82 billion approved for 21 projects
European Union: Tacis Program	Finances technical assistance and investment projects, including the development of an east-west transport corridor from Central Asia to Europe	111.9 million since 1991
European Bank for Reconstruction and Development (EBRD)	Provides assistance through loans to encourage financial reform, the privatization of industry, and investment in natural resources, oil, and gas	587.4 million in signed projects since 1993
Asian Development Bank (ADB)	Encourages transition to a market-based economy by providing loans to support government reform, infrastructure development, education and training, industry, agriculture, and private-sector development	$525 million provided in loans since 1993

Appendix 8
Privatization in Kazakhstan, 1991–1999

	1991	1992	1993	1994	1995	1996	1997	1998	1999
Share of small firms privatized (%)	–	–	27.3	41.7	60.0	79.5	100.0	–	–
Privatization revenues (cumulative, as % of GDP)	0.0	3.4	6.1	6.4	6.7	8.9	12.3	16.2	18.0
Private sector share in GDP (%)	5.0	10.0	10.0	20.0	25.0	40.0	55.0	55.0	60.0

Source: European Bank for Reconstruction and Development, *Transition Report 2000* (London: EBRD, 2000), p. 176.

Appendix 9
Foreign Investment in Kazakhstan

Table A9-1. Foreign Direct Investment in the Kazakhstan Economy by Country, 1993–1999 (USD millions)

Country	1993	1994	1995	1996	1997	1998	1999	1993–1999
United States	966.9	412.0	153.3	164.2	208.1	399.3	709.3	3,013.1
Republic of Korea	0.0	0.5	270.5	442.6	720.0	31.9	18.1	1,483.6
Great Britain	0.0	25.7	152.8	483.7	311.4	86.5	85.9	1,146.0
Turkey	55.3	78.9	79.3	75.6	65.0	88.8	29.1	472.0
China	5.0	5.0	2.0	0.0	313.0	86.7	30.2	441.9
Canada	0.0	16.0	35.1	132.3	22.8	30.6	8.4	245.2
Indonesia	0.0	0.0	0.0	0.0	124.3	55.0	0.0	179.3
The Netherlands	0.0	0.0	0.0	0.0	0.0	0.0	218.1	218.1
Other countries	244.2	121.6	291.3	375.2	342.4	454.4	264.1	2,093.2
Used	1,271.4	659.7	984.3	1,673.6	2,107.6	1,233.3	1,363.2	9,292.6
Repaid	0.0	0.0	–20.1	–536.9	–785.7	–81.3	–161.1	–1,585.0
Total	1,271.4	659.7	964.2	1,136.8	1,321.3	1,152.0	1,202.1	7,707.6

Note: According to the Agency of the Republic of Kazakhstan on Investment (ARKI), 150 contracts, totaling $1,302.5 million, were signed in the priority sectors of the economy from 1997 to 1999, and investment into fixed assets reached $1,166.3 million. This created 5,640 additional employment positions from 1997 to 1999.
Source: Agency of the Republic of Kazakhstan on Investment.

Table A9-2. Foreign Direct Investment in the Kazakhstan Economy by Industry, 1993–1999 (USD millions)

Industry	1993	1994	1995	1996	1997	1998	1999	1993–1999
Oil and gas	975.7	544.1	315.1	387.1	717.9	824.5	1,145.3	4,909.7
Nonferrous metallurgy	0.0	17.9	344.5	706.5	761.3	77.4	45.4	1,953.0
Ferrous metallurgy	0.0	0.0	102.1	122.9	110.6	12.5	13.3	361.4
Energy sector	0.0	0.0	0.0	126.1	128.3	86.2	26.9	367.5
Food industry	44.7	41.8	38.5	41.7	70.6	42.9	42.6	322.8
Communication	0.0	27.8	34.9	20.4	126.4	4.6	5.4	129.5
Mining industry	0.0	0.0	0.0	118.6	67.7	0.0	0.0	186.3
Other industries	251.0	28.4	149.2	150.3	124.2	185.2	84.3	972.3
Total	1,271.4	659.7	984.3	1,673.6	2,107.0	1,233.3	1,363.2	9,292.6

Source: Agency of the Republic of Kazakhstan on Investment.

Appendix 10
Foreign Development of Oil and Gas Resources in Kazakhstan (Major Projects)

Company	Joint Venture (JV) Partners	Description
Tengizchevroil	Chevron (US), Kazakhoil (Kazakhstan), LUKoil (Russia), Exxon-Mobil (US)	JV to develop 6-9 billion barrels of reserves at the Tengiz and Korolev fields
Caspian Pipeline Consortium (CPC)	Agip (Italy), British Gas (UK), Chevron (US), LukArco (US and Russia), Exxon-Mobil (US), Oman, Rosneft-Royal Dutch/Shell (Russia, UK, and Netherlands)	Project to build and operate 1.2 million barrels/day crude oil pipeline from Tengiz field to Black Sea port of Novorossiisk
AgipKCO*	Agip (Italy), Statoil (UK), Inpex (Japan), Exxon-Mobil (US), Royal Dutch/Shell (UK and Netherlands), TotalFinaElf (France), Phillips Petroleum (US)	Oil exploration project at the Kashagan deposit located on the Caspian Sea shelf, thought to be the world's fifth largest oil deposit
China National Petroleum Corporation (CNPC), Uzenmunaigaz	Kazakhstan	Development of Uzen and Zhanazhol fields in Aktobe; estimated 2.5 billion barrels of oil reserves
Hurricane-Kumkol KV	Hurricane (Canada), Occidental Petroleum (US), Yuzhneftegaz (Kazakhstan), Yuzhkazgeologia (Kazakhstan)	Development of 442 million barrels of crude oil at Kyzl Kiya
Kumkol-LUKoil	LUKoil (Russia)	Production of more than 600 million barrels of reserves at Kumkol
Karachaganak PSA	British Gas (UK), Agip (Italy), Texaco (US), LUKoil (Russia)	Development of Karachaganak oil and gas field in northwest Kazakhstan; estimated 2 billion barrels of oil reserves, 28 trillion cubic feet of gas reserves
Demunai	Caesar Oil (US)	Developments of fields in Aktobe
Stepnoi Leopard	Snow Leopard Resources (Canada), Snow Leopard International	Development of Teplovsko-Tokareyev fields with more than 100 million barrels of estimated oil reserves
American International Petroleum Corporation (AIPC) Exploration License	AIPC (US)	Exploration drilling at Altai; estimated reserves of 3.8 billion barrels oil equivalent
CCL Oil	Kazakhstan	Five-year concession (begun 1996) for the Pavlodar refinery

Appendix 10 (continued)
Foreign Development of Oil and Gas Resources in Kazakhstan (Major Projects)

Company	Joint Venture (JV) Partners	Description
Tractebel	Kazakhstan	Lease to operate Kazakhstan's gas pipeline system
Ertismunai	IPI (US), Kuat Holding (Kazakhstan)	Development of estimated 4.0 billion barrels oil reserves at Munai
Aktobe Preussag	Preussag Gmbh (Germany)	Exploration near Zharkamys
Temir PSA	Royal Dutch/Shell (UK/Netherlands), Veba Oil (Germany)	Development of more than 300 million barrels of oil reserves at Temir
Mertvyi Kultuk PSA/Ostrovnaia	Exxon-Mobil (US), Oryx/Kerr-McGee (US)	Development of 150 million barrels of oil reserves

*OKIOC was formed in 1993; in September 1998, Kazakhstan sold its share of the consortium to Philips Petroleum, based in the United States, and Inpex of Japan. Kazakhstan will continue to profit from the consortium, however, through taxes, royalties, and bonuses. In the summer of 2001, after Italy's ENI Agip became sole operator, OKIOC was renamed AgipKCO.

Appendix 11
Social Statistics for Kazakhstan, 1991–1999

	1991	1992	1993	1994	1995	1996	1997	1998	1999
Expenditures on health and education (as % of GDP)	–	6.1	6.5	5.3	7.5	7.2	7.1	6.2	6.5
Mortality rate (per 1,000 male adults)	–	–	–	–	–	–	383.0	382.0	–
Basic school enrollment ratio (%)	94.4	94.2	94.0	93.6	94.3	94.6	93.7	93.2	–
Unemployment (annual average as % of labor force)	0.4	0.6	7.5	11.0	13.0	13.0	13.0	14.0	14.1

Source: European Bank for Reconstruction and Development, *Transition Report 2000* (London: EBRD, 2000), pp. 176–77.

Appendix 12
Partial List of Nazarbayev Family Holdings and Reputed Holdings

Holding	Description	Nazarbayev Family Member
Air Kazakhstan Group	Kazakhstan's national air carrier	Allegedly controlled by Timur Kulibayev's group, through Kazkommertsbank
"Akzept" Corporation	Corporation of companies involved in production and trade, including grain and raw materials, telecommunications, scientific research, securities, and real estate	Allegedly controlled by Timur Kulibayev's group
Alautransgas	Supplier of liquid gas to five oblasts of Kazakhstan, servicing 30 percent of Kazakhstan's population; purchases gas from Tengizshevroil, Uzenmunaigaz, Shymkentneftetorgsyntez, and Pavlodar Oil Refinery	Allegedly controlled by Timur Kulibayev's group
Almatinskiy torgovo-finansovy bank (Almaty Trade and Finance Bank)	Influential bank in Almaty	Allegedly controlled by Timur Kulibayev's group
Bank account at Swiss branch of Credit Agricole-Indosuez	$80 million	Account belongs to Nursultan Nazarbayev, according to authorities in Geneva.
Bank account in Swiss Pictet et Cie Bank	Unknown	Account allegedly belongs to Nursultan Nazarbayev
BN Munai	Joint venture with U.K.-based Atlantic Caspian to develop the Akkul oil field	Thirty percent of the shares belong to BN Consultancy, owned by Bulat Nazarbayev (brother of the president).
"Bobek" Children's Fund	Created to provide assistance to children; allegedly collects money from akims and businesses on a regular basis	Sara Alpysovna Nazarbayeva heads the fund.
Eurasia Travel Company	Services and pays for Nazarbayev's family vacations in expensive resorts around the world	Alleged to be closely connected with Nursultan Nazarbayev
Europe Plus Kazakhstan	Radio station	Founded by Rakhat Aliyev
Hyatt Rakhat Palace Hotel	Luxury hotel in Almaty	Allegedly linked to Rakhat Aliyev's group

Entity	Description	Notes
Informika Media Holding	Includes television channel KTK (Commercial Television of Kazakhstan), the *Karavan* newspaper, and Franklin Publishing House	Allegedly controlled by Rakhat Aliyev
International Fund for the Development of Kazakhstan (Kazakhstan Fund)	Registered in 1995, the fund opened account 35877 with United Overseas Bank in Geneva; allegedly, up to $19 million was transferred through the account annually.	Timur Kulibayev was appointed secretary of the fund; Nursultan Nazarbayev was allegedly given the right to make all transactions and transfer money from the fund to a personal account.
KazAgroFinance	Agriculture equipment leasing company	State-owned, allegedly controlled by Timur Kulibayev's group
Kazakh Academy of Physical Training, Sports, and Tourism	Joint stock company	Thirty-eight percent of the shares owned by Sara Alpysovna Nazarbayeva
Kazakhoil	Major oil company operating in Kazakhstan	Allegedly controlled by Timur Kulibayev's group
Kazakhstan Temir Zholy	Kazakhstan's railway system	Allegedly controlled by Timur Kulibayev's group
Kazatomprom	National Atomic Company	Allegedly controlled by Rakhat Aliyev since it falls under the auspices of national security; Aliyev heads the KNB (National Security Committee)
Kazkommertsbank	Kazakhstan's largest bank; includes subsidiaries Kazkommerts-Policy, Kazkommerts securities brokerage, Unified Payment System, and two financial companies registered in the Netherlands, Kazkommerts Inter-national B. V. and Kazkommerts Capital-2 B. V.	Allegedly controlled by Timur Kulibayev's group
Kazphosphor	Phosphorus company	Allegedly controlled by Timur Kulibayev's group
KazTransOil	Oil company	Allegedly controlled by Timur Kulibayev's group; Kulibayev is the president.
KEGOC: Kazakhstan Electricity Grid Operating Company	Electrical grid manager for Kazakhstan	Government stock company; allegedly controlled by Timur Kulibayev's group
Khabar Information Agency	Includes television channel, radio station, and several newspapers and magazines	Headed by Dariga Nazarbayeva
Korinth Trade and Investment	An investment group that acquired a controlling interest in Nelson Gold, a Canadian mining outfit	Allegedly controlled by Timur Kulibayev's group

Appendix 12 (continued)
Partial List of Nazarbayev Family Holdings and Reputed Holdings

Mangistaumunaigaz	Gas company	Allegedly controlled by Rakhat Aliyev and Dariga Nazarbayeva
Nazarbayev Educational Fund	Fund for educational development in Kazakhstan	Chaired by Dinara Nazarbayeva
Neftianoy tsentr (Oil Center)	Chain of gas stations in Kazakhstan	Allegedly controlled by Rakhat Aliyev and Dariga Nazarbayeva's group
Nelson Gold	Canadian-based firm that controls 50 percent of the development of the Alibekmola and Kozhasai oil fields (the combined proved reserves of the two fields are 264 million barrels); 70 percent of ownership held by Kazkommertsbank	Allegedly controlled by Timur Kulibayev's group
Novoe pokolenie	Newspaper	Allegedly owned by Rakhat Aliyev
NSBK Group	Includes Narodny Bank, Kazakhstan's Eximbank, and KazakhInStrakh (an insurance company)	Allegedly controlled by Timur Kulibayev's group
Nurbank	Bank active in Kazakhstan	Founded by Dariga Nazarbayeva. Nurbank is allegedly used for serving the businesses controlled by her and Rakhat Aliyev.
Orel and Berkut	Offshore companies	Used to make transactions with oil money, these companies allegedly belong to Nursultan Nazarbayev and James Giffen
Panorama	Newspaper	Allegedly owned by Rakhat Aliyev and Dariga Nazarbayeva
Pavlodar Oil Refinery	Oil refinery	Allegedly partly controlled by Timur Kulibayev's group
Radio "NS"	Almaty radio station	Allegedly owned by Timur Kulibayev
Rakhat Group	A group of 28 companies involved in the oil and gas industry, trade in metals, mining, construction, telecommunications, media, and hotel management; the group also finances the Almaty-based "Rakhat" volleyball and water polo teams (formerly called Dinamo)	Allegedly linked to Rakhat Aliyev
Real estate abroad	Property worth tens of millions of dollars, including: a villa in Saint-Tropez, France, a villa on the Turkish coast of the Mediterranean, a house in the French Alps, and a nineteenth-century residence in downtown London	Allegedly purchased by the Nazarbayev family

Sakharny Tsentr (Sugar Center)	Kazakhstan's major sugar company	Founded and headed by Rakhat Aliyev
Shymkentneftetorgsyntez (ShNOS)	Private oil company	Allegedly controlled by Timur Kulibayev's group through Kazkommertsbank
TransNefteGaz	Holding company	Newly created national oil and gas monopoly headed by Timur Kulibayev

Sources: Akezhan Kazhegeldin, "Otkrytoe pismo Akezhana Kazhegeldina generalomu prokuroru RK Yuriu Khitrinu," October 7, 1999, as published on Internet web site Eurasia.org.ru: <www.eurasia.org.ru/1999/tribuna/10_13_AK_Khitrin.htm>; Liza Brichkina, "Otkrovennoe Khanstvo," *Profil*, vol. 168, no. 46 (December 6, 1999); Xavier Pellegrini, "Kazahstanskie sanovniki poaplis v zhenevskie seti," *L'Hebdo*, February 3, 2000, as translated on Internet web site Eurasia.org.ru: <www.eurasia.org.ru/2000/inter_press/02_12_Launder_rus_.htm>; Sagyndyk Mendybayev, Nikolay Fomin, and Victor Shelgunov, "Kak razvorovali stranu," as published on Internet web site Eurasia.org.ru: <www.eurasia.org.ru/family/01.html>; Eldar Merlink, "Vvedenie v kazakhstanskuiu oligarhologiu Razdelennaya elita 2. Kto est Kto, Gde I s Kem v sovremennom Kazakhstane (dannye na mart 2000)," Institut aktualnyh politicheskih issledovaniy, March 31, 2000, as published on Internet web site Eurasia.org.ru: <www.eurasia.org.ru/2000/top5/03_31_anal.htm>; Vitaly Khlupin, "Kazakhstanskaya politicheskaya elita: mezhdu modernizatsiey I traibalizmom," paper presented at the Second All-Russia Congress of Political Scientists, Moscow, MGIMO, April 22, 2000, as published on Internet web site Kazhegeldin.kz: <www.kazhegeldin.kz/articles/About_27_05_00_002.htm>; Denis Lomov, "Sekrety sem'I Nazarbayeva" *Vremya*, N12, May 30, 2000, as published on Internet web site Eurasia.org.ru: <www.eurasia.org.ru/2000/top5/05_30_ss30.05.htm>; Sagyndyk Mendybayev, Nikolay Fomin, and Victor Shelgunov, "Kak priatali dengi v Shveitsarii—1," July 5, 2000, as published on Internet web site Eurasia.org.ru: <www.eurasia.org.ru/2000/analitica/07_05_stole1.htm>, "Kak priatali dengi v Shveitsarii—2," July 7, 2000, as published on Internet web site Eurasia.org.ru: <www.eurasia.org.ru/2000/analitica/07_07_stole2.htm>; "Kak priatali dengi v Shveitsarii—3," July 12, 2000, as published on Internet web site: <www.eurasia.org.ru/2000/analitica/07_12_stole3.htm>; Steve LeVine, "Sem'ia Nazarbayeva vyshla na mezdunarodnyi rynok," *Wall Street Journal*, October 10, 2000, as translated on Internet web site Business.ru: <www.business.ru/information/stories/2000/10/11/003_1028_vedomosti.html>; Paul Sampson, "Nazarbaev Cultivates Central Asian Dynasty," *Reuters Business Briefing*, November 2000, as translated on Internet web site Kazhegeldin.kz: <www.kazhegeldin.kz/english/About_22_11_00_en.htm>; Nikolay Skripnik, "Kazakhskaya interventsia na ukrainskiy rynok kak sredstvo legalizatsii kazakhskih tenevyh kapitalov," *USA Today*, December 1, 2000, as published on Internet web site Ferghana.ru <www.ferghana.ru/news03/559.html>; "Schet N35877 grazhdanina s pasportom 0000001," *Novaya gazeta*, N4, January 22, 2001, as published on Internet web site Novayagazeta.ru: <www.2001.novayagazeta.ru/nomer/2001/04n/n04n-s18.html>; Tair Farabi, "Za obschim dastarhanom," February 10, 2001, as published on Internet web site Eurasia.org.ru: <www.eurasia.org.ru/2001/tribuna/02_10_Dastarh.htm>; and "Govorit i pokazyvaet Sem'ia," February 19, 2001, as published on Internet web site Eurasia.org.ru: <www.eurasia.org.ru>.

Notes

The complete publication information for any source appearing here in shortened form may be found in the bibliography or at first mention in these notes.

Chapter 1
Introducing Kazakhstan

1. Chinua Achebe, *The Trouble with Nigeria* (London: Heinemann, 1983), p.1.

2. See Olcott, *The Kazakhs*; and Martha Brill Olcott, *Central Asia's New States* (Washington, D.C.: United States Institute of Peace, 1996).

3. Wood MacKenzie, quoted in Jaffe, *Unlocking the Assets*, table 3.

4. Quoted in George Lenczowski, "The Arc of Crisis: Its Central Sector," *Foreign Affairs*, vol. 57, no. 4 (spring 1979), p. 796.

5. Samuel Huntington, *The Clash of Civilizations and the Remaking of the World Order* (New York: Simon and Schuster, 1996).

6. The Commonwealth of Independent States (CIS) was formed by Belarus, Russia, and Ukraine on December 8, 1991, and membership was extended to the remaining former Soviet republics on December 21, 1991. Eventually all of the former Soviet republics, except Latvia, Lithuania, and Estonia, joined the CIS.

7. Strobe Talbott, *American Policy in the Caucasus and Central Asia*, address to the Central Asia Institute, Johns Hopkins School of Advanced International Studies, July 21, 1997.

8. In his press conference of December 8, 1999, President Clinton stated: "We got the Caspian pipeline agreements, which I believe 30 years from now you'll look back on and say that was one of the most important things that happened this year." Source: *RFE/RL Newsline*, vol. 3, no. 238, part 1 (December 9, 1999).

9. It is becoming more accepted with time for the English language press to use the word *Kazakh* to refer to all those who live in Kazakhstan, regardless of their ethnic origin.

10. For a more detailed discussion of Kazakhstan's economy at the time of independence see Martha Brill Olcott's chapter on Kazakhstan in *Kazakhstan, Kyrgyzstan, Tajikistan, Turkmenistan, and Uzbekistan: Country Studies* (Area Handbook Series), ed. Glenn E. Curtis

(Washington, D.C.: Library of Congress Federal Research Division, 1997). See also Boris Z. Rumer, ed., *Central Asia in Transition: Dilemmas of Political and Economic Development* (New York: M.E. Sharpe, 1996); and Richard Pomfret, *Economies of Central Asia* (Princeton, N.J.: Princeton University Press, 1995).

11. According to Kazakhstan's first census, in 1999 there were 14,953,000 people living in Kazakhstan, down from 16,199,100 in 1989. For complete demographic information, see appendices 1 and 2.

12. A claim made at a news conference held by Foreign Minister Yerlan Idrissov in Astana on May 8, 2001, as reported by the Interfax news agency on that same date.

13. In 1989, 40.1 percent of Kazakhstan's population were ethnic Kazakhs, and 37.4 percent ethnic Russians; in 1999, 53.4 percent were ethnic Kazakhs, and 30.0 percent ethnic Russians. For more detailed information, see appendix 2.

14. The present-day city of Almaty and the oblast of the same name were known as Alma Ata during the Soviet period. The oblast, or province, is a territorial and administrative unit used in Russia and Kazakhstan. Contemporary Kazakhstan is composed of fourteen oblasts and two urban administrative areas, Astana and Almaty.

15. This figure is based on projections through 1999. See Victor Shelgunov's analysis in "The Flight from the Oasis: Economic Crisis and the Migration Level," *Central Asian Bulletin,* December 6, 1998, no. 15. See appendices 1 and 2 for more demographic information.

16. This phrase was dropped from the 1995 constitution.

17. Known as *Kiev* until the end of the Soviet period, Ukraine's capital city is now known as *Kyiv.* The Soviet-era name is retained here for historical correctness.

18. Nazarbayev, *Bez pravykh,* p. 26.

19. The phrases *glasnost* (opening) and *perestroika* (reconstruction) became the watchwords of reform after Mikhail Gorbachev came to power in 1985.

20. The Soviet Union was effectively dissolved when the leaders of the Belarusan SSR, Ukrainian SSR, and Russian Federation (RSFSR) met outside Minsk on December 8, 1991, and declared the 1922 Treaty of Union that had created the Soviet Union to be null and void.

21. "We the People" are the first three words of the preamble of the U.S. Constitution.

22. The 1995 constitution preserves Russian as an official "language of international communication." Kazakh remains the sole "state language."

23. See appendix 6 for Kazakhstan's trade statistics.

24. An expanded version of the Shanghai Five, which originally included Russia, China, Kazakhstan, Tajikistan, and Kyrgyzstan, was created in April 1996. Uzbekistan joined the newly named Shanghai Cooperation Organization in June 2001.

25. In July 1994.

26. *Interfax,* August 29, 1995, as quoted in FBIS–SOV–95–168, August 30, 1995, p. 65.

27. Kazakhs turned on local Russian settlers and officials after learning that "the natives" would be forced to serve in labor brigades at the front. For more on the 1916 Kazakh uprising, see Olcott, *The Kazakhs,* pp. 118–126.

Chapter 2
Reluctantly Accepting Independence

1. Olcott, "Kazakhstan: Pushing for Eurasia," p. 556.

2. U.S. Information Agency (USIA) polls in October and November 1997 showed his approval rating at 65 percent (*Opinion Analysis*, USIA Office of Research and Media Reaction, October 16, 1997, November 17, 1997.)

3. The Giller Institute Poll in July 1997 showed that 33.4 percent of the population supported his economic policies. Reported in *Interfax*, July 27, 1997, as translated in *BBC Summary of World Broadcasts*.

4. Even before the collapse of the Soviet Union gave Moldova its independence, local officials in Transdniesteria declared this region an independent Soviet Socialist Republic and began to set up a separate republic government. After Moldova's independence, the separatist movement in Transdniesteria continued to grow stronger, and it received vast support from Moscow. Russia's Fourteenth Army was stationed in the region, making a Moldovan military victory impossible. There are several possible explanations for Russia's disproportionate support for the Transdniesterian separatists vis-à-vis, for example, the Russians in northern Kazakhstan. One possibility is that Moscow wished to retain a bargaining chip that it could use to "encourage" a reluctant Moldova to join the CIS. Unlike Moldova, Kazakhstan was a strong supporter of post-Soviet integration. Another factor was certainly the prominence of the Moldovan issue in the Russian press, a condition that Russian nationalists were exploiting. The plight of Russians in Kazakhstan did not receive this kind of media exposure and thus was not such a point of contention between Russian nationalists and moderates. Crowther, "Moldova," pp. 316–49.

5. To be his "eyes and ears" during this period Nazarbayev sent Kanat Saudabayev, later Kazakhstan's ambassador to Turkey, the United Kingdom, and the United States, to be his personal representative in Moscow.

6. It has been repeatedly rumored that Nazarbayev was invited to attend the Minsk summit in December 1991 and declined.

7. For more biographical information on Nazarbayev, see Tolmachev, *Lider*; Shepel' and Kasymbekov, *Pervyi Prezident Respubliki Kazakhstan*; Zhigalov and Sultanov, *Pervyi Prezident Respubliki Kazakhstan*. For Nazarbayev's autobiographical works, see Nazarbayev, *Nursultan Nazarbayev: Adiletting aq zholy*; *Bez pravykh*; *V potoke istorii*; and *Piat' let nezavisimosti*.

8. The present-day city of Almaty and the oblast of the same name were known as Alma Ata during the Soviet period. The oblast, or province, is a territorial and administrative unit used in Russia and Kazakhstan. Contemporary Kazakhstan is composed of fourteen oblasts and two urban administrative areas, Astana and Almaty.

9. For more on the reformers' targeting of Kunayev, see Olcott, *The Kazakhs*, pp. 245–53.

10. Gennady Kolbin, an ethnic Russian, was appointed by Moscow to replace Kunayev as first secretary of the Communist Party of Kazakhstan in December 1986. Nazarbayev took over from him in June 1989.

11. For more on the 1986 Alma Ata Uprising, see first the documentary volume *Alma Ata 1986* and Kozybaev's *Dekabr' 1986*. See also *Literaturnaia gazeta*, November 28, 1990, p. 11; *Kazakhstanskaia pravda*, September 28, 1990, p. 1, and December 17, 1991, p. 2.

12. The protests of 1986 were reevaluated in 1989–1990 by a committee led by Mukhtar Shakhanov; see "Zakliuchenie Komissii Prezidiuma Verkhovnogo Soveta KazSSR po okonchatel'noi otsenke dekabr'skikh sobytii 1986 goda v Alma-Ate i drugikh oblastiakh Kazakhstana," Alma-Ata, 1991.

13. *Sovetskaia Rossiia,* October 19, 1989, as translated in *FBIS Daily Report,* SOV–89–107, October 27, 1989.

14. Nazarbayev as quoted in Yuri Kulchik, "Central Asia after the Empire: Ethnic Groups, Communities and Problems," in *Central Asia: Conflict, Resolution, and Change,* Roald Z. Sagdeev and Susan Eisenhower, eds. (Washington, D.C.: Center for Political and Strategic Studies, 1995).

15. See Nazarbayev's speech to Seventeenth Congress of the Kazakhstan Communist Party in *Kazakhstanskaia pravda,* June 8, 1990, pp. 2–4.

16. One such group was the Kazakh language society called the *Kazakh tili.* Founded in the late 1980s, its purpose was to advance the role of the Kazakh language in public life.

17. Russian speakers were particularly concerned about a clause in the draft language law that would require some professionals and officials to know two or three languages, as well as a clause mandating which languages must be offered in schools (*Itar–Tass,* September 22, 1989).

18. The Kazakh nationalist party called Azat (freedom) dates from this period. It was founded in 1990 and advocated more autonomy for Kazakhstan within the Soviet Union. It called for Kazakhstan's sovereignty and the possibility of its secession from the USSR and for the creation of local military groups (Brown, "New Political Parties in Kazakhstan").

19. An example of late Soviet power-sharing arrangements with the republics was a program put forward in March 1989 giving the republics limited control over their own budgets. Most major industries, however, remained in the hands of the center. Bohdan Nahaylo, "Why the Empire's Subjects Are Restless," *Index on Censorship,* vol. 18, no. 5 (May/June 1989), p. 27.

20. Azat joined with the Republican Party of Kazakhstan and the Kazakh nationalist Zheltoksan Party in 1992, but the group soon broke up. It is led by Chairman Kozha Akhmet Khasen. Alash is a Kazakh nationalist party that also has an Islamist tinge. Its current leader is Sovetkazy Akatayev. See "Major Political Parties and Public Associations in the Republic of Kazakhstan," on the Official Kazakhstan Internet web site: <www.president.kz/main/msainframe.asp?lng=en>.

21. Olzhas Suleimenov said this in an interview with *Sovershenno sekretno* (no. 9, 1990, pp. 22–23).

22. Since 1989 Armenia and Azerbaijan have clashed over Azerbaijan's ethnic Armenian enclave of Nagorno-Karabakh. After several years of fighting, Armenia now controls a portion of the secessionist territory, and the region's final status is still undetermined. Georgia's Abkhazia region has been trying to win its independence through violent struggle since 1989. The region now enjoys de facto independence, but tensions remain high.

23. The Treaty on the Union of Sovereign States that came out of the Novo-Ogarevo meeting sought to remake the Soviet Union to fit the realities of 1990. It proposed a union in which the sovereignty of the constituent republics would be guaranteed, as would their rights to "decide independently all issues of their development." The treaty spelled out which powers would belong to the Union and which would be jointly exercised by the union and its con-

stituent republics. It also set out the procedures for the implementation of those powers (draft of Novo-Ogarevo Agreement, published in *Pravda*, June 27, 1991, p. 2).

24. The term *nomenklatura* refers to managers, enterprise owners, bureaucrats, advisers to the president, and others who constitute the traditional communist elite.

25. For a discussion on the sovereignty debate, see Olcott, *The Kazakhs*, pp. 264–68.

26. Nazarbayev played the role of power broker at this meeting, offering a new version of the union treaty that would have been signed had the coup not taken place.

27. Vladimir Akimov, *Itar–Tass*, February 22, 1994. Suleimenov left the fray of Kazakhstan's political scene in 1995 when he accepted an appointment as Kazakhstan's ambassador to Italy.

28. The highlights of Nazarbayev's plan for the EAU were published in *Izvestiya*, June 8, 1994, p. 2, as translated in RusData DiaLine, *Russian Press Digest*. Additional information is available in *Itar–Tass*, April 21, 1994.

29. Nursultan Nazarbayev, remarks at the Carnegie Endowment for International Peace, April 23, 1999.

30. When Kozyrev began his stint as the foreign minister, he was known for his liberal, pro-Western policies. By 1994, his rhetoric had undergone a significant shift, and he had joined the voices advocating the protection of Russian speakers in the "near abroad" and insisting on Russia's right to assume a "special role" in countries of the former Soviet Union. See Kozyrev, "The Lagging Partnership."

31. *Rossiiskaia gazeta*, April 2, 1996, p. 3.

32. An acronym formed by the first letter of each member country: Georgia, Ukraine, Azerbaijan, and Moldova.

33. For more information on the GUUAM group, see: Olcott, Åslund, and Garnett, *Getting It Wrong*, pp. 66–70.

34. Ibid., pp. 26–27.

35. President Nazarbayev's statement at a news conference in October 2000 during Putin's official visit to Kazakhstan. See "Agreements Signed with One of Russia's 'Closest Partners,' " *BBC Monitoring*, October 9, 2000.

36. For example, Syzdyk Abishev, who was appointed the minister of External Economic Relations of the Republic of Kazakhstan in 1991.

37. *USIA Opinion Research*, 1993, found that 29 percent of the population "completely agreed" with this statement, and 32 percent "agreed more than they disagreed" with the statement. By nationality the breakdowns were as follows: Kazakhs (18 percent, 35 percent), Russians (39 percent, 34 percent), and others (32 percent, 24 percent).

38. The United States' Nunn-Lugar Cooperative Threat Reduction Program oversaw the denuclearization of Kazakhstan, including the 1994 airlift of weapon-grade uranium to the United States, dubbed Operation Sapphire.

39. The 1994 agreement provided for the joint training of Russian and Kazakhstani border guards and for a joint council composed of the heads of the two countries' border services. The 1995 document set up joint Russian-Kazakh border forces and allowed for a small Russian border detachment to be deployed in Kazakhstan, but Kazakhstan retains the sole right to defend its borders.

40. Nazarbayev and Yeltsin signed the treaty, called the Declaration on Eternal Friendship and Alliance Oriented to the Twenty-first Century, on July 6, 1998. For a comprehensive

discussion of Russian-Kazakh defense relations, see Alexandrov, "Military Relations between Russia and Kazakhstan," pp. 18–25.

41. "Russia Strengthening Its Relationship with Kazakhstan." *Nezavisimaia gazeta*, February 15, 2000, p. 2.

42. Tom Dalyell, "Keeping the Nasties under Lock and Key," *New Scientist*, February 4, 1995, p. 47.

43. CENTRASBAT was formed in 1995 under UN auspices. Since then, it has participated in two major multinational military exercises organized by NATO's Partnership for Peace program. These exercises have taken place in all three CENTRASBAT countries and have included troops from the United States and other countries in the region. Most recently, military personnel from Kazakhstan and the United States participated in Exercise "Zhardem '99," a month-long practice exercise in providing aid during natural disasters.

44. In 2001, Russia will provide Kazakhstan with twenty million dollars' worth of arms and military hardware. See "Russia to Export to Kazakhstan 20m-Dollars' Worth of Arms," *BBC Monitoring*, January 12, 2001.

45. Nazarbayev in an interview in November 2000. See "Kazakh President Upbeat on Eurasian Economic Community's Future," *BBC Monitoring*, November 15, 2000.

46. International Monetary Fund, *Direction of Trade Statistics Yearbook* (Washington, D.C.: IMF, 1998).

47. International Monetary Fund, *Kazakhstan: Recent Economic Developments*, Staff Country Report, no. 96/22 (Washington, D.C.: IMF, March 1996), p. 106.

48. In June 2000, Putin approved a new foreign policy concept for Russia. The document emphasizes the importance of further developing relations and maintaining "strategic partnerships" with Russia's neighbors.

Chapter 3
The Challenge of Creating Kazakhstanis

1. These include Alash, which is named after the mythic founder of the Kazakh party and traces its roots to the nationalist movements founded in 1990, and Azat. Both of these groups support special rights for Kazakhs.

2. For a study of the nature of boundaries in Central Asia, see A. Malashenko and M. B. Olcott, eds. *Mnogomernye granitsy Tsentral'noi Azii* (Moscow: Carnegie Moscow Center, 2000).

3. "Kak nam obustroit Rossiu," *Komsomolskaia pravda*, September 19, 1990, and Aleksandr Solzhenitsyn *Publitsistika* (Yaroslavl: Verhne-Volzhskoe knizhnoe izdatelstvo, 1995), vol. 1, pp. 540–41, 543.

4. See, for example, Nazarbayev's interview with Manfred Quiring, "Now He Is Keeping His Distance from Moscow," *Berliner Zeitung*, February 11, 1994, as translated in *FBIS Daily Report*, SOV–94–030, February 14, 1994. He did sign two agreements with Moscow in January 1995, which, respectively, defined the treatment of citizens of one state permanently residing in the other.

5. See Martha Brill Olcott, *Central Asia's New States* (Washington, D.C.: United States Institute of Peace Press, 1996), pp. 62–70.

6. Conference on Security and Cooperation in Europe, "Recommendations to the Government of Kazakhstan," letter of Max van der Stoel, the Commission for Security and Cooperation in Europe (CSCE) High Commissioner on National Minorities, The Hague, April 29, 1994.

7. Turkmenistan and Russia signed a dual citizenship agreement in December 1993, at which time Boris Yeltsin very symbolically accepted Turkmen citizenship.

8. The "Treaty between the Kazakhstan Republic and Russian Federation on the Legal Status of Citizens of the Kazakhstan Republic Permanently Residing in the Russian Federation and Citizens of the Russian Federation Permanently Residing in the Kazakhstan Republic," printed in *Kazakhstanskaia pravda* (January 21, 1995), as translated in *FBIS Daily Report*, SOV–95–019 (January 30, 1995), made it easier for such permanent residents to become citizens of the state in which they lived ("Agreement between the Republic of Kazakhstan and the Russian Federation on Simplification of the Procedure for Obtaining Citizenship by Citizens of the Republic of Kazakhstan Arriving for Permanent Residence in the Russian Federation and Citizens of the Russian Federation Arriving for Permanent Residence in the Republic of Kazakhstan"), *Kazakhstanskaia pravda*, January 21, 1995, as translated in *FBIS Daily Report*, SOV–95–017, January 26, 1995.

9. A. G. Vishnevskii, *Naselenie Rossii 1995*, p. 82, quoted in Olcott, "Demographic Upheavals," p. 542.

10. Ethnic Russians appointed to the Kazakh government between 1994 and 1996 included: Vladimir Karmakov, minister of energy and the coal industry (appointed June 14, 1994); Vyacheslav Kostuychenko, minister of industry and trade (appointed June 17, 1994); Vladimir Skolnik, minister of science and new technologies (appointed August 19, 1994); Viktor Khrapunov, minister of energy and the coal industry (appointed March 15, 1995); Konstantin Kolpakov, minister of justice (appointed October 3, 1995); Nikolay Bayev, minister of ecology and biological resources (appointed October 3, 1995); and Nikolai Radostovets, chairman of the State Committee on Anti-Monopoly Policies (appointed April 22, 1996). Skolnik and Khrapunov have remained fixtures in Kazakhstan's political life.

11. *Karavan*, December 15, 1995, p. 2.

12. Delorme, *Mother Tongue, Mother's Touch*, pp. 67–70.

13. *Kazakhstanskaia pravda*, May 29, 1996, p. 3.

14. *Kazakhstanskaia pravda*, October 9, 1993, insert, as translated in *FBIS Daily Report*, USR–94–003, January 12, 1994, p. 44.

15. Ibid.

16. The statement that political authority arose exclusively from "the Kazakh people" was eliminated from the 1995 constitution, but the new constitution still states in its preamble that the people of Kazakhstan are charged with the task of "creating a state on the indigenous Kazakh land."

17. Nazarbayev, "Ideological Consolidation," p. 45.

18. Ibid., p. 40.

19. *Kazakhstanskaia pravda*, May 25, 1996.

20. Lev Gumilev served the first part of a 1950–1956 term in a camp in Karaganda. See Gershtein, *Memoirs*, pp. 347–48.

21. Gumilev's works include *Drevniaia Rus' i Velikaia Step'* (Moskva: T-vo Klyshnikov, Komarov i Ko., 1992); *Drevnie Tiurki* (Moskva: "Klyshnikov-Komarov," 1993); *Ritmy Evrazii:*

Epokhi i Tsivilizatsii (Moskva: Ekopros, 1993); and *Iz Istorii Evrazii* (Moskva: Izd-vo "Iskusstvo," 1993).

22. Eitzen, *Scenarios on Statehood*, p. 191.

23. Nazarbayev's remarks during a speech in 1993.

24. See K. Nurlanova, "The Kazakh National Ideal," *Nauka Kazakhstana*, nos. 4, 6, and 8 (1994).

25. Karimov, *Uzbekistan na poroge XXI veka*, pp. 48–66.

26. See N. A. Nazarbayev, *Na poroge XXI veka* (Moscow: Oner, 1996), especially section 1, which is on the collapse of the USSR.

27. For more information on this period, see Olcott, *The Kazakhs*, pp. 28–53.

28. The three most prominent members of the early, pro-Russian Kazakh secular elite were Chokan Valikhanov (1835–1865), Ibrahim Altynsarin (1841–1889), and Abai Kunanbayev (1845–1904). All three were also celebrated during the Soviet period, and their writings were published in full. For writings by these men, see Chokan Valikhanov, *Sobranie sochinenii v piati tomakh* (Alma-Ata: Glav. red. Kazakhskoi Sov. Entsiklopedii, 1984–1985); Ibrahim Altynsarin, *Sobranie sochinenii v trekh tomakh* (Alma-Ata, 1925–1938); Abai Kunanbayev, *Izbrannye sochinenia* (Alma-Ata, 1980).

29. In June 1916, the Russian tsar ordered the conscription into labor units of eighteen- to forty-three-year-olds from territories corresponding to the present-day regions of the Caucasus and Central Asia, sparking an anti-Russian insurgency throughout the Kazakh territory. For a more detailed discussion of these events, see Olcott, *The Kazakhs*, pp. 118–26.

30. Martha Brill Olcott, "The Collectivization Drive in Kazakhstan," *Russian Review*, vol. 40, no. 2 (1981), pp. 122–42.

31. For more on Kazakh attitudes toward their native language and the use of bilingual education to spread "Kazakhness," see Delorme, *Mother Tongue*.

32. Gudkov, *Russkie v Kazakhstane*.

33. LAD is a registered political group formed in 1993 and initially led by Aleksandra Dokuchaeva, who now lives in Moscow.

34. See Gudkov, *Russkie v Kazakhstane*, p. 17, table 8.

35. See the public opinion survey in ibid., p. 17–18.

36. *Jamestown Monitor*, November 26, 1997.

37. See Eitzen, *Scenarios on Statehood*; Laitin, *Identity in Formation*; N. M. Lebedeva, *Novaia russkaia diaspora: Sotsial'no-psikhologicheskii analiz* (Moskva: Institut etnologii i antropologii im Miklukho Maklaia RAN, 1997); Vitkovskaya, *Russians in the Non-Russian Former Republics*.

38. See in particular Laitin, *Identity in Formation*, pp. 105–57.

39. Tishkov, "Ethnicity and Power," p. 50.

40. See Gudkov, *Russkie v Kazakhstane*, pp. 17–18 and 31–32.

41. Ibid., table 16.

42. From 1920 to 1924 the territory around Orenburg was merged into the Kirgiz (Kazakh) Autonomous Soviet Socialist Republic, but in 1924–1925 it was returned to Russia. See Kozybayev, *Kazakhskaia Sovetskaia Entsiklopediia*, maps on pp. 176–77, 200–201.

43. See "Cossack Chiefs Back Putin for President," *BBC Monitoring*, March 18, 2000, and Pamela Johnson, "Zyuganov Promises to Raise Salaries, Help the Cossacks," *The Russia Journal*, 13 March 2000, as published on the Internet web site of ISI Emerging Markets: <securities.com.ru/c/s.dll/plquer>.

44. See Grigorii G. Kosach, "The Regional Version of the Russian-Kazakhstan Transborder Cooperation: The Case of Orenburg Oblast," unpublished manuscript, 2000, p. 48.

45. See Galina Vitkovskaya and Aleksei Malashenko, eds. *Vozrozhdenie kazachestvo: nadezhdy i opaseniia* (Moscow: Carnegie Moscow Center, 1998).

46. *Kazakhstanskaia pravda*, November 22, 1995, as translated in *FBIS Daily Report* SOV–95–225.

47. This was part of a February 27, 1996, broadcast (*OMRI Daily Digest*, February 28, 1996).

48. "Konstantin Zatulin Discusses the Fate of the CIS," *Nezavisimaia gazeta*, December 10, 1997, p. 3.

49. See Gudkov, *Russkie v Kazakhstane*, p. 11.

50. Ibid.

51. Sabit Jusupov, 1995, 1996 (unpublished material). The survey did not list potential alternatives to Nazarbayev.

52. See survey in Gudkov, *Russkie v Kazakhstane*, pp. 27–30.

53. Sixty-six percent of the Russians supported this idea, versus 35 percent of the Kazakhs (United States Information Agency, *USIA Opinion Analysis*, M203–97, December 10, 1997).

54. Emelian Pugachev was a Don Cossack who claimed to be Peter III and led a 1773–1774 Russian peasant uprising.

55. "East Kazakh Security Service Detains Group of 'Terrorists' from Russia," *BBC Monitoring*, November 20, 1999, as published on the Internet web site of ISI Emerging Markets: <securities.com.ru/c/s.dll/plquer>.

56. Lariokhin and Charodeev, "'Pugachev Rebellion' Suppressed," p. 3.

57. Gudkov, *Russkie v Kazakhstane*, p. 12.

58. Ibid., p. 10.

59. United States Information Agency, *Opinion Analysis*, August 18, 1995.

60. United States Information Agency, *Opinion Analysis*, M–202–97, USIA Office of Research and Media Reaction, December 11, 1997.

61. Sabit Jusupov, commissioned research, 1995.

62. *FBIS Daily Report*, SOV–92–167, August 27, 1992, p. 62.

63. The border demarcation began as a unilateral Uzbek effort. See Marat Gurnov, "Uzbek Secret Services Become Active in the South of Kazakhstan," *Central Asian Bulletin*, February 3, 2000.

64. Kazakhstan Census, January 12, 1989, reported in *Alma-Ata Yegemendi Qazaqstan*, as translated in *FBIS Daily Report*, USR–92–144, November 11, 1992.

65. *OMRI Daily Digest*, August 19, 1996.

66. Gulnar Tankaeva, *Karavan*, August 2, 1996, p. 10.

67. Merhat Sheripzhan, "Kazakhstan's Security," *Central Asia Monitor*, no. 6 (2000), p. 21.

68. "Uighur Minority Stages Second Protest in Almaty," *Info-Prod Research (Middle East)*, November 18, 1999.

Chapter 4
Trying Pluralism and Abandoning It

1. See Mendybayev, Fomin, and Shelgunov, *Kazakhgeit;* and Shelley, "Corrupt Oil Practices."

2. Vrichkina, "Otkrovennoe Khanstvo."

3. Zheltoksan (December) was named for the month in 1986 when former republic leader Dinmuhammad Kunayev was replaced, prompting riots. Alash was named in honor of the legendary founder of the Kazakh people and also recalls the name of the first Kazakh political party and government in 1918–1920.

4. Semipalatinsk oblast was merged into East Kazakhstan in 1997. The Kazakh name for Semipalatinsk is *Semey*, but common usage remains *Semipalatinsk*.

5. See Atakhanova, "The Monster of Semipalatinsk."

6. Olzhas Suleimenov got into trouble for writing *Az i Ya*, first published in 1976, which offered a pro-Turkic view of early Russian history. He survived politically because he enjoyed the backing of Kazakh party boss Kunayev and so became a target of Gennady Kolbin.

7. Suleimenov continued his writing career in Italy, See his *Iazyk pis´ma*.

8. Kazakhstan's National Security Committee and the Procuracy accused the joint-stock company Nevada-Semey, established under Suleimenov's Nevada-Semipalatinsk movement, of illegal export practices involving a shipment of copper (*Izvestiya*, April 7, 1993, p. 2, as translated in *FBIS Daily Reports*, Central Asia, USR–93–051, April 24, 1993).

9. This practice was introduced as a control measure during the 1989 USSR Congress of Peoples Deputies elections and was a feature in legislative elections in the Russian republic as well.

10. The method of voting used in Kazakhstan at the time was to select a representative by crossing out the names of the other candidates; 1,229 candidates contested 270 parliamentary seats allocated for territorial representatives, while 544 candidates vied for the 90 seats intended for public organizations. Voter dissatisfaction was sufficient to unseat some of the old-line politicians.

11. Nazarbayev received 98 percent of the vote in the December 1991 race, with 80 percent of the electorate participating. His only potential opponent reportedly failed to gather the 100,000 signatures necessary to have his name on the ballot.

12. Tereshchenko was Kazakhstan's prime minister from 1991 to 1994.

13. For more on post-Soviet party formation, see Herbert Kitschelt, Zdenka Mansfeldova, Radoslaw Markowski, and Gabor Toka: *Post-Communist Party Systems: Competition, Representation, and Inter-Party Cooperation* (Cambridge, U.K.: Cambridge University Press, 1999); and for a comparison with Russia, see Michael McFaul, "Party Formation and Non-Formation in Russia," Carnegie Endowment Working Paper 12 (Washington, D.C.: Carnegie Endowment for International Peace, May 2000).

14. Zinaida Zakaeva and Zaure Sarsenbayeva, *Mezhetnicheskie Otnosheniya v sovremennom Kazakhstane* (opyt kompleksnogo sotsiologicheskogo analiza).

15. These figures are for the Kazakhstan Communist Party, whose members consider themselves heirs to the CPSU. The Kazakhstan Communist Party was founded in September 1991 but was denied registration as an official party until March 1994. Membership figures and information are available on the Internet web site Eurasia.org: <www.soros.org/cen_eurasia/departments/election/kazakhstan/index.shtml>.

16. "Preliminary Kazakhstan Election Results," *Intercon Daily Report on Russia*, October 13, 1999.

17. Information on political parties is available at the official Kazakhstan Internet web site: <www.president.kz/main/mainframe.asp?lng=en>.

18. Opposition parties have complained of harassment, surveillance, denial of access to the state-run media, and arbitrary banning from registering candidates, according to Freedom House's *Freedom in the World 2000–2001* (New York: Freedom House, 2001).

19. See appendix 4 for information on political parties and the results of parliamentary elections.

20. See Luong and Weinthal, "The NGO Paradox."

21. From the "Constitution of the Republic of Kazakhstan," section 8, as published on the official Kazakhstan Internet web site: <www.president.kz/main/mainframe.asp?lng=en>.

22. See Luong, "Ethno-politics and Institutional Design."

23. The powers of the *maslikhat* include: approving of plans, economic and social programs for the development of the territory, and the local budget; making decisions on issues of local administrative-territorial organization in their jurisdiction; considering reports by the heads of local executive bodies; and forming standing commissions and other working bodies of a *maslikhat*.

24. See chapter 15, "The Constitution of the Republic of Kazakhstan," adopted January 28, 1993, for the rights and responsibilities of local government.

25. Luong, "Ethno-politics and Institutional Design," pp. 323–30.

26. This was true on the Kazakh-Russian, the Kazakh-Kyrgyz, and the Kazakh-Uzbek borders. The population along the Kazakh-Turkmen border was far less dense than along the other three.

27. Chernykh, "Russia and Kazakhstan," p. 9.

28. The northern oblasts clustered in three groups: the northwest (Uralsk, renamed West Kazakhstan, Kostanai, and Aktiubinsk), the north (Akmola, Petropavlovsk, renamed North Kazakhstan, and Pavlodar), and the northeast (Ust-Kamenogorsk, including Semipalatinsk which was incorporated in 1997, renamed East Kazakhstan).

29. Grigorii G. Kosach reports that only three of the twelve *raion* heads of border districts have close ties with their Kazakh counterparts. See his unpublished paper, "The Regional Version," pp. 16–17.

30. "Nazarbayev Opposes the Election of Governors," *RFE/RL Daily Report*, April 1, 1999.

31. A local businessman, Kayrat Baybaktinov, won the election with almost 53 percent of the vote (1,773 votes), beating seven other candidates, including the incumbent *akim* (Baymuratov, "Kazakhs").

32. *BBC Monitoring Service*, April 13, 2001.

33. See Luong, "The Path Least Resisted."

34. On April 22, 1997, Taldy Kurgan (pop. 721,000) became part of Almaty region, and Turgai's territory (pop. 315,000) was divided between Kostanai and Akmola regions. On May 3, 1997, Zhezkazgan (pop. 496,000) was incorporated into Karaganda, Kokchetau (pop, 664,000) into North Kazakhstan, and Semipalatinsk (pop. 838,000) into East Kazakhstan. All population statistics are from the 1989 census as published in *Naselenie SSSR 1988* (Moscow: Goskomstat SSSR, 1989), pp. 26–28.

35. Brichkina, "Otkrovennoe Khanstvo."

36. Privileged communications to author.

37. "Kazakhstan's New Parliament," *Izvestiya*, May 12, 1994, p. 4.

38. "New Faces in Parliament," *Sovety Kazakhstana*, November 2, 1994, pp. 1–2, as translated in *FBIS Daily Report*, Central Eurasia, USR–94–124, November 15, 1994, p. 87.

39. See appendix 4.

40. The position of parliamentary speaker went to Abish Kekilbayev of SNEK, who was also acceptable to the Kazakh president. See "Kazakh Parliament Chooses New Speaker," *RFE/RL Daily Report*, no. 76 (April 21, 1994).

41. The Respublika group bears no direct relation to the RNPK that was formed in 1998.

42. This first Otan also bears no relation to the mass party of the same name that was organized in 1999.

43. Karashal Asan-ata (Asanov), author of the trilogy *Prizrak nezavisimosti* (The Spectre of Independence), was arrested in November 1998 for "insulting the honor of the presidency" at a political rally in Almaty. See "Kolonka Vadima Boreiko," *Nedel'ka*, November 11, 1998, p. 3.

44. According to Kazakh government statistics, on September 1, 2000, there were 1,258 mass media and information agencies in the country of which 76 percent were privately owned. Kazakhstan, Country Reports on Human Rights Practices, U.S. Department of State, February 2001.

45. A journalist was dismissed from the television station *31 Kanal* for taking a critical position of the government. See *Civil Society List*, April 20, 2000.

46. Human Rights Watch, *Kazakhstan*.

47. Boris Giller, together with director Sergei Bodrov, produced the award-winning film *Prisoner of the Mountains*, released in 1997.

48. Giller's printing operation, Franklin Printing, was originally supported with an investment and loan from the Central Asian American Enterprise Fund and printed materials from the independent press of Kazakhstan and Kyrgyzstan.

49. For an account of pressure on the press see Sharipzhan, "Mass Media in Kazakhstan," pp. 13–15.

50. For an example of the international protest of the shutdown of *XXI Vek*, see the letter written by Ann K. Cooper, executive director of the Committee to Protect Journalists (CPJ) to Nursultan Nazarbayev as published on the CPJ Internet web site: <169.132.35.44/protests/98ltrs/kazakstan30sept98.html>.

51. Human Rights Watch, *World Report 1999: Kazakhstan*, published at Human Rights Watch Internet web site: <http://www.hrw.org/worldreport99/europe/kazakhstan.html>.

52. Human Rights Watch, country report for Kazakhstan, 1998.

53. The new law introduces limitations on transmissions by foreign media and stricter controls on publishing Internet newspapers.

54. These complaints are detailed in Human Rights Watch's report *Kazakhstan*.

55. These included 136 from the Ministry of Internal Affairs, 14 from the court system, 10 from the prosecutor's office, 26 from customs agencies, 30 from tax agencies, 9 from the banking system, 62 from local self-government bodies, and 210 from other state authorities. "Kazaks Crack Down on Corruption in Judiciary," *Interfax-Kazakhstan*, April 20, 2000.

56. "Unemployment, Corruption, Top Kazakh Worry List, Polls Show," *Nachnem s ponedelnika*, April 7, 2000.

57. "Independent Newspapers Shut Down for Reprinting Corruption Allegations from Foreign Media," *CSJ Action Alert*, August 9, 2000.

58. See the Eurasia Information and Analysis Center's *Freedom of Speech and Mass Media in Kazakhstan* as published in 1998 on the Internet web site of the International Eurasian Institute for Economic and Political Research: <iicas.org/english/publruss.htm>.

59. Jusupov, "Analiz predposylok," p. 11.

60. Other candidates included Serik Abdrakhmanov of SNEK and Olzhas Suleimenov of the Congress Party. Like Suleimenov, Abdrakhmanov (a former Komsomol leader) had formed his own nationwide ecology group, Elim-ai, and was also said to have used the money from dues to amass a personal fortune. Both men receded from public life without the charges having been proved, Abdrakhmanov to private business.

61. Abdildin became the first secretary of the Communist Party of Kazakhstan in April 1996.

62. "Kazakh Parliament Steps up Challenges," *Sovety Kazakhstana*, November 2, 1994, pp. 1–2, as translated in *FBIS Daily Reports*, Central Eurasia, USR–94–124, November 15, 1994, p. 87.

63. See *Almaty Panorama*, March 11, 1995, p. 2, as translated in *FBIS Daily Reports*, Central Asia, SOV–95–049, March 14, 1995; *Kommersant-Daily*, March 15, 1995, p. 4, as translated in *FBIS Daily Reports*, Central Asia, SOV–95–067–S, April 7, 1995; *Kazakhstanskaia pravda*, March 15, 1995, p. 1, as translated in *FBIS Daily Reports*. Central Asia, SOV–95–052, March 17, 1995. For the text of the court's ruling, see *Kazakhstanskaia pravda*, March 16, 1995, p. 3, as translated in *FBIS Daily Reports*, Central Asia, SOV–95–055, March 22, 1995.

64. Suleimenov, a major general in the Ministry of the Interior, had previously served as the head of the Kazakh Communist Party Central Committee Department of Administrative Affairs during Kolbin's cleanup. Leonid Nikitinsky, "The Journalist against the Central Electoral Commission," *Moskovskiye novosti*, no. 31, April 30–May 7, 1995, p. 14, as translated in *FBIS Daily Report*, SOV–95–97.

65. In December 2000, Suleimenov became the first deputy minister responsible for Kazakhstan's interior troops, and in June 2001, he was appointed the commander of interior troops.

66. He retained the power to name his cabinet (still subject to parliamentary approval) and all other government officials and gained the power to sponsor all legislation and to declare states of emergency that put the constitution in abeyance.

67. These goals were: to secure the independence and sovereignty of Kazakhstan; to break away fully from the old economic and political system; to provide economic and political freedom—but not at the expense of social security; to develop Kazakhstan's human resources; to develop Kazakhstan's natural resources; to make good use of the nation's land; to provide political stability; and to strive for an atmosphere of tolerance and mutual respect in Kazakhstan's population.

68. These were the strengthening of national security through the development of the energy sector and by formulating a military doctrine; promoting the internal stability of the country; encouraging economic growth; creating a good investment climate; and improving the quality of government service; as well as eliminating corruption.

69. The 67 seats in the 1995 Majilis were divided as follows: People's Union Party, 24 seats; Democratic Party, 12 seats; Peasants Union, 5; Trade Unions Federation , 5; Communist

Party of Kazakhstan, 2; independents and others, 19. (Central Intelligence Agency, *CIA World Factbook 1999*, Kazakhstan entry. See appendix 4 in this volume.)

70. The debt of the State Pension Fund accounted for 20 percent of the 1996 budget. The privatization of the electric power and oil companies throughout 1997 generated signing bonuses of more than $300 million that was used to pay down the debt. See Business Information Service for the Newly Independent States (BISNIS), "Commercial Overview of Kazakhstan," *BISNIS Report*, June 1998.

71. "Pension Reform Looms in Kazakhstan," *Jamestown Monitor*, June 13, 1996.

72. "Under Pressure, Kazakhs Pass Pension Bill," *Panorama*, June 14, 1996, p. 3.

73. See the text of the Language Bill N–151–1, published in Russian: "Zakon Respubliki Kazakhstan ot 11 iiulia 1997 goda N 151–1: O Iazykakh v Respublike Kazakhstan," passed into law July 11, 1997.

74. "Kazakhs Pass Language Bill," *Itar–Tass World Service*, July 15, 1997, as translated in *FBIS Daily Reports*, Central Eurasia, SOV–97–196, July 16, 1997.

75. Cummings, *Kazakhstan*, p. 60.

76. Baildinov, "Kazakh Government Reorganizes."

77. Marchenko was credited with the development of Kazakhstan's stock market and its security-based pension scheme ("Security Commission Chair Resigns," *United States–Kazakhstan Council News Wires*, October 15, 1997).

78. The former deputy prime minister left public life under a cloud of corruption in September 1994 ("New Kazakh Ministers Appointed," *United States–Kazakhstan Council News Wires*, October 17, 1997).

79. In February 1999, Kalmurzayev was appointed the head of the president's administration, and in April 2001, he was made the head of Kazakhstan's State Property Committee.

80. In April 1998, Nurlan Kapparov was named the head of Kazakhoil, the Kazakh state oil company, and Mukhtar Ablyazov of Astana Holding became the minister of energy, trade, and industry.

81. Among the ranks of the "young Turks" were Bulat Abilov, the president of Butya, a large trading company; Mukhtar Ablyazov of Astana Holding, one of the biggest trading and industrial groups in Kazakhstan; and Kapparov, who before heading Kazakhoil ran a vodka and sugar trading company.

82. "Mynbayev Narrowly Escapes Impeachment," *Panorama*, no. 41 (October 1998).

83. "Kazakhstan to Hold Early Presidential Elections," *Intercon Daily Report on Russia*, October 8, 1998.

84. Kazymzhomart Tokayev remained as foreign minister, Kairbek Suleimenov as interior minister, and Muhtar Altynbayev as defense minister.

85. "Kazakh Security Committee Chair Dismissed," *Moscow Interfax*, August 9, 1999, in FBIS–SOV–1999–0809, August 9, 1999.

86. "Majilis Threaten No Confidence Vote," *Moscow Interfax*, February 12, 1999, FBIS–SOV–1999–0212, February 12, 1999.

87. "Opposition Leader Seeks Position of Prime Minister," *Moscow Interfax*, November 23, 1998, FBIS–SOV–98–327.

88. "Nazarbayev Slams Cabinet," *Moscow Interfax*, September 1, 1999, in FBIS–SOV–1999–0901.

89. "Budget Debate Continues in Astana," *Moscow Interfax*, September 2, 1999, FBIS–SOV–1999–0902, September 2, 1999.

90. Tokayev was confirmed by parliament as prime minister on October 13, 1999.

91. The Agency for Economic Planning changed to the Ministry of Economy; the Agency for Strategic Planning and Reforms was split into the Agency for Strategic Planning directly under the president, and all its former financial and economic functions were transferred to the Ministry of Economy; the Ministry of Education, Health, and Sports, and the Ministry of Science and Higher Education merged into a single Ministry of Education and Science. The other functions were handed over to the new Agency for Health and Agency for Sports and Tourism, which are not part of the government. The Atomic Energy and Space Ministries were transferred from the former Ministry of Science and the Ministry of Higher Education to the Ministry of Energy, Industry, and Trade.

92. "Tokayev Government Settles In," *Panorama*, no. 8 (February 15, 1999).

93. The new government had three Russians: Vladimir Schkolnik, a former head of the ore-enriching combine in Aktau; First Deputy Prime Minister Aleksandr Pavlov, who had served in the Tereshchenko government; and Nikolai Radostovets, formerly in charge of the antimonopoly committee, who became the minister of labor and social security.

94. Michael Dobbs reports that in this period Akin, Gump received $1 million in fees, the Carmen Group $700, 000, and Mark A. Siegel Associates $470,000 (Michael Dobbs, "Investment in Freedom Is Flush with Peril," *Washington Post*, January 25, 2001, p. 1).

95. This author received several phone calls from Mark Siegel Associates during the run-up to the election and a visit from Mark Siegel himself.

96. See Address of the President of the Republic of Kazakhstan to the People of Kazakhstan, "The Situation in the Country and the Major Directions of Domestic and Foreign Policy: Democratization [and] Economic and Political Reform for the New Century," September 30, 1998.

97. The movement was formed on October 2, the demonstration held on October 10, and Kazhegeldin was convicted on October 15.

98. *Moscow Itar–Tass*, April 20, 1996, as translated in *FBIS Daily Reports*, Central Asia, SOV–96–078, April 23, 1996.

99. This was more than a hundred times the minimum monthly wage at the time.

100. See the OSCE's report, "The Republic of Kazakhstan Presidential Election, January 10, 1999, Assessment Mission," released on February 5, 1999, available on the OSCE Internet web site. <www.osce.org/odihr/election/kazak1-2.htm>.

101. See International Foundation for Election Systems (IFES) Election Guide, as posted on the Internet: <http://www.ifes.org/eguide/resultsum/kazakhstanres.htm>.

102. It also stipulated that political parties should receive at least 7 percent of the popular vote to be able to contest ten seats in the Majilis. For each party member on the party list the Central Election Commission should receive a deposit equivalent to twenty-five times the minimum wage. Parties that clear the 7-percent barrier are reimbursed for this expense.

103. "Kazakh Opposition to Try to Get the Existing Government to Resign," *Interfax-Kazakhstan*, September 16, 1999.

104. Otan received 30.89 percent of the vote; the Communists, 17.75 percent; the Agrarian party, 12.63 percent; the Civil Party, 11.23 percent; the Azamat, 4.57 percent; the People's

Congress of Kazakhstan, 2.83 percent; the Alash party, 2.76 percent; the Revival Party 1.97 percent; and the Labor Party, 1.38 percent (*Interfax*, October 17, 1999).

105. Without specifying the reasons, the Central Election Commission declared invalid the results of the second round of voting in four of forty-seven districts. New elections in those districts were held on December 26, 1999.

106. The composition of the Majilis was as follows: Otan received 20 seats in single-mandate districts, for a total of 24 seats; the Civil Party received 9 for a total of 11; the Communist Party received 1, for a total of 3; the Agrarian Party received 1, for a total of 3; RNPK received 1, for a total of 1; People's Cooperatives received 1, for a total of 1; business groups received 10, for a total of 10; progovernment candidates received 20, for a total of 20; and other groups received 4, for a total of 4. Source: OSCE/ODIHR report. See appendix 4.

107. "CIS Sees No Irregularities in Kazakh Elections," *Moscow Interfax*, October 11, 1999.

108. "Unsuccessful Candidate Seeks Asylum in the UK," *Itar–Tass*, October 27, 1999, as translated by FBIS–SOV–1999–1027.

109. To examine some of the claims being made surrounding Nazarbayev's alleged hidden assets, see "Otkrovennoe Khanstvo," filed under Nazarbayev on the Internet web site of Compromat.ru: <www.compromat.ru/main/Nazarbayev/a.htm>.

Chapter 5
Economic Development or Stealing the State?

1. *Karavan-Blitz*, July 12, 1996, p. 2, as translated in *FBIS Daily Report*, SOV–96–140, p. 45.

2. See appendix 5 for the GDP of Kazakhstan, 1991–2001.

3. UN Development Program, *Human Development Report 2001* (New York: Oxford University Press, 2001), p. 146.

4. *The Former Soviet Union in Transition*, papers submitted to the Joint Economic Committee, Congress of the United States, May 1993, vol. 2, p. 937. The net material product is a measure formerly used by most centrally planned economies but now largely superseded. It purported to measure the output of goods and services but excluded certain public services and thus has a narrower coverage than the GNP.

5. See the work of David G. Tarr in "The Terms-of-Trade Effects of Moving to World Prices on Countries of the Former Soviet Union," *Journal of Comparative Economics*, vol. 18, no. 1 (February 1994), pp. 1–24.

6. During this time, the railway fees for transit through Russia were raised as part of an attempt to increase Kazakh dependence on Russia.

7. See the discussion of the ruble zone in Olcott, Åslund, and Garnett, *Getting It Wrong*, pp. 46–48.

8. Four countries introduced their national currencies before Kazakhstan: Azerbaijan (August 1992), Belarus (July 1993), Kyrgyzstan (May 1993), Georgia (August 1993), and Ukraine (November 1992).

9. "Economic Crisis Spills into Kazakhstan," *Interfax*, October 21, 1998. By January 2001, the tenge traded at $1 to 145.42 tenge.

10. *Interfax*, "Investment Report of Central Asia and Caucasus," December 27, 1999–January 9, 2000, vol. 3, no. 1 (58), in FBIS–SOV–2000–0111, January 11, 2000.

11. Economist Intelligence Unit, *Country Report, Kazakhstan*, November 22, 1999.

12. *Interfax*, December 27, 1999–January 9, 2000, vol. 3, no. 1 (58), in FBIS–SOV–2000–0111, January 11, 2000.

13. Economist Intelligence Unit, *Country Report, Kazakhstan*, August 18, 1998.

14. *Interfax*, December 21, 1998, in FBIS–SOV–98–355, December 21, 1998.

15. For 1999 figures, see *Interfax*, January 24–30, 2000, vol. 3, no. 4 (61), in FBIS–SOV–2000–0131, January 31, 2000.

16. For 1999 figures, see *Interfax*, February 7–13, 2000.

17. For 1999 figures, see International Monetary Fund, *Direction of Trade Statistics Quarterly* (Washington, D.C.: IMF, 2000), p. 145.

18. "Russia Gains Control of Power Grid in Debt-Equity Swap," *Financial Times*, January 28, 1997, p. 6.

19. Former KGB boss Yuri Andropov succeeded Leonid Brezhnev as General Secretary of the Communist Party of the Soviet Union.

20. For a dissenting perspective on this, see Anders Åslund, "The Myth of Output Collapse after Communism" (Washington, D.C.: Carnegie Endowment for International Peace, December 2000). See Carnegie Internet web site: <*http://www.ceip.org/files/publications/aslund-output.asp?pr29from=pubauthor*>.

21. For 1999 figures, see European Commission, *Economic Trends: Kazakhstan*, April–June 1999, p. 31.

22. Ibid., p. 164.

23. Sander Thoenes, "Kazakhstan's Sale of the Century," *Financial Times*, October 25, 1996, p. 28.

24. Auezov, "Corporate Securities," p. 12.

25. Kalyuzhnova, *The Kazakhstani Economy*, pp. 75–76.

26. Twenty of the funds managed to accumulated more than 60 percent of the vouchers, while another nineteen funds gathered about 20 percent.

27. The Kazhegeldin government passed significant legislation on property rights and in the 1995 Civil Code established the basic freedoms of entrepreneurial activity, including the right to own and operate a business without government interference.

28. *Itar–Tass*, "New Stage of Kazakh Privatization," March 20, 1996, in FBIS–SOV–96–057, March 20, 1996.

29. *Interfax-Aif*, January 27, 1997, no. 4, issue 82.

30. See Kalyuzhnova's description of "privatization through the individual projects" in *The Kazakhstani Economy*, p. 76.

31. The Pavlodar Aluminum Plant went to White Swan Ltd., the Sokolov-Sarbai Mineral Conglomerate to Ivedon International Ltd., and KazChrome to Japan Chrome Corp. These contracts to subsidiaries of Trans-World Metal Corporation attracted scrutiny in the press. See Richard Behar, "Capitalism in a Cold Climate," *Fortune*, June 12, 2000, pp. 194–200.

32. Lev and Mikhail Chernoy engaged in a business partnership with the Trans-World Group only to eventually become apparent rivals. Both were accused of links with organized crime by Russian Interior Minister Anatoly Kulikov in 1997. Mikhail Chernoy, who has been banned from entering Bulgaria, France, Great Britain, Switzerland, and the United States

because of suspicions he has links to the criminal world, is rumored to have been involved in the murder of competitors in the aluminum industry. See Behar, "Capitalism"; "Lev Chernoi, Kak Zerkalo Banditskogo Kapitalizm," as published on the Internet web site Kompromat.ru: <www.compromat.ru/main/chernoy/zerkalo.htm>; and "Mikhail Chyorny Looks for Land to Call His Own," *Moscow Times*, November 11, 2000, pp. 2–3.

33. Peck, "Foreign Investment," p. 477.

34. "Turning Cheap Steel Mills into Gold," *Business Week*, May 27, 1996, p. 108 E–4.

35. See Horton, "Bankruptcy Kazak Style," pp. 349–56.

36. Vera Avaliani, "Kazakhstan Privatization to Go On," *United Press International*, March 13, 1996.

37. *Interfax Kazakhstan*, January 28, 1998, in FBIS–SOV–97–019.

38. The Kazakh government decreed on June 6, 1997, that the shares of the following enterprises would be offered through the stock exchange by the end of 1997: metal producers Kazakhstan Aluminum Company, Kazchrome, Shymkent Lead Plant, Jezkasgantsvetmet, Ust-Kamenogorsk Titanium Magnesium Combine, Sokolov-Sarbai Mining Production Unit, and Yuzhno-Toparskoye Ore Mining Company; oil producers Mangistaumunaigaz and Aktyube-munaigaz; Borly Coal Mines; Halyk Savings Bank, the country's largest bank; and Atakent, the top exhibition and trade center in Almaty. Auezov, "Corporate Securities," p. 15.

39. "Small Business Privatization Winds Down in Kazakhstan," *Financial Times*, London edition, June 26, 1998, p. 31.

40. European Commission, *Kazakhstan Economic Trends, Third Quarter 1998* (Brussels: European Commission, 1998), p. 178. This source also lists privatization for principal sectors of the economy. In industry, 82.2 percent of small enterprises, 11.3 percent of medium enterprises, and 6.5 percent of large enterprises were privatized as of the third quarter of 1998. For construction, these figures were 86.9, 9.7, and 3.4 percent, respectively. Of small agricultural enterprises, 64.5 percent were privatized by that point, as were 17.9 percent of medium enterprises and 18.0 percent of large enterprises. The transportation and communication sector had privatized 77.6 percent of its small enterprises, 16.3 percent of medium enterprises, and 6.1 percent of large enterprises. For trade and catering, the figures were 95.6, 3.8, and 0.5 percent, respectively. Finally, personal and public services had privatized 94.1 percent of small enterprises, 4.9 percent of medium enterprises, and 1.0 percent of large enterprises by the third quarter 1998.

41. 1998–2000 KAMAL Consortium, Pavlodar, Kazakhstan, *Reuters*, January 12, 2000. See <http://www.pavlodar.com/nfrk/nfrknews.shtml?datfile=vJ9iwI8hqrCsFwst0aHz12d7FvHvY_qtSi>.

42. In addition, no more than 40 percent can be invested in second-level band deposits, no more than 30 percent in international financial organization securities, and no more than 30 percent in Kazakh Stock Exchange A–listed securities. *Interfax Daily Business Report*, February 14, 2000.

43. "Wonderful Business Opportunities Offered by This Former Soviet Republic," *Financial Times*, Asia Intelligence Wire, March 22, 2000.

44. "The Extent of Corruption," *Karavan*, May 20, 1994, p. 2.

45. "News and Issues: Kazakhstan," *Watson Wyatt Worldwide*, May 1999, published on the Watson Wyatt Internet web site: <www.watsonwyatt.com/homepage>.

46. In May 2001, the government of Kazakhstan created a new company, TransNefteGaz, which combined KazTransOil, KazTransGaz, and a number of other companies, including a 50-

percent stake in KazTransFlot. The new company will handle marketing, operate oil and gas pipelines, organize financing, develop feasibility studies, build new pipelines, and take part in all Kazakhstan's domestic and international hydrocarbon transport projects.

47. "Privatization Stalled in Kazakhstan," *Jamestown Monitor*, vol. 6, no. 105 (May 30, 2000).

48. OKIOC was formed in 1993; in September 1998, Kazakhstan sold its share of the consortium to Phillips Petroleum, based in the United States, and Inpex of Japan. Kazakhstan will continue to profit from the consortium, however, through taxes, royalties, and bonuses. In the summer of 2001, after Italy's ENI Agip became sole operator, OKIOC was renamed AgipKCO.

49. Nursultan Nazarbayev, *Kazakhstan 2030*, as published on the official Internet web site of Kazakhstan: <www.president.kz/main/mainframe.asp?lng=en>.

50. For 1999 figures, see "Foreign Direct Investment in Kazakhstan," as published on the Internet web site of the Agency of the Republic of Kazakhstan on Investments: <http://www.kazinvest.com/eng/default.htm>.

51. For 2000 figures, see *Interfax Kazakhstan*, March 1, 2000.

52. Samsung first entered Kazakhstan in 1995 when Samsung Deutschland Gmbh received a management contract for Zhezkazgantsvetmet. For an account of their problems, see Peck, "Foreign Investments," p. 481.

53. See Matthew J. Sagers, "The Nonferrous Metals Industry of Kazakhstan," *Post-Soviet Geography and Economics*, vol. 39, no. 9 (1998), p. 507. The remaining 22.6 percent of shares are held by undisclosed individuals.

54. The IMF provided a $290 million loan in 1994. The economic reform program touted by the IMF sought to reduce inflation and stabilize the exchange rate, along with encouraging deregulation, privatization, and reform of the social insurance system.

55. See appendix 7 for a description of these programs. For a discussion of the role of international financial institutions in Kazakhstan, see Richard M. Auty, *The IMF Model and Resource-Abundant Transition Economies: Kazakhstan and Uzbekistan*, United Nations Working Paper 169, November 1999.

56. See International Monetary Fund, *Kazakhstan IMF Economic Review* (Washington, D.C.: IMF, May 2000).

57. He has remained in Nazarbayev's inner circle, serving briefly as Kazakhstan's ambassador to Belgium, where he is said to have involved himself in the Tractebel transaction scandal (discussed later in this chapter) and then was briefly named mayor of Almaty. Later he headed the Kazakh mission to NATO, and in May 2001 he was appointed the minister of Agriculture.

58. "Foreign Investors Dominate Kazakhstan's Industry," *OMRI Daily Digest*, December 13, 1996.

59. Wood MacKenzie, quoted in Jaffee, *Unlocking the Assets*, table 3.

60. For an extensive discussion of Kazakhstan's oil and gas potential, see Ebel, *Energy Choices*, chapter 4.

61. James Giffen, a former New York banker who now heads Mercator and who is also an official adviser to Nazarbayev, was placed under investigation by the U.S. Justice Department for laundering money to Switzerland. Giffen, who had served as an adviser to Nazarbayev during the negotiations with Western oil companies for drilling rights, is also under investigation by the Justice Department for violating the Foreign Corrupt Practices Act. Giffen claims

that his post as Nazarbayev's adviser makes him an official in a foreign government and hence not subject to the provisions of the act. See the following: Louise Shelley, "Corrupt Oil Practices Implicate President Nazarbayev," *Central Asia/Caucasus Analyst*, July 19, 2000; Paul Sampson, "Middleman Caught Up in Kazakh Oil Inquest," *Oil Daily*, July 7, 2000; and Michael Dobbs, David Ottaway, and Sharon LaFraniere, "American at Center of Kazakh Oil Probe; Insider Linked to Payments to Foreign Officials," *Washington Post*, September 25, 2000, p. A1.

62. Hugh Pope, "Corruption Stunts Growth in ex-Soviet States—Struggle in Kazakhstan is the Apparent Spark for U.S. Investigation," *Wall Street Journal*, July 5, 2000, p. A17.

63. These consortia are described in appendix 10.

64. The figures for 1997 are taken from Economist Intelligence Unit, *Country Reports, Kazakhstan*, 1998; all other figures are found in *EIU Reports*, 1997.

65. International Monetary Fund, *Kazakhstan*.

66. Crude oil production data are from the International Energy Agency's Internet web site: <www.iea.org>.

67. According to Minister for Energy, Industry, and Trade Asygat Zhabagin, the four pipeline projects with the highest priority for the Kazakh government are: rebuilding and upgrading the Atyrau-Samara pipeline, which ships oil to Russia; the CPC's pipeline connecting the Tengiz oil field and Russia's Novorossiisk-2 terminal; a new Transcaspian pipeline through Aktau, Baku, and Turkey to the Mediterranean; and a pipeline connecting Kazakhstan and China (*Petroleum Report*, vol. 6, no. 14 [327], March 27–April 3, 1998, p. 19). The remaining two are the economical but controversial pipelines through Iran to the Persian Gulf and the similarly controversial route through Afghanistan (Alfa Capital Kazakhstan, "The Kazakh Economy," August 13, 1998).

68. Economist Intelligence Unit, *Kazakhstan: Oil and Gas Report*, February 23, 2000.

69. See Julia Nanay, "Export Markets for Oil from the CIS and the Caspian Region," presentation at the Oil and Gas Transportation in the CIS and Caspian Forum, Vienna, October 10, 2000.

70. *Neftegazovaya Vertikal*, "Chevron Verit v Kazakhstan, Kazakhstan Verit v Chevron," September 30, 2001.

71. "Kazakhstan Economy," published on the Internet web site of the U.S. Energy Information Agency: <www.eia.doe.gov>, April 4, 2000.

72. This group is the Oman Oil Corporation, controlled by the Omani government, which was instrumental in arranging the financing of the CPC pipeline.

73. Martha Brill Olcott, *Central Asia's New States* (Washington, D.C.: United States Institute of Peace Press, 1996), p. 79.

74. Olcott, *The Kazakhs*, p. 294.

75. A few years later, Chevron paid the government of Kazakhstan $660 million for a similar 5 percent stake. Moscow *Interfax*, October 3, 1997, as translated in *FBIS Daily Reports*, SOV–97–276, October 6, 1997.

76. Officials cite the Russian-Iranian Treaty of 1921 and the Soviet-Iranian Treaty of 1941.

77. For a more detailed analysis of the territorial dispute over the Caspian, see Bolukbasi, "Caspian Sea Mineral Resources."

78. For a discussion of Kazakhstan's earlier position on the Caspian and the evolution of its relations with Russia on oil questions, see Babak, "Kazakhstan."

79. The agreement, signed on July 6, 1998, divides the seabed and mineral resources of the northern Caspian between Russia and Kazakhstan. It leaves the waters and biological resources of the sea under the common control of the littoral states. It specifically states that it "does not preclude" a future agreement between all five littoral states as to the permanent legal status of the Caspian.

80. "Pipeline Politics in Istanbul," *Financial Times*, November 19, 1999, p. 17.

81. Nursultan Nazarbayev, speech at the Baker Institute, Rice University, Houston, November 21, 1997.

82. TotalFina Elf, BG Plc, and Agip were said to be a part. *Kazakhstan Weekly Business News*, as reported by *Turkestan Newsletter*, December 22, 2000.

83. Economist Intelligence Unit, *Kazakhstan: Oil and Gas Report*, February 23, 2000.

84. Jaffee, "Unlocking the Assets."

85. A production-sharing agreement (PSA) is a contract between an investor and a national government that grants the investor exclusive rights to prospect for and extract mineral resources from a specific site and provides the investor with a guaranteed tax and royalty structure, generally including temporary tax relief.

86. Chinese sources estimated that the Uzen field contains 207 tons of recoverable resources (*Beijing Xinhua*, November 6, 1997, as translated in *FBIS Daily Report*, CHI-97-310, November 7, 1997). According to *Itar–Tass*, it is second in size only to the Tengiz oil field. *Itar–Tass*, September 24, 1997, as translated in *FBIS Daily Report*, SOV-97-267, September 24, 1997.

87. *Itar–Tass*, September 24, 1997, in *FBIS Daily Report*, SOV-97-267, September 24, 1997. Kazakhstan was able to justify giving China the rights to Uzen because China was the only country that offered to build a pipeline. Even though Uzen is second in size in Kazakhstan to the Tengiz field, it is still small by world standards and would not normally justify such construction.

88. *RFE/RL Newsline*, April 9, 1999.

89. For a detailed discussion of the situation, see *Interfax Oil and Gas Report*, January 28–February 3, 2000, vol. 4, no. 419.

90. Access Industries is hoping to arrange to swap oil from the Uzen field, bringing it to refineries in Tiumen until the Chinese complete their pipeline.

91. Itera is reputed to be a foreign-based and privately owned spin-off of Russia's Gazprom.

92. The new company, TransNefteGaz, in addition to combining KazTransOil, KazTransGaz, and a 50 percent stake in KazTransFlot, also includes a 90-percent stake in Aktiubinskneftesvyaz, 99 percent of Munai-Impex, 90 percent of Kaztranssvyaz, 100 percent of the Atyrau international airport and helicopter company Euro-Asia Air, and 3.5 percent of the communication company Bailanys.

93. Interfax, "Central Asia Report," July 30, 1998.

94. Nazarbayev announced the creation of the National Oil Fund in May 2000. The fund was meant to be an extrabudgetary institution that would help Kazakhstan set aside profits from the sale of oil and gas to avoid "the Dutch disease." In 2001, Kazakhstan announced that it had deposited $660 million from the sale of its stake in the Tengiz field.

95. *Kazakhstan NewsWire*, February 15, 2000.

96. See the Internet web site of *Report on Business Magazine*: <http://www.robmagazine.com/archive99ROBdecember/html/moving_target.html>.

97. Scott Horton, "The Investment Environment in Kazakhstan," *CISLawNotes*, July 1998. See also: <http://www.bbwt.ru/Resources/newsletters/cis98b006.html>.

98. Economist Intelligence Unit, *Business Eastern Europe*, July 27, 1998.

99. International Energy Agency, *Caspian Oil and Gas* (Paris: IEA, 1998).

100. *Interfax Central Asia*, December 14, 2000.

101. In December 2000 Kazakhoil lost the right to participate in production-sharing agreements on behalf of the state and to receive royalties (*Interfax Central Asia*, December 14, 2000).

102. *Interfax Central Asia*, July 17, 2000. The struggle for the Pavlodar refinery is described by Peck, "Foreign Investment," pp. 476–77.

103. For more, see Scott Horton, "The Investment Environment in Kazakhstan," *Central Asia Monitor*, no. 5 (1998).

104. "Kazakh Potential: Endangerment by Lack of Stable Business Climate," *Hart's Asian Petroleum News*, vol. 3, no. 42 (October 25, 1999).

105. *Karavan*, March 1, 1996, p. 5.

106. *Interfax Central Asia*, September 19, 1997.

107. *OMRI*, November 1, 1996.

108. FBIS–SOV–97–358, December 24, 1997.

109. This occurred when a signing bonus for the OKIOC deposit seems to have gone astray. See *OMRI*, January 5, 1996.

110. Based on reports by *Jamestown Monitor*, June 4, 1996, FBIS–SOV–94–18, September 16, 1994, and by *Nezavisimaya gazeta*, April 18, 1995, p. 1.

111. Aleksandr Samoilenko, *Literaturnaya gazeta*, November 3, 1993.

112. "Dela Kazhegeldina," *Nezavisimaya gazeta*, April 18, 1995, p. 3.

113. Sander Thoenes, "Breathing Life into Kazakh Smelters," *Moscow Times*, January 5, 1997, pp. 3–4.

114. Vladimir Lesin was one of the top figures in Trans-CIS Commodities, a branch of the Trans-World Group registered in Monaco. See Richard Behar, "Capitalism in a Cold Climate," *Fortune*, June 12, 2000, p. 194.

115. "Russian Minister's Dismissal Surrounded by Allegations of Corruption," *Wall Street Journal*, January 28, 1997, p. 1.

116. *Moskovskii Komsomolets*, December 5, 1995, p. 2, as translated in *FBIS Daily Report*, SOV–245–S, December 21, 1995, p. 17.

117. In late 2000 the Eurasian group held the Sokolov-Sarbai complex, Kazakhstan Aluminum Company, Aksu Ferroalloys Plant, Eurasian Energy Corporation, JSC Ferrachrome, and the Donsk Mining Enrichment Plant.

118. Valerii Stepshin, "Penistyi okatysh: Tsentral'no aziatskii bulleten,'" December 4, 2000.

119. "Trans-World Settles with Kazakhstan," *Financial Times*, February 28, 2000, p. 8.

120. Sabton Limited, registered in Cyprus and a subsidiary of Leviev's Africa Israel Investment Ltd., won control of Tselinnyy in April 1999, outbidding Kazatomprom. See "Limping Uranium Plant Sold to Israeli Company," *Interfax Kazakhstan*, May 7, 1999. Sabton has promised investment of $100 million for a production program from 2000 to 2005, but it remains to be seen whether this commitment will be met.

121. *Interfax Oil and Gas Report*, January 28–February 3, 2000.

122. Internet web site of Eurasia.org: <www.eurasia.org>, February 3, 2000, report of an Almaty news conference by Mashkevich. In June 2001, Mashkevich was charged with money

laundering involving the purchase of a villa outside Brussels by a Belgian judge. During this time it was also reported that he was under investigation for a payment to him by Tractebel. See Steve LeVine, "Three Prominent Kazakhstan Businessmen Are Charged in Money Laundering Feud," *Wall Street Journal*, July 6, 2001, p. 3.

123. For the campaign contributions of the Blavatnik family, see the disclosure reports of the United States Federal Election Commission, published on its web site: <herndon1.sdrdc.com/cgi-bin/qind>. For more on Blavatnik, see Dan Morgan and Michael Dobbs, "Washington Lobbying Oils Russian Capitalism," *Washington Post*, October 27, 1999, p. A1.

124. Halliburton, Inc., will receive $292 million of those funds to refurbish the massive Samotlor oil field in Siberia that is owned by TNK.

125. *Interfax Daily Business Report*, February 14, 2000.

126. The Vasilkovskoe deposit has been billed as Kazakhstan's largest gold deposit and the fourth largest undeveloped gold deposit in the world. It is located in Akmola oblast and was discovered in the mid-1960s. Vasilkovskoe is estimated to hold 382 tons of gold. Bakyrchik, located in East Kazakhstan oblast, contains an estimated 326 tons of gold. It is rated as one of the largest gold deposits, not only in the former Soviet Union, but in the world. See Matthew J. Sagers, "Gold Production in Central Asia," *Post Soviet Geography and Economics*, vol. 39, no. 3 (1998), pp. 140–41.

127. European Commission, *Kazakhstan Economic Trends* (Brussels: European Commission, 1998), April–June 1998, table 9.2, p. 132.

128. Kazakhstan's gold production increased from 8.9 tons in 1998 to 9.6 tons in 1999 and was estimated to have increased further in 2000. See Economist Intelligence Unit, *Country Report for Kazakhstan*, November 2000.

129. Loutchansky, described by *Time* as "the most pernicious unindicted criminal in the world," heads Nordex, a company based in Vienna that, according to former CIA director John Deutch, is "an organization associated with Russian criminal activity." Among other allegations, Nordex is said to be involved in the smuggling of nuclear materials ("60 Minutes Interviews Grigori Loutchansky," December 6, 1998).

130. Leviev was born in Tashkent, Uzbekistan, and emigrated to Israel. He now controls the Africa Israel Investment Ltd., one of the world's leading producers of diamonds. He also reportedly has close ties with both Nazarbaev and Putin. See Hanan Sher, "Sabbath Warrior," *The Jerusalem Report*, April 17, 1997, p. 22.

131. Arkady Gaidamak was born in the Soviet Union but emigrated to Israel in the early 1970s. He was alleged to be involved in supplying illegally obtained Russian arms to the government of Angola, in addition to money laundering in partnership with Jean-Christophe Mitterrand, the son of the late French president. See Dmitry Babich, "The Mafia in Angola," *Moscow News*, January 24, 2001, p. 4.

132. The article links Vasilkovskoe to Floodgate Holding, Ltd., in the Dutch West Indies. See A. Isaev and V. Shtyrkov, "Levaev i pustota," *Aziopa*, June 5, 2001.

133. In August 1996, the Friedland-controlled Indochina Goldfields, which already held 15 percent of the Bakyrchik Ltd. stake in the mine, bought an additional 65 percent from its partner in a $65 million deal. In December 1996, Indochina bought a 60-percent share in the mine from the government of Kazakhstan.

134. "Bakyrchik Rises Again," *Mining Journal*, June 1, 2001, p. 423.

135. The total payment for the 60 percent was to include $60 million in cash, paid in four installments, and a $5 million signing bonus. Only half of the promised $60 million was paid, however, because in 1999 Ivanhoe transferred shares back to the government to eliminate its remaining payment obligation. See John Schreiner, "Indochina Goldfields to Get Larger Stake in Kazakh Mine," *Financial Post*, December 17, 1996, p. 12.

136. The Kazakh government estimated FDI to be $1.5 billion in 2000.

137. For 1998 projections, see International Monetary Fund, *World Economic Outlook* (Washington, D.C.: IMF, May 1998), p. 155.

138. Economist Intelligence Unit, *Kazakhstan*, October 1997.

139. *Interfax*, March 4, 1998, as translated in *FBIS Daily Report*, SOV–98–063.

140. Marat Yermukanov, "Hard Times for North Kazakhstan Farmers," *Central Asia Caucasus Analyst*, December 6, 2000.

141. Simon, "Republic of Kazakhstan," p. 2.

142. Ibid., p. 3.

143. *Jamestown Monitor*, September 15, 1998.

144. "Troubled Kazakh Economy Gasps for Breath," *Financial Times*, London edition, December 20, 1996, p. 6.

145. "Kazakhstan Regulations: Investors to Get Corruption Cover," *Financial Times*, February 23, 2000.

146. *United States–Kazakhstan Business Council News Wires*, August 24, 1998.

147. See "Kazakhstan Repays the IMF Ahead of Schedule"; IMF External Relations Internet web site: <www.imf.org/external/np/sec/nb/2000/nb0035.htm>.

148. *Interfax*, "Kazakhstan's External Debt Payments in 2000 Total USD 473.3 million," June 19, 2000.

149. For 1999 figures, see International Monetary Fund, *Trade Statistics Yearbook* (Washington, D.C.: IMF, 1999); and *Direction of Trade Statistics Quarterly* (Washington, D.C.: IMF, 2000).

150. *Interfax Moscow*, September 30, 1998.

151. *Interfax Central Asia*, December 14, 2000.

152. *Interfax Central Asia*, October 23, 2000.

Chapter 6
A Divided Society

1. *Itar–Tass*, January 29, 1999, as translated in *FBIS Daily Report*, SOV–99–029, February 1, 1999.

2. *Itar–Tass*, World Service in English, April 19, 1999, as translated in FBIS–SOV–1999–0419.

3. "Kazakh Prosecutor-General: Bureaucrats Brake Fight against Corruption," *Interfax-Kazakhstan*, July 23, 1999.

4. The Nazarbayev family allegedly has used offshore accounts and holding companies to divert capital from Kazakhstan. One of the allegations is that Nazarbayev used the Kazakhstan Fund, set up in 1995, with an account at United Overseas Bank in Geneva, to spirit millions

of dollars out of the country and into an anonymous and protected bank account ("Shchet no. 35877 grazhdanina s pasportom 0000001," *Novaia gazeta*, January 22, 2001).

5. The Corruption Perceptions Index is a composite index that draws on seventeen polls and surveys from ten institutions ("New Corruption Index Released by Transparency International," *Preventing Business Fraud*, June 2000, p. 4). In the 2001 Transparency International Rankings, Kazakhstan improved its ranking to seventy-first but still remained behind deeply corrupt states like Moldova (sixty-third), although ahead of Russia (seventy-ninth). See the Internet web site of Transparency International: <www.transparency.org>.

6. See appendix 2: "Population of Kazakhstan by Nationality, 1989 and 1999."

7. UNDP figures for 1997 show that ethnic Kazakhs made up 50.6 percent of the population, with Russians making up 32.2 percent, and other nationalities 17.2 percent (UN Development Program, *Kazakhstan 1998*, p. 77).

8. Kaiser and Chinn, "Russian-Kazakh Relations."

9. "Internal Migration in Kazakhstan for the 1Q of 1998," *Delovaya nedelya*, July 31, 1998.

10. Ethnic Kazakhs make up a minority of the population in Akmola oblast (37.4 percent of the total), East Kazakhstan oblast (48.5 percent), Karaganda oblast (37.6 percent), Kostanai oblast (31.1 percent), Pavlodar oblast (38.2 percent), North Kazakhstan oblast (29.5 percent), Astana city (40.9), and Almaty city (38.5) (*Pervaia natsional'naia peripis' naseleniia*, 1999).

11. According to the 1999 census, ethnic Kazakhs account for 18.8 percent of the population in Kostanai, 24.2 percent in Karaganda, and 24.0 percent in Pavlodar. In other principal cities, ethnic Kazakhs remain a minority: 40.9 percent of the population in Astana, 38.5 percent in Almaty, 36.0 percent in Kokchetau, 13.9 percent in Petropavlovsk, 7.5 percent in Rudny, 48.8 percent in Semipalatinsk, 11.8 percent in Temirtau, 35.5 percent in Uralsk, 18.5 percent in Ust-Kamenogorsk, 48.7 percent in Shymkent, and 37.4 percent in Ekibastuz (*Pervaia natsional'naia peripis' naseleniia*, 1999).

12. Statistics show a steady decline in the birthrate: during the period 1970–1975, it was 3.3 (births per woman); for 1980–1985, 3.1; and for 1993–1998, 2.0 (World Bank, *2000 World Development Indicators*).

13. *Agence France-Presse*, March 17, 1999.

14. Vitkovskaya, *Emigration*, p. 13.

15. Some 175,000 Russians left Kazakhstan in 1992; 170,000 in 1993; 283,000 in 1994; 162,000 in 1995; 121,000 in 1996; 175,000 in 1997; 144,369 in 1998; 91,742 in 1999; and 185,371 in the first eleven months of 2000 (Shelgunov, "Flight from the Oasis"). The 1999 official figure is from "Migratsia naseleniia Respubliki Kazakhstan za 1991–1999 gody," as published on the ASTEL's Internet web site: <www.asdc.kz/kazstat/111/migr.htm>. The figures for 2000 are from Interfax-Kazakhstan as reported by Justin Burke of Eurasia.net in *Kazakhstan Daily Digest*, January 23, 2001.

16. Sabit Jusupov, commissioned research, 1995.

17. *Rossiiskaia gazeta*, April 23, 1997, p. 7.

18. In 1997, 11,582 Kazakhs immigrated to Kazakhstan, while 11,759 left; in 1998, 10,955 immigrated, and 9,270 left ("Perepis' Naseleniia 1999," *Kazakhstan Government Statistical Report*, 1999).

19. This figure was reported by Zauytbek Turysbekov, the director of the state's migration and demography agency, and quoted in *Itar–Tass*, December 12, 1998, as translated in *FBIS Daily Report*, TEN–98–346, December 15, 1998.

20. Sabit Jusupov, commissioned research, 1998.

21. Aleksandr Alekseenko, "Migratsionnoe dvizheniie kazakhov za predely Kazakhstana:otsenki iprognosi," unpublished manuscript, 2000. Alekseenko quotes the newspaper *Do iposle ponedel'nika*, from June 16, 2000, as the source for the higher figure, offering a 76,000 figure from a report of a parliamentary committee (on migration from Kazakhstan from 1993 to 1999).

22. Vitkovskaya, *Emigration*, pp. 15, 20. The outmigration of Kazakhstan's other ethnic communities was considerably smaller.

23. Ibid., pp. 24, 31.

24. Ibid., p. 27.

25. For a detailed discussion of Kazakhstan's language policy, see Fierman, "Language and Identity.""

26. "Ethnic Relations in Public Opinion," commissioned research conducted by Kazakh specialists, 1996, unpublished.

27. Only in rural Kyzylorda did less than 50 percent of the rural population (47.4 percent) claim to speak fluent Kazakh. See Alekseenko, "Migratsionnoe dvizheniie kazakhov."

28. Izdibayev, "Kazakh Attitudes."

29. Report by the Kazakh Institute for Socioeconomic Information and Forecasting, September 1999.

30. Zinaida Zakaeva and Zaure Sarsenbayeva, "Mezhetnicheskie Otnosheniya v sovremennom Kazakhstane" (opyt kompleksnogo sotsiologicheskogo analiza), unpublished manuscript, 1998.

31. Shelgunov, "Flight from the Oasis."

32. *Globe*, December 27, 1998.

33. This figure was 14 percent in Almaty and 3 percent in Astana.

34. These figures vary by source. Kazakh Minister of Culture Mukhtar Kulmuhammed claimed that 36 percent of the population of Kazakhstan had a full command of Kazakh, and 20 percent of the Kazakhs lacked a full command of Kazakh. This statement was made at the international seminar "Monitoring Inter-Ethnic Relations in Kazakhstan: Experience, Effectiveness, and Prospects." *Interfax*, May 24, 2001.

35. *Kazakhstanskaia pravda*, December 20, 1996, p. 4, as translated in *FBIS Daily Report*, SOV–97–042–S.

36. "Kazakh Parliament Deputy Criticizes Ministers for 'Illiteracy,'" *RFE/RL Newsline*, August 10, 2000.

37. "Speaking of Camels," *Economist*, February 15, 1997, p. 34.

38. "It Will Be Difficult Not to Speak Kazakh," *Azia-tranzit*, September 24, 1998.

39. For a comparative study on how well the Russians in Kazakhstan are doing, see Laitin, *Identity in Formation*.

40. Smetanina, "Nazarbayev Was Asked a Russian Question."

41. Masanov and Savin, *Kazakhstan*, p. 107.

42. The figure was 53 percent in Astana and 55 percent in Almaty (*Globe*, December 27, 1998).

43. Sabit Jusupov, commissioned research, 1995.

44. U.S. Department of State, *Order Trumps Liberty for Many in 3 Central Asian Nations: Ethnic Differences Brewing?* Opinion Analysis, Office of Research, M-60-00, May 26, 2000, p. 7.

45. I am choosing to use the term *clan* for the sake of continuity rather than to engage in the current social science debate over how to best describe these subethnic lineage identities in tribal (or segmented) societies.

46. See Schatz, "The Politics of Multiple Identities," pp. 489–506.

47. Contributed by Timothy Soggs, private Internet web site: <http://members.spree.com/sip/ananias/>.

48. Syzdyk Abishev died in 1997 after suffering a head injury while on vacation in Turkey with Nazarbayev. He served as the first deputy trade minister of the Kazakh SSR from 1983 to 1988, as the general director of the republican self-financing amalgamation under the Kazakh SSR Council of Ministers from 1988 to 1990, and as the minister of external economic relations of the Republic of Kazakhstan from 1990 to 1994, working closely with President Nazarbayev.

49. "Ethnic Relations in Public Opinion," 1996, unpublished research.

50. From 1938 to 1986 Kazakhstan had eight ethnic Russian first secretaries and only two who were ethnic Kazakh, Z. Shaiakhmetov and D. Kunayev. See Olcott, *The Kazakhs*, pp. 199–224.

51. Vitaly Khlyupin, "Kazakhstan's Zhuzes: Tribalism of the Twenty-first Century," published on the Internet web site Eurasia: <www.eurasia.org.ru/book/sbornik23.html>.

52. See Nurbulat E. Masanov, "The Clan Factor in Contemporary Political Life in Kazakhstan," *Prism*, vol. 4 (February 6, 1998).

53. Shelgunov, "Flight from the Oasis."

54. Akhmetzhan Yesimov was named the first head of the State Investment Committee and the first deputy prime minister. Yesimov lasted until February 1998, when he was appointed head of the presidential administration. He then served as Kazakhstan's ambassador to Belgium, where he is said to have interested himself in the Tractebel transaction scandal (discussed here in chapter 5) and then was briefly named the mayor of Almaty. After heading the Kazakh mission to NATO, he was appointed the minister of agriculture. Nurtai Abykayev was the director of the National Security Committee but was dismissed to the reserves in the wake of a scandal that developed after Kazakhstan illegally delivered forty MiG–21 fighter aircraft to Pyongyang, North Korea. See Khlyupin, "Kazakhstan's Zhuzes."

55. Vrichkina, "Otkrovennoe Khanstvo."

56. The republican headquarters for the struggle against organized crime and corruption was established on April 28, 2000.

57. "Kazakh Regional Security Chided for 'Repressive' Measures against Corruption," Khabar televisions, May 28, 2000, as reported by BBC Monitoring Central Asia Unit, May 29, 2000.

58. Zakaeva and Sarsenbayeva, "Mezhetnicheskie Otnosheniya."

59. See Alekseenko, "Migratsionnoe dvizheniie kazakhov."

60. Economist Intelligence Unit, April 10, 2001.

61. Huttenbach, "Whither Kazakhstan?" p. 583.

62. Rowland, "Urban Population Trends," p. 543.

63. FBIS–SOV–95–127, 3 July 1995, p. 71, as translated from *Kazakhstanskaia pravda*, June 23, 1995.

64. Elena Brusilovskaya, "Stanem novoselam i ty, i ya. Vas zdes' ne zhdut," AiF, no. 21 (261).

65. Zauresh Zaitova, "Problems of Regional Development in Kazakhstan," Kazakhstan News from the *Globe*, May 18, 2001.

66. These economic figures are from Jusupov's report, "Analiz predposylok."

67. Sabit Jusupov, "Otchet po teme analiz predposylok sotsial'nykh konfliktov v Kazakhstane," commissioned research, unpublished, 1997.

68. See appendix 5 for more details.

69. Local authorities meet 78.9 percent of the expenditures for education versus 21.1 percent by the republic, 83.5 percent of health care, and 13.8 percent of social security and welfare. The latter burden was shifted to the central authorities when the pension system was changed.

70. VAT is an indirect tax on consumer expenditure, charged and collected at each stage of the production process and at the point of sale. In 2001, the VAT was reduced from 21 to 16 percent in an effort to give people an incentive to pay it.

71. The exact same pattern is found in the collection of VAT as well (see International Monetary Fund, *Republic of Kazakhstan*, p. 45.

72. S. Zhusupov and K. Ezhenova, *Dinamika obshchestvennykh, protsessov v Kazakhstane*, Almaty, 1997, p. 43.

73. "Crime Up in Southern Kazakhstan in the First Quarter of 2000," *Interfax*, May 6, 2000.

74. "Security Service Sums up 1999 Results," *Interfax-Kazakhstan*, January 14, 2000.

75. Cummings, *Kazakhstan: Centre-Periphery Relations*, p. 20.

76. Ibid., p. 9.

77. *Interfax Central Asia*, May 13, 1999.

78. For more on the rural-urban divide in Kazakhstan, see Cynthia Buckley, "Rural/Urban Differentials in Demographic Processes: The Central Asian States," *Population Research and Policy Review*, no. 17 (1998), pp. 71–89.

79. *Karavan*, February 1, 1997, as translated in *FBIS Daily Report*, SOV–97–062, April 2, 1997.

80. "Zvezda-konechnaya vstrecha sostoyalas," *Zvezda irtysha*, December 2, 2000.

81. See appendix 3.

82. For more on the economic dynamics in such places, see Rama and Scott, "Labor Earnings."

83. UN Development Program, *Human Development Report: Kazakhstan 1999* (Almaty: UNDP, 2000), p. 39. Poverty is particularly acute in the oblasts of South Kazakhstan (pop. 1,976,689) and Zhambyl (pop. 983,935).

84. Savin and Alekseenko, "Problemi emigratsii v Yuzhnom Kazakhstanie."

85. *Rossiiskaia gazeta*, April 12, 1994, p. 6.

86. The 1999 census revealed that Almaty city was one of the few areas of Kazakhstan that had experienced population growth; currently there are 1,071,927 residents in Almaty, 105.4 percent of the 1989 population (*Kratkie Itogi Perepisi Naseleniia 1999 goda v Respublike Kazakhstan*, Almaty, 1999, p. 6).

87. Andrei Zhdanov, "Kochevie v pol'zu gorodov," *Karavan*, May 29, 1998.

88. The figures are taken from national statistics and direct communications from national statistical offices to UNECE secretariat, published in UN Economic Commission for Europe, *Economic Survey of Europe* (Geneva: UNECE, 2000), p. 230.

89. "Kazakhstan," Economist Intelligence Unit Report, April 10, 2001.

90. Shelia, "Snow Leopard," p. 7. An article in *Pravda* said that one million people were unemployed in Kazakhstan, as compared with the official CIS number of 257,000 registered

at unemployment offices. Aleksandr Pavlov, "The Temperature of Public Life in the CIS," *Pravda*, April 23, 1998, as translated in *FBIS Daily Report*, SOV–98–128, May 12, 1998.

91. *Kazakhstanskaia pravda*, July 2, 1996.

92. European Commission, *Kazakhstan Economic Trends*, April–June 1998 (Brussels: European Commission, 1998), p. 90.

93. Kazakhstan's population aged fifteen to sixty-four increased from nine million in 1980 to eleven million in 1996. See World Bank, *1998 World Development Indicators* (Washington, D.C.: World Bank, 1998), p. 51.

94. *Globe*, December 23, 1998.

95. *United States-Kazakhstan Council News Wires*, August 15, 1998.

96. *NTV*, February 20, 1998, as translated in *FBIS Daily Report*, SOV–98–051.

97. *Interfax Moscow*, November 12, 1997, FBIS–SOV–97–316.

98. For an account of their joint meeting with Leonid Solomin, see "KSPK predlagaet vlastiam mirnym uregulirovat' situatsiiu s sudebnym protsessom nad zhanatastsami," *Panorama*, March 13, 1998.

99. Karaganda workers staged strikes in January and June of 1992 and threatened another strike in February 1994.

100. *Ekspress-K*, January 18, 1995, p. 2, as translated in *FBIS Daily Report*, SOV–95–014, January 23, 1995.

101. *RFE/RL Newsline*, July 16, 1997.

102. "Solomin Case Is Closed," *Union of Councils for Soviet Jews News*, September 15, 1997, as published on the UCSJ Internet web site: <www.uscj.com/stories/091597news.shtml>.

103. See U.S. Department of State, "Kazakhstan, 1999 Country Report."

104. *Itar–Tass*, March 13, 1998, as translated in *FBIS Daily Report*, SOV–98–072.

105. *Interfax Moscow*, July 29, 1999.

106. UN Development Program, *Poverty in Transition*, p. 13.

107. The Organization for Economic Cooperation and Development defines Purchasing Power Parity as currency conversion rates that both convert to a common currency and equalize the purchasing power of different currencies. In other words, they eliminate the differences in price levels between countries in the process of conversion. (Figures from UN Development Program, *Central Asia 2010*, p. 172.)

108. *Jamestown Monitor*, November 19, 1997.

109. Central Intelligence Agency, *Handbook*.

110. CIS Interstate Statistical Committee, *1997: Statistical Yearbook*, p. 317.

111. For all Kazakhstan, 34.6 of urban respondents and 38.2 of rural respondents reported that they could not feed their families. See Alekseenko, "Migratsionnoe dvizheniie kazakhov."

112. See Serdar Svas and G. Gedik, "Health Care Reforms in Central Asia," in *Central Asia 2010*, pp. 144–61.

113. *OMRI Daily Digest*, April 2, 1996.

114. According to the Kazakhstan State Statistical Administration, the number of pediatric beds dropped from 37,300 to 22,700 from 1995 to 1998, and the number of maternity beds dropped from 16,500 to 10,500. Available at its Internet web site: <*http://www.asdc.kz.kazstat/new/zdrav.html*>.

115. UN Development Program, *Poverty in Transition*, p. 215.

116. See especially *Kazakhstanskaia pravda*, May 31, 1995, p. 2.

117. *Panorama,* January 30, 1998, p. 11, as translated in *FBIS Daily Report,* SOV–98–051, February 20, 1998.

118. *Ekspress,* January 16, 1998, p. 1, as translated in *FBIS Daily Report,* TEN–98–021, January 21, 1998.

119. This is according to Klara Sultangalieva, the director of the Center for Promoting a Healthy Lifestyle in Atyrau. Institute for War and Peace, "Reporting Central Asia," no. 39, February 6, 2001.

120. World Bank, *1998 World Development Indicators,* p. 105.

121. Ibid., p. 47.

122. Akanov and Suzhikova, "Kazakhstan," p. 237.

123. *Delovaya Nedelya,* December 16, 1997, p. 7, as translated in *FBIS Daily Report,* SOV–98–003.

124. For more on the linkage between the environment and public health, see the World Bank, *World Development Report 2000/2001,* p. 78.

125. For more on the Caspian Sea, see Namazi, "Caspian's Environmental Woes," pp. 121–36.

126. Lipovsky, "Deterioration of the Ecological Situation," p. 1119.

127. Ibid., p. 1120.

128. Ibid., p. 1109.

129. "Special Report: The Aral Sea Crisis," *BBC Water Week,* 27 March 1998.

130. Rakhimova, "Health Condition."

131. UN Development Program, *Human Development Report,* p. 82.

132. UN Development Program, *Poverty in Transition,* p. 214.

133. U.S. Department of State, *Order Trumps,* p. 3.

134. U.S. Department of State, *Charms of Market: Private Sector Continue to Elude 3 Central Asian Republics,* Opinion Analysis, Office of Research, M-38-00, April 17, 2000, p. 5.

135. UN Development Program, *Poverty in Transition,* pp. 71, 72.

136. *Delovaya Nedelya,* December 16, 1997, p. 7, as translated in *FBIS Daily Report,* SOV–98–003.

137. Herrick and Sapieva, "Perceptions," p. 28.

138. See Buckley, "Suicide."

139. *United States–Kazakhstan Council News Wires,* May 5, 1998.

140. Oleg Kvyatkovskiy, "Old Problems Beset New Department," FBIS–SOV–96–083–S, February 8, 1996.

141. The survey was taken by the Youth for the Future of Kazakhstan Public Foundation. The results were published in the *Globe,* Almaty, December 27, 1998.

142. See W. Baldridge, "Pension Reform in Kazakhstan," in *Central Asia 2010,* pp. 176–81.

143. Independent union leader Madel Ismailov got thirty days in jail for holding an unauthorized rally of pensioners in Almaty on January 30, 2000.

144. Article 23 of Kazakhstan's 1997 Budget Law, published in *Kazakhstanskaia pravda,* January 8, 1997, as translated in *FBIS Daily Report,* SOV–97–019, January 30, 1997.

145. Ibid., Article 16.

146. This is according to the data released at a government-sponsored conference held in Astana on April 11, 2001, Megalopolis.

147. Aleksandr Mashkevich heads the Federation of Jewish Communities of Kazakhstan, while Leviev sponsors Chabad Lubavitch Kazakhstan. In 1997, Chabad Lubavitch Kazakhstan

completed the construction of a new synagogue and community center in Almaty, the Beis Menachem Center.

148. For example, this view of Islam is found in a series of articles by K. Nurlanova that define "the Kazakh national idea" (*Nauka Kazakhstana*, nos. 4, 6, and 8, 1994).

149. *Panorama*, May 28, 1994, p. 10.

150. *Interfax*, September 7, 1998, as translated in FBIS *Daily Report*, SOV–98–250.

151. *RFE/RL Newsline*, August 14, 1998.

152. On February 16, 1999, six explosions occurred simultaneously in Tashkent, concentrated around Independence Square, where key government buildings are located. These explosions killed fifteen people and injured 130 but did not harm President Karimov, whom many suspected was the target of the bombings. See Saradzhyan, "Bombs Shake Iron Rule." In the late summer of 1999, Islamic militants invaded Kyrgyzstan from Tajikistan, seizing villages and taking hostages. The guerrillas planned to fight their way into the Ferghana valley of Uzbekistan but were beaten back by Kyrgyz forces with CIS assistance. In August 2000, Islamic militants entered Uzbekistan from Tajikistan and there clashed with Uzbek security forces.

153. Kazakhstan had a defense budget of $115 million in 2000. See the International Institute for Strategic Studies, *The Military Balance 2000–2001* (Oxford, U.K.: Oxford University Press, 2001), p. 171.

154. "Kazakhstan May Allow Overflights for Strikes on Afghanistan, TV Says," *BBC Monitoring*, May 26, 2000.

155. One year later, Uzbek security forces were still alleging the existence of Islamic training camps in southern Kazakhstan, although the existence of such camps has yet to be proved conclusively. See "Islamic 'Guerrillas' Training in Kazakhstan," *Mashhad Voice of the Islamic Republic of Iran*, January 15, 2000, translated as FBIS–SOV–2000–0115.

156. Institute of Development of Kazakhstan, "Uroven' religioznosti."

157. Aidosov, "Mirovozzrencheskie." See also Talgat Ismagambetov, "Is Islamic Fundamentalism a Threat in Kazakhstan?" *Prism*, vol. 4, no. 7 (April 3, 1998).

158. U.S. Information Agency, *Opinion Analysis*, M–211–97, December 24, 1997.

159. When this question was asked again in 2000, 68 percent said that they favored secular law. U.S. Department of State, "Central Asians Differ on Islam's Political Role, but Agree on a Secular State," Office of Research, Opinion Analysis, July 6, 2000, p. 5.

Chapter 7
Can Kazakhstan Regain Its Promise?

1. The homicide rate (per 100,000 people) rose from 15.7 in 1994 to 16.5 in 1997, although statistics showed that the rate dropped to 16.3 in 1998 (UN Development Program, *Human Development Report: Republic of Kazakhstan, 1999*, p. 60).

2. For more on the trade in illicit drugs in Central Asia, see Martha Brill Olcott and Natalia Udalova Zwart, *Drug Trafficking on the Great Silk Road: The Security Environment in Central Asia*, Carnegie Endowment Working Paper 11 (Washington, D.C.: Carnegie Endowment for International Peace, 2000).

3. In July 1998, police officers in Almaty charged with extortion physically resisted arrest by officers of the National Security Committee (Vladimir Akimov, "Kazakhstan: Kazakh Secu-

rity, Police Clash over Corruption Incident," *Itar–Tass*, July 11, 1998, translated as FBIS–SOV–98–192.

4. In April 2000, Nazarbayev accused Kazakhstan's law enforcement agencies of resorting to "sadistic" torture to extract confessions. See "Kazakhstan's President Says Police Resort to Torture," *IPR Strategic Business Information Database*, April 24, 2000. This problem is also referred to in the U.S. State Department's Human Rights Report for Kazakhstan for 2000.

5. See Richard M. Auty's *Sustaining Development in Mineral Economies: The Resource Curse Thesis* (London: Routledge, 1993); and *Patterns of Development: Resources, Policy and Economic Growth* (London: Wiley, 1995). See also Karl, *Paradox of Plenty*. In addition, see A. H. Gelb and Associates, *Oil Windfalls: Blessing or Curse?* (New York: Oxford University Press, 1988).

6. Stalin distinguished between nations, nationalities, and ethnic groups. Only the first, which had complex economies, fixed historic territories (which abutted foreign countries in every case), unique languages and cultures, and a population of significant size, were given their own union republics in the USSR. Many nationalities received autonomous republics or, in some cases, autonomous oblasts, which were of even more limited juridical status, while the peoples were entitled to more limited forms of cultural protection.

7. For a list of companies and enterprises tied or allegedly tied to the Nazarbayev family, see appendix 12.

8. UN Development Program, *Human Development Report 1998*, p. 10.

9. Jusupov, "Analiz predposylok," p. 54.

10. In April 2000, a Russian An–12 military transport aircraft, which was the property of Kazakhstan's Infrakos state enterprise, left Baikonur, where it was to be taken to the Moscow suburban town of Zhukovskiy as scrap metal. Instead, the plane ended up in the Congo, where it was illegally sold. It is alleged that other military equipment from Baikonur has been sold abroad, although precise figures for missing hardware are not available. See "Kazakh Military Aircraft Sold to Congo as 'Scrap Metal,'" *BBC Worldwide Monitoring*, April 29, 2000.

11. Nazarbayev's middle daughter, Dinara Kulibayeva, heads Kazakhstan's education fund, named for her father.

12. In case of the death or incapacity of the president, his term shall be completed by the presiding officer of the senate, according to Article 48 of the constitution.

13. International Monetary Fund, *Statistics Yearbook 2001*, pp. 220–21.

14. *Moscow Interfax*, December 8, 1992, as reported in *Daily Reports Central Eurasia*, FBIS–SOV–92–236, Dec. 8, 1992, p. 36.

15. *ABV*, 30 May 1994, p. 6.

16. *Nezavisimaia gazeta*, June 29, 1993, p. 3.

17. See International Institute for Strategic Studies, *The Military Balance 2000–2001* (Oxford, U.K.: Oxford University Press, 2000), p. 164.

18. See appendix 7 for U.S. and international aid and assistance projects in Kazakhstan.

Selected Bibliography

"Agreement between the Republic of Kazakhstan and the Russian Federation on Simplification of the Procedure for Obtaining Citizenship by Citizens of the Republic of Kazakhstan Arriving for Permanent Residence in the Russian Federation and Citizens of the Russian Federation Arriving for Permanent Residence in the Republic of Kazakhstan." *Kazakhstanskaia pravda*, January 22, 1995.

Aidosov, S. B. "Mirovozzrencheskie orientatsii studentov: Otnoshenie k religii." Trans. Mark Eckert. *Sayasat*, no. 9 (1997), pp. 48–49.

Akanov, Aikan, and Balzhan Suzhikova. "Kazakhstan," *Social Sector Issues in Transitional Economies of Asia*. Oxford: Oxford University Press, Asian Development Bank, 1998.

Akhmetalimov, Amangeldy, and Gennady Kulagin. "Kazakhstan President on the Need to Strengthen CIS." *Itar–Tass*, December 23, 1993.

Akimov, Vladimir. "Kazakhstan: Kazakh Security, Police Clash over Corruption Incident." *Itar–Tass*, July 11, 1998. Trans. as FBIS–SOV–98–192.

———. "Kazakhstan: Final Results of Parliamentary Elections Issued." *FBIS–SOV–94–053*, March 18, 1994.

Alexandrov, Mikhail. "Military Relations between Russia and Kazakhstan in Post-Soviet Era (1992–1997)." *Central Asia Monitor*, no. 2 (1998), pp. 10–15, and no. 3 (1998), pp. 18–25.

Alma Ata 1986. Almaty: Altyn Orda, 1991.

Ardayev, Vladimir. "One Hundred Days of Nursultan Nazarbayev." *Izvestiya*, March 11, 1992.

Atakhanova, Kaisha. "The Monster of Semipalatinsk." *Initiative for Social Action and Renewal in Eurasia*, September 26, 2000. <www.isar.org/isar/archive/ST/Semipalatinsk.html>.

Auezov, Magzhan M. "The Development of a Corporate Securities Market in Kazakhstan." *Central Asia Monitor*, no. 3 (1998), pp. 12–19.

Babak, Vladimir. "Kazakhstan: Big Politics around Big Oil." In *Oil and Geopolitics in the Caspian Sea Region*. Ed. Michael P. Croissant and Bulent Aras. Westport, Conn.: Praeger, 1999.

Baildinov, Yergali. "Kazakh Government Reorganized." *Panorama*, April 11, 1997. Trans. in *FBIS Daily Reports. Central Eurasia, SOV–97–117*, April 29, 1997.

Beisenova, Aliya. "Environmental Problems in Kazakhstan." In *Sustainable Development in Central Asia*. Ed. Shirin Akiner, Sander Tideman, and John Hay. New York: St. Martin's Press, 1998, pp. 159–85.

Bolukbasi, Suha. "The Controversy over the Caspian Sea Mineral Resources: Conflicting Perceptions, Clashing Interests." *Europe-Asia Studies*, vol. 50, no. 3 (1998), pp. 397–414.

Brichkina, Liza. "Otkrovennoe Khanstvo." *Profil'*, vol. 168, no. 46, December 6, 1999, published on Internet web site Compromat.ru: <www.compromat.ru/main/Nazarbayev/a.htm>.

Brown, Bess. "New Political Parties in Kazakhstan." *Radio Liberty*, August 23, 1990.

Buckley, Cynthia. "Rural/Urban Differentials in Demographic Processes: The Central Asian States." *Population Research and Policy Review*, no. 17 (1998), pp. 71–89.

———. "Suicide in Post-Soviet Kazakhstan: The Role of Stress, Age, and Gender." *Central Asian Survey*, vol. 6, no. 1 (1997), pp. 45–52.

Central Intelligence Agency (CIA). *Handbook of International Economic Statistics*. Washington, D.C., September 1997.

Chernykh, Nikolai. "Russia and Kazakhstan Begin Building an Economic Union." *Kommersant*, May 25, 1993.

Chinn, Jeff, and Robert Kaiser. *Russians as the New Minority: Ethnicity and Nationalism in the Soviet Successor States*. Boulder, Colo.: Westview Press, 1996, pp. 185–205.

Clark, Jennifer Cook, Allen L. Clark, and Koh Naito. "Emerging Mineral Policy and Legislation in the Economic Development of the Central Asian Republics." *Resources Policy*, vol. 24, no. 2 (1998), pp. 115–23.

Commission on Security and Cooperation in Europe. *Report on Kazakhstan's Presidential Election*. Washington, D.C.: Organization for Security and Cooperation in Europe, January 10, 1999.

Crowther, William. "Moldova: Caught between Nation and Empire." *New States, New Politics: Building the Post-Soviet Nations*. Ed. Ian Bremmer and Ray Taras. Cambridge, U.K.: Cambridge University Press, 1997, pp. 316–49.

Cummings, Sally N. *Kazakhstan: Centre-Periphery Relations*. London: Royal Institute of International Affairs, 2000.

Dalyell, Tom. "Keeping the Nasties under Lock and Key." *New Scientist*, February 4, 1995, p. 47.

Dave, Bhavna. *Politics of Language Revival: National Identity and State Building in Kazakhstan*. Ph.D. diss., Syracuse University, 1996. Ann Arbor: UMI, 1996, 9737807.

Delorme, R. Stuart. *Mother Tongue, Mother's Touch: Kazakhstan Government and School Construction of Identity and Language Planning Metaphors*. Ph.D. diss., University of Pennsylvania, 1999. Ann Arbor, Mich.: UMI, 1999, 9926116.

"Draft of Novo-Ogarevo Agreement." *Pravda*, June 27, 1991.

Ebel, Robert E. *Energy Choices in the Near Abroad*. Washington, D.C.: Center for Strategic and International Studies, 1997.

Economist Intelligence Unit (EIU). *Country Reports, Kazakhstan*. Issues from years 1997 to 2000.

Eitzen, Hilda Carper. *Scenarios on Statehood: Media and Public Holidays in Kazakhstan*. Ph.D. diss., Columbia University, 1999. Ann Arbor, Mich.: UMI, 1999.

European Commission (EC). *Kazakhstan Economic Trends, 1998*. 4 vols. Brussels, 1998.

Fierman, William. "Language and Identity in Kazakhstan: Formulations in Policy Documents 1987–1997." *Communist and Post-Communist Studies*, vol. 31, no. 2 (1998), pp. 171–86.

Forced Migration Projects. *Kazakstan: Forced Migration and Nation Building*. New York: Open Society Institute, 1998.

The Former Soviet Union in Transition. Papers submitted to the Joint Economic Committee, Congress of the United States, May 1993. 2 vols. Washington, D.C., 1993.

Gershtein, Emma G. *Memoirs*. St. Petersburg: INAPRESS, 1998.

Gudkov, Lev. "Russkie v Kazakhstane." Tsentr Issledovanii Russkikh Men'shinstv v Stranakh Blizhnego Zarubezh'ia. Moscow, 1995.

Gurgen, Emine, et al. *Economic Reforms in Kazkhstan, Kyrgyz Republic, Tajikistan, Turkmenistan, and Uzbekistan*. Occasional Paper 183. Washington, D.C.: International Monetary Fund, 1999.

Haghayeghi, Mehrdad. "Kazakstan's Declining Agriculture." *Central Asia Monitor*, no. 1 (1996), pp. 4–7.

Hale, Henry Ewing. *Statehood at Stake: Democratization, Secession, and the Collapse of the Union of Soviet Socialist Republics*. Ph.D. diss., Harvard University, 1998. Ann Arbor: UMI, 9822897.

Heleniak, Tim. "The Changing Nationality Composition of the Central Asian and Transcaucasian States." *Post-Soviet Geography and Economics*, vol. 38, no. 6, (1997), pp. 357–78.

Herrera, Yoshiko M. *Imagined Economies: Regionalism in the Russian Federation*. Ph.D. diss., University of Chicago, 1999. Ann Arbor: UMI, 1999, 9920146.

Herrick, Rebekah, and Almira Sapieva. "Perceptions of Women Politicians in Kazakhstan." *Women and Politics*, vol. 18, no. 4 (1997), pp. 24–32.

Horton, Scott. "Bankruptcy Kazak Style: The Karmet Case." *BNA East European Reporter*, May 20, 1996, pp. 349–46.

Human Rights Watch. *Kazakhstan: Freedom of the Media and Political Freedoms in the Prelude to the 1999 Elections*, vol. 11, no. 11 (October 1999). <www.hrw.org/hrw/reports/1999/Kazakhstan>.

Huttenbach, Henry R. "Whither Kazakhstan? Changing Capitals: From Almaty to Aqmola/Astana." *Nationalities Papers*, vol. 26, no. 3 (September 1998).

Institute of Development of Kazakhstan. "Uroven' religioznosti i konfessional'nye orientatsii naseleniia respubliki Kazakhstana." July 1996.

Interfax. *Investment Report of Central Asia and Caucasus*. 1994–2000.

International Monetary Fund (IMF). *International Financial Statistics*. Vol. 51, no. 6 (June 1998). Washington, D.C.: 1998, pp. 910–35.

———. "Kazakhstan Repays the IMF Ahead of Schedule." External Relations Department, June 1, 2000. <www.imf.org/external/np/sec/nb/2000/nb0035.htm>.

———. *Republic of Kazakhstan: Selected Issues and Statistical Appendix*. Washington, D.C.: International Monetary Fund, 2000.

Interstate Statistical Committee of the Commonwealth of Independent States (CIS). *Commonwealth of Independent States in 1997: Statistical Yearbook*. Moscow, 1998.

Ismagambetov, Talgat. "Is Islamic Fundamentalism a Threat in Kazakhstan?" *Prism*, vol. 4, no. 7 (April 3, 1998).

Isopoved gosurdarya. Moscow: Shelkovyi put, 1999.

Izdibayev, Toulegen. "Kazakh Attitudes toward Other Ethnic Groups Remain Neutral and Cordial." *Panorama*, February 27, 1998.

Jaffee, Amy. *Unlocking the Assets: Energy and the Future of Central Asia and the Caucasus*. Houston, Tex.: Rice University Center for International Political Economy and James A. Baker III Institute for Public Policy, April 1998.

Javeline, Debra. "Response Effects in Polite Cultures: A Test of Acquiescence in Kazakhstan." *Public Opinion Quarterly*, vol. 63, no. 1 (1999), pp. 1–28.

Jusupov, S. E. "Analiz determinant migratsionnykh protsessov v Kazakhstane (po materialam konkretno-sotsiologicheskogo issledovaniia)." Almaty, 1999. Unpublished research.

————. "Analiz predposylok sotsial'nykh konfliktov v Kazakhstane." Almaty, 1998. Unpublished research.

————. "Mezhetnicheskikh otnoshenii v Kazakhstane." Almaty, 1999. Unpublished research.

Kaiser, Robert, and Jeff Chinn. "Russian-Kazakh Relations in Kazakhstan." *Post-Soviet Geography*, vol. 36, no. 5 (May 1, 1995).

Kalyuzhnova, Yelena. *The Kazakhstani Economy: Independence and Transition*. London: Macmillan, 1998.

Karimov, Islam. "Uzbekistan na poroge XXI veka: Ugrozy bezopasnosti, uslovia i garantii progressa." Tashkent, Uzbekistan: 1997.

Karl, Terry Lynn. *The Paradox of Plenty: Oil Booms and Petro-States*. Berkeley, Calif.: University of California Press, 1997.

Kasymbekov, M. B, and Vladimir N. Shepel'. *Pervyi Prezident Respubliki Kazakhstan Nursultan Nazarbaev: khronika deiatel'nosti*. Almaty: Ana tili, 1997.

Kaupova, N., et al. "Trends and Causes of Maternal Mortality in Kazakhstan." *International Journal of Gynecology and Obstetrics*, no. 63 (1998), pp. 175–81.

Kazakhstan. Official government web site. September 26, 2000. <www.president.kz/>.

"Kazakhstan Census, 12 January 1989." Reported in *Alma-Ata Yegemendi Qazaqstan*. Trans. in *FBIS Daily Report*. USR–92–144, November 11, 1992.

Kazakhstan Embassy Bulletin. Vol. 1 (March 31, 2000). Washington, D.C.

Kazakhstan, Government of. "Perepis' Naseleniia 1999." Kazakhstan Government Statistical Report, 1999.

Khazanov, Anatoly. *After the USSR: Ethnicity, Nationalism, and Politics in the Commonwealth of Independent States*. Madison, Wisc.: University of Wisconsin Press, 1995.

Khlyupin, Vitaly. "Kazakhstan's Zhuzes: Tribalism of the Twenty-first Century." <www.eurasia.org.ru/book/sbornik23.html>.

Kozybaev, Manash Kabashevich. *Dekabr' 1986 goda fakty i razmyshleniia*. Almaty: Istoriia i Etnologiia, 1997.

————, ed. *Kazakhskaia Sovetskaia Entsiklopediia*. Alma-Ata, 1981.

Kozyrev, Andrei. "The Lagging Partnership." *Foreign Affairs*, vol. 73, no. 3 (May/June 1994), pp. 59–71.

Laitin, David D. *Identity in Formation: The Russian Speaking Populations in the Near Abroad.* Ithaca, N.Y.: Cornell University Press, 1998.

Lariokhin, Taras. "Kazakhstan President Addresses Global Panel Conference." *Itar–Tass*, November 26, 1993.

Lariokhin, Taras, and Gennadi Charodeev. "'Pugachev Rebellion' Suppressed." *Izvestiya*, November 25, 1999, p. 3.

Latypova, Ye. "Kazakhstan's Russian, Slavic, and Cossack Organizations Formed an Association." *Panorama*, May 1, 1998.

Lipovsky, Igor. "The Deterioration of the Ecological Situation in Central Asia: Causes and Possible Consequences." *Europe-Asia Studies*, vol. 47, no. 7 (1995), pp. 1115–32.

Luong, Pauline Jones. *Ethno-Politics and Institutional Design: Explaining the Establishment of Electoral Systems in Post-Soviet Central Asia.* Ph.D. diss., Harvard University, 1998.

———. "The Path Least Resisted: The Politics of Economic Decentralization in Kazakhstan." Paper prepared for presentation at the annual convention of the Association for the Study of Nationalities, April 13–15, 2000, Columbia University, New York.

Luong, Pauline Jones, and Erika Weinthal. "The NGO Paradox: Democratic Goals and Non-Democratic Outcomes in Kazakhstan." *Europe-Asia Studies*, vol. 51, no. 7 (November 1999), pp. 1267–84.

Masanov, Nurbulat, and Igor Savin. *Kazakhstan: Model' Etnopoliticheskogo monitoringa.* Moscow: Institut etnologii i antropologii RAN, 1997.

Matzko, John R., and Brian Butler. "ICBMs and the Environment: Assessments at a Base in Kazakhstan." *Post-Soviet Geography and Economics*, vol. 40, no. 8 (1999), pp. 617–28.

McLure, Charles E., Jr. "Tax Reform in Kazakhstan." *Bulletin for International Fiscal Documentation*, vol. 52, no. 8–9 (1998), pp. 375–88.

Mendybayev, S., N. Fomin, and V. Shelgunov. *Kazakhgeit.* Moscow: Kompaniia Sputnik, 2000.

Morgan, Dan, and Michael Dobbs. "Washington Lobbying Oils Russian Capitalism." *Washington Post*, October 27, 1999, p. A1.

Nahaylo, Bohdan. "Why the Empire's Subjects Are Restless." *Index on Censorship*, vol. 18, no. 5 (May/June 1989), p. 27.

Namazi, Siamak. "The Caspian's Environmental Woes." *The Caspian Region at a Crossroad.* Ed. Hooshang Amirahmadi. New York: St. Martin's Press, 2000, pp. 121–36.

Naselenie SSSR 1988. Moscow: Goskomstat SSSR, 1989.

Natsional'noe Statisticheskoe Agenstvo Respubliki Kazakhstan. *Chislennost' naseleniia Respubliki Kazakhstan po oblastiam, gorodam, raionam, raionnym tsentram i poselkam na nachalo 1998 goda*. Almaty, 1998.

Nazarbayev, Nursultan. *Bez pravykh i levykh*. Moscow: Molodaia Gvardiia, 1991.

———. "The Ideological Consolidation of Society as a Condition of Kazakhstan's Progress." *Kazakhstanskaia pravda*. October 9, 1993. As translated in *FBIS Daily Report* USR–94–003, January 12, 1994.

———. *Na poroge XXI veka*. Moscow: Oner, 1996.

———. *Nursultan Nazarbaev: Adiletting aq zholy*. Almaty: "Qazaqstan," 1991.

———. "On the Situation in the Country and Major Directions of Domestic and Foreign Policy: Democratization, Economic and Political Reform for the New Century." Address to Kazakhstani nation delivered September 30, 1998.

———. *Piat' let nezavisimosti: Iz dokladov, vystuplenei, i statei Prezidenta Respubliki Kazakhstan*. Almaty: Ana tili, 1996.

———. *V potoke istorii*. Almaty: Atamura, 1999.

Olcott, Martha Brill. "Central Asia's Catapult to Independence." *Foreign Affairs*, vol. 71, no. 3 (summer 1992), pp. 118–28.

———. "Demographic Upheavals in Central Asia." *Orbis*, vol. 40, no. 4 (fall 1996), pp. 537–50.

———. *The Kazakhs*. 2nd ed. Stanford: Hoover University Press, 1995.

———. "Kazakhstan: Pushing for Eurasia." *New States, New Politics: Building the Post-Soviet Nations*. Ed. Ian Bremmer and Ray Taras. Cambridge, U.K.: Cambridge University Press, 1997, pp. 547–70.

Olcott, Martha Brill, Anders Åslund, and Sherman W. Garnett. *Getting It Wrong: Regional Cooperation and the Commonwealth of Independent States*. Washington, D.C.: Carnegie Endowment for International Peace, 1999.

Organization for Security and Cooperation in Europe (OSCE). "Republic of Kazakhstan Parliamentary Elections 10 and 24 October 1999 Final Report." Office for Democratic Institutions and Human Rights. January 20, 2000. <www.osce.org/indexe-se.htm>.

———. "The Republic of Kazakhstan Presidential Election, January 10, 1999, Assessment Mission." OSCE web page. February 5, 1999. <www.osce.org/odihr/election/kazak1–2.htm>.

Peck, Anne E. "Foreign Investments in Kazakhstan's Mineral Industries." *Post-Soviet Geography and Economics*, vol. 40, no. 7 (1999), pp. 471–518.

Rakhimova, Kulimkhan. "An Assessment of the Health Condition of the People of Semipalatinsk Region Who Have Repeatedly Suffered External and Internal Exposure to Radiation." *Kapnemma*, June 2, 1999. Published on the Internet:<w.afsc.org/nero/pesp/rakhimova.htm>.

Rama, Martin, and Kinnon Scott. "Labor Earnings in One-Company Towns: Theory and Evidence from Kazakhstan." *World Bank Economic Review*, vol. 13, no. 1 (1999), pp. 185–209.

Rowland, Richard H. "Urban Population Trends in Kazakhstan during the 1990s." *Post-Soviet Geography and Economics*, no. 7 (1999), pp. 539–56.

Ruffin, M. Holt, and Daniel Waugh, eds. *Civil Society in Central Asia*. Center for Civil Society International, Seattle, and Central Asia-Caucasus Institute, Nitze School of Advanced International Studies, Johns Hopkins University, Washington, D.C. Seattle: University of Washington Press, 1999.

Rumer, Boris Z., ed. *Central Asia in Transition: Dilemmas of Political and Economic Development*. New York: M. E. Sharpe, 1996.

"Russkie v Kazakhstane: Osnovnye rezul'taty reprezentativnykh oprosov obshchestvennogo mneniia, provedennykh noiabria 11–dekabria 2, 1994, goda v 10 oblastiakh respubliki (57 punktov oprosa). Obshche chislo oproshennykh(1000 russkikh, 1000 kazakhov." Moscow: Tsentr issledovanii Russkix Men'shinstv v s Stranakh Blizhnego Zarubezh'ia, 1995.

Sachs, Jeffrey D., and Andrew M. Warner. "Natural Resource Development and Economic Growth." Harvard University Development Discussion Paper No. 517a (October 1995).

Sagdeev, Roald Z., and Susan Eisenhower, eds. *Central Asia: Conflict, Resolution, and Change*. Chevy Chase, Md.: CPSS Press, 1995.

Saradzhyan, Simon. "Bombs Shake Iron Rule in Uzbekistan." *Moscow Times*, February 18, 1999.

Sarsembayev, Azamat. "Imagined Communities: Kazak Nationalism and Kazakification in the 1990s." *Central Asian Survey*, vol. 18, no. 3 (1999), pp. 319–46.

Savin, Igor, and Aleksandr Alekseenko. "Problemi emigratsii v Yuzhnom Kazakhstane." *Sovremenniye etnopoliticheskiye protsiessi i migratsionnaya situatsiya v Tsentral'noi Azii*. Ed. Galina Vitkovskaya. Moscow: Carnegie Moscow Center, 1998, pp. 113–18.

Schatz, Edward. "The Politics of Multiple Identities: Lineage and Ethnicity in Kazakhstan." *Europe-Asia Studies*, vol. 52, no. 3 (2000), pp. 489–506.

Sewall, Bella Katy. "Transboundary Water Management in Central Asia: Have Donors Made a Difference?" Ph.D. diss., Harvard University, 1998.

Sharipzhan, Merhat. "Kazakhstan's Security." *Central Asia Monitor*, no. 6 (2000).

———. "The Mass Media in Kazakhstan." *Central Asia Monitor*, no. 1 (2000), pp. 13–15.

Shelgunov, Viktor. "The Flight from the Oasis: Economic Forecasts and the Migration Level." *Tsentral'noaziatskii bulleten*, no. 15 (December 6, 1998).

Shelia, Vakhtang. "We Call This Snow Leopard Just Home Cat." *Novaya gazeta*, March 16, 1998, p. 7.

Shepel', Vladimir N., and M. B. Kasymbekov. *Pervyi Prezident Respubliki Kazakhstan Nursultan Nazarbayev: Khronika Deiatel'nosti*. Almaty: Ana tili, 1997.

Shevelev, Anatoly. "Kazakhstan President Comments on Relations with CIS Countries." *Itar–Tass*, August 24, 1994.

Simon, Alexander. *Republic of Kazakhstan: Livestock and Products, Livestock Update*. Washington, D.C.: Foreign Agricultural Service, U.S. Department of Agriculture, 2000.

Smetanina, Svetlana. "Nazarbayev Was Asked a Russian Question." *Kommersant*, June 7, 1998.

Smith, David R. "Kazakhstan." In *Environmental Resources and Constraints in the Former Soviet Republics*. Ed. Philip R. Pryde. Boulder, Colo.: Westview Press, 1995.

Suleimenov, Olzhas. *Iazyk pis´ma: Vzgliad v doistoriiu—O proiskhozhdenii pis´mennosti i iazyka malogo chelovechestva*. Almaty: RIAL, 1998.

Sultanov, B. K, and K. V. Zhigalov *Pervyi Prezident respubliki Kazakhstana: Khronika deiatel'nosti, ocherki vnutrennei i vneshnei politiki*. Almaty: Fond polit. issl. "Kazakhstan-XXI vek," 1993.

Tishkov, Valery. "Ethnicity and Power in the Republics of the USSR." *Journal of Soviet Nationalities*, vol. 1, no. 3 (fall 1990), pp. 48–63.

Tolmachev, Gennadii. *Lider*. Almaty: Dauir, 2000.

"Trans-World Settles with Kazakhstan." *Financial Times*, February 28, 2000, p. 8.

Umarov, Khojamakhmad. "The Demographic Boom and Its Impact on the Mountain Regions of Tajikistan." In *Sustainable Development in Central Asia*. Ed. Shirin Akiner, Sander Tideman, and John Hay. New York: St. Martin's Press, 1998, pp. 186–94.

United Nations Development Programme. *Human Development Report: Kazakhstan, 1998*. Almaty, 1998.

———. *Poverty in Transition*. New York: Regional Bureau for Europe and the CIS, 1998.

U.S. Department of State. *Kazakhstan Country Report on Human Rights Practices for 1998*. Washington, D.C.: Bureau of Democracy, Human Rights, and Labor. February 26, 1999.

————. *Order Trumps Liberty for Many in Three Central Asian Nations: Ethnic Differences Brewing?* Washington, D.C.: Opinion Analysis, Office of Research. M–60–00. May 26, 2000.

Vishnevskii, A. G., ed. *Naseleniie Rossii 1995.* Moscow: Institute of Economic Forecasting of the Russian Academy of Sciences, 1996.

Vitkovskaya, Galina. *Emigration of the Non-Titular Population from Kazakhstan, Kyrgyzstan, and Uzbekistan.* 1999. Unpublished manuscript.

————. *Russians in the Non-Russian Former Republics and Forced Migration to Russia.* Conference report on Geo-Demographic Problems in Russia. Radford University, August 5–8, 1994.

Vitkovskaya, Galina, and Aleksei Malashenko, eds. *Vozrozhdenie kazachestvo: Nadezhdy i opaseniia.* Moscow: Carnegie Moscow Center, 1998.

Weinthal, Erika Sora. *Making or Breaking the State? Building Institutions for Regional Cooperation in the Aral Sea Basin.* Ph.D. diss., Columbia University, 1998, 9910676.

World Bank. *World Development Report 2000/2001: Attacking Poverty.* New York: Oxford University Press, 2000.

Zhigalov, K. V., and B. K. Sultanov. *Pervyi Prezident Respubliki Kazakhstan: Khronika deiatel'nosti, ocherki vnutrennei i vneshnei politiki.* Almaty: Fond politicheskih issledovaniy "Kazakhstan-XXI vek," 1993.

Index

About the Author

Martha Brill Olcott, a specialist in Central Asian and Caspian affairs and inter-ethnic relations in the Soviet successor states, joined the Carnegie Endowment in 1995. She is also a professor of political science at Colgate University. Ms. Olcott co-directs the Carnegie Moscow Center's Project on Ethnicity and Politics in the former Soviet Union, which organizes seminars, conferences, and publications on problems of state building in multi-ethnic Soviet successor states and on regional and ethnic conflicts within Russia. She has previously served as a special consultant to Acting Secretary of State Lawrence Eagleburger and as director of the Central Asian American Enterprise Fund.

Ms. Olcott received her graduate education at the University of Chicago and has been a member of the faculty at Colgate University since 1975. A prolific author on Central Asian affairs, her books include *Getting It Wrong: Regional Cooperation and the Commonwealth of Independent States*, co-authored with Anders Åslund and Sherman Garnett (Carnegie Endowment, 1999); *Russia After Communism*, edited with Anders Åslund (Carnegie Endowment, 1999); and *The Kazakhs* (Hoover Institution Press, 1987, and 2nd ed. 1995).

Carnegie Endowment for International Peace

The Carnegie Endowment is a private, nonprofit organization dedicated to advancing cooperation between nations and promoting active international engagement by the United States. Founded in 1910, its work is nonpartisan and dedicated to achieving practical results.

Through research, publishing, convening, and, on occasion, creating new institutions and international networks, Endowment associates shape fresh policy approaches. Their interests span geographic regions and the relations between governments, business, international organizations, and civil society, focusing on the economic, political, and technological forces driving global change. Through its Carnegie Moscow Center, the Endowment helps to develop a tradition of public policy analysis in the states of the former Soviet Union and to improve relations between Russia and the United States. The Endowment publishes *Foreign Policy*, one of the world's leading magazines of international politics and economics.